MIAMI

BEACH

A HISTORY

BY HOWARD
KLEINBERG

CONTENTS

PHOTO EDITOR:
 Arva Moore Parks
CURRENT PHOTOGRAPHER:
 John Gillan
EDITORS:
 Donna K. Born
 Martha Reiner
ART DIRECTION/BOOK DESIGN:
 James Kitchens
PROJECT DIRECTOR:
 Regina Dodd

Miami Beach: A History
is an official project of
Miami Centennial '96

LIBRARY OF CONGRESS CATALOGUE CARD
 Number: 94-068440
 ISBN: 0-9629402-3-2

To my mother and father,
who brought me South;
and to my wife Natalie,
who took over from there

———•·•———

PREFACE

(Claude Matlack)

Far away from Miami Beach, on the Mediterranean coast of the Sinai Peninsula just below the Gaza Strip, is an area close to the Egyptian town of Al Arish. When I passed through it more than 25 years ago, it was as a journalist on the way to the Suez Canal during a time of daily exchanges of rifle and rocket fire between Egyptian and Israeli soldiers.

Nevertheless, I thought to myself as I saw the hundreds of date palms shading the magnificently white beach, what a tourist attraction this place could be.

Another Miami Beach.

How odd, I continued thinking, that despite the centuries of incursions by Roman legions, Ottoman Turks and, more recently, Israelis and Egyptians, the swatch of land remained with its potential unrecognized.

It used to be that way with Miami Beach, a place known by other names until its incorporation in 1915. It was the Tongue of the Mainland, Boca Ratonnes, the peninsula, Ocean Beach, Alton Beach and, ultimately, Miami Beach. Like Al Arish, it sat there, not waiting to be discovered—it already was— but to be acknowledged as something with greater potential than simply the barrier sandbar it was; mangrove trees on the west collecting the sand that created the beach on the east.

As one who has spent nearly a lifetime on the Miami side of Biscayne Bay, I, too, knew Miami Beach was there, but had not yet discovered it fully. As a teenager, my knowledge of Miami Beach was the sizzling beach at 14th Street, where we haphazardly pursued giggling girls who wouldn't be caught. As a young adult, Miami Beach was a place to see big name stars in the plush hotels. But it was not until I began doing research for this book in the spring of 1992 that I fully began to understand the tangled, miraculous, sometimes erroneous, often exaggerated but never-ending story of Miami Beach.

This story has been pursued as a journalist would chase it, as that is what I am. For two years, I have attempted to overturn thousands of illusory seashells in search of information that had not yet been known before, or that needed clarification, and blend it in with that which we already knew, or should have known.

What follows is the result. Come discover Miami Beach with me.

Howard Kleinberg
Miami, Florida
September 1994

v

Ten minutes of the Greatest Circle

Ten Common English miles

No. 15th Section containing Cape Florida, with part of Baha...

CHAPTER ONE

THE LONG SANDBAR

"Special chart of Cape Florida" by William Gerard DeBrahm, 1765. (HASF)

Undoubtedly, the *cacique*, himself, had gone there; brought his canoe from the river on the western edge of the bay to this seemingly endless jungle of mangrove trees on the east. The Spanish would call these indigenous wanderers of Southeast Florida after the chief they met in their first encounter: Tequesta, or Chequescha. The narrow peninsula was an extension of the mainland—largely inhospitable, populated by hundreds of crocodiles and millions of mosquitoes. It ranged down toward an island that eventually would be called Key Biscayne. When the tide rode out, the *cacique* could dip into the mangroves and seize the crabs as they scrambled over the exposed roots. Or he could set out in search of bigger prizes, dragging his canoe just a quarter-mile east across the narrow spit of land to the ocean sea. His people had lived in this area for thousands of years.

These original people of Biscayne Bay were semi-nomadic. In the summer, their domain was the wide, shallow bay—ringed by mangroves, inhabited with a bounty of sea life. In the winter, they moved south, to the islands the Spanish called the Martires; the Florida Keys. There was a substantial village where the river flowed from the west into the bay. Juan Ponce de Leon sailed the length of Florida's peninsula in July 1513, south from his first landfall near St. Augustine. When he reached its southern tip, he probably probed the waters to see if entrance to the bay was possible there. It wasn't; Bear Cut was too shallow. More likely, he rounded the tip of Key Biscayne, or Caesar's Creek below Elliott Key, to

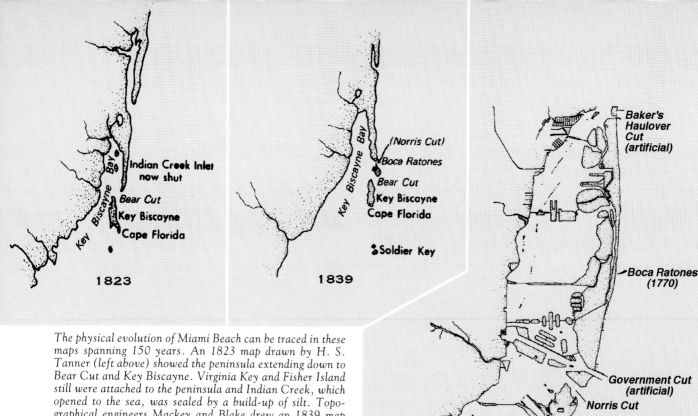

The physical evolution of Miami Beach can be traced in these maps spanning 150 years. An 1823 map drawn by H. S. Tanner (left above) showed the peninsula extending down to Bear Cut and Key Biscayne. Virginia Key and Fisher Island still were attached to the peninsula and Indian Creek, which opened to the sea, was sealed by a build-up of silt. Topographical engineers Mackey and Blake drew an 1839 map (center above) for General Zachary Taylor in his war against the Indians. In that map, Virginia Key appeared as an unnamed island south of the new, hurricane-driven Norris Cut. The southern tip of the peninsula, then called Boca Ratones, is today's Fisher Island. A contemporary map (right) shows the creation of Government Cut and the many man-made islands in Biscayne Bay. (Roland Chardon)

search for fresh water which was plentiful in natural springs in the bay. Ponce de Leon either learned of or met Tequesta, and his expedition recorded the settlement at the river as "Chequescha." Through the centuries, the name—like the land—has been altered: Tegesta, Tekesta, Tequesta. Another village existed on the eastern peninsula, where today's Surfside is located. There may have been yet another village farther south. Until the third decade of the 19th century, the southern tip of this peninsula was today's Virginia Key. That's where the other Tequesta village might have been.

Few early maps show the area in detail. A German-born surveyor and cartographer, William Gerard DeBrahm, made the first detailed chart of the Biscayne Bay region after he visited it in 1765. England had acquired Florida from Spain in exchange for Cuba in 1763. DeBrahm's map comprised part of a 1772 report on Florida to the Earl of Hillsborough. In it, DeBrahm renamed most of the previously Spanish-named places with British names; for example, Biscayne Bay became the Gulf of Sandwich.[1]

In 1771, a Dutch-born British surveyor, Bernard Romans, found himself in southern Florida charting its lands, bays and inlets. Romans, who at one time had worked for DeBrahm, mapped the state

from the Atlantic side, all the way around southern Florida, then up the west coast to Pensacola. His detailed map of the Biscayne Bay region was more revealing than was DeBrahm's, particularly the peninsula on the bay's eastern edge. Romans' peninsula was much the way later map-makers showed the land composition. The promontory stretched south, but instead of an elongated mass of land, it was cut in two by a narrow body of water that emptied into the Atlantic Ocean. That was today's Indian Creek at a time when it cut all the way through the land; silt has long since blocked it off from the sea.[2]

The Tequesta village at Surfside was uncovered in 1923 when the Tatum Brothers' development company, clearing land for a residential section called Altos Del Mar, disturbed a mound of skulls and other bones. So excited—and publicity hungry—were the Tatums and their press agents, that they concocted tales of ancient pirate treasure that received considerable coverage in the *Miami Metropolis*. Botanist John Kunkel Small debunked the pirate legend in 1929 when, in a book on the demise of Florida vegetation, he reported the bones in a mound to be those of aboriginal Indians. Small claimed that simply by reaching under the loose sand, a skull could be located anywhere. But he, too, held out the prospect that some of the bones were those of Europeans. "Many of them indicated death by violence; as a pierced skull or fractured skull," Small wrote. "The superficial burials may represent the period just after the discovery of America, for some of the skulls seem to be other than Indian and would thus represent the remains of the shipwrecked Europeans who may have been killed in attacks by the red men, or have died natural deaths while prisoners, or have been the victims of sacrificial ceremonies which were practiced among the aborigines."[3]

The Tatums, unfortunately repeating the actions of John Sewell at the site of a similar Tequesta burial mound on the north bank of the Miami River in 1896, scattered the bones and paved over most of the site.

In 1934, State archeologist Vernon Lamme excavated what was left of the mound. His archaeologists found more than 60 skeletons of the peninsula's first residents and another mound that included types of pottery. It was estimated that remains in the burial mound, with its various levels, could be dated as far back as 3,000 years ago and as recently as the period of the first European contact early in the 16th Century. Lamme crated the bones and artifacts and shipped them by train to the Smithsonian Institution in Washington, D.C. Tragically, they were either stolen or lost. Either way, early Miami Beach man never reached the showcase of our nation's attic.[4] Present-day Dade County archaeologist Bob Carr claims excavations in some of the back yards of that vicinity today would reveal more skulls and bones.

The Tequestas are extinct, victimized by European disease, enslavement, dispersion and attacks from other Indian tribes. Since they left no written or pictorial record, we know little about their lives. They may have grown crops, or they may have been non-agricultural. Letters from the 1568 Spanish mission on the Miami River indicate that they were a peaceful people until provoked—and they were provoked by the proselytizing Spaniards and encroaching Seminoles. Many anthropologists link the Tequestas to the Calusa tribe of Florida's lower west coast. Indeed, Spanish documents of the period forge the link to the Calusas—subjugating the Tequestas to the Calusas' powerful King Carlos.

An eyewitness report from Hernando D'Escalante Fontaneda, for 17 years a prisoner of the Calusas and the only one of the hundreds of shipwrecked sailors to live and recount his adventures, testified to the Calusa/Tequesta cultures. He mentioned a place the Indians called "Tequesta" and said that these Indians lived north of the Martires. "These Indians have no gold," he wrote in his memoir, "less silver and less clothing. They go naked, except only some breechcloths woven of palm, with which the men cover themselves; the women do the

Mrs. John K. Small and friend sit atop the Surfside burial mound; skulls and other bones were uncovered there. In addition to the mound, the site included a triangular shaped village. (Small; SPA)

Charles Hardman's mural, that was done for the Miami Beach Post Office by the New Deal's WPA in 1936, depicts a meeting of the Spanish and Native Americans on Florida shores. (SPA)

like with certain grass that grows on trees [Spanish moss]. This grass looks like wool, although it is different from it. The common foods are fish, turtles, snails (all of which are alike fish), and tunny and whale."[5]

No one is certain when the last of the Tequestas died or left the peninsula. Documents show Tequestas living in the Keys as late as 1732, when Florida still was under Spanish rule. Although the Spaniards failed to convert most of the Tequestas to Christianity, they succeeded in establishing a working relationship with the natives. In the early years of the 18th Century, bands from the Creek Federation called Uchises and Yamases (now known as Seminoles) began penetrating the Tequesta lands.[6] Spanish correspondence documents that the Tequestas sought removal to Havana, claiming that their villages were being destroyed and that the Seminoles were selling their victims to the British as slaves. The Spanish attempted to remove the Tequestas by boat, but funds ran short and only 270 were transported to Cuba.[7] The majority of them died of illness in Havana; the few who survived eventually returned to Florida.[8] What remained of the shrinking nation was less hospitable to the Spanish when they returned in 1743 for another effort to establish a mission in the Biscayne Bay region—an idea that was quickly abandoned. Twenty years later, when Florida became a British possession, the remaining Indians, fearful of British slave trading, emigrated to Havana.[9]

The British quickly gave up on Florida, returning it to Spain in 1784. However, the British presence in the Bahamas continued to haunt the Spanish. Bahamian families took up residences on the mainland and participated in salvaging wrecked ships. In 1817, a Nassau newspaper advised shipwreck victims who might find themselves stranded on the long sandbar that eventually became Miami Beach: Placed every four miles along the beach were signposts "on which there is an inscription in English, French and Spanish indicating where Wells of fresh water have been properly dug."[10] Multi-linguism had an early start in Miami Beach.

One of nature's strongest forces—the hurricane—is presumed to have created Norris Cut (which was variously known in early days as Narrow Cut, Narrows Cut and Narres Cut[11]) and which separates what we call Virginia Key from the remainder of the peninsula. Geographer Roland Chardon concluded that 1838 was the most probable date of the creation of the cut, since maps drawn prior to that date show no opening to the sea in that vicinity, while an 1839 map clearly does. Chardon wrote:

While no major storm is known to have struck the Biscayne Bay area itself in 1838,

two powerful hurricanes are recorded as having crossed the region, one in 1835 and the other in 1837. I have favored the south Florida hurricane of 1835, whose center apparently passed squarely over northern Biscayne Bay, as the most probable major agent that formed Norris Cut.[12]

From a slight opening (Narrow Cut) it grew to become noticeable to map makers. By 1838, Chardon theorized, the cut was big enough to be identifiable. The southern tip of the peninsula had separated; Virginia Key became an island.

It was the last time Nature cut a parcel of land away from what would be Miami Beach. The dredge and the steam shovel did the rest. Fisher Island was taken away from the peninsula with the creation of Government Cut in 1905 and, with the furrowing of Haulover Cut in 1926, Miami Beach, too, became part of an island.

Although Florida became a territory of the United States in 1821 and achieved statehood in 1845, the lifestyle of settlers in South Florida remained the same. It centered on shipwrecks. Vessels that struck the Florida reefs lost their cargoes to salvors, many of whom helped perpetuate the actual shipwrecks by extinguishing lights and removing markers. Congress took aim at unscrupulous practitioners in 1821 when it required salvors to obtain occupational licenses from the judge of the U.S. District Court in Florida. It was not until 1876, however, that the U.S. government began building five stations along the southeast coast to aid shipwreck victims who had previously had to make do for themselves in the hostile natural environment.

Earliest known photo (1884) of Biscayne House of Refuge. (Munroe; HASF)

Mangrove trees surround Crocodile Hole at the entrance to Indian Creek. Allison Island was created at this site. (Small; SPA)

One of those life-saving stations, the Biscayne House of Refuge, was in today's Miami Beach, on a 10-acre oceanfront parcel running north from today's 72nd Street. Study of the Biscayne House's log from 1883 to mid-1900 reveals that the station was of frame construction, with three rooms and a small kitchen downstairs and a loft upstairs with a dozen cots. The Biscayne House, which stood on top of the ridge overlooking the beach, had an unscreened porch on three sides, a brick chimney in the kitchen, a cistern and a boat house for a surf boat. A path led through the matted jungle behind the house, through a mangrove swamp, to a dock on the bay where the keeper maintained a supply boat also used for taking stranded people to Miami or Biscayne (Miami Shores).[13]

It is questionable that the Biscayne House of Refuge was the first non-Indian settlement on the long sandbar. A single sentence in the reminiscences of Rose Wagner Richards advises about a man named John Braman. Mrs. Richards, the daughter of William Wagner, who settled on the mainland in the 1850s, reported the arrival of Braman on the beach sometime prior to 1861. "One man arrived named Braman who settled on the beach opposite Miami, somewhere near where the harbor entrance is to be made," she recalled in 1903.[14] The U.S. census of 1860 shows John Braman to be a resident of the Biscayne Bay area and also of Key West. Braman, a ship's carpenter, was a naturalized American who was born in the Bahamas. He was recognized as one of the first Bahamians to have settled in Key West.[15] He married Mary Kemp of Key West on March 21,

1839 and was naturalized in 1849.[16] In the 1860 Dade census, Braman does not appear with any family. But in the Monroe County census of the same year, he is listed along with wife Mary and two sons and a daughter as living in Key West. Braman is not in any subsequent Dade County listings but he does continue to show on census lists of Monroe County. He died in Key West on August 22, 1889 and was buried in the Key West city cemetery.[17]

In name confusion, various documents mention Bremon's Landing in Miami Beach, as well as Brama's Landing and Brahman's Landing.[18] The site most likely was on the west side of the peninsula below today's 11th Street and probably as far south as today's Fisher Island, which was part of the peninsula until 1905. There would have been plenty of work for a ship's carpenter in the Biscayne Bay area, and perhaps Braman combed the shore of today's Miami Beach for lumber that had washed up from shipwrecks with which to build or repair small vessels. Or perhaps Braman was himself a salvor. There is no doubt that Braman was there and did something on the bay side of Miami Beach. What remains in question is what he did and whether he actually put up the first structure.

It has been reported in several histories, but without documentation, that, in 1870, Henry B. Lum and his 15-year-old son Charles arrived on the long sandbar on a visit of curiosity. Lum, an adventurous sort who participated in the 1849 California Gold Rush, reportedly became infatuated with the several coconut trees he saw growing on the beach.

Settlers from the western edge of the bay also came to the unnamed beach to spend the day or perhaps to camp out in the open. One of their favorite spots was a place called Crocodile Hole, about two miles south of the Biscayne House of Refuge. In an 1887 letter to his hometown newspaper in Concord, Massachusetts, Alfred Munroe, uncle of Coconut Grove pioneer Ralph Munroe, described a trip to Crocodile Hole:

We enter the pond from the [Indian] creek by a narrow opening through the mangrove woods and as soon as we get sight of it we also see four or five crocodiles, some of them floating like logs on top of the waters, others on the banks, but as soon as they get sight of us make a plunge into the deep pond, and all are quickly out of sight. The pond is some 300 feet long by 40 wide, and is very deep. There are probably a hundred or more crocodiles in it, and it would be dangerous to expose oneself in its waters for a single moment.

In an earlier letter to his sisters on February 21, 1887, Alfred Munroe wrote about a visit to the House of Refuge, sailing down Indian Creek from Biscayne Bay.

There we landed and took a pathway across the narrow land to the Life Saving Station on the seashore. It is in charge of Mr. [Jack] Peacock, our landlord's brother,[19] a curious compound of wit and fun whose brain is full of wonderful stories about his past experiences here and elsewhere and he tells them well. He kept us in roars of laughter till about 11 o'clock when we retired on one of the government cots. I slept well to the music of the roaring waves.

Jack Peacock was not the first to man the life saving station in Miami Beach. That honor fell to William J. Smith, who was on the job for only a few months—from October 7, 1876 to July 3, 1877—before moving on to homestead on the mainland near today's 36th Street in Miami. The loneliness of the station keeper's life certainly must have contributed to Smith's short tenure. The keeper would sometimes go for days without seeing a person other than his own family. His role, according to the 1879 annual report of the federal life saving service, was:

[To] succor shipwrecked persons who may be cast ashore, and who, in the absence of such means of relief, would be liable to perish from hunger and thirst in that desolate region. Crews of surfmen are not needed here, but the keepers and members of their families are required to go along the beach, in both

directions, in search of castaways immediately after a storm.[20]

Food and supplies were obtained either from ships sent up from Key West or by the keeper of the house sailing his own boat from the bay side of the federal property across and down Biscayne Bay to William Brickell's trading post at the mouth of the Miami River.[21]

British-born seaman Edward Barnott succeeded Smith and stayed in the position until November 15, 1882. A month before he began his duties, he took as his bride Mary Ann Sullivan, who was said to be only 13 years old at the time. Years later, Mrs. Barnott claimed she had buried several babies in the dunes behind the House of Refuge.[22] When a new superintendent was appointed for the entire life saving station district, Barnott—as well as three of the four other keepers—was fired. He was replaced by Hamilton D. Pierce, who had been the first keeper of the Orange Grove House of Refuge south of Lake Worth.[23] All keepers were required to write in an official log, but Pierce's log beginning January 28, 1883 is the first to survive. It reflects the humdrum of a keeper's life—repairing signposts and cots, sighting ships passing. Providing refuge for sailors is mentioned only once, when, in July 1884, three men in two skiffs received shelter for the night.

His wife's failing health prompted Pierce to resign in November 1884. "Jolly Jack" Peacock, an Englishman who had served as an indentured apprentice prior to coming to America at the age of 20, took over the life saving station.[24] Ralph Munroe referred to Peacock as "one of the most humorous and frolicsome, original and ingenious, eccentric, good-hearted and wayward of men."[25] Peacock had earlier been sheriff and tax assessor of Dade County, which then stretched from the edge of the Florida Keys all the way to today's Martin County. His brother Charles followed "Jolly Jack" to southeast Florida and established the first hotel in the region, the Bay View House, later known as the Peacock Inn. It stood where Coconut Grove's Peacock Park now is located.

Shortly after beginning his duties, Jack Peacock penciled in this entry at the bottom of the page for February 10, 1885: "Local stranger arrived."[26] He was referring to his daughter Rafaela, the seventh child born of his marriage to Martha Snipes. A similar entry on November 4, 1886 noted the birth of his son Richard. Two weeks earlier, Peacock awakened to an amazing sight. "The beach is packed with wreckage and pipes of wine more or less for 60 miles," he wrote. "The bulk of the wine is salt water damaged and the best of it of such low grade that the wreckers don't think it will pay charges to work it. The vessel or vessels broke up somewhere and the current brought the drift here."[27]

The ship was bound from Bordeaux to Havana and broke up in a hurricane at sea. Barrels of assorted wines floated to shore along the southeast coast of Florida as far north as Lake Worth. Although Peacock was displeased with the salt-damaged quality of the wine, he did the next best thing: he bathed in it, believing it to offer a cure for his rheumatism.[28] Ralph Munroe, with practically all the other settlers of the area, including Seminoles, gathered up his share of the wine. Munroe reported that casks of Madeira wine were not ruined "Many of us", he wrote, "tried to save some of it, thinking it might age into good quality. Within a few weeks, however, the kegs commenced to leak, mysteriously, and having no means of bottling it, we lost it all. It seemed that a peculiar small worm had bored the casks."[29]

Upkeep on the House of Refuge was difficult. Peacock was plagued with mosquitoes year-round; his requisitions to the government for more screening went unfulfilled. At first he mended the screens with cloth, but soon even that was not enough to do the job. Happily, on April 16, 1888, Peacock reported receiving 20 pieces of wire screening from New York via Key West. Peacock's tenure of five and one-half years made mention of numerous vessels, including a Spanish steamer that ran aground eight miles south of the station, near Norris Cut—then the southern tip of Miami Beach.

According to the logs of Peacock and his successor, William Fulford, the station began to decline physically. Peacock complained that his large surf boat was rusted out and useless, and that he was unsuccessful in his attempt to paint the house. Fulford, who replaced Peacock in 1890, called attention in some of his earliest entries, to two worthless boats and a partially painted house, with most of its bedding old and worn out.[30]

But the days of isolation were ending. Henry Lum saw a commercial future in the farming of coconuts on the beach. He was soon to interest two Quakers from New Jersey, Elnathan Field and Ezra Osborn, in the project. Shortly, the House of Refuge would no longer be the only structure on the beach. First, portable houses arrived by boat. Then, in 1886, Lum's son Charles built a home on the long sandbar.

The isolated beach was about to become more than a haven for shipwrecked sailors.

When the coconut planters arrived, Norris Cut, as seen in this 1884 photograph, marked the southern end of the peninsula that included Miami Beach. (Munroe; HASF)

CHAPTER TWO

THE COCONUT PLANTATION

Trying to earn a living out of Miami Beach did not originate with the first tourism promoters. While the Spanish, and the English who followed them to the southeast coast of Florida, apparently saw no streets lined with gold, Henry Lum viewed the peninsula as another kind of financial opportunity. Streets lined with coconut trees would be just fine with him.

The story is told that Lum and his son Charles visited the peninsula in 1870 and found three coconut trees growing in the sand of the southern shore. This inspired Lum to grow coconuts commercially. The three coconut trees would not have been unique to the area. Just across the bay, at the mouth of the Miami River, coconut trees were reported to be growing in the late 18th Century. Coconut trees originated on the islands of the Indian Ocean and were brought to the Western Hemisphere.[1]

Much of what we know of early Lum comes to us from Charles Edgar Nash, a Pennsylvanian who wrote the first history book of Miami Beach in 1938.[2] According to Nash's account, Lum was born in 1820 on a farm alongside Pennsylvania's Susquehanna River. As a teenager, he worked his way by raft down river to Baltimore, where he taught school for one term. Lum later walked from Baltimore to Bloomington, Ohio—a distance of nearly 400 miles as the crow flies. There, he bought an acre of land and went into the nursery business. In 1849, when Lum was a 29-year-old nurseryman, gold was discovered in California so he went west. Luck seemed to evade the young man. He found no gold and opened a bakery instead. There, he literally struck gold, being paid in gold dust by miners for his breads and cakes. After he amassed $2,000, Lum hit the road again—going to Sandusky, Ohio, where he purchased 50 acres and began anew in the nursery business. He moved to the Middletown-Red Bank, New Jersey area in 1866 and continued as a nurseryman.[3]

Despite the significance of the role Lum played in Miami Beach history, it isn't certain if or why he and his son were in the Biscayne Bay area in 1870, other than looking for new adventures. According to Nash, the Lums sailed across Biscayne Bay from the Miami River and made landfall on the southern tip of the peninsula—today's Fisher Island. It was there that Lum saw his coconut trees. Who planted them? Braman? It is extremely rare for a coconut to be washed ashore, to sprout and to prosper unattended. Coconuts in that location would have to have been planted by people. From seed to first crop of nuts would take about seven years. Trees of about 20 feet in height would be 10 to 12 years old.[4] What also is puzzling is that Florida State surveyors' field notes of 1873 made no reference to Braman's Landing. How could a surveyor miss a dock or small building? He could not. The answer lies somewhere akin to the mystery of the disappearance of the dinosaurs. Something—perhaps a hurricane, perhaps the persistence of the jungle—erased any trace of coconut trees or man from the lower section of Miami Beach by 1873. While Ralph Munroe refers in his memoirs to a Brama's Landing for Braman's Landing, it must be asked whether there was anything there other than a clearing to beach a small boat.

Henry Lum went back to New Jersey and, with his nurseryman's and business-oriented mind, began planning to go into the coconut plantation business. Accompanied by daughter-in-law Effie's brother, Stillwell Grover of Red Bank, New Jersey, Henry Lum returned to the Biscayne Bay area in 1882, coming up from Key West in a 16-foot boat. "The journey itself was a bit of courageous pioneering for them," wrote Munroe, "since they knew nothing whatever of sailing, and actually worked up along

Ralph Munroe (right) stands in front of a mature coconut tree on the beach in 1884. (Munroe)

the keys with jib hauled flat amidships all the way, being blown out into the Gulf Stream more than once, and taking four weeks for the trip."

Munroe wrote that Lum was looking for a place to grow coconuts. The sands of Miami Beach must have been quite a sight to Henry Lum and Grover after the rocky shorelines of the Florida Keys. It would appear that Lum cast his eyes upon a section of land where John Braman had settled two decades earlier. Munroe wrote that Lum bought a tract "just north of Narres [Norris] Cut, then called Brama's landing, and later did some planting."[5]

Lum's presence on the ocean beach is documented by two letters he wrote to state officials. The first, in December 1882, sought a government survey of "the point of land across the bay from Miami from the south line of Township 53S to the cut below. . . as I am ready to purchase the same."[6] The south line of Township 53S would cut across 12th street of today's Miami Beach. Obviously not having received a response, Lum wrote again in January 1883, seeking the information. In the second letter, Lum enclosed a sketch of the shape of the land he wanted in relationship to the surveyed land north of it. "The land in question is within the dotted lines on accompanying slip," he said of his sketch. "I would like a part of the land and other parties here would take the remainder."[7] The "other

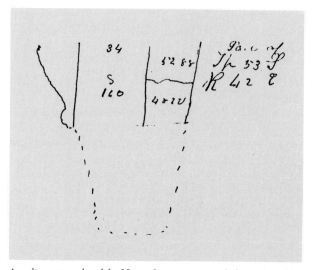

A rudimentary sketch by Henry Lum was part of a letter from him to state officials in 1883 seeking a survey of some of his property. The sketch shows the southern tip of Miami Beach—now Fisher Island—and the property just north of it. (Joe Knetsch)

parties" certainly were Ezra Osborn and Elnathan Field and their families. Lum, Osborn and Field, the latter two Quakers, were living in Middletown, New Jersey in 1880. Field was in his early 40s and was a farmer. It appeared that he was successful because he employed two domestic servants and three farm laborers.[8] Osborn, in his mid-50s, was a surveyor, as was his son Frank. But Ezra also must have dabbled in farming as he had a farm laborer living in his household.[9]

None of them was the first actually to acquire deeds to property on the beach. The former mayor of Key West, William D. Cash, received a deed to land along the west side of Indian Creek in June 1881, more than a year before Osborn and Field. There is no indication of Cash's intention or that of another purchaser, William Gleason, a mainland carpetbagger who for a brief period claimed to be Lieutenant Governor of Florida. He bought nearby land on the peninsula in 1882.[10]

It could not be just coincidental that three men from Middletown, New Jersey suddenly found themselves on a remote South Florida beach in 1882 with the same goal in mind. While Field and Osborn are continually linked through documents, Lum remains on the fringe. Ralph Munroe wrote that Osborn was a friend of Lum in New Jersey; that Field was Osborn's foreman on the coconut project. However, state and federal records show Field and his family to be partners with Osborn and his family on land purchases. If Lum still was seeking to buy land on the beach in January 1883, Osborn and Field already had. On November 20, 1882, Susan Osborn, Ezra's 20-year-old daughter, and Elnathan Field received deeds. A month later, on December 19, Frank Osborn, Ezra's 26-year-old son, and Field received deeds to additional land.[11] All this land was north of today's 11th Street, and north of the parcels being sought by Lum as late as January 1883. Records do show, however, that Lum purchased two lots from the federal government along the ocean north of 11th Street on January 6, 1883.[12] The lands cost between 75 cents and $1.25 an acre. Osborn and Field involved other New Jersey investors and, with minor breaks, purchased all the coastal land between Key Biscayne and Jupiter. Eventually, Lum received the lands he was seeking from the state south of 11th Street and probably took advantage of whatever improvements remained of Braman's Landing to settle himself, as Munroe makes constant reference to Lum's place being across the bar and on the bay.

Next came the task of buying the coconuts, transporting them to the Florida coast and planting them. Nash wrote that Osborn, Field and Lum hired 25 men from New Jersey life saving stations, bought some condemned lifeboats from the government and repaired them, then loaded the men, boats, mules, wagons, tents, a small portable house, tools and provisions for 100 days on a Mallory line vessel for Key West. There, they chartered the schooner *Ada Doan* to bring them to what would become Miami Beach. With no dockage available, the vessel anchored offshore and the equipment floated ashore in the surf. The job completed, the *Ada Doan* then lifted anchor and set sail for Trinidad where it would take on a load of coconuts for the planters-to-be. While the ship was off to Trinidad, the men made camp about four miles south of the House of Refuge—near today's Lummus Park—and cut trails about 30 feet apart from the beach back to the mangrove swamp to the west. These trails were where the coconuts were to be planted.[13]

Charles Pierce's memoir, published years later, gives eyewitness testimony to the unloading of the *Ada Doan*. In the fall of 1883, Charles was 19 years old and living with his father, Hamilton Pierce, who had been keeper of the Biscayne House of Refuge for almost a year. As would any youth of that period, in that environment, he led an outdoors life: hunting,

Coconut planters pose in front of a surf boat for Ralph Munroe's camera in 1883. Workers unloaded the coconuts from a schooner and brought them ashore in these boats. (Munroe)

sailing and fishing. But now his curiosity was stimulated by news that a ship was coming up from Trinidad with a load of coconuts for the newcomers. Charles' father had been appointed by the customs house in Key West to be a special inspector for the unloading of the cargo of the ship; his job was to make certain only coconuts were unloaded. The young man accompanied his father to the camp where they met Field, Frank Osborn and J. W. Mathieson and his wife—the latter two from Staten Island, New York. In due time, the schooner *Ada Doan* appeared about a half mile off the coast.[14] "When the *Ada Doan* arrived, Field said he needed me as an oarsman in one of his boats to help with the unloading," wrote Pierce.

> We arrived alongside the schooner, which was anchored about a half mile from shore, and found another boat was ahead of us. As we had to wait for her to leave before we could load, I went on board to look around. The *Ada Doan* was a flush deck craft, just open low rail along amidship. Part of the schooner's crew were down in the hold throwing the nuts on deck. Others were tossing them to the men in the surfboats alongside who would drop them into the boat. This was kept up until the bottom of the boat was covered with nuts two or three deep. Then the men in the boat would stand aside and let the men on deck throw them into the boat until she was loaded. Then the boat was manned, lines were cast off, and the boat was rowed to shore where she was beached and unloaded. Then the same operation was performed again. It was a slow way to unload a ship, and a hard one at that. . . .All day from early morning until night the work went steadily on. It was hard and I was extremely tired when the last trip was made that day.[15]

Pierce wrote that the work continued the next day but he had to quit because his hands were blistered on the palms through constant use of a big oar. He left the job just after dinner, "which consisted of Irish stew, bread, butter and coffee, the regular menu at Field's camp."[16] Nash wrote that the schooner contained 100,000 nuts, with 38,000 unloaded on what would become Miami Beach; the remainder destined for other sections of the southeast Florida coast. The *Ada Doan* returned to Trinidad for another cargo of nuts for the beach. The following winter, a different ship arrived with a cargo of

Wife of J.W. Mathieson; she and her husband came to the coconut plantation from Staten Island, N.Y.(Munroe; HASF)

coconuts to be planted on Field and Osborn properties on Virginia Key and Key Biscayne. A year later, another ship came with coconuts for the coast from Boca Raton to Lake Worth.[17]

Traveling from New Jersey as part of the planting crew was 20-year-old Richard Carney, also of Middletown, who had been hired by Osborn and Field to work on the project. Carney worked on his father's farm until becoming a practical civil engineer. He signed on with Osborn and Field, lured by the promise of adventure. Carney was to tend to the coconut plantation while Osborn and Field returned to New Jersey and only occasionally came back to the beach. Nash wrote that Carney's task was monumental. "Trees, vines, and underbrush were so thickly interlaced that no lines at all could be laid out on the ground. Some of the men climbed tall trees and sighted the distant marker, while others

Temporary houses for coconut planters stand alongside the shore in the vicinity of today's Lummus Park in Miami Beach. One of them was home to Richard Carney who eventually moved it to Coconut Grove.(Munroe)

struggled through the brush below, carrying long bamboo stakes as directed at 20-foot intervals across a strip about 100 feet wide. When working in the dense growth in the swamps, accurate planting was facilitated by having men roped together at 20-foot intervals."[18] The planting was doubly difficult as a result of the constant swarms of mosquitoes and sand flies as well as the presence of coral snakes and occasionally, rattlesnakes. As soon as the workers finished planting on Miami Beach, they packed up their gear and huts and moved down to Key Biscayne to continue the process. When the year turned, the crews moved their camp nearer the House of Refuge to plant in that vicinity. The little house put together in what today is Miami Beach's Lummus Park was disassembled often and moved around, first to near the House of Refuge, later near Lake Worth and elsewhere along the coast. Nash wrote that the Lums planted 10,000 nuts on their property; the rest were planted by Osborn and Field.

Little Tiger came to Lum's camp with venison. (Munroe)

As soon as the first nuts sprouted in the Miami Beach area, it became evident there were going to be problems. The peninsula was infested with rabbits. As the sprouts came out of the ground, rabbits discarded their previous diet of salt sea oats and fed on them. In a 1936 newspaper interview with Carney, he claimed that the planters sent North for corn, dosed it with strychnine and spread it among the young trees. But the rats that also were devouring the young coconut sprouts had never before seen corn and ignored the bait. The article went on to say

Monroe often sailed his boat, the Kingfish, *across the bay to Miami Beach, sometimes just to visit, other times to bring food supplies to the coconut planters.* (Munroe; HASF)

that the planters then laced apples with strychnine but that also failed to attract the culprits. Nevertheless, the planters persisted and coconuts were placed into the ground for 65 miles along the lower southeast coast with varying results. By the end of the third year, Osborn and Field had exhausted their funds. They stopped planting and awaited the growth of the young trees. In the meantime, they sought new backers.[19] Nash wrote that Field met an old horticulturist friend, a fellow Quaker, at a meeting in New Jersey and so interested John S. Collins in what was happening on the Florida coast, that he invested $5,000. All told, 60 other investors were found. Lum, searching for additional funds, also lured Henry Robinson of New York City into his project.

Ralph Munroe, established across the bay in an area whose name was then spelled Cocoanut Grove, was a frequent visitor to Lum's property and the Osborn and Field coconut camp. On January 3, 1884, after catching a dozen kingfish in the ocean opposite the House of Refuge, Monroe noted in his diary that he sailed past the coconut camp and into the bay, despite taking strong waves over his stern. After entering the bay, Munroe sailed to the Lum property, left bananas and fish and continued home to Coconut Grove. The next day he was back at both Lum's and the coconut camp and made note that the Little Tiger was at the camp with venison. A week later, Munroe returned, reporting that he found everything going well, that he took tea with Lum and sailed home. Munroe must either have been infatuated with the coconut operation, despite his feelings that it never would succeed, or he was terribly bored and had little else to do. On January 16, according to his diary, he again returned to Lum's property, reported that Lum was not there but that Field was. January 18 found Munroe at Crocodile Hole where he came upon a dead crocodile. He propped it up on the bank and took a photograph of it. There are numerous references to Munroe spending time at Lum's, taking Lum over to Miami, returning people to Lum's. On February 2, he noted that he made a delivery to the coconut camp of fish, pineapples, bananas and tomatoes. On February 20, he again photographed the Lum place, then walked to the coconut camp for dinner.

Charles Lum was quickly becoming prominent in the Biscayne Bay community. He was appointed superintendent of Dade County Schools in 1885 and participated in the first recorded school board meeting on June 27. In 1886, Charles Lum built a two-story house on the southern portion of the beach

In Nash's *Miracle of Miami Beach*, there is a sketch purported to be that of the Charles Lum house. It depicted a two-story building with a porch, a thatched-top small building and a third, barn-like structure. What is most interesting about the sketch, drawn by Charles Lum's wife Effie, is that it shows four mature coconut trees growing on the property. Were these the trees the Lums supposedly saw in 1870? If they were, why did Effie put four of them into the sketch instead of three? If they are not those trees, but trees planted by Lum in 1882-1883, then the sketch would have to be dated later because the trees could not have grown to that height in so short a time.

to house him and his bride. "The newly-wed Lums lived a happy but lonesome life here on the beach for three years," Nash wrote:

Bears and wildcats then prowled through the thickets. Green turtles could be captured in breeding season on the beach and their eggs, according to Mrs. [Effie] Lum, made delectable omelets, while fish in abundance could be had at any time. Oysters were plentiful in Indian Creek and cocoplums, which made a tasty sauce when cooked, were common on the low dunes. Westward the mangrove, wild grapevines, poisonwood and seagrape held sway, occasionally relieved by fragrant acacia trees and patches of blossoming verbena and lantana.[20]

The Lums raised chickens and had a garden with lima beans, cabbage, beets, tomatoes, celery, bananas and bread-fruit. They went over to the mainland to gather wild oranges, lemons, limes and guava; they bought venison from the Indians. The House of Refuge, the Lum house and Dick Carney's 12 by 22 feet portable house were the only domiciles on the ocean beach in 1886.

Carney had moved back to the lower beach from Hillsboro when he finished planting there and, in 1894, shipped it across the bay when the planting venture was ended. He put it on land he was homesteading in Coconut Grove. He later placed it in the backyard of his property at 2935 South Bayshore Drive, where it stood for many years thereafter. In his later years, Carney was given to exaggerating his role in the ocean beach enterprise. He gave a newspaper interview which contended that it was he, rather than Osborn and Field, who bought almost all of Miami Beach and that he, at one time, was one of the wealthiest men in the country.[21] When Carney left the beach, he became a

close friend of Ralph Munroe. The commodore referred to him as "sailor, cook and comrade, all in one, and expert in all three roles."[22]

By 1887, it was evident that the battle was going against the planters. A method of placing chicken wire and palmetto leaves around the trees to fend off rabbits had been put into effect but Osborn, in New Jersey, seemed frustrated in not hearing how it was working. "After thee gets all the wire on," Quaker Osborn wrote Carney on March 3, 1887, "[I] wish [thee] would go over the whole plant stating how each section is. Number now growing, number eaten off and killed, number eaten off and sprouted again, number wired, heighth of plant. How the wired ones are working." Not all was a disaster, however. Osborn referred to plants at Andrews as doing "first rate so far. Rabbits not eating any. It is supposed that wild cats there kill all the rabbits." Osborn most likely was referring to Stephen Andrews, who was keeper of House of Refuge No. 3, five miles south of Lake Worth. Osborn and Field owned the coastal properties in that area as well.

It would appear that the two groups—the Osborn/Field team and the Lum team—operated independently of each other, but together as well. Osborn and Field were partners; Lum was a totally separate operator. Being from the

Richard Carney, foreman of the Osborn/Field operation. (Munroe)

same part of the country, having encouraged each other into their respective ventures and having found themselves thrown together on an exotic enterprise on a remote strip of beach more than a thousand miles from home, they naturally worked for the common good. As Osborn inquired of Carney as to the condition of his trees, he also expressed professional interest in Lum's. "Has Lum suffered as we have in our plants?" he asked Carney in a letter written February 2, 1887. Two letters written early in 1888 raise the question as to whether Osborn had more than just coconut trees in mind with his property. They also showed that Osborn's prime interests ranged beyond the strip of land between Biscayne Bay and the ocean and closer to Lake Worth. On April 29, 1888, Osborn wrote that he was sending four large letters cut out of black muslin that he wanted Carney to nail to "the shanty put on the bluff next to the ocean so as to be seen by passing vessels." The letters were *P A R K*. He asked that Carney paint a five-foot-wide strip of white across the building to help show the letters better. In his letter, he sketched a shack and the positioning he sought on the letters. In that same document, he also drew a sketch of city blocks running from the ocean to Lake Wyman, where he also indicated a hotel. That would pinpoint Osborn's interest on the beach opposite today's Boca Raton, where Lake Wyman is located. There is nothing to indicate that Osborn ever built his hotel, but partner Field is noted in Charles Pierce's memoir as having come to Lake Worth "after the winter of 1891-92 and bought the George Charter beach ridge homestead and built Manalapan Cottage to use for a winter hotel."[23] (Manapalan also is the name of a town on the New Jersey coast not far from Middletown.) The hotel was not successful, and was sold to two men, one whom he identified only as Baird and the other as John Collins,[24] who soon was to figure prominently in the growth of Miami Beach.

Lum, also struck with a lack of success in the coconut project, was looking elsewhere. In February 1884, Lum received from the United States as part of the Public Lands Act property that would include all of today's Miami Design District in Buena Vista. He also bought coastal property in today's Broward County at state auction in March 1885. In that same month, he received deed from the state to lands that now comprise much of the Dade County Civic Center and Jackson Memorial Hospital complex in the City of Miami. As early as May, 1886 he sold more than 270 acres of his land on the beach to his son Charles as well as to Henry Robinson of New York.[25]

By 1890, the Lums had gone back to New Jersey where father and son settled in Red Bank, across the Navesink River from Middletown. Charles became a prosperous farmer there. Henry spent winters in Florida. In May 1895, 85-year-old Henry Lum and his 37-year-old daughter Minnie died within hours of each other. The father had suffered for a long time with a heart condition while the daughter was the victim of a disease that paralyzed her legs. The family went to Florida in November 1894, but their health declined and they returned to New Jersey the following May in deplorable condition, the daughter traveling the entire distance on a cot. They both died a few days after their return.[26] The dreamer supposedly inspired by three coconut trees 25 years earlier had paid his last visit to the remote strip of land by the ocean.

John Collins, the $5,000 investor in Osborn and Field's endeavor, was not about to accept defeat. He was determined to rescue the operation.

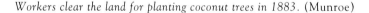

Workers clear the land for planting coconut trees in 1883. (Munroe)

CHAPTER THREE

JOHN COLLINS' AVOCADO GROVE

John Collins (MN)

When Henry Lum, Ezra Osborn and Elnathan Field began their venture into the coconut business in late 1882, they most likely were unaware of the planning being done by Dr. John Wescott of St. Augustine. Beginning at the time of Reconstruction, Wescott dabbled in several Florida ventures, including railroads in the northern part of the state and the gathering and canning of oysters at Indian River for shipment north. He was a physician who later became Surveyor-General of Florida.[1] It was Dr. Wescott's goal to create an inland waterway along the entire east coast of Florida with a series of canals linking the natural bodies of water that lay just west of the Atlantic Ocean. In 1881, he established the Florida Coast Line Canal and Transportation Company. He proceeded to raise funds, obtain land and begin actual operations on a project that would connect the St. John's River near Jacksonville to Biscayne Bay, 340 miles away. Wescott, like Lum, was a dreamer and his ambitious plans soon outran his capital. But his vision ultimately led to what we now know as the Intracoastal Waterway. Wescott saw a commercial future for Southeast Florida that few others saw at the time. In a January 1882 letter, months before the New Jerseyites began buying land to plant coconuts on the ocean beach, Wescott recognized the potential of the Biscayne Bay region as a significant shipping center. At the time, there was no railroad south of the Jacksonville-St. Augustine area. In his letter to a Col. Coryell, Wescott wrote:

This coast line perfected, fruit & vegetables could be delivered from Biscayne Bay to Jacksonville in 24 hours, in Savannah 8 hours more, there to be distributed to every part of the U.S. A new City will soon develop at Biscayne Bay or Barnes Sound, Larger & better than Key West, and open a New line of Commerce for our western products, and direct the course of Exportations for large quantities of such Commercial products as is consumed in all the large and Small towns of Cuba, and the English Islands [Bahamas]. . . .[2]

A waterway such as planned by Wescott would have been of tremendous help to successful coconut planters. Rather than having to ship their products first by small boat to Key West for transfer to larger vessels headed north, they could have used the waterway to ship north directly. It turned out to be a moot point, however. The coconut planters on the ocean beach never harvested enough nuts to provide a single shipload in any direction. Meanwhile, Wescott used state incorporation laws to obtain alternate sections of state land on either side of the proposed canal: 3,840 acres for each mile of construction.[3] Thus, by 1890, Wescott's Florida Coast Line Canal and Transportation Company had title to a major chunk of what would become Miami Beach, stretching along the mangrove side of the narrow strip from today's 44th Street to Sunny Isles, including today's Normandy Isle. The Wescott project was a disaster, with canal diggers improvising as they moved down the state from the Matanzas River south of St. Augustine. There were no detailed plans for a route. Despite the blundering, which resulted in "circuitous routes and awkward elbows,"[4] the Internal Improvement Trustees continued to favor Wescott's enterprise and awarded his company lands as far south as Key West.

Eventually, Wescott found himself out of the picture and George L. Bradley of Washington, D.C., took over running the reorganized company. In the 1890s, Bradley brought in Henry Flagler as an investor. Flagler was on the verge of making his imprint on the Florida scene with his railroad. The state had given 516,480 acres of public land to the Florida Coast Line Canal and Transportation Company. Financially strapped, the canal company had only land for assets. And land was what Flagler wanted. He invested $100,000 in the canal company. In exchange, he would receive 1,500 acres of land for each mile of the railroad extension that was completed from West Palm Beach to Miami.[5] By 1896, at a time when Flagler's railroad was reaching

Miami—Wescott's anticipated new city—the *New York Times* reported that the canal company had made significant progress on the section of the waterway between Lake Worth and Biscayne Bay. Nevertheless, the final links were not completed until 1912, six years after Bradley's death. By then, Flagler's railroad had cornered the market on transportation to the north, and the canal was not to be a significant player in shipping fruit and vegetables. At a depth of five feet and a width of 50 feet, the waterway was too shallow and narrow for ships large enough to carry substantial cargo.[6] By 1927, Congress, under pressure from the Florida delegation, took over the canal as a federal project, enlarging and deepening it. Rather than developing as a commercial waterway, the canal grew to become the highly popular and convenient Intracoastal Waterway enjoyed so much by pleasure boaters. For men like the ambitious John Collins, it would serve no purpose.

Horticulturist (and thrifty) Collins, frustrated by his partners' inability to grow coconuts commercially on the ocean beach, sought to salvage his investment. He decided to travel to Florida from his prosperous family businesses in Moorestown and Merchantville, New Jersey. It was a trip that was to further deepen his involvement in the future not only of Miami Beach but of Palm Beach County.

There is a vagueness about when Collins first came to South Florida. Most references, including a 1922 *Miami Herald* interview with the then 85-year-old patriarch, say only that he came here in the 1890s.[7]

Collins's ownership of land in South Florida can be traced back to February 1891 when he, along with David Baird of Manapalan, New Jersey and Elnathan Field, purchased the George Charter homestead on Lake Worth for $7,500. In July 1892, Collins, Baird and Field purchased more land at Hypoluxo Beach for $18,000.[8]

Other books, newspaper articles and family interviews tend to support his first trip as having occurred before the 1894 arrival in West Palm Beach of Henry Flagler's railroad. He was not to locate in what would become Miami Beach until after the turn of the century. His investment in southern Florida, however included the coconut–raising business and the Hypoluxo Beach real estate partnership whose object was to "purchase real estate and for the improvement and sale of lands. . . ."[9] Field is recorded by the *Tropical Sun* of February 4, 1892 as having arrived at Hypoluxo Beach on January 28, 1892 "with a force of men—preparing to build."[10] Collins, considered a pioneer in areas of fruit development, developed an interest in South Florida during a meeting with Field in New Orleans at a National Pomological Convention, an association

Thomas Pancoast, Collins' son-in-law, came to the ocean beach to check on Collins' agricultural venture. He is seen here in the jungle near the Crocodile Hole around 1905. (Pancoast Family)

dedicated to fruit cultivation. It was there that Field first interested Collins in the new area. It led to his $5,000 investment in the soon-to-fail coconut venture.

Hypoluxo Beach became Collins' winter home. He was wealthy and could afford a second home. And he was ambitious. John Collins was not the type of man who would accept defeat with the failed coconut-planting project.

Like Osborn and Field, Collins was a Quaker. He was born in Moorestown, New Jersey on December 29, 1837, the son of Isaac and Sarah Collins. His father was a farmer and John was the sixth generation of Collinses to live and work on the New Jersey homestead. The family history in America was traced to 1678 when Francis Collins, who came from Radcliff, Middlesex, England to Burlington, New Jersey where he built the first Quaker meeting house. [11]

John Collins recognized his calling early. Educated in public and private schools in Moorestown, he experimented with growing strawberries commercially as a youth and entered the fruit-growing and nursery business in 1855 after his father gave him a quarter acre of land. He planted half in blackberries and half in strawberries. In that first year, he harvested 1,080 quarts of berries for the Philadelphia market. Collins later established the Pleasant Valley Nurseries and opened builders' and farmers' supply yards in Moorestown and Merchantville. He was the founder of the New Jersey Horticultural Society and an innovator in plant culture. He used the profits from Pleasant Valley Nurseries to buy additional property in the area. His reputation grew with his experimentation with and commercialization of the Wilson blackberry and the Kiefer pear. [12] It didn't hurt his bank account, either.

On January 17, 1861, Collins married Rachel A. Rogers. Their 55-year marriage, which ended with Rachel's death in 1914, produced five children:

Mary, Katherine, Arthur, Irving and Lester. John Collins' enterprise reached out to his children. He financed each of his sons in business, as well as his son-in-law Thomas Pancoast, who was married to Katherine. Pancoast also was to figure significantly in the history of Miami Beach.

The firm of Collins and Pancoast in Merchantville, five miles from Moorestown, sold agricultural products, farm machinery, hardware, coal and lumber. [13] Pancoast, born in Moorestown in 1865, was in the wholesale cloth business in Philadelphia for eight years before joining with his father-in-law in 1888. Lester, who was the last son to be married, was put in charge of the Collins farms, allowing the patriarch of the family more time to devote to his Florida projects. Arthur remained at the Collins homestead, farming the land and, in 1911, entered the nursery business himself ten miles away in Burlington. Irving Collins ran the family hardware, lumber and coal business in Moorestown. Although Quakers, the Collins' extended family, with the exception of matriarch Rachel, did not wear traditional Quaker clothing or adhere to the strictest principles of the religion.

John Collins' investment in Florida coconuts followed a venture into a rare metals mine in North Carolina that also lost money. With this background, he was determined to cut his losses. His eyes turned toward that strip of land across Biscayne Bay from the new City of Miami. It was on the western shore of the bay that oil and railroad mogul Henry Flagler had focused his interest. Prodded by widow Julia Tuttle to extend his railroad from West Palm Beach to the Miami River, Flagler negotiated a contract with Tuttle whereby he received half her lands on the north bank of the river and some of William Brickell's in the settlement of Fort Lauderdale in exchange for bringing in the railroad. When the first train arrived in April 1896, Flagler's people already were busy at work building the Royal Palm Hotel in what would be downtown Miami, which, when completed, was said to be the largest wooden structure in the world.

Incorporated in July 1896, the new City of Miami became America's southern frontier. Laborers and entrepreneurs flooded the new area in hope of being in on the ground floor of something big. Few, however, saw much value to the barrier strip immediately east of the city other than for an afternoon sojourn in the surf.

Charles Edgar Nash wrote that Collins first came to the Miami area in 1896, which would coincide with the arrival of Flagler's railroad, the birth of the city and the availability of a hotel room. Collins hired two men to row him across the bay to the beach. This was where Osborn and Field planted

Collins chose the high ground in the center of the island north of today's 23rd Street for his agricultural venture. (Small; SPA)

many coconut trees; this was where his $5,000 had gone. Whenever his first visit occurred, he undoubtedly stood on the desolate strip, saw some coconut trees grown to adulthood, and envisioned a new frontier of horticulture, far different from the long-established patterns of his New Jersey home. Still distressed by the inability of his earlier partners to be successful, he was determined that he would make things grow. He knew about early and late fruits and of the marketing of them. When he looked upon the western shore of Indian Creek, he knew avocados could be grown there. The soil was not salty. Pine and palmetto trees flourished there, and they do not grow in salty soil. He also felt no frost would bother him this far south.[14]

In 1907, seven years after the death of Ezra Osborn, Collins bought a half interest in the lands originally shared by Field and Osborn, running from Jupiter to Norris Cut. A great deal of time and money was spent clearing the land suitable for planting but what to plant became an issue. Field was a believer in planting grapefruit as citrus already was growing well on the other side of the bay. Collins, his horticultural interests aroused by the thought of introducing something that wasn't already plentiful, wanted to plant alligator pears, as avocados then were called, as well as mangoes. The disagreement in philosophies was settled when Collins bought out Field's interest in their partnership and became sole owner of everything on today's Miami Beach between 14th and 67th streets, from the bay to the ocean. At first Collins remained at his Hypoluxo Beach residence and employed a foreman to handle his property. He built a shack near today's 41st Street to serve as a residence for the foreman. [15]

Collins planted 2,945 avocado trees on the west side of Indian Creek.[16] The massive planting was unlike the coconut operation of 24 years earlier.

This time there was no boat up from the Caribbean to dump its cargo of nuts in the ocean to be picked up by laborers. Collins' avocados—at one dollar apiece—were coming from across the bay, from the nursery of George B. Cellon, who arrived in Miami in 1900 and built a fruit grove and nursery near Buena Vista.[17] (His father, John Cellon, is credited with bringing the first citrus to Florida in the vicinity of Gainesville in the mid-18th Century.)

Crews of black laborers, armed with axes, machetes, plows and harrows, were brought in to clear land where just a quarter century earlier it had been cleared in the same primitive manner for Lum, Osborn and Field. This time, however, the laborers complained loudly about the conditions. Tangled roots were particularly difficult to clear. Collins reached into his pocket, sent money north and brought in 16-ton, 35-horsepower tractors with wheels fitted with special knives for cutting the palmetto roots.[18] It was estimated that clearing of the land by manual labor was costing Collins $70 to $300 an acre. The power-driven tractors cut his cost to about $30 an acre. With his newly-bought machinery, Collins cleared 160 acres on land 1,000 feet east of the ocean off Indian Creek. His orchard was a mile long and 700 feet wide. To run the farm, Collins transferred Charles Spyer from one of his New Jersey groves.[19]

When Collins planted his avocados in 1907, the beach was by no means a totally deserted strip of land. Typical of attention to the beach was this brief article that appeared in the August 7, 1896 issue of the *Miami Metropolis*, one week after Miami was incorporated:

One day early this week, A. E. Kingsley chartered the launch 'Edith R' for a trip to Norris Cut. Mrs. S. Graham and Miss Clements accompanied him. The party had a lunch basket and bathing suits along and enjoyed themselves immensely bathing in the surf. They returned in the evening hav-

Rows of young avocado trees at the beach in what today is known as the Orchard Subdivision. (Pancoast Family)

Avery Smith's "Fairy Land" ferry boats left from Henry Flagler's Fair Building, which stuck out into the bay at the foot of S. E. 1st Street. (Smith)

ing had a good time. They were well sunburned and as hungry as bears are said to be. There is a very nice beach and good surf just north of Norris' Cut, but no shade. If a pavilion and a few bath houses were erected on the beach so that people could find a shady spot to shelter them from the sun when they wished to sit down to luncheon or where they could take refuge in case of a rain squall, we believe a hundred people would go over to Norris' Cut every Sunday. There are a thousand people at Miami who have nothing to do and no where to go every Sunday, and there must be at least one in ten who enjoy looking at the 'sad sea waves' and taking a dip in the old ocean. We understand a club is being formed to build a commodious pavilion, elevated about seven feet above the ground, so as to permit the space underneath being partitioned off into a number of bath houses. If this project is carried out, Norris' Cut will be a favorite resort. . . .

Tourism, in its rudimentary stages, had appeared. Richard M. Smith, a former Connecticut schooner captain, played a role in that. Smith moved to Miami by 1900, became Miami city clerk in 1902 and was elected Dade County tax assessor in 1904. He is credited with putting up a two-story building near the southern edge of the ocean beach, one much like the pavilion project being described in the 1896 article. An undated newspaper story said Smith built the place in 1904 as a dance hall and inaugurated ferry service between the beach and Miami. A

1926 newspaper article referred to the structure as being old and ramshackle by 1908. E. V. Blackman, in his 1921 *History of Miami and Dade County*, wrote that Dick Smith built it as a bathing house. In 1907, the Miami Ferry Company was transporting people across the bay to the old Smith place but improvements were lacking. Later, another Smith, Avery Smith (no relation) and his partner, James C. Warr, entered the picture.[20]

Avery Smith, of Norwich, Connecticut first came to Miami in 1908. He recalled years later that the beach then:

had remained a jungle, practically as nature had designed it. I had the curiosity to see what there was beyond that curtain of trees to view more closely the land, the ocean and the beach. I engaged a fisherman and his launch to carry me over to the island. . . .We landed our launch about where the north side of the government cut or channel from the ocean enters the bay on the island's west shore, and followed a zigzag

Richard Smith's Casino was little more than an open air shelter; Avery Smith enclosed and improved it and re-named it Fairy Land. (Matlack; HASF)

THIS PIER THE ENTRANCE TO
FAIRY-LAND
IS THE PRIVATE PROPERTY OF
THE BISCAYNE NAVIGATION Co
ALL PERSONS OTHER THAN THOS
LANDED BY BOATS OF SAID Co
WILL BE CHARGED 25 CENTS EAC
ADMISSION FEE BISCAYNE NAVIGATION

Fairy Land guests walk the boardwalk from the bay side dock to the ocean front casino on the southern tip of the beach. (Smith)

course through the underbrush to the opposite or ocean side of the land. Our only guide through the tangled mass was an occasional view of the roof of an old building that had been built there as a clubhouse by [Smith]. The building was mostly roof, very high and shaped like the famous pyramids of Egypt, and it served us well as a guide through the jungle.

There were coconut trees, palmettos, sea grapes, coco plum bushes, yellow cactus and purple beach verbenas in profusion. There were fat little, shiny eyed raccoons, cotton-tail rabbits, and a considerable number of ferocious looking, but absolutely harmless black and orange mottled chicken snakes, to be seen, good sized ones, all of which added to the novelty of our trip of exploration, and made us think of the experience of Robinson Crusoe on his South Sea isle. We saw the land, the sea and all that nature had put there but that was about all there was at that time. I was greatly impressed with what I thought was an opportunity to establish a pleasure resort, and transportation proposition in connection with it, and to grow up with Miami and Miami Beach.[21]

Avery Smith purchased the lease to a portion of land with Dick Smith's building on it and had that lease assigned to him by the owner of the land, Charles Lum. "I then became owner of the only building at the beach," he boasted.[22] Obviously, Smith was oblivious to Collins' farm north of him. In the jungle that was that area then, it would be easy to regard the Collins property a mile or so away as being in another world. Smith returned to Connecticut where he had been operating excursion steamers. But in the summer of 1909, he suggested to his friend, James C. Warr of Wareham, Massachusetts, that he come to Florida with him to develop a resort at the beach and provide transportation from the mainland. Smith and Warr formed a partnership called the Biscayne Navigation Company and in the fall came

to Florida and started building boats at Huffstettler's Miami River boat yards. They also began constructing wharves at Miami and at the beach.[23] They purchased and remodeled a boat, the *Lady Lou*, and put her into operation immediately. They also bought and repowered the *Sallie*. Later, two 60-foot, double-decked boats were built at Huffstettler's and placed in service. Jocularly, these boats were called the *Mauretania* and *Lusitania*, named after two of the most prominent ocean-going vessels at the time.[24]

The *Sallie* left for the beach daily at 2:30 p.m. On Sundays, there were two trips, one at 10 a.m. and another at 2:30 p.m.[25] Smith and Warr fixed up the old Smith building, built a pier and boardwalk and named the enterprise Fairy Land. Vessels left the Biscayne Navigation Company pier at the foot of today's East Flagler Street in Miami twice daily, at 9:15 a.m. and at 2:15 p.m.[26] Advertisements purchased in the *Miami Metropolis* described Fairy Land as:

The People's Play Ground. Excellent all year-round sea bathing establishment. Average temperature of sea water 76 degrees, winter season. All modern improvements. Large recreation pavilion for picnics.

Smith and Warr's fleet also offered excursions up the Miami River, into the Everglades and around Biscayne Bay.

By then, Miami Beach's geography had undergone a dramatic change. The southern tip of the peninsula was cut away to create a new, deeper channel to the sea. As early as 1902, the Flagler interests, frustrated with the shallow waters of Biscayne Bay and of the equally shallow channels leading to the ocean, sought ways to better provide for shipping. If South Florida was to become a great seaport, there had to be a better way to get from the ocean to the ports on the west side of the bay. At the time he was extending his railroad from West Palm Beach to Miami, Flagler deepened the channel leading from Cape Florida to the Miami River. In its natural state, the bay was dangerous to ships drawing more than six feet.[27] Flagler's dredges deepened a channel from 12 to 15 feet. Still, this was not the most convenient way to get to the ocean. A straight line from the port would be more adequate, but the beach blocked the way. Flagler sent Harold Parrott, the president of his companies, to Washington, D.C., to lobby for federal assistance in cutting a deeper harbor running from west to east. Parrott told a Congressional committee that if the federal government would cut across the narrow peninsula north of Norris Cut, the Flagler interests would dredge an 18-foot-deep channel from the port of Miami to the western edge of the beach.[28] In the 1901 session, Congress, approved a $300,000 appropriation to cut an 18-foot channel through the peninsula and to dredge a basin 1,200 by 600 feet inside the bay. Flagler, through Parrott, agreed to spend a like amount to dredge a channel of the same depth from the Miami wharf to the peninsula.[29] Thus, Miamians such as Dick Smith knew as early as 1901 that soon there would be a new southern tip to the Ocean Beach. That would explain why Smith did not erect his two-story building at the southern tip of the remote peninsula. Instead, he built a bit further up-land, where the new southern extremity would be located.

John Sewell, who built the Royal Palm Hotel for Flagler and also cleared Miami's first streets, recalled in his memoirs the day when U.S. House Rivers and Harbors committee officials came to Miami to select the exact spot to slice the peninsula for the new channel, now known as Government Cut:

> Congressman Burton [Theodore Burton, R-Ohio] brought his entire committee to Miami to look over the location of the new cut, bringing Mr. Davis [Robert Davis, D-Palatka], representing this district, with them. Mr. Flagler furnished his steamship *Martinique*, in command of Captain George Dillon, going out around Cape Florida and up the coast to inspect the location for the cut. I, as mayor, accompanied the committee on the trip. The wind was blowing and we had a rough sea. When we got to the point where the engineers had cut an opening through the brush for their stakes, Mr. Burton was up in the pilot house with his field glasses and when we got to where he could see the City of Miami through this opening across the seven hundred feet of land he said, 'This is fine— and we will make the cut right through according to the engineers' stakes, and let's get back inside the ship.' More than half of the party had gotten seasick and had to go to staterooms.[30]

The strip chosen for the cut still was owned by Field, who took the government to court over the value of the condemned land. Sewell claimed the court gave Field a good price on land that was assessed at $1.25 an acre.

On March 14, 1905, the cut was completed between the bay and the ocean, but not without some last minute exertion. Capt. G. Duncan Brossier, who came to Miami several years before it was incorporated and later went into the real estate business, recalled in an article he wrote for the *Miami Herald* in 1930:

> For several months, the P. Sanford Ross Dredging Company had been engaged in digging the channel from [the] Miami side of the bay to the ocean. They had proceeded far enough with their dredging operations that the honorable mayor of Miami, then John Sewell, declared a holiday for the purpose of witnessing this great event. The entire population of 3,500 people were present and it was a gala day. There was a great deal of excitement, as with each dip of the dredge the workers would cut a few feet closer to the ocean. The people were lined up on both sides of the cut making merry, forecasting, prophesying what the completion of this channel would mean to Miami. Then, for some unknown reason, the dredging operation stopped—the dipper dug its nose in the sand and refused to budge. Something had gone wrong. When the superintendent of the dredge announced that he had experienced a breakdown, and that the joining of these two waters would

The waters of Biscayne Bay (left) are about to meet the ocean as thousands of spectators watch the creation of Government Cut in 1905. (MN)

have to be postponed for another day, you can imagine the great disappointment to the patriarchs who had come so far, under such trying conditions, to witness this event. However, John Sewell, the man who never had been found wanting in any crucial moment, came to the rescue. With a spade he began to dig and soon the sand was flying in every direction. In less than 30 minutes a little stream from the bay, following the line of the trench made by Mr. Sewell, joined the waters of the Atlantic Ocean The current being very rapid and the pressure on the bay side rather strong, it was only a few hours until the cut widened from a foot to nearly ten feet, and the next day, those of us who visited the scene, found that the bay had cut a path through the island to a width over 500 feet.[31]

The assembled crowd apparently did not react with frustration at the first sign of the delay. It remained good natured and accepted the discomfort of going without dinner or liquid refreshment, as the digging by Sewell and others took until dark to complete.[32] Interestingly, no accounts mentioned formal names of either the elongated peninsula that had just been abbreviated or of the new island that had been formed between the new cut and Norris Cut to the south. They had none.

Five days after the cut was made, it had its first fatality. The chief engineer of the rock breaker dredge still working in the cut fell from the vessel and drowned.[33] He was Luther Greer, and no one named anything in his memory.

This was the land to which John Collins had come to farm in 1907—accessible by scheduled ferry boats, site of an oceanside bath house and lanced by dredges seeking a better way to carry goods to and from the 11-year-old City of Miami to the west and the Atlantic Ocean to the east. At first, it appeared his efforts with avocados would parallel the failure of earlier coconut plantings. In the case of avocados, the wind sweeping in off the ocean across the narrow strip and Indian Creek and into his orchards was damaging the crop. He was growing not only avocados and mangoes but tomatoes and potatoes as well which he planted between the trees.[34] He also planted Australian pine trees, because they grew quickly and served as excellent wind breaks.[35] Irrigation was a continuing problem. He further reduced his fortune by installing special pumping machinery, first as an overhead irrigation system, then, when he realized he was losing much water to evaporation, to an underground system.

Australian Pine trees still line the drive that was named for them. They were planted as protection from the wind when the area was part of John Collins' grove. (Fishbaugh; SPA)

As Flagler and the citizens of Miami envisioned the need for a channel to the sea for the new city to grow, Collins also had ideas about transportation. Taking his crop over to the railroad in Miami was a tedious process. It first had to be hauled overland to the western edge of the beach, then barged up the east side of the bay, across the northern portion and then down the west side to Miami, a distance of seven miles. It was the overland route Collins first sought to eliminate. He decided, in 1911, that he needed to build a canal from Indian Creek to Biscayne Bay, which would allow him to barge his avocados directly to the city. To avoid the shallow and still reptile-infested Crocodile Hole to the north, Collins cut his canal from a grass-covered pond on the southern edge of Indian Creek southwest to the bay, the spoil bank becoming today's Dade Boulevard. But cash was running low and he turned to his children in New Jersey for help.

It was logical for Collins to look to them; after all, he had set them up in business. Rather than an immediate response, they suggested they come to South Florida to see for themselves what he intended to do. The visiting party was comprised of Lester, Arthur and Irving Collins, Irving's wife, and Thomas and Katherine Pancoast.[36] The Collinses and Pancoasts checked into the Halcyon Hotel in downtown Miami, which is where John Collins had been living. They stayed in the area about three weeks but those three weeks were history-making because it was then that the groundwork was laid not only for a canal on the beach but for a bridge across the bay as well.

Shortly after their arrival in Miami, the family crossed the bay by boat to see what it was that had captured John Collins' undivided attention, as well as his money. After looking over the farm, the family was less than enthusiastic; at least about a future of avocado farming, or even of his successful Red Bliss potato crop that produced 18 carloads to ship north in 1911. They were loathe to pour a lot of money into the operation because they had their own plans for expansion back in New Jersey and would prefer to retain their money for those projects.[37] But these people were insightful. They saw something else in the narrow strip of land—a future resort center. That is what the Collinses and Pancoasts talked about when they returned to their hotel in the evening. Even before they left Miami, the family decided they would be willing to give John Collins money for his canal if he would build a bridge across the bay.[38] This would open the beach to motor traffic, enhance the value of the family real estate there and be the basis for great development of the heretofore remote strip of land. John Collins never turned down an opportunity to plow new fields. He immediately accepted their offer, saying that the beach could become another Atlantic City. But he still was a farmer at heart. Give him the money that he asked for his farm and he would work with them on their

dreams and ambitions. Out of this agreement came the Miami Beach Improvement Company, a firm invested in by the entire family and perhaps the first time the name "Miami Beach" appeared on any legal document.

But John Collins could not handle all this enterprise by himself. He already was 74 years old. He needed help and when his sons declined to leave the family homesteads in New Jersey, Thomas and Katherine Pancoast stepped forward. It was a courageous decision. Not even John Collins' wife had accompanied him on earlier trips to Miami. She would join him at the winter home in Hypoluxo Beach but would not come to Miami until the farm was built. Even then she stayed at the Halcyon. None of the Collins daughters-in-law wanted to come to the new frontier.[39] Thomas Pancoast would come first to Miami to get things started, then be joined by Katherine. Later, their son Russell, who had been sent to live with his aunts and uncles, would be brought down.

Work on the canal and bridge was to run almost simultaneously, but it didn't happen that way. When the Biscayne Navigation Company found out that Collins planned to span the bay, the company went to the county and complained that their ferry business would be ruined. Prompted by his lawyer Frank Shutts, owner of the *Miami Herald* and counsel for Henry Flagler, Collins drove his automobile to the Biscayne Navigation Company dock in Miami and demanded that one of the ships take him and his car over to the beach. None of Smith and Warr's vessels could accommodate an automobile. Collins' point was made, and he was awarded a franchise to build what would be called the world's longest wooden bridge.

The Collins Bridge began where the Collins Canal met the bay. Permission to span the bay came from the U.S. War Department in May 1912; the permit caused a flurry of excitement. Property owners on the peninsula properly anticipated a rush of real

John Collins built the canal from his avocado groves to Biscayne Bay to more easily move his crop to market. The fill from the Collins canal was used to create Dade Boulevard. (Matlack; HASF)

estate sales. Upon word of War Department approval, the realty firm of Bendle and Anderson advertised that "Ocean Beach is destined to become a great commercial port, a veritable Treasure Island, a year-round residence section and winter play ground for the multitudes."[40] Bendle and Anderson were selling 50x130 foot lots from $400 to $1,200, cautioning "procrastinators to BUY, and BUY NOW!"[41] The people of Miami took note of John Collins. He no longer was the quiet little Quaker who farmed out on the peninsula. On July 6, 1912, the *Miami Metropolis* brought him out to page one with a story headlined: "The Great Improvements Now Being Made At Collins' Ranch, Across Bay." It noted his investment in land on the beach 20 years earlier. "The investment, it is safe to assume, did not represent such a tremendous amount," wrote the *Metropolis*. "Bought at the time it was, the taxes were small and it was not until four years ago that a start was made on what it is now proposed to make the show place of all show places in Dade County." (Perhaps the *Metropolis* did not think his investment was consuming his pocketbook, but Collins and his family knew better.) The story went on to detail his success with avocados, mangoes and potatoes, then added:

Interest in the Collins ranch has been revived greatly within the last few months by reason of its close association with the bridge that is to be built across the bay, starting at a point about a mile above the city limits. [Northeast 15th Street]. When it was decided to improve the property, but before thoughts of a bridge across Biscayne Bay had been dreamed of, Mr. Collins concluded a short cut to the ocean beach would be necessary. . . . The canal, it was intended, should cut directly across the peninsula to a small lake at the head of what is known as Indian Creek, though slough would be a better name for it. . . . Two machines are now within a few hundred yards of each other and by September 25th, according to the estimate of Thomas J. Pancoast, secretary and treasurer of the company, they will have met and the public will be invited to inspect one of the neatest propositions to be found in the entire county. . . .

According to Mr. Pancoast, work is to be begun on the bridge across the bay immediately. The eastern end of it will first strike land on Bull's [Belle] Island, which is crossed, and then comes a couple of small spans and the peninsula is reached directly at the mouth of the canal now being dug. Fifty feet back from the north bank of the canal has been cleared and for a mile the boulevard [Dade Boulevard] that is to be a continuation of the bridge follows that bank.

The *Metropolis* gave too much credit to Collins, citing him rather than his conservative sons and son-in-law for the land development that was to follow. "Though primarily intended as a big fruit ranch, Mr. Collins has decided the proposition offers too many advantages to be kept from the public, and has laid out four tiers of blocks containing 415 lots facing the beach boulevard," wrote the *Metropolis*. "These are being improved as rapidly as possible and by fall will be ready to be offered to the public."

Several months later, Miami's newest newspaper, the *Miami Herald*, showed its enthusiasm with a page one story. The newspaper, while calling attention to the phenomenal growth throughout the Miami district, concentrated on the beach, saying a trip there "will astonish the average individual if he has not been there for a month or two."[42] The newspaper began by predicting:

Five years from now—that is the maximum, mind you—there will be an East Miami. That may not be the name of it, but the suburb will be there just the same. It will occupy land that is now a mass of mangrove, palmetto and tangled jungle and the location will be on the peninsula just across the bay from the city. Sooner than it will be realized there will be a bridge across the bay, and when the ocean side is accessible without a tedious ride of a half hour in a boat anything but comfortable, and with paved roads running up and down a perfect beach, then will homeseekers and investors grab at a chance to secure holdings in a place so ideally located.[43]

But there was frustration and difficulty aplenty on the horizon for Collins and his family. Building the bridge was not as easy as they expected, and certainly more costly than ever they imagined. While it made things difficult for them, it paved the way for the entry into the beach scene of a man who was to shape the destiny of the land in his own dynamic image.

Carl Fisher was about to step on stage.

CHAPTER FOUR

"MEET ME IN MIAMI ...NICE LITTLE TOWN"

Carl Fisher's arrival in South Florida was not planned. He was supposed to join his yacht in Jacksonville, but when John Levi sailed out of the Gulf of Mexico, around Cape Sable and into Biscayne Bay, he wired the Indianapolis magnate to meet him in Miami. (HASF)

To begin building the bridge from Miami to the beach, Collins and Pancoast turned to Miami as well as New Jersey banks for funding. The Lummus brothers—J. E. and J. N.—both arrived in Miami before the railroad and, by 1912, were established in the banking business. J. E. Lummus, as president of the Southern Bank & Trust Company, loaned Collins $10,000 and J. N., as president of the Bank of Bay Biscayne, loaned him $15,000.[1] The Collins and Pancoast plans for the beach were not lost on the Lummuses; they saw an opportunity building. In May 1912, before work even began on the Collins bridge, a company headed by the Lummus brothers bought 500 acres of land on the southern end of the beach from Charles Lum and Edmund Wilson. The price: $80,000. In October, they bought an additional 80 acres from Jennie Richardson of Detroit, land J. N. Lummus later reported was all swamp, mangrove and palmetto—some of it under water at high tide.[2] The Lummuses sometimes get lost in history, particularly in the shadow of soon-to-arrive Carl Fisher, but it was they who actually pioneered sales on the beach. The Lummuses called their company Ocean Beach Realty Company. On July 9, 1912 they filed the first plat on the beach; five months before Collins and six months before Fisher. (Fisher did not file his first plat until January 15, 1914.[3]) In subsequent newspaper interviews as well as in J. N. Lummus' 1940 personalized history, *The Miracle of Miami Beach*, it becomes evident that the man who loaned Collins money to *start* his bridge, who sold the first lots and who became the first mayor when the City of Miami Beach was incorporated in 1915, was envious of the attention historians paid to Fisher. (The Lummus brothers are barely mentioned in Nash's *The Magic of Miami Beach*. Only two widely separated sentences and no photographs identifying the Lummuses appear in the 144-page book, which could be one of the reasons J. N. published a history of his own two years later.) While not detracting from the gigantic role Fisher played in development of the beach, Lummus was adamant that the public be aware that he and his brother were Miami Beach's first developers.

James E. Lummus and John N. Lummus were brothers who preferred to use their initials rather than their first names, a decision that brought about confused identifications by historians and reporters beyond the lifetimes of the two men. J. E. was born six years earlier than J. N., in 1867. Both were born in Bronson, in Florida's Levy County, the sons of Ezekial and Frances Lummus, originally of Georgia. Ezekial, a farmer, was a Confederate veteran who relocated to Bronson shortly before J. N.'s birth. While J. E. pursued a business career, J. N. took up telegraphy and worked as a telegraph operator for railroads.[4] "Coming to Miami. . . in 1895, before the Flagler Railroad was completed into the city," J. N. later wrote, "I saw that there was a great future here. I remained in Miami until after the first train of the Florida East Coast Railway puffed its way into the village over wobbly tracks."[5] He returned a year later as a train dispatcher and held that job for seven years. Meanwhile, J. E. sold his business interest in Bronson and came to Miami in February 1896 to open a general merchandise store that he maintained until 1908. During that period, J. E. won a commissary contract with the Florida East Coast Railway to supply materials for the railroad extension to Key West. J. N. became associated with his older brother, traveling by boat once a week to the railroad camps along the Florida Keys to collect money and check the inventory. In 1908, J. E. turned to banking, joining the Bank of Bay Biscayne and becoming its president in 1909. Brother J. N. went into the title abstract business and remained in that business while serving

J. N. Lummus was the first to plat land and begin selling lots on what now is Miami Beach. (MB)

as one of the founders of the Southern Bank and Trust Company in 1911. When John Collins and Thomas Pancoast came in pursuit of loans the following year to begin the bridge across the bay, J. E. and J. N. were in positions to loan them money—and to take note of the possibilities the bridge would create.[6]

Thomas Pancoast arrived in Miami on July 1, 1912 to close contracts for construction of the Collins Bridge. Pancoast was secretary and treasurer of the new Miami Beach Improvement Company with John Collins as president. Work on the bridge began on July 22.[7] It was estimated that the bridge would cost $75,000 to build and would consist of a million and a half feet of lumber, 2,000 barrels of cement, 3,000 pilings and tons of nails and bolts. The George F. Cook Company was chosen to do the building and J. I. Conklin, who had drawn the plans and specifications, was retained as supervisor of the project.[8] It was first thought that the two-and-one-half-mile long bridge—13,000 feet long, to be precise—would require from four to six months to complete. Instead, it took 10 months.

While the bridge originally was supposed to be entirely of wood, it quickly became evident that bare wood pilings would not last long. Marine worms of several descriptions threatened to eat away at the pilings. The price of the bridge went up by $10,000 and time was lost when Collins was forced to order sheet iron that would slip over the submerged wood pilings. It was into those iron tubes that concrete would be poured around the timber. Pancoast returned to Miami in late August, boasting that Florida would be his future home for good. "Mrs. Pancoast and our youngest son will join me as soon as I can arrange for the accommodation," he told a reporter in Miami, "and with the completion of the bridge we will build a home of our own across the bay."[9] Avery Smith, having lost the battle with Collins to keep the bridge from being built, remained active with his Fairy Land resort on what now was Lummus property. Realizing that his boats no longer would monopolize transportation from Miami across the bay, but that auto traffic would bring even more people to the beach, Smith and his partners proceeded

To keep up with the competition, Avery Smith added amenities to his casino. (Fishbaugh; SPA)

to upgrade the old Smith Casino property. (In the lexicon of the day, a casino was a building used for dancing and other entertainment but not necessarily for gambling.) Smith wrote to the *Miami Herald* in August 1912 that 50 more bath houses were being added to the casino, making 155 in all. He also said a large piazza would be added in front of the pavilion, with wicker chairs for guests. In obvious response to the speed with which people in automobiles soon would be able to cross over on Collins Bridge, Smith installed new and heavier powered motors on his vessels for "a quicker and more frequent service" between the beach and the mainland.[10]

At the same time, Smith also was getting another competitor, in the bathing house business. Where Collins' and Pancoast's bridge loomed as a threat to his cross-bay transportation system, a group headed by Dade County sheriff Dan Hardie planned a second beach front amusement and recreation center. Originally referred to as "Coney Island,"[11] the new ocean casino which came to be known as Hardie's Casino, had a strong list of officers and subscribers including Hardie, J. N. Lummus, editor S. Bobo Dean of the *Miami Metropolis*, meat purveyor Phillip Ullendorf, hotelier Gus Muller and

local clothier E. B. Douglas. Hardie's was a storied name in the area. History recorded him as the last of the frontier sheriffs based on the rhetoric of his campaigning and the operation of his office. "I am for arresting suspicious characters first, and letting them explain afterwards," he boasted in his 1908 campaign that swept him into the sheriff's office.[12]

John Collins still spent his summers in New Jersey and would not return to Miami until November. It was obvious that Collins' son-in-law was assuming command of the family interests. Thomas Pancoast negotiated and signed the contracts; he made the public statements. But Collins certainly did not relinquish all his authority. In the summer of 1912, he offered free park land on the beach to the City of Miami, no strings attached. The 10 acres of land is between today's 21st and 22nd streets, eventual site of the Miami Beach Public Library, the Bass Art Museum and the parking lot that goes down to the beachfront. The mainland city took Collins up on the offer and accepted the park, even though it was well outside and across the bay from the city limits.[13] (In 1919, the four-year-old City of Miami Beach bought the park from Miami for $1,000 and devoted several thousand more dollars to clean up what was said to be "one of the few eyesores on Miami Beach."[14])

While Pancoast, as the on-the-scene executive of the Miami Beach Improvement Company, claimed the cross-bay bridge project was running ahead of schedule, he reported there were some problems. Pilings that arrived for the west side of the bridge were too short and work had to be shifted over to the eastern side of the bridge, at Bull's Island.[15] In December, it was reported that pile driving for the bridge was reaching completion and that it was expected that the bridge would be completed and ready for traffic by February 1, 1913.[16] Then there was a lack of barges, delaying the planking. February 1 came and went. On February 11, the *Miami Herald* reported there still were 4,000 feet of

In 1912, Hardie's Casino (left) opened just north of Smith's (right). A wooden boardwalk connected the two south beach casinos with the Collins Casino at 23rd Street. (Alice Wood)

the bridge to be planked before reaching its eastern terminus.[17]

In late 1912, Collins and Pancoast had run out of credit and cash. The bridge was a half–mile short of reaching the beach. Pancoast later said that eventually the family could have raised the money to finish the project. But, as 1912 began to fade, fresh funds or credit needed to be realized quickly or the project would have to stop. And the notoriety of a

work stoppage would be devastating to the land sales that the Miami Beach Improvement Company was conducting. By then, a new face came upon the scene. He was Carl Fisher, a high-living industrialist from Indiana who made a fortune with Prest-O-Lite automobile headlamps and who built the Indianapolis Speedway.

Fisher was a relative newcomer to the area. He had met Collins and was impressed that a man his age would take on such a huge adventure. When he learned of Collins' financial difficulty, Fisher decided to bail him out—and include himself in. On January 21, 1913, he advanced Collins $50,000 in bonds to complete the bridge and, in turn, was given 200 acres of land on the beach. It ran from the ocean to the bay, 1,800 feet wide north and south.[18] It was but a beginning for Fisher, who was to carve an empire out of it. For Collins and Pancoast, it was a good deal as well. They needed the money to finish their bridge (and canal) and get on with the selling of lands they retained. Already, there was a competitor on the southern tip in the Lummuses' Ocean Beach Development Company. Collins and Pancoast knew they had to get the Miami Beach Improvement Company moving quickly or risk losing land sales business to the Lummuses and their partners. And surely they realized that Carl Fisher would not be far behind.

Ironically, the first link completed between Miami and what would be Miami Beach came just two days after the death of Henry Flagler, the man

Ocean Beach Realty Company employees and J. N. Lummus' daughter Helen pose before raising the American flag in front of the company's south beach office on March 17, 1913. **Above top:** *1913 advertisement for lot sales for J. N. Lummus' Ocean Beach Realty Company. Lots on the South Beach section sold for between $650 and $800 each. (Miami Metropolis)*

who forged the first link from civilization to the emerging jungle on the bay. Despite the sadness of that loss, there could not help but be a jubilant feeling as the bay finally was conquered. On May 22, 1913, Thomas Pancoast and his family had the honor of being the first persons to cross the new span. Accompanying the Pancoasts on the historic journey were builders, contractors and newspaper writers. John Collins was not there; he remained back in New Jersey, a further indication of the aging Collins' acquiescence to Pancoast as the functioning head of the family projects.[19] The Collins Bridge did not reach all the way to the peninsula until June 12. It ended at Bull's Island, the only natural island in that area of Biscayne Bay. From there, a foot bridge provided visitors access to the beach. However, a dredge was busy filling in land for a dirt road between Bull's Island and the beach over which automobiles eventually would drive. For the time being, cars had to be turned around on Bull's Island for the trip back to the mainland. The bridge was two laned, and had a four foot high railing its entire length. Pancoast claimed it was the world's longest bridge, saying he had investigated the matter thoroughly and could find no record anywhere of a bridge of such length.[20] The drawbridge, on the west side of the bridge, was one that revolved rather than raised.[21] In the three weeks between the time Pancoast led his invitation-only caravan across the bridge and when it was opened to the public, finishing touches, such as the bridge tender's house and toll gates, were completed. The toll for pedestrians and bicycles was five cents, while motorcycles and one-horse riders were charged 10 cents. Toll for one-seat automobiles was 15 cents;

When autos reached the Bull's Island east end of Collins Bridge, a turntable was used to point them back toward Miami. (Pancoast Family)

two-seats were charged 20 cents. Sightseeing vehicles were charged anywhere from $5 to $15, depending upon the horsepower of their engines.[22]

As the bridge was being built, competition for land sales and recreational tourism on the beach was growing. Newspaper ads placed by both the Lummus and the Collins interests pointed to a new bridge opening the way for Miamians to come over to the island and invest. Ocean Beach Realty Company, with Joseph McDonald—one of Flagler's most capable associates—as president, former judge and state attorney John Gramling as vice president, J. N. Lummus as secretary-treasurer, and Avery Smith as a partner, was selling lots on the old Lum property for from $650 to $1,000, with 10 per cent cash as a down payment. Ocean Beach Realty referred to the peninsula as "A Tropical Isle, between the Mighty Atlantic and Beautiful Bay Biscayne"[23] and boasted of the anticipated increase in value of the properties with each improvement made in the area. Ocean Beach Realty had cleared, graded and built streets on 40 acres of the property as early as January 15. It also was building a 10-foot wide boardwalk along the ocean side and had constructed two cement bungalows for sale or rent on Atlantic Boulevard, later to be renamed Collins Avenue. Ocean Beach Realty was spending a lot of money—money that it did not have. The company started with a cash capital of $50,000 and borrowed additional funds at eight per cent from the two banks of the Lummus brothers. Other investors sought a quick fortune and it wasn't there. They offered to sell out and the Lummus brothers took them up on it.[24] With a lot of property to develop and very

Spectators watch first autos set out from Miami across the Collins Bridge enroute to the beach. (Alice Wood)

31

A long string of autos crosses the two-and-one-half-mile long Collins Bridge on its June 12, 1912, opening day. Thomas Pancoast claimed the bridge to be the longest wooden bridge in the world. (HASF)

little cash, the Lummuses were in a tight spot as 1913 began. It was then that Carl Fisher dropped into the Ocean Beach Realty office on today's Flagler Street, introduced himself to J. N., and questioned why the Lummuses weren't developing all their properties simultaneously. When J. N. explained the cash problem, Fisher loaned the company $150,000 at eight per cent interest. The Lummuses gave Fisher 105 acres on the north end of the Ocean Beach property plus a mortgage on all swamp lands Ocean Beach owned west of what would be Washington Avenue but then was called Miami Avenue.[25]

In February, Ocean Beach Realty resident agent Capt. John H. Welch reported that an average of a lot a day had been sold in the previous two weeks.[26] John Gramling, an officer of the company, was building a house on the street facing the ocean and John W. King, architect for the Ocean Beach group, was putting up two bungalows just above the Gramling house. Construction on Hardie's new casino, on today's Ocean Drive between Biscayne and First Streets, also was well under way. "Conditions are changing rapidly on the ocean beach. . . ," the *Miami Metropolis* reported on January 10, 1913:

It is beginning to assume the appearance of a seaside resort. What the imagination of the incorporators of the Ocean Beach Realty

Company depicted last summer is beginning to take definite shape. It took faith to undertake the job of making the waste of sand and the mangrove swamp into an attractive and habitable place, but faith marches at the head of progress, and there are now few doubters as to the ultimate outcome.

Lummus' men were at work creating a 20-foot-wide rock road from where the Collins Bridge would reach through the entire Lummus tract. To drive from the heart of Miami, across the bridge and down to the southern end of Ocean Beach Realty property would be a distance of seven miles. "A big force of men is now at work on this road under the supervision of Mr. Frank Hardee," the *Metropolis* continued. "Looking northward from First Street, it presents a long vista flanked with cocoa palm and other forms of wild shrubbery. The completed plan calls for various kinds of palms and ornamental trees along the highway.

Thus, the image of the beach as a remote and vast jungle waiting to be tamed by Carl Fisher is not entirely accurate. Men already were at work. J. N. Lummus wrote:

We hauled kerosene to the beach by the barge loads to burn the palmetto and

land sales business. The Miami Beach Improvement Company scheduled an auction for 100 ocean front lots. The four-day sale was restricted to 25 lots per day. A written five year guarantee for free use of the Collins Bridge went with the sale of each lot. Also assured was an infrastructure of sewer and water connections, electricity, cement sidewalks and an elevated boardwalk at the ocean front.[29] To conduct the auction, Collins and Pancoast hired Edward "Doc" Dammers who, it later was observed, "was the type of salesman who could make a good living selling ice cream to the Eskimos."[30] Dammers was to hold similar auctions on behalf of the Lummus and Collins interests, later becoming a dominant factor in land sales in mainland Miami and, eventually, Coral Gables where he became the city's first mayor. It was Dammers' style to lure prospective customers to the scene with giveaways. For the Miami Beach Improvement Company auction, 400 prizes were prepared for distribution to anyone who took advantage of a free boat ride across the bay from Miami and listened to Doc's sales pitch. The prizes included leather goods, clocks, opera glasses, vases, dinner sets and oriental rugs.[31] In the four days, all 104 lots were sold, four more than were supposed to be. Depending upon size and location, some lots sold for as little as $760; the highest price, $3,700, was paid by Miami businessman S. A. Belcher.[32]

This was the frenzied frontier environment that Carl Fisher found when he began acquiring land in exchange for loans. And he loved it. As a result of his acquisitions, Fisher now owned a nice chunk of the peninsula, from the northern edge of Ocean Beach Realty property to the southern side of Miami Beach Improvement. He called his property Alton Beach, a name with no specific meaning. Fisher is credited with deciding upon that name while riding in a train to Indianapolis. He saw a freight train with "Chicago, Northwestern and Alton Railroad" on one of its cars and decided he liked the name Alton.[33] In a short while, he would begin transforming the barrier strip into a playground for millionaires based on a genius for marketing that eclipsed his colleagues in land sales and development of Miami Beach.

How Fisher got to be the man who built Miami Beach is an adventure in itself. After he died, much of his early life was told by his first wife Jane Fisher in her 1947 book *Fabulous Hoosier*, but Jane had a reputation for embellishment. In his lifetime, however, Fisher apparently was loathe to hold still for biographical studies. His collected papers, on file at the Historical Association of Southern Florida, include a decade-long series of letters from the *National Cyclopedia of American Biography* pleading with him to complete the biographical forms sent him for their publication. The pleas continued after

mangrove. Only the small stuff would burn, so we chopped up the remainder and used the logs and stumps for reinforcing the dredged materials as it was pumped in, until it was built up from three to five feet. We were bothered with rattlesnakes, hundreds of coons, thousands of rats and millions of mosquitoes. The rattlesnakes were dangerous, the coons a nuisance and the rats and mosquitoes were pests.[27]

There is no doubt that Fisher was the catalyst by which the beach grew rapidly, but prior to any Fisher enterprise, work on the beach was already impressive. As Lummus' Ocean Beach Realty Company pressed hard on land sales, Collins' and Pancoast's Miami Beach Improvement Company worked hard at keeping abreast. With the bridge still under construction and the canal nearing completion, Collins and Pancoast first responded to the improvement of Smith's Casino and the construction of Hardie's. On December 27, 1912, work began on a Collins casino, located between today's 22nd and 23rd streets. The building was two stories high, its lower floor a dressing room for bathers and a portion of the upper floor was a dance hall.[28]

As the pages on the calendar turned to 1913, Collins and Pancoast entered into the thick of the

MIAMI BEACH
AUCTION SALE 3 DAYS

Wednesday, Thursday and Friday
FEB. 18--19--20
From 10 A. M. until 11:30 A. M.
Each Day at Miami Beach

OWNERS
The Miami Beach Improvement Co.
210 Twelfth Street, Miami, Florida

Sale Conducted By
DAMMERS & GILLETTE
of 47 West 34th Street, New York

The Miami Beach Improvement Company advertised its first-ever auction of property for three days in February 1913. To conduct the auction, Collins and Pancoast hired Edward "Doc" Dammers and offered 400 prizes to people who took the free boat ride across the bay to the auction. (SPA) **Right:** Edward "Doc" Dammers was a dynamic salesman of Miami Beach and, later, Coral Gables property. He became the first mayor of Coral Gables. (HASF)

his death in 1939 but to Carl's widow, Margaret Collier Fisher, his second wife. She continued to ignore the requests and tucked the partially completed form into the file of his personal papers. Fisher also never appeared in *Who's Who*, an indication that he did not cooperate with that publication, either.

Fisher's arrival in the Miami area was accidental. He had ordered a yacht built for cruising Lake Michigan, near where he had a summer home. He called it the *Elph* after a dog he once owned. Realizing the delivery date corresponded with winter months on the lake, he devised an inaugural—and business—trip down the Mississippi River. The December 1909 trip was to take place when his marriage to the former Jane Watts was less than two months old but Jane wasn't invited. A friend, Henry Buchmann, was. So was William Galloway, his trusted black servant and man Friday. And so was an engineer named John Levi, who designed the *Elph* at Seabury Shipyards in New York.

When Jane found out she wasn't invited, the teen-aged bride threw a fit. Carl ultimately relented but subjected her to a manly lifestyle aboard, including having her chew on a plug of tobacco. Jane

rationalized the episode by writing that Carl loved her but that he was, and always would be, a bachelor at heart.[34]

Christmas Eve 1909 found the *Elph* in New Orleans, where Carl and his friends went ashore for a night of revelry and left Jane stewing. A few days later, while cruising in the Gulf of Mexico near Mobile Bay, either a navigation problem or a storm blew the *Elph* onto a sandbar.[35]

After the mishap, the Fishers left the vessel and returned to Indianapolis, leaving Levi to ship the *Elph* by railroad flatcar to Jacksonville where the Fishers would meet him. However, it was discovered that there was a bridge across the tracks somewhere between Mobile and Jacksonville under which the *Elph* could not fit. Levi was left with no choice but to sail the ship to Jacksonville. Hiring a cook and pilot, he embarked on the journey only to find his pilot was without merit. After three days of not sighting land, Levi took control of the *Elph* and headed due east. His landfall was at Cape Sable on Florida's lower coast. From there, and with the assistance of a fisherman guide he hired near Cape Sable, he turned up toward Florida's southeast coast en route to Jacksonville.[36] Two weeks after leaving the ship, Fisher received a telegram from Levi. "Meet me in Miami instead of Jacksonville," it said. "Nice little town."[37]

An epic-making relationship was about to begin.

Below: *In an obviously playful mood, Carl and Jane Fisher framed their faces in holly wreaths for their Christmas card for pioneer Miami Beach photographer Claude Matlack. (Matlack; HASF)*

CARL FISHER BEFORE FLORIDA

Carl Fisher was born in Greensburg, Indiana, January 12, 1874, son of Albert and Ida Graham Fisher. He did not go past the sixth grade, choosing instead to drop out in 1886. At the age of 12, he sold newspapers and candy on the train that passed through Greensburg, about 50 miles southeast of Indianapolis.[1]

When he was 17, his mother divorced her heavy-drinking husband and moved with her three sons to Indianapolis. Carl used $600 in savings to open a bicycle repair shop there with his brothers Rolly and Earle.[2] Carl became adept at racing bicycles. At times he appeared with future auto racing star Barney Oldfield in county fair bike races in Indiana, Illinois and Ohio. Ever competitive, Carl never won any championships but he was popular.

His business grew on the strength of his advertising, his racing renown and the mechanical skills he and his brothers possessed. It wasn't long, however, before the automobile attracted Carl's attention. After opening a garage in Indianapolis, he began racing at Midwest dirt tracks. In 1904, Fisher drove two miles in 2.02 minutes around a Chicago track, a record then. [3]

Among his ambitions was a race track in Indianapolis. Simultaneous with that dream was a $10,000 gamble with a new auto product that would produce millions for him. In 1904, few cars had more than dim, kerosene-powered headlamps. Not only did they not throw off enough light, but they kept blowing out as motorists increased their speed. On a visit to Dayton, Carl met Fred Avery, who had obtained the French patent for compressed acetylene but was being monumentally frustrated by the instability of the gas. Carl was ready to jump at any idea that would light the night roads brightly. He put $10,000 into development of the lamp.[4]

In its early days, the Prest-O-Lite company endured explosion after explosion. No window in Indianapolis appeared safe from the blasts of the Prest-O-Lite company. But the tanks that were successfully filled began to sell. More and more automobiles drove around with the Prest-O-Lite tanks strapped to their sides providing light during darkness.

Prest-O-Lite's new, less dangerous, plant rose on a 400-acre farm outside Indianapolis. And nearby, he

began to fulfill his greatest dream at the time, the Speedway. Union Carbide, which had been following the Prest-O-Lite success story with great interest, sought to obtain the company. Fisher was heavily involved in his auto race track and, in seeking the financial freedom and time to do it, he sold his controlling interest in Prest-O-Lite to Union Carbide for $9 million, then turned sole attention to the speedway.[5]

The Indianapolis Motor Speedway was chartered in February 1909 with a capital of a quarter-million dollars. In the first featured race on Aug. 19, 1909, a driver and his riding mechanic crashed and were killed. On the third day, two spectators and a car's mechanic were killed. Three days of racing and five dead.[6] What's more, the tar-and-gravel track was disintergrating under the wheels of the racing cars. Humiliated by the track conditions and mortified by the deaths, Fisher halted the race after 235 miles and promised better things in the future. He and his partners put their heads—and money—together and ordered 3.2 million bricks to put over what was left of the scandalized surface.[7]

Races held in 1910 drew small crowds and Fisher realized he would have to do something spectacular to reestablish his race track. And he did. He created a 500-mile-long auto race in 1911 and, in doing so, boasted: "We're talking about the greatest automobile race ever put on anywhere on the face of the earth."[8]

A crowd estimated to be near 80,000 paid $1 apiece to see Fisher's first 500-miler in 1911. He had snatched his speedway from the jaws of defeat. While still in its infancy, the event already would be called the greatest spectacle in sports. In 1912, Fisher doubled the original $25,000 prize money. With each new year, he made improvements; the Memorial Day race continued to grow in attendance, purses and popularity.

While Fisher's first love may have been his speedway, he had another. She was 20 years his junior. Jane Watts met Carl Fisher when she was but 15 years old and he was 35. Their courtship was whirlwind, and they married on October 23, 1909 in a small home ceremony attended only by family.[9]

It was shortly thereafter that Carl's already dynamic life story was to add its greatest chapter: Miami Beach.

A. J. Bendle's Miami Beach residence, begun in 1913 and completed the next year, is credited by some as being the first house built on the beach. Those who so credit Bendle ignore the fact that Charles Lum built a residence on the beach in 1886. (MB)

FISHER'S HOT AIR BALLOON STUNT

To spur sales of his Stoddard-Dayton, Packard and Reo automobiles, Carl Fisher devised a stunt in Indianapolis in October 1908 that would carry his white Stoddard-Dayton roadster into the sky dangling from a hot air balloon. He promised to drive the car back from its landing site.

The balloon lifted the roadster and carried it 10 miles out of the city. Shortly, Carl drove into Indianapolis with the collapsed balloon in the back seat. It caused a sensation that attracted nationwide attention.

Jane Fisher, his first wife, wrote in her 1947 book *Fabulous Hoosier* that it was a hoax; that what the public did not know was that Carl's brother Rolly had driven a like car out to the landing site. The auto that had been lifted by the hot air balloon had no engine in it, she contended. That's how it was able to be lifted.

When Carl descended in the balloon, she wrote, he switched cars and drove into Indianapolis.

CHAPTER FIVE

A TOWN IS CREATED

The Lummus Investment Company Building at Biscayne Avenue (now Biscayne Street) and Ocean Drive was the site of Miami Beach's incorporation meeting and earliest city business. (HASF)

When Carl and Jane Fisher arrived by train in Miami in February 1910, the warm breezes certainly must have made an impression upon them. Ever since Christmas, all the northern states and much of the Deep South had been numbed by winter cold. As 1909 closed, even Miami was to feel the cold blasts. Temperatures bottomed out in Miami at 33 degrees. But winter spells are much milder and shorter in South Florida compared to the North. Carl Fisher had been back in frozen Indianapolis for several weeks when he received the telegram from John Levi to come to Miami. Temperatures had returned to being warm by the time they stepped off the train to meet Levi aboard the *Elph* anchored in the Miami River. Neither the *Miami Metropolis* nor the *Miami Morning News-Record* made note of the Fishers' presence in Miami then, which was unusual, as both newspapers usually reported famous and/or rich people and their yachts visiting Biscayne Bay. The Fishers did not stay long; it was getting to be the time when advance preparations had to be made for the Memorial Day races at Speedway. They sailed aboard the *Elph* as far as Jacksonville but disembarked there and took the train back to Indianapolis.[1]

Buying a home in Miami appeared farthest from Carl's mind in the late spring and summer days of 1910, but when he received an advertisement for a house in Miami, he bought it unseen. The seller was a Civil War veteran named Alonso Bliss who had achieved wealth in herbal medicine and real estate. Bliss was one of Washington, D.C.'s largest real estate holders. He later made real estate investments in Miami and spent his winters there in a home near today's Southeast 14th Street and Brickell Avenue.[2] Carl and Jane Fisher named their new home *The Shadows* because, Jane wrote, of the shadows thrown across the property by the Australian pine trees. This was not Fisher's first home away from home. Earlier, he bought land, also sight unseen, in St. Joseph, Michigan, just north of Indiana on the east side of the lake. He built the first of their summer homes there and also planned a resort. (It now is the St. Joseph Yacht Club.)

If Carl had any intentions about retiring to Miami, he kept it hidden. He was not yet 40 and was fully involved with his motor speedway. But his vacations in Miami would be fun times. It was a place to bring his boat, and to party. It did not take long, however, for wealthy Carl Fisher to become a target. On the evening of February 20, 1912, while the Fishers were entertaining house guests, their Brickell Avenue home was robbed of $2,000 in cash and jewelry. A theft of that significance was major news in Miami. The robbery occurred while the Fishers and their guests were in the ballroom. When Jane discovered the theft in another part of the house, Carl immediately set bonfires around the property in anticipation that the burglar still was on the premises.[3] The crime went unsolved. Among the lost property were Jane's ruby ring, two small diamond rings, one garnet necklace, a black opal and diamond ring, other jewelry and cash.[4]

The year 1912 was otherwise momentous in Carl Fisher's life. He reached great wealth—his share of the sale of Prest-O-Lite to Union Carbide that year was greater than $5 million. Before the year had ended, he would be a party to building a new town outside Indianapolis; he would embark on one great venture running the breadth of the United States

A wide swath through dense growth became Miami Beach's famous Lincoln Road. (Pancoast Family)

and he would prepare to start another in creating a tourist mecca where, only a few years earlier, a remote sandbar stood. Early in the year, he, his friend Jim Allison and Frank H. Wheeler laid out the town of Speedway to the west of Indianapolis and adjacent to his auto race course. Jane recalled that Carl originally conceived the idea as a town to house the workers at the Prest-O-Lite factory. "And I won't have a damned horse in the streets," the man made rich by automotives told his wife.[5] Many of its streets were—and still are—named for automobiles: Ford, Nash, Buick, DeSoto, Cadillac, etc. A stipulation in the deeds—said no longer to exist by the Speedway city clerk—was that no land ever be sold or rented to a black person and that no black be allowed to own or operate a business within the city.[6] This may be the first indication of a class conscious and/or racist trait that was not particularly evident in Fisher's early years but became an issue late in his life and has remained so posthumously.

In the fall of 1912, Fisher, ever the promoter, began to think that one way to create a market for more automobiles and automotive products would be to have more and better roads. Just a better road or two through Indiana or Ohio was not in his thinking. He envisioned one all the way across the United States. At the time, the only cross-country routes were railroads and the old wagon trails. Only 28 of the then-48 states spent any money on roads; the grand total of their expenditures amounted to $11 million. Carl wanted to spend $10 million on one road alone.[7] The idea of driving an automobile from the east all the way to the west coast was a dream but Carl believed in making dreams come true. His mind conjured up what he called, at first, the Coast-to-Coast Rock Highway.

He called together Indianapolis' leading automotive manufacturers and presented them with an idea: Help him with finances on building this coast-to-coast road and they would more than realize their money back in immensely increased automobile traffic and, therefore, snowballing automotive sales.[8] Fisher estimated it would take 18 months to build the highway, which would later be renamed the Lincoln Highway. The dinner party for the Indianapolis men was fruitful. Before the evening had ended, he had a pledge of $300,000 from Frank Seiberling of Goodyear Tire and Rubber Company. Within a month, he published the *Ocean-to-Ocean Highway Bulletin*, citing contributors to date and telling of the significance of a coast-to-coast highway-jobs, transportation,

Dredge churns fill out of Biscayne Bay to create land on the western side of Miami Beach. (Pancoast Family)

On January 21, 1913, Fisher received 200 acres of land on the beach from John Collins.[11] Fisher had loaned Collins $50,000 in late 1912 to complete his bridge. To cement the deal, Collins threw in the 200 acres as a bonus. Carl Fisher now owned an undeveloped, rugged piece of the peninsula. His young wife was particularly distressed.

No one knew why Carl wanted this ribbon of swamp. "I could not imagine nor could anyone else. When later we went by boat to inspect the new property, I protested. We walked, stepping gingerly and slapping at mosquitoes, skirting the swamp going toward the beach…I can recall how disgruntled I was that day. The mosquitoes were biting every inch of me. I refused to find any charm in this deserted strip of ugly land rimmed with a sandy beach. But Carl was like a man seeing visions.[12]

This was a challenge to Fisher. He told his bride that some day a great city would rise where they stood. Fisher not only had the recent background of the planning of Speedway and developing a beach resort in Michigan but he was able to look out the south windows of his *Shadows* estate in Miami and see dredges pumping out bay bottom to create land

Workman takes on seemingly impenetrable mangrove trees that dominated the Miami Beach landscape. (Matlack; HASF)

access, urban growth, and farm-to-market. He followed that with personal appeals to people in high places, including Henry Ford. The designer of the Model T remained a holdout, despite pleas from President William Howard Taft to join in the project. Ford defended his position by contending that as long as private industry built the roads, the public never would feel an obligation to road building.[9] As the months passed and believers backed his project with dollars, Fisher created the Lincoln Highway Association to plan the route and handle the day-to-day operations. Choice of the route was highly political. Fisher and the association intentionally kept it secret so as to keep interest high. When the route was announced at a meeting in Colorado—and excluded going through that state—Coloradans immediately reneged on their contributions. The route roughly paralleled today's Interstate 80 and was completed in 1915, although some spurs were not finished until 1930. It did not come easy. There were many years of continued battling for funds and involvements with major American corporations and presidents. Fisher turned much of the road project over to Henry B. Joy, who became the association's president while Carl accepted the role of vice president.[10]

During the period when he first planned the road and its completion, Fisher also become totally immersed in another major project on Biscayne Bay.

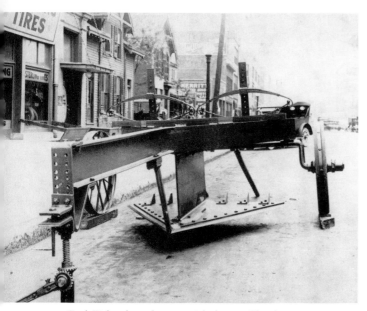

Carl Fisher brought a special plow to Florida to uproot mangroves. The Collins Bridge could not support its weight, so Fisher had it shipped from Miami to the beach by barge. (MB)

for Locke Highleyman's Point View project that adjoined the Fisher home on Brickell Avenue. But Fisher was not in Miami when the land deal with Collins was announced. Instead, John Levi, who had become his confidante and business associate, announced that a sea wall would be built on the bay side of the property and the bay dredged to a considerable depth, creating a channel which would allow yachts to put in on the west side of the ocean beach for the first time. Levi said the entire tract, running 1,800 feet wide from the bay to the ocean between the Lummus and Collins properties, would be cleared except for the best trees. He said thousands of others would be planted and that the tract soon would be divided into building lots.[13] There now would be three companies at work developing the beach: John Collins and Thomas Pancoast's Miami Beach Improvement Company to the north; Fisher's soon-to-be-named Alton Beach Realty Company in the center; and J. N. Lummus' Ocean Beach Realty Company south to Government Cut. For all parties, the arrival of Fisher and the completion of the Collins canal and bridge were the seeds from which would grow a great tourist resort.[14]

As part of J. N. Lummus' continuing rancor about being third-man-out at the hands of historians, he contended that he was the first to give land on the beach to Fisher.[15] This is not borne out by legal documents that show Fisher received Collins' land on January 23, 1913.[16] Lummus did not make his deal with Fisher until March 27, 1913.[17] He borrowed $150,000 from Fisher at eight per cent interest and turned over to him 150 acres of Ocean Beach Realty west of today's Washington Avenue—the

mangrove swamp. This gave Fisher 350 acres of land on the beach.[18]

Shortly, Fisher interests were hard at work clearing the land, pumping up bay bottom and laying out streets. Fisher's plan included platting 77 city blocks, building streets and wide boulevards, improving Bull's (Belle) Island and dredging the channel in the bay all the way to Government Cut.[19] Clearing the land, as Lummus and Collins already knew, was no easy task. The huge mangrove roots had to be dealt with. Jane Fisher related a story of how Fisher was sitting in his Indianapolis Motor Speedway office one day in the spring of 1913 and talking with an auto mechanic. The mechanic told him of a big plow he was building to clear some land in California. "Carl slapped his hand on the desk in a wild burst of hope," recalled Jane. " 'Build one for me, Al,' he exclaimed. 'The biggest plow you can build.' "[20] Fisher had the plow shipped to Miami where he bought a tractor to lug it around to the beach. Unfortunately, the tractor and plow were too heavy for the just-completed bridge and both had to be sent across the bay in a barge.[21]

Parallel to Fisher's endeavor, there were other happenings on the beach. In April 1913, the second casino on the peninsula opened. This was the casino that was to carry Dan Hardie's name. It was situated on Ocean Beach property between Biscayne and First Streets. With 160 changing rooms, lounges, 400 assorted bathing suits for hire, dining room and dance pavilion,[22] it painted a picture of the beach quite different than the total wilderness depicted by Jane Fisher. Also, Collins and Lummus had been selling lots for months, with some houses already being constructed in the Lummus section. In May, Frank B. Shutts—like Fisher, an Indiana native—purchased 47 acres of swamp land between the Fisher and Lummus properties. Shutts, who came to Miami in 1909 and was Fisher's Miami attorney and founder of the *Miami Herald*, said he would fill in the land and put it on the market several years hence. The subdivision, he said, would be called Aurora, after his Indiana home town.[23]

Fisher's project was not moving fast enough to satisfy him. The sooner his land was cleared, platted and built with streets, the quicker he would be able to sell lots and regain some of the money that was pouring out of his bank accounts. Fisher had so many businesses and bank accounts at the time that he was able to juggle his dollars from one account to another, confusing not only himself but the tax collectors as well. He sold some of his Union Carbide stock for cash, traded some of it for other stock or borrowed from it for his adventures at Speedway and the beach east of Miami. No one, not even Carl, could keep up

While clearing out the jungle-like growth of the beach, workmen also collected a maze of crocodiles. (Pancoast Family)

with where he was getting his money from or where he was sending it to.[24]

A 1925 newspaper article ignored Lummus' contribution to the dredging of the bay side of the peninsula only a dozen years earlier. The task of Fisher's men clearing the land required eight months, the article said. It reported that in addition to the crews of laborers cutting a swathe across the land, Fisher employed dredging crews of 150 men to bulkhead the west side of his land, then pump in sand and water from the bay. When the water drained off, the sand remained; the process built up the land to the bulkhead height. In addition to the workers, the article continued, Fisher employed three pumping boats, two digging boats, 15 barges, five supply boats, two oil tugs, two anchor boats and an 18-inch pipeline one mile in length.[25]

Lummus had a different story. He wrote that Shutts, representing Fisher, and he, representing the Lummus interests, traveled to Tallahassee together to obtain the first ever dredging permit issued by the State of Florida. Following that, attorney Crate D.

Bowen, representing Fisher, and Lummus went to Washington to secure a federal permit for the dredging. "According to the plans," wrote Lummus, "we had to move six million cubic yards of bay bottom onto the land. When I speak of 'we,' I mean Carl Fisher and the Lummus Company let the contract [with the Clark Company of Baltimore] and the work was done at a cost of ten cents per cubic yard, or in other words, $600,000 for the dredging. Our [the Lummus Company's] part was $315,000 and Fisher's was $285,000."[26]

Lummus also shared credit with Fisher for the first automobile road on the beach. It was built in the second half of 1913, after the Lummus Brothers, Collins and Fisher hosted county commissioners on the peninsula in hope of convincing them to contribute public funds to the road. "When the commissioners looked over what the Collins crowd, the Fisher interests, and the Lummus Company were doing and planned to do, they agreed to accept a deed to the land where Collins Avenue is now located, and the road along Collins Canal to the bay

41

to connect with Collins Bridge," wrote Lummus. "Dade County was to pay one-third of the cost of building these roads, the Lummus Company one-third, and Fisher one-third. It took ten men one week to cut a right-of-way from where Mr. Collins was then having the canal dug...I started cutting right-of-way at South Beach and Fisher met with his cutting at Fourteenth Lane, or midway on the Carney tract. This was the first road suitable for automobiles built on Miami Beach, and it was completed in 1913."[27] (He did not say why Collins did not share in the cost although it can be assumed that he did not because little, if any, of the road ran on his property.)[28]

Fisher's first project was to fill in swampy Bull's Island, a name he changed to Belle Isle in 1914. In August 1913, the dredge *Florida* pumped constantly for four days to complete the fill, leaving the island with 32 acres of land. Fisher cleared practically all the trees, dumped 300,000 cubic yards of sand onto the island and completed the road from where the Collins Bridge left off.[29] In September, Fisher began construction of a narrow-gauge railroad alongside the canal. The railroad would carry materials closer to his building sites, including the major thoroughfare he was creating across the narrow strip of land: Lincoln Road. Rock was taken partway up the canal on barges, then loaded onto miniature railroad cars, hauled to the spot desired and dumped.[30] The *Metropolis* seemed awed by Fisher's energies and accomplishment. On December 10, 1913, the day Fisher opened his land sales under the name Alton Beach, the newspaper published a recap of his activity on the beach for the year. Under the headline

The Collins/Pancoast Casino at 23rd Street had Miami Beach's first public swimming pool. It later became Fisher's famous Roman Pools. (MH)

Wilderness Transformed Into Beautiful Alton Beach, the *Metropolis* observed, in part:

Transformed from a wilderness to a park, almost in an instant, as though by waving of a magic wand, Alton Beach today seems a fairyland, and the story if its development during the last twelve months reads like a romance, to which however 'finis' has by no means been written, for each day sees some new beauty added to it.

When Carl G. Fisher purchased three hundred and fifty acres on the peninsula, a year ago, the land was a sandy waste along the ocean side, while skirting Biscayne Bay was a seemingly impenetrable mangrove swamp. Today the entire tract has been cleared of the jungle-like growth, millions of cubic yards of sand have been pumped in; more than a hundred acres is covered with a velvety carpet of fine grass, homes are in course of construction, streets and boulevards made, shrubbery and trees planted, a golf course laid out, and other improvements planned which will bring the total expenditure of money on the property beyond the million dollar mark. Already over $300,000 has been spent on the beach and, according to Mr. Fisher, the work has only begun.[31]

As 1913 turned into 1914, a land rush of sorts ensued. All three land companies on the beach were holding lot sales and auctions. Lummus' Ocean Beach Realty was far ahead of the crowd. On January 22, Ocean Beach advertised the names of 178 persons and companies that had purchased lots. Significantly, most of the purchasers were from just across the bay, in Miami. Their idea was twofold: one, as speculation for future resale and, two, as sites for a beach home on weekends and holidays.[32] By June, 21 houses were under construction on Ocean Beach property, all to be completed by the end of the year. The houses were to be built of concrete and averaged $4,000 in cost.[33] To stimulate a home building program, Lummus advertised that he would give away 25 lots on what today is Collins Avenue to people who contracted to actually construct a house by January 1, 1915, costing not less than $3,000. The response was heavy and somewhere along the line Lummus lost track of numbers. By the time he caught up, he had signed contracts to give away 32 instead of 25 lots.[34] Collins and Pancoast, meanwhile, had completed their own casino, the third on the beach. What was unique about this one was that it had a concrete swimming pool. The Hardie and Smith casinos did not have pools, just direct access to the beach. Collins' and Pancoast's Miami Beach Realty

was selling ocean front lots from $1,500 to $1,875 and lots on Indian Creek from $450 to $1,500. It also boasted that the largest avocado orchard in the country—the fruit of Collins' labors—was on the property.[35] Still, visitors to the beach had no facilities for spending the night, unless they were among those building cottages. The idea of a hotel was on the minds of the managers of all three projects. Miami Beach Realty was the most forward about it, advertising that it had a hotel site on 600 feet of ocean front and that it would offer "special inducements and liberal terms to parties who will erect the class of hotel desired."[36] Fisher already had announced his intentions to turn the beach into a tourist mecca, and it would be only a matter of time before the first hotel would be erected on the peninsula. Fisher, meanwhile, announced that the first house soon would be built on newly filled-in and bulkheaded Belle Island. He saw the south side of the island as an excellent vantage point for motor boat races he hoped to conduct in a newly-deepened channel.

Fisher's desire for a yacht channel was strengthened by his growing interest in boat racing. The man had a lifetime of racing competition, beginning with his bicycles and extending to automobiles and even hot air balloons. According to an unauthorized article submitted to a boating magazine by one of his employees, Fisher's love for boating precluded those avocations, beginning when, as a youth, he put his first boat—also called *Elph*—

Spectators gather to watch early Miami Beach boat race in Biscayne Bay. (Fishbaugh; SPA) Fisher's Mid-Winter regattas were among the highlights of the tourist season and brought into competition some of the biggest names in racing. (Matlack; HASF)

into the White River near his Indianapolis home.[37] Much of Fisher's attraction to South Florida was based on his love for boats and boat racing. His impetus for creating channels on the west side of the beach was his anticipation of great boat races to be held there. Simultaneous with the clearing of land for his developments, Fisher's dredges were at work preparing a boat race course in Biscayne Bay. It was in his thinking that spectacular water sports events would lure some of the top names in racing—and those who followed them—and bring abundant free publicity to his land development.

FLORIDA TOURS

Carl Fisher's promotional brochure for Dixie Highway lured people to Miami Beach. (MB)

Indirectly, Fisher's ambition for world-class boat racing in Biscayne Bay led to the huge mid-winter sports spectacle called the Orange Bowl Festival. When business leaders on the Miami side of the bay began talking about a mid-winter festival to lure tourists, it fit right in with Fisher's plans for a huge boat race. The first Magic Knights of Dade Festival was planned for January 1915. Fisher's attorney, Frank Shutts, was one of the organizers of the five-day festival and it did not take much for Fisher to join in. He personally financed the Miami Mid-Winter Regatta, which was a part of the Magic Knights Festival, and continued to do so for a number of years before turning it over to the Miami Chamber of Commerce. The first festival began on January 11, 1915 with a salute of 100 guns, the assembling of invited governors, a proclaimed prince and princess and a coronation ball.[38] The following day brought a parade depicting Miami's history, the Spanish settlers, the Indians, Columbus' landing in the New World and military units. The remainder of the festival included field sports, a nighttime illuminated parade of automobiles, an industrial parade featuring 20 different towns in the area, fireworks and, finally,

OUTLINE OF **Dixie Highway**

Rogers & Company, Chicago

Above: *Dixie Highway had multiple routes, two beginning in Upper Michigan and one starting in Chicago. All ended in Miami.* (MB) **Left:** *Dixie Highway pathfinders are welcomed in Miami in 1915.* (Alice Wood)

Jane and Carl Fisher's first Miami Beach home was at the foot of Lincoln Road, fronting on the ocean. (Chase Family)

two days of speedboat racing over a two-mile course on the bay. Fisher entered his own boats in several events, winning one with the first of his large cruisers, *Shadow*.[39] While the Magic Knights of Dade Festival did not last too many years—World War I intervened—it was the seed that later sprouted the Palm Festival and, ultimately, the Orange Bowl Festival.

Fisher was incapable of keeping his attention focused on one project; he had to have an overload at all times. With the Lincoln Highway started and responsibility transferred to others, but with the massive ground-clearing and dredging of his Alton Beach going at full-speed—and draining his wallet—Carl, along with Hoosier Motor Club chief W. S. Gilbreath, conjured up another huge undertaking: the Dixie Highway. There is no telling when this idea first entered Fisher's mind, but by 1914, he already was lining up routes and participants. If there was a need for an east-west highway across the United States, why not a north-south road as well? And what would be a better way to make it easier for tourists and investors to reach his new South Florida project than to create a highway from Chicago all the way to Miami? (The highway ultimately reached

as far north as the Straits of Mackinac in Upper Michigan and had two branches as it snaked its way to Miami.)

Much as happened with the Lincoln Highway; the idea appealed to a great many towns and states which hoped to be included in the route. There were plenty of jobs on the line, and the prospect of caravans of autos stopping off at small towns along the way for gasoline, food and lodging was mouth-watering. An organizing conference was called for Chattanooga in April 1915. From the outset, even prior to the organizing meeting, Miami was to act quickly to get this road started. Dade County pledged to have 68 miles of oil road built as part of the Dixie Highway. "If all the counties between Miami and Chicago were to act as quickly as Dade County is doing, the road would be the longest continuous road in American in less than 12 months," wrote one Dixie Highway principal.[40] Much of the enthusiasm for the highway was drummed up with motorcades along the projected route. At the end of the line of these motorcades was a young Miami ready and willing to show its zeal for the road. When the motorcade reached downtown Miami on October 14, 1915, after a 1,500-mile journey from Chicago,

'THE MOSQUITOES WERE BEYOND BELIEF'

John Collins' son-in-law Thomas Pancoast built a home for his wife and three sons in 1914 on the banks of the southern end of Indian Creek, where it flowed into a body of water that has come to be called Lake Pancoast. The precise address, it later would be designated, was 2600 Collins Avenue. (The family patriarch, Collins, continued to split his year between Florida and New Jersey, and was not to construct his beach house until the following year at what would be 2432 Collins Avenue.) At first, Pancoast built a small garage for two cars with a combination bedroom-living room, and a kitchen and dining room above. His son Russell remembered that there was no room for the three Pancoast boys and they lived in tents along the creek. "My younger brother and I had one tent, and my older brother, who was just finishing college, had a tent by himself. Along the shore in front of the tents, the crocodiles used to sun themselves on the beach. They didn't bother us and we didn't bother them. We got quite used to them. In fact, we missed them later on when they disappeared." The large Pancoast house finally completed, the boys packed their tents and moved indoors. But even indoors, life still was considered a bit rugged. "My mother really had, I think along with most women of that time, the real problems of pioneering," Russell Pancoast recalled. "And this *was* pioneering on the beach at that time. The mosquitoes were beyond belief. Also the sand flies were bad, and if anyone went into the house, they were sprayed immediately after they came through the screen door—which was always opened out instead of opening in...Then, after you sprayed yourself and the mosquitoes, you were able to go through the rest of the house." Pancoast reminisced that the workmen had to put newspapers under their stockings to make it difficult for the mosquitoes to bite their ankles and feet, and wore wide-brimmed hats with nets hanging over their faces. "The mules, which were doing a great deal of the roadwork, would be attacked by the mosquitoes so badly that sometimes they would break out of the mule pen and go into Indian Creek. Sometimes they would drown, and others had to be pulled out with a truck." (Source: Oral history interview of Russell Pancoast conducted by Georgia Moretz for the Junior League of Greater Miami, Aug. 26, 1970.)

Mrs. Katherine Pancoast dons mosquito netting to survive the ever-present mosquitoes. (Pancoast Family)

in Chicago and touching Indianapolis, Louisville, Nashville, Atlanta and into Florida at Tallahassee. Both roads converged on the terminus: Miami.[42] Fisher's frustration with the lack of progress of the highway is evident in a letter he wrote in 1921 to Judge M.M. Allison, president of the Dixie Highway Association.

> It seems to me that it would be quite easy to have a very effective propaganda just now if, for instance, a battleship could be traded for either 1,000 or 10,000 miles of good highway, Some of the. . . battleships cost 50 to 75 million dollars—so one good one would be enough to build a first class highway clear across the United States. This sort of propaganda might take very well with the farmers and if we could get the eyes of the Nation concentrated on a North and South Highway and an East and West Highway, it would be a good thing.[43]

If Fisher was to convince people that his Alton Beach was a good place to build a home, or estate, he needed to set an example. In March 1914, he announced he would build a home at the foot of Lincoln Road at the ocean. Next to the huge Deering Estate (Viscaya) being built on the Miami side of the bay, it was the largest home to be constructed in the area at the time. On a lot 300 by 400 feet, Fisher built a house that was two stories high except for a portion that rose three stories in the center. This first of his Miami Beach homes to be called—what else?—the *Shadows*, was designed in Italian Renaissance style and included a swimming pool and tennis courts. It was estimated to have cost $65,000.[44] Jane Fisher wrote that her new home had a curved twin stairway, framed with the golden tubes of the pipe organ. "The green lawn and the moving Atlantic seemed to enter the 300 square feet of ceiling-high window frontage and become part of the immense drawing room with its sea-green carpets and large sofas and chairs lushly padded with down and covered with pale green cotton damask. . . . That house was Florida. Even the table china I ordered from Lennox was made with an orange-tree design, and our silver bore the same device."[45]

The Fishers' house was impetus for others. T. J. Nolan of Omaha announced he would build a home on property adjoining Fisher's. Carl's Speedway associate, Frank Wheeler, also said he would build a house nearby.[46] Lummus' Ocean Beach Realty was already busy putting up houses, including one for J. N. Lummus at what would be 1200 Ocean Drive.

Nevertheless, while Fisher, Lummus and their colleagues made huge improvements in the mangrove swamp and jungle that was so repulsive to Jane Fisher a little more than a year earlier, most of the beach

thousands turned out to greet it. Fisher, who had participated in the motorcade but who intentionally reached Miami early enough to be part of the greeting delegation, was elated with the reception. "You got'em beat to death," he exclaimed, comparing the Miami reception to those of other communities. "You've sure got'em beat to death. Just look at 'em coming. This is the best yet."[41]

The Dixie Highway was to have a long and arduous struggle over more than a decade before it was a fully-completed route between Miami and the Midwest. Acrimonious arguments over the route the highway would take ate up much of the pure enthusiasm for the project. Fisher and the governing Dixie Highway Association literally cut the baby in half, creating an eastern route that began at Sault Sainte Marie on the Upper Michigan peninsula and traveled through and past Toledo, Dayton, Cincinnati, Asheville, Augusta, Savannah and into Florida at Jacksonville; and a western route, beginning

A year before Miami Beach was incorporated, Lummus advertised Ocean Beach with a thought that it might become East Miami in the future. (HASF)

still was closer to a primitive state than a tourist and residential community. Builders were dependent upon the mainland for supplies and upon their own resourcefulness to get through the day. "My mother had been used to having all the vegetables, fruit, etc., in a grocery store handy to her," Thomas and Katherine Pancoast's son Russell recalled of his New Jersey days:

Here there were no stores, and nowhere to buy food directly without a major undertaking. Also, the ice might come over on a barge one day but might not come over on the barge the next day. There was no fresh milk in the beginning, and canned milk was something my mother had never used, and she had to learn how to use it. Then she had to learn how to use the various vegetables and fruits that were strange to her.[47]

They grew on her father's nearby farm. In 1914, John Collins still had 200 acres of avocados under cultivation, 25 acres of mangoes, 15 of pastureland and 25 of winter truck vegetables in 1914.[48] The hardship extended to the boys as well, as the nearest school was on the other side of the bay. The two younger Pancoast brothers rode a bicycle six miles across the Collins Bridge to the school in downtown Miami, and six miles back each day. "On the return," Russell Pancoast reminisced, "if you were fast enough,

you could get ahold of a handle on a car...and then you could get a tow across the bridge."[49] Another youngster on the beach at the time also was having to reach the city for schooling but he got there in a different manner. Jesse Weiss was six years old when his parents, Joe and Jennie, sent him off to school in the ferry boat that left from the dock at the southwest tip of the beach in 1913. Joe Weiss, a native of Hungary, had come to the beach from New York that year and got a job at the Smith's Casino lunch stand. Later he was to open his own restaurant across the street from the casino, the one that grew world famous as Joe's Stone Crab. To add to the stories told by Russell Pancoast of a near pristine beach, Jesse Weiss told of his early days on the lower tip of the peninsula:

There were a half dozen of us who grew up together. We played on the beach, we wrestled, we swam, we went shark fishing, we'd turn turtles when they came up; turn them on their backs. They came to lay eggs, then covered them. We used to walk along the beach and eat seagrapes off the trees. They tasted very much like guavas, but were a little sweeter. One bad thing was mosquitoes in summer. They were absolutely terrible.[50]

No one appears to have recorded whose idea it was but Collins, Fisher and Lummus got together early in 1915 and decided to incorporate their land. It took 25 registered voters to become a town and the beach had 33 among a population of 150.[51] (It would take 300 registered voters to become a city, something that did not occur until 1917.) How the town came to be called Miami Beach, rather than Ocean Beach or Alton Beach is both mysterious and confusing. In his book, Lummus again takes credit. "As eighty per cent of the population in the area was living on the Lummus development," he wrote, "I suggested to Fisher and Collins that the town should be named Miami Beach."[52] This is indeed puzzling as Lummus' property was called Ocean Beach, while Collins' was Miami Beach. In the incorporation paper of March 26, 1915, while stating the town would be named Miami Beach, it was noted that the incorporation meeting took place at the offices of the Ocean Beach Realty Company, "at Ocean Beach, Florida." At the incorporation meeting, Lummus established another first. He was elected Miami Beach's first mayor. Seven aldermen were chosen, including Thomas Pancoast. In all, 30 ballots were cast for and none against the proposed slate, which included the mayor, aldermen, clerk and combined marshal and tax collector.[53]

Of the 30 voters present, one-third were elevated to public office in Miami Beach's first-ever election.

CHAPTER SIX

THE EARLY HOTELS

After Carl Fisher purchased the Collins/Pancoast Casino in 1916, he built a Dutch-style windmill that became the signature of his Roman Pools. (Matlack; HASF)

A town ranging from Government Cut on the south to today's Fontainebleau Hilton Hotel on the north had been incorporated, streets graded, small homes built, larger homes planned, a deeper channel dug, electricity introduced, boat races and land auctions held but still there was no hotel. If Miami Beach was to be a resort as well as a residential community, the tourists needed to have a place to sleep. There were hotels across the bay in Miami, but that was miles away–across the big wooden bridge, or by ferry boat. Surely, there had to be a more convenient location for tourists who preferred walking visits to the shore–and who someday might be convinced to buy lots and build homes on the peninsula. Through their announcements, all three developers had called for hotels but none had yet been built, or even started by early 1915. In March, a story appeared in the *Miami Herald* speculating that a 250–room hotel built by a New York syndicate "will likely be situated on the beach." The story went on, without publishing documentation, that there would be baths, a great pier, tennis courts and all sorts of amenities at the new hotel.[1] The story did not speculate as to whether the hotel would be built on property controlled by Collins, Fisher or Lummus. No matter; no such grand hotel materialized anywhere on the beach at that time. Miami Beach's first hotel was a small one, not particularly heralded and with hardly the special services as speculated in the *Miami Herald* story. Once again, J. N. Lummus got the opportunity to claim a first in his section. In April, William J. Brown purchased a lot from Mrs.

A. E. Rickmers in the Ocean Beach development, beginning 150 feet north of Smith's Casino, and began building a two–story structure.[2] The announcement said it would have a dozen hotel rooms on the upper floor with a bath between each two. On the first floor would be kitchenette apartments and dressing rooms. Brown anticipated future growth, planning the building so more floors and walls could be added. He even said that although the hotel was built of pine, it was his intention ultimately to stucco it. He first said he would call the

Miami Beach's first hotel was built by William J. Brown in 1915. Although modified significantly, it remains today as the Star Apartments at First Street and Ocean Drive. (MB)

BROWN'S LAYERS

Brown's Hotel has survived the years and today is the Star Apartments at 112 Ocean Drive. Around its lifetime, legends have grown. On June 9, 1919, the *Miami Metropolis* carried Brown's claim that the hotel was built atop the stern of a hulk of a ship that was at least a century old. Brown told the newspaper that during excavation for the hotel, he exposed the entire outline of the ship, claiming its oak planking was at least four inches thick. He reported that the wood was rotting badly, but with solid sand beneath it, he continued to build his foundation over the wreck. When Hurricane Andrew blew through Miami in 1992, its winds ripped a portion of stucco from the upper floor of the Star Apartments, exposing its original pine panels. Also exposed were painted signs on opposite sides of the building, one advertising it as Brown's Hotel, the other calling it the Rainbow Hotel. Miami Beach's building director described the hurricane-exposed wood as looking like it were new.

place the Ocean Beach Hotel but changed it prior to opening to the Atlantic Beach Hotel.[3] He also changed his mind on the number of hotel rooms because, by July 1915, while the building still was under construction, it was reported to contain 36 hotel rooms with baths. The hotel has come down through history, myriad owners and name changes, and countless modernizations—including stuccoing—to be known as Brown's Hotel.

Brown, born in Scotland, came to New York City in 1894; where he apprenticed as a plumber. The lure of new opportunity brought him to Miami shortly after the turn of the century where he resumed his work as a plumber, eventually owning his own business. In 1912, he purchased the Biscayne Hotel in Miami and began a new career as a hotelier.[4] Brown had his Miami Beach hotel ready for the start of the 1915–1916 winter season, thus beating Fisher and Collins to the claim of the first hotel on the beach. Brown sold in April 1922 to Louis Levin and Charles Optener of Chicago, who in turn, sold it a little more than a month later to N. B. T. Roney, a man whose name soon would become synonymous with Miami Beach hotel history.[5]

Lummus may have had the first hotel in his district and a bunch of other firsts but what he didn't have was the cash reserve that Fisher and, to a lesser degree, the Collins and Pancoast interests had. It has been suggested that a lack of money was one of the reasons Lummus cooked up the sale of a mile of oceanfront to the new town of Miami Beach in August 1915. It would have been a tough sell today but back then there was nothing wrong with Ocean

J. N. Lummus, Miami Beach pioneer and its first mayor, built his home on the northwest corner of 12th Street and Ocean Drive. (MB)

In 1915, J. N. Lummus sold Miami Beach the land that is Lummus Park for $40,000. The park would become the front porch of the Ocean Drive Art Deco District. (Matlack; HASF)

Beach Realty, of which the town mayor was an officer, selling a large parcel of land to the town. One could argue that Lummus did not pick up an immense amount of cash for the sale—$40,000—so money was not the factor. It also could be argued back that Lummus, in selling the land, not only got $40,000 but also got a lot of property off his tax bill and, by insisting in the contract that the city plant and beautify the strip, created at taxpayer expense a lovely front lawn for his own home at 12th and Ocean and increased the property values of the adjacent land. Lummus, of course, saw it differently. While he, too, recognized the need for a park in perpetuity, thus preventing anyone from building on the ocean side of the street, he said the narrow 20-acre tract, while sold at $10 per front foot, actually was worth $100 per front foot.[6] Lummus saw himself as a great sacrificer for the good of the community and, as it turned out, he was. It matters not whether Lummus pulled off a sweet deal because the park, now known as Lummus Park, running from Fifth to Fifteenth streets at Ocean Drive, became the front porch of the internationally-acclaimed Art Deco District. Years later, Lummus recognized that he had made a mistake and sold short on the park land. He asked the City of Miami Beach for reversionary rights so the park could be sold for commercial purposes. The city council turned him down. In the context of establishing Miami Beach parks, Lummus' bitterness toward both Collins and Fisher for their popularity,

again reveals itself. Lummus complained about Collins' gift of a park to the City of Miami in 1912. In his book, Lummus wrote: "Just why the Collins crowd deeded Collins Park to the City of Miami instead of the City of Miami Beach was a mystery to me as Mayor of Miami Beach." The answer was obvious: In 1912 there was no City of Miami Beach or any other incorporated territory on the peninsula. Collins could not have deeded a park to Miami Beach. When the town was incorporated three years later, however, the City of Miami offered to turn the park over to the new town but asked for $1,500 for funds it had expended on the park. By Lummus' own account, the offer was denied because Miami Beach, he said, did not have that much cash. In 1919, Miami Beach did buy the park from Miami for $1,000 and spent several thousand more fixing it up.[7]

All three entrepreneurs had different selling styles and ambitions for their portions of Miami Beach, although Fisher and Collins were much closer to each other in goals for their properties. Lummus' Ocean Beach Realty was working toward a residential community of modest means, with small hotels for visitors. The Collins family seemed more interested in attracting well-to-do persons anticipating a quiet retreat on the beach, much as was happening just north in Palm Beach. Fisher was after the new young lions of American industry—colleagues in the automotive world and others who had recently come upon their fortunes and loved to spend their dollars on fast boats and cars, polo ponies and ostentatious parties that he didn't like to attend. Both Collins and Fisher envisioned several grand hotels.

There continues to be debate as to Fisher, Collins and anti-Semitism. It has been claimed that they had put into their deeds restrictions against Jews owning land or living on their properties. Yet, typical deeds involving Fisher, Collins and Lummus found in the Dade County Records Department do not show their properties excluding Jews. All three had restrictions limiting ownership to Caucasians. Typical was this deed in a transaction between Fisher and his Alton Beach Realty Company:

The party of the second part, Carl G. Fisher, or assigns, legal representatives, or the owner or owners of said real estate by virtue of any judicial proceedings, is not and shall not be permitted to sell, lease, or rent the said real estate in any form, manner, by and title, either legal or equitable, to any person or persons other than of the Caucasian Race; nor to any firm or corporation of which any persons or persons other than of the Caucasian Race shall be a member or stockholder.[8]

This was common wording in most deeds throughout the South and in sections of the North, as well as Fisher's covenants in Speedway documents. But to assume that Jews could not own land as a result is to assume incorrectly as Jews were Caucasians as defined by the old divisions which recognized three races: Caucasoid, Mongoloid and Negroid.[9] While the Caucasian–only clause clearly discriminated against Asiatics and blacks, it left open the door to Caucasian Jews. Instead of a legal restriction, however, it became an open practice of not renting or selling to Jews. It was so overt that it was part of advertising campaigns to say that the apartments or hotels were "Restricted" or, in other words, "For Gentiles Only." While one doesn't have to agree with what was happening, one also has to understand the context of the times. In the first decades of the 20th century, racial hatreds surfaced with a passion. Minorities were forced to form organizations to fight discrimination. The National Association for the Advancement of Colored People organized in 1909 and, in 1913, the Anti-Defamation League of B'nai B'rith came into being. Huge waves of immigrants coming from Eastern Europe, combined with the smoldering desire of the children of former slaves seeking the life they thought they were assured in the Constitution, kept the majority of America's citizens, those of Northern European background, on edge.[10] Among the most prominent of anti-Semites was Henry Ford, the automobile magnate who refused to join in with Fisher on the Lincoln Highway. Ford's

tirades against Jews are well documented, particularly in the anti-Semitic weekly newspaper *The Dearborn Record*, which he published. Jews were seen as different kind of people. Those who saw them that way claimed it was the bearing of the Jews that created that image. As an example, the founder of Anti-Defamation League, Sigmund Livingston, wrote to the editor of *Outlook Magazine* in 1911 protesting an article that implied there were characteristics in Jews that brought about the prejudice. The editor, Lyman Abbot, wrote back saying that although some Jews were his warm personal friends and that they had made great contributions to society, some "render themselves offensive" seek "the highest and best places, not always . . . by the most honorable means [and are given to] ostentatious display."[11] This popular attitude extended to Fisher. While he numbered some Jews as his friends, they were wealthy Jews who were totally assimilated into American society. The remainder, which included most of America's Jews at the time, were of a lower class to Fisher and he dealt with them differently. What Fisher and Collins did in practice—exclude Jews—was common throughout the United States at that time and for several decades afterward. Historian Polly Redford found Fisher's anti-Semitism odd because, she claimed, before Fisher met Jane, he was engaged to a Jewish woman. Redford also was puzzled by the Collins restrictions because both the Collinses and the Pancoasts were from religiously tolerant Quaker backgrounds. Lummus did not place such restrictions on sales or rentals. Had he done so, Joe Weiss would have been prevented from living and operating a business in South Beach and it would have to be left to someone else to bring stone crabs to the dinner table. Discrimination against blacks was another matter. They were precluded by deed and it was not

Joe and Jennie Weiss stand in front of their Biscayne Street restaurant in 1918. Shortly, the Weisses would serve up stone crabs to its customers and go on to become the internationally-known Joe's Stone Crab. (Jo Ann Bass)

Carl Fisher built the Lincoln Apartments at the southwest corner of Lincoln Road and Washington Avenue in 1916. When it opened in January 1917, the Lincoln made some of the rooms into hotel rooms. (Chase Family)

until the 1960s that rigid enforcement of this discrimination began to cease.

As World War I was being fought in Europe and America found itself teetering on the edge of involvement, Fisher's Lincoln Road grand boulevard was sorely in need of enhancement. By 1915, *The Shadows* at the eastern end of the street and his land sales office further west were about all there was to the place. Sales were not going as well as expected for any of the three entrepreneurs on the beach. Potential investors appeared to have a wait-and-see attitude. Giveaways of free lots, a gimmick used by both Lummus and Fisher, did not accelerate the sale of other properties. The war, of course, was a major culprit. In 1916, however, Fisher built the first of his hotels, the Lincoln, on the southwest corner of what now is Washington Avenue and Lincoln Road. By later Fisher standards, it was small—only 32 rooms. When originally announced, it was to be an apartment house.[12] Fisher called for 12 apartments, 10 of them consisting of two bedrooms, a living room, a bath room and a screened porch. The main floor of the three-story building had a kitchen and dining room. It was close by the golf course Fisher was building and equally close to the glass-enclosed tennis court he had built. Architect for the building was August Geiger, who also had designed Fisher's house. A resident of Miami since 1905, Geiger was to become the designer of some of the area's finest buildings. For the Lincoln, he designed one of Italian Rennaissance appearance, highlighted by decorated stucco with marble inserts. There was a garden in the back and a Spanish tile roof. The $40,000 apartment hotel opened on January 20, 1917.[13] As Miami Beach grew, so did Fisher's Lincoln. An addition was completed in 1922 and an annex in 1924, bringing the hotel to 65 rooms.[14] The Lincoln, like all future Fisher hotels, was restricted and so-advertised. Ironically, when it was sold in 1940 by the Fisher estate shortly after his death, the purchaser was a Jewish man, Moses Ginsburg of New York.[15] Ginsburg

razed the Lincoln to construct the Mercantile Building.

Lummus' Ocean View Realty was stuck in the morass of financial despair. It was hocked to the hilt and the slow movement of lot sales impeded meeting its debt service. In April 1916, Lummus bundled up a bunch of his land on the west side of the beach and joined in with Fisher to create the Miami Ocean View Company. The new company was composed of Fisher, both Lummus brothers, James Snowden, Jim Allison, John Levi and E. B. Lent. Wealthy oilman Snowden, who was to build a large estate on John Collins' property—later sold to Harvey Firestone and eventually becoming the site of the Fontainebleau Hotel—was president of the new company. Lummus lots valued at $175,000 were sold to the company which, announced immediately that all the avenues through the property would be paved, water mains and sewers installed, trees planted and a number of houses built in the first year.[16] At the time, it was the largest cash transaction ever recorded in Dade County. The new company held property from Fifth Street to the start of Fisher's Alton Beach at 11th Street, and from Washington Avenue (then called Miami Avenue) west to Alton Road. They promised that a grand hotel soon would be built, thus setting the stage for Fisher's first totally planned resort hotel, the Flamingo, which was to come along several years later. With the organization of the Miami Ocean

JANE'S "SKIMPY" SWIM SUIT

Jane Fisher claimed the first of an almost endless string of Miami Beach bathing beauties to be none other than herself. In her book *Fabulous Hoosier*, she wrote that women who came to bathe at husband Carl Fisher's pavilion wore long black dresses, black stockings, bathing shoes and mop caps. One day, she wrote, she was working on her latest swimming stroke, the Australian crawl, when she felt the need for "greater freedom in the water." She reassembled herself in a skirt that dropped only to her knees, and anklets instead of long black stockings. Jane was bare from just above her ankles to just below her knees and, according to her, it caused a scandal—particularly in Miami's church circles. Carl, recognizing free publicity, backed—even encouraged—Jane. This led to other women following Jane's lead until "within a few weeks of my public pillorying, not a black cotton stocking was to be seen on the Beach."

View Company, Fisher had for all practical purposes bought out most of Lummus' holdings.

To the north, Fisher also was active. In 1916, he purchased the Collins Pavilion from the Miami Beach Improvement Company, brought in an Indianapolis contractor and announced that he would construct a Dutch windmill which, in addition to being a spectacle of sorts, would pump water from holding tanks into two swimming pools.[17] An idea Fisher got from a similar windmill at Chicago's Green Gardens, the oceanside windmill went on to become a Miami Beach landmark. (It later burned and was demolished for a Holiday Inn.)

In 1916, aviation pioneer Glenn Curtiss, who already had established flying schools near San Diego and Newport News, Virginia, announced that he would move his Virginia school to Miami Beach. As early as 1912, vanguard pilots such as Charles C. Whittmer and Deckwith Havens flew the first Curtiss seaplanes over Biscayne Bay[18] It was speculated that Curtiss chose Miami Beach for his experimental planes, particularly seaplanes, because he felt their presence might draw the interest of wintering millionaires who might invest in his projects. J. N. Lummus, seeking publicity, had given land to Curtiss for a flying field, providing it rent free until 1915. That field was located on bayside land that later became the site of the Fleetwood Hotel near West Avenue and Eighth Street.[19] (The land now is occupied by the South Bay Club and Southgate Towers.) In 1916, with a war in Europe going on and America's entry possible, it also was speculated that a branch of Curtiss' newly announced flying school would be created to train military pilots.[20] An airplane hangar was constructed on Lenox Avenue just south of Lincoln Road.[21] By January 1917, less than three months before the United States entered the war, Army reserve flight students were flying over Miami Beach. They also trained at a field on the mainland at the site of today's Civic Center, where the first flight over Miami took place in 1911. After America declared war on Germany, plans for enlarging the Curtiss field on the mainland were announced and no further mention was made of Miami Beach.[22] The Miami Beach presence was not exactly palatable to the new residents and vacationers who were on the beach for peace and relaxation. The noise of low-flying planes caused a rash of complaints. According to one anecdote, the straw that broke the camel's back occurred when a student pilot, courting a beach girl, tied a note to a grapefruit, intending to drop it on her lawn. The drop was off target and crashed through the roof of her house.[23] The Curtiss Army flying school on the beach was short-lived.

Simultaneous with the formation of the Miami Ocean View Company was an idea of J. N. Lummus:

The James Snowden estate sat in the wilderness on the site that later would become the Fontainebleau Hotel. (Alvin Samet)

another auto route across Biscayne Bay. While the Collins Bridge was a convenient way to get from the mainland to the beach, the wooden structure was of questionable quality. Besides, it did not reach the beach close to the Lummus properties. Lummus drew an imaginary line from his property across the bay to the burgeoning city of Miami. The line reached the mainland at today's 13th Street; there Lummus took an option on bayside land. He then suggested that the county build a causeway from Point A to Point B, taking advantage of bay bottom dredged up in creating a still-deeper ship channel from the port of Miami to the ocean. He had somewhat of an ace in the hole. Sam Belcher, who was chairman of the Dade County Commission, also had a home in Miami Beach— more specifically, in the South Beach section owned and developed by Lummus. In preparation for calling a bond issue, Lummus' engineer, Roy Wilson, and a county-hired engineer, Isham Randolph of Chicago, drew plans for a causeway and submitted them to Washington D.C. for approval to cross the bay.[24] There was considerable opposition in Miami to a $600,000 bond issue that would do more to attract people and development to the beach than provide any benefits to the city, which is where all but a few of the hotels were located. Lummus needed to convince Dade's voters that a causeway would be in the best interests of the county. "Carl Fisher sent me $2,000 and our company spent $4,000 to acquaint voters of the necessity of access to the ocean, and the election went over two to one," wrote Lummus of the 1916 bond issue.[25] Work started on the County Causeway in February 1917 and was expected to be completed in a year. Less than two months after construction began, the United States entered World War I. The causeway would have to wait until the war was over.

There were other ideas brewing. While the dredge *Davis* was piling up bay bottom near the Fisher and Lummus properties in 1913, it also was creating two small islands immediately to the west. They were not intentional; it just happened that way as the *Davis* deposited sand as it deepened the channel on the bay side of Miami Beach.[26] Those two unintentional islands became Flagler Island, where Fisher would construct a memorial to the railway magnate who opened the way to Miami, and Star Island, where, in 1919, the Miami Ocean View Company began building exclusive new residences. The development of Star Island inspired similar landfills to create new islands in the bay, such as the soon-to-be Palm and Hibiscus islands, the Venetian Isles and the County Causeway. In doing so, developers forever affected the natural flow of water in the bay—and drew the wrath of naturalists much as did the draining of the Everglades.

Miami Beach, despite America's participation in World War I, was beginning to look more like a town than the jungle it was carved from. By 1918, residences dotted the landscape of South Beach beginning at Biscayne Street, while oil storage tanks occupied a chunk of the lower west side of the island. Apartment houses were springing up in the Lummus section and estates were beginning to appear in the

Fisher and Collins developments. The 1918 Sanborn Insurance Company map of Miami Beach claimed a population of 500. It identified the J. H. Hannan estate on the ocean immediately to the north of the Carl Fisher estate—shortly to be sold to Goodyear magnate F. A. Seiberling—and the H. R. Duckwall estate a block north. To the south of Fisher's home was the estate of Arthur C. Newby.[27]

Fisher had become enthralled with polo, much as he had been caught up earlier in bicycle, auto and boat racing. But there was more to this polo craze than just love of the sport. Some of the richest people in America played the sport and if Fisher could create a polo paradise on Miami Beach, he could lure those people to his tropical paradise and sell them on investing in and promoting his adventure. To that end, he built the first of his polo fields and stables in 1918 just east of Alton Road near Lincoln Road. Fisher's interest in polo was fed by financier Harold Talbott, Jr., who was to serve as Secretary of the Air Force in 1953. Talbott was just what Fisher wanted. Not only did he introduce him to a sport Carl found stimulating, but he also wrote to all his wealthy polo-playing friends urging them to ship their polo ponies to Miami Beach for the 1918–1919 winter season. The Flamingo Polo Grounds opened on February 20, 1919. More than 2,000 persons—including many socially prominent people who were wintering in South Florida as well as many others who came in for the event—were estimated to have watched the first match, in which Talbott was the star of the "Reds" team over the "Whites."[28] Fisher, despite his enthusiasm for the sport, did not play in the first match. Most likely, he was too busy working the crowd. In advance of the match, it was announced that parking spaces for cars would be provided, as well as seats for spectators. Members of Fisher's new polo club were provided special spaces. All streets to the field were to be closed once the game began,

Left: A polo team of Cuban army officers came to Miami Beach on February 23, 1921 to play against an American team. The two squads are shown lined up before the match. (Matlack; HASF) **Below:** Spectators from both nations fill the grandstand to watch the Cuban-American polo match in Miami Beach. (Matlack; HASF)

except for Lincoln Road.[29] Thus, Fisher's recreational enticements now included a polo field, a golf course that ran just north of Lincoln Road and the glass-enclosed tennis courts east of Washington Avenue. All of this, of course, was further enhanced by the improvements Fisher made in the old Collins Casino on 23rd Street, where he put in his windmill-powered Roman Pools, added a second pool, tore down the inferior original structures, created new buildings, a grand ballroom and parties galore for his wife and friends.

Belle Isle—last stepping stone of the Collins Bridge—was a quick success story. Fisher, as promised, began development of the island shortly after completion of the bridge. In 1915, Charles G. McCutcheon, president of the American Gear and Manufacturing Co. of Jackson, Michigan, bought the north half of the island for $2,500 an acre. He already owned two lots in the south half and agreed with Fisher's idea to build exclusive residences there as well as boat houses and docks. With Fisher promoting boat races on the bay, Belle Isle was the perfect location for aficionados of that sport. The *Miami Metropolis*, in its January 1, 1916 edition, reported that:

> The improvements on the beach include improvements on Belle Isle, formerly a mangrove thicket, now a thing of beauty and a joy forever. One $9,000 residence owned by . . . McCutcheon . . . has been built there, and three other palatial homes are being built on the island. The more pretentious of these is that for Commodore Robt. Henkel of Detroit, the cost being estimated at $30,000. In this home will be installed a $22,000 pipe organ, one of the largest in the south. Commodore Charles W. Kotcher of Detroit, is building a $10,000 residence and boat house and O.J. Mulford

of Detroit also is to build a beautiful home on the island.

It was no accident that a group of "commodores" built there; it was in proximity to the boat racing course and Edward Purdy's boat yards just over the most easterly span of the Collins Bridge. It also was directly at a point in the bay where the water was calmest, the lee side of Miami Beach, which afforded protected waters for their yachts. This fact soon was soon to play into Fisher's thinking as he planned his first big hotel.

Despite the achievement at the beach, the city across the bay, where more than 30,000 people already lived, was growing at a much faster pace. By 1917, the City of Miami had enough hotel rooms to accommodate 8,000. And it was seen as not sufficient because 10,000 to 15,000 tourists were expected for the 1917–1918 season despite the war. Miami Beach had the Lincoln Hotel and Apartments and Brown's small hotel, fewer than 60 rooms in all. One Miami hotel alone, the Royal Palm, had 400 rooms. There were 200 rooms at the Halcyon, and just over 100 each at four other mainland hotels. Even Miami's YMCA was able to accommodate 84 visitors. "At

The Breakers was originally an apartment house but under the new ownership of Mrs. Tatum Wofford, it reopened as a hotel for the 1917–18 tourist season. (MB)

the peak of the season," reported the *Miami Metropolis* on November 27, 1917, "one might imagine himself in a great metropolis, the streets present such a busy appearance. Automobiles are so numerous that the downtown business district is frequently congested with parked cars." This was not the case in Miami Beach. None of the developers there wanted anything resembling Miami's busy lifestyle but they certainly wanted to compete for the tourist dollar. Miami Beach had three apartment buildings of note: the Breakers, the Toldeo and the Pratt. The Breakers opened for the 1917–1918 tourist season and advertised itself as "facing east upon the Atlantic Ocean overlooking the Gulf Stream . . . the boat landing and yacht basin are opposite the west entrance on Lake Chipola."[30] (The southern edge of Indian Creek, dug out and deepened by the Collins/Pancoast interests when they were building the Collins Canal, mysteriously became known as Lake Chipola for a short period of time. Later, its name was changed to Indian Lake, then Lake Pancoast.) A widow, Mrs. Tatum Wofford, having first run a guest house on the beach at 23rd and Collins, concluded that there was a great market for exclusive hotel

rooms. She leased the Breakers Apartments, improved the rooms, sold some of her diamonds to pay for it and reopened it as the Breakers Hotel.[31] Then she did something really outrageous. She charged $25 a day, an astonishing amount at that time. Her idea was to cater only to the most wealthy patrons. Brown's Hotel had no such exclusivity and Fisher's Lincoln still was more an apartment house than a hotel. Her business acumen reaped rewards. In stages over four years, she built the Wofford Hotel next door to the Breakers at 2400 Collins Avenue, immediately south of John Collins' home. It became a Miami Beach landmark but fell into disrepute years later under different ownership. Eventually, it was torn down.

There was a need to build more hotels, to complete the County Causeway, to have major sports and entertainment on the Beach to stir sales. The end of the war in November 1918 provided that opportunity. A new development entered the scene, beginning just north of the old Biscayne House of Refuge at 72nd Street. It was called Tatum's Ocean Park Company.[32] The Georgia-born Tatum Brothers had been in the real estate business on the mainland since 1902 when J. H. Tatum established there. He was joined in 1903 by Smiley Tatum, later by brothers B. B. and J. R.[33] At one point, the Tatums owned the *Miami Metropolis*. Their Tatum Brothers Real Estate & Development Company eventually subdivided to become separate companies for each of their real estate developments, which ranged from the ocean to the Everglades, then just a short distance west of downtown Miami. Tatum's Ocean Park Company held land from one side of the narrow peninsula to the other, beginning immediately north of the House of Refuge and continuing north to about 87th street. or where today's Surfside begins. (The Tatums later were to expand further north with their Altos del Mar developments to what would become Surfside. The Tatum's Ocean Park property also came to be a part of the Altos del Mar developments.) They had 31,000 feet of ocean footage and built a road the length of the property. As 1919 began, the Tatums planned to sell 20 lots 100 feet wide and from 790 feet in length up to more than 2,000 feet —both ends facing the water.[34] Of note was a January 2, 1919 advertisement in the *Miami Herald* that located Tatum's Ocean Park as being "just a little way north of the point where it is proposed to cut the canal connecting the ocean and the bay." It was in the area of the House of Refuge where the peninsula was particularly narrow. The closest exit from the bay to the sea was Government Cut, two and one-half miles to the south. How much more convenient it would

Carl Fisher's Alton Beach Company office was at 331 Lincoln Road in 1922. (Fishbaugh; SPA)

be for boaters higher up the beach if a canal connected the two bodies of water several miles up the bay. As it turned out, the proposed canal referred to by the Tatums was not cut at that point, but further north— at Baker's Haulover—and not until 1924.

Speculation about a cut to the north appeared as early as 1916 and it centered on Baker's Haulover. The property was owned by John Collins and Elnathan Field. While Collins was amenable, Field was another matter. He had become a difficult person with which to deal. Anticipating problems with Field, it is most likely that a second choice was made for the cut, the one referred to by the Tatums.

Fisher had a chance to own the property eventually purchased by the Tatums. But he passed on it and then spent the next few years trying to figure out deals with which he could have another try at it. Seeking to interest Goodyear Tire magnate Frank Seiberling, Fisher wrote to his winter-time neighbor about the prospects of purchasing land and bay bottom held by the Tatums in the vicinity of today's Bay Harbor Islands and Bal Harbour, as well as bayside property to the south owned outright or controlled by Fisher companies. Part of the letter included his desire to put together a group to purchase the land from Tatum. "I have one man here who will put $250,000 into a company, and I myself would put in $250,000," he wrote Seiberling on February. 3, 1919, "I am just taking a long shot at you, thinking that possibly you may be interested. You are one of the few men who have seen this property who can appreciate the possibilities, and who can realize that I made a mistake in not purchasing the property several years ago when I could have had it for about one-fifth the price I should have to pay for it now."[35]

A day later, he wrote Seiberling again, this time talking about the prospects of building canals through the Tatum property from the bay to the ocean.

It would make a wonderful improvement to cut an opening through to the sea at places marked in red. Those openings would not have to be jettied, but bulk–headed by driving piling. They could be made for $25,000 apiece, and by bridging these openings, you could have a tremendously interesting development. At least 12 or 15 islands could be built in the bay from the riparian rights that go with the property, as the water near the shore is only about a foot deep at low tide. I estimate the islands could be made for $800 an acre, or less.[36]

Fisher outlined in his February 3 letter what he saw as his dreams for post-war Miami Beach:

Lake Pancoast and Indian Creek, looking north in 1914. Thomas Pancoast's house is at the top of the lake. To the left are the avocado orchards placed by Pancoast's father-in-law John Collins. Collins Avenue is at the right, Indian Creek Drive is on the east shore of the creek and Pine Tree Drive is off to the left. (Alvin Samet)

I am sending you under separate cover a blueprint showing all the property belonging to the Tatum Brothers, or approximately 5 miles, which we looked at some few days ago," he wrote Seiberling. "I am also sending you a marked map of the developed part of the peninsula, showing the property which belongs to me, and the property of the Ocean View Company. . . . On this map is shown also the undeveloped property to the north. I have outlined various schemes which can be worked out. This property [today's Sunset Islands and Bayshore Golf Course], together with the five miles of [Lummus-owned] ocean front, can be sold for almost any figure you care to name. . . . $1,500,000 would purchase the property and fill it, lay out the roads and do the first planting. For this sum you could also lay out an additional golf ground. This hotel will cost about $1,000,000. As soon as the building of the hotel is announced, which will have to be within the next 30 or 40 days, it will be impossible to purchase the property to which I refer for twice what it can be got for now.

That hotel he so dearly wanted was very much on his mind. As 1919 matured, it was about to come to fruition.

CHAPTER SEVEN

THE FLAMINGO HOTEL

The Flamingo Hotel, which opened on the last day of 1921, was Carl Fisher's first major hotel. (Matlack; HASF)

Perhaps before obtaining his first rough sketch of the building, Carl Fisher already had a name for his hotel: the Flamingo. Jane Fisher wrote that the name came to him much as Alton Beach had come to him on a train ride years earlier—on impulse. She related a story that Fisher and some friends had gone on a fishing trip to Andros Island in the Bahamas and "saw a cloud of flame they took to be a sunset. Then they realized it was in the wrong direction for the sun. The pink cloud lifted and they saw the wings of thousands of gloriously colored flamingos."[1] Fisher saw endless decoration possibilities revolving around the unusual bird. He inspired his old Prest-O-Lite partner Jim Allison to go in with him on the hotel, but as the projected costs skyrocketed, Allison bowed out. (He had another activity in the wings—an aquarium that he would locate at the foot of the new causeway when it was completed.) Fisher, who had been spending lavishly, finally began feeling a pinch. He had to borrow as the hotel's costs grew from a projected $750,000 to double that. For the Flamingo, however, Fisher wanted nothing but the best—and there was a huge price tag attached to "the best."

Soon after he had announced his plans for the Flamingo in 1919, but before any construction began, he sought out a man to manage the hotel. That man was Charles S. Krom, who, with the possible exception of Fisher, was to become more identified with the Flamingo over the years than anyone else. He managed the Flamingo for 28 winter seasons. In July 1919, Fisher's friend, Indianapolis stock yard operator Charles Rauh, recommended Krom after visiting the Griswold Hotel in New London, Connecticut, which Krom managed. "I advised Krom to write you personally and frankly think is one of your kind of men,"[2] Rauh wrote. Fisher wrote back that he already had corresponded with Krom and that a lot of others were boosting him. Krom was born in High Falls, New York in 1884. A graduate of Colgate University, he served at several hotels, including some along the New Jersey seashore. Fisher hired Krom early enough for him to oversee construction of the hotel. With 200 rooms and baths in each room, the Flamingo was to become the Miami Beach hotel that was well worth the wait. To design it, Fisher went to the Indianapolis firm of Rubbish and Hunter; he chose C. B. Floyd, also of Indianapolis, to be in charge of construction. What made the Flamingo unique was the dome at the top of its 11-story-high central tower. Lit at night, with changing colors, it was a landmark. In addition to the hotel, Fisher built a series of cottages on the grounds, which fronted on the bay and 15th Street. As construction took place, Krom and Fisher continued to exchange letters discussing rental rates, decorations and murals by naturalist artist Louis Fuertes and children's book illustrator N. C. Wyeth (father of Andrew) that were to adorn the hotel lobby and other public rooms. Both had ties to *National Geographic Magazine* as contributing artists and, thus, most likely were introduced to Fisher by John Oliver LaGorce, who was associate editor of the magazine, and who had become fast friends with Fisher. Fisher and Krom had their first clash over the murals and Krom soon found out that what Carl Fisher wanted, Carl Fisher got. Krom wrote that he did not feel murals highlighting flamingos were proper, that he had consulted with decorators and architects and that the planned murals and plaster casts were not in

As part of the ambiance of the Flamingo, gondolas plied the bay waters just offshore from the hotel. (Albertype; SPA)

During the 1920s, tea dances on the Flamingo grounds were popular with both tourists and local residents. (Fishbaugh; SPA)

keeping with the architecture of the public rooms. Fisher responded that this was what he wanted and it was going to stay that way.[3]

By the beginning of October, with the hotel 80 percent complete, Fisher hoped to free his money through the the sale of bonds guaranteed by his realty company which, he said, had assets of $7 million. He issued $500,000 worth of bonds at seven and one-half per cent interest and wrote letters soliciting buyers who could handle the issue.[4] Fisher estimated then that he had a total of about $1.25 million sunk into the Flamingo exclusive of the grounds, servants' quarters, walks, etc. and was anticipating earnings between $125,000 and $150,000 per season. As time neared for the Flamingo opening, Fisher showed genuine excitement about his latest creation. In a letter to LaGorce, he boasted:

I wish I could tell you in time about the gondolas we are building. I had Purdy [boat-builder Edward Purdy] come down on a rush order and we are going to build six of them

The lobby of the Flamingo included a mural of flamingos that caused a clash between Fisher and his hotel manager. (Matlack; HASF)

in twenty days. I have some of the most wonderful Bahama negroes you ever saw to push these gondolas around. They are all going to be stripped to the waist and wear big brass ear rings. And possibly necklaces of live crabs or crawfish.[5]

If there was one thing that Fisher yearned for but couldn't accomplish, it was live flamingos at his hotel. He attempted to bring some in from Andros Island but they died en route. Instead, he decorated his hotels with images of flamingos. (In 1921, naturalist Harold H. Bailey succeeded in bringing a young flamingo from Andros to Allison's aquarium bird display, a second dying en route.[6]) In December, the *Miami Metropolis* reported that room rates at the Flamingo would be $15 a day and upwards including meals. Doubles started at $20. On December 31, 1920, the hotel opened with a posh private party followed the next day with the formal, public opening. Fisher's hotel, while years late in arriving, had created an entirely new image of Miami Beach: opulence where just several years before, the ocean beach had been a rat-infested jungle. The *Metropolis*, on January 4, 1921, said the opening event "was like a chord of music, filled with color, beauty and emotion. It was a cameo of human interest, a scene as palpitating and prismatic as a metropolitan night."[7] Across the bay, in Miami, there already were hotels the size of the Flamingo and with their own degree of elegance, but for Miami Beach, this was the breakthrough.

Even before the Flamingo opened, Fisher was at work hoping to lure a major celebrity to his hotel-to-be. In November, Ohio Senator Warren G. Harding won the presidential election over Ohio Governor James M. Cox and became prime quarry for Fisher. He invited the president-elect to vacation at his hotel "where a suite will be at your disposal . . . every possible privacy would be yours, and no overdraft on your time and nature permitted."[8] In trying to lure Harding, which would put the Flamingo firmly on the map, Fisher catered to Harding's fondness for fishing, telling him that there were 600 varieties of fish in the Gulf Stream and that Fisher would put his cruiser, along with guides, at the president-elect's disposal. Harding turned him down. He wrote: "It is very tempting [but] we shall not be able to stay."[9] In the little more than two weeks between that letter and Harding's arrival in Biscayne Bay on January 29, 1921, things changed. How Fisher turned matters around is hazy at best but, suffice to say, he not only drew gigantic publicity to his month-old hotel and the Miami Beach area, he literally snatched Harding away from officials and promoters of the City of Miami. Harding's agenda was fluid, so much so that he arrived in the Miami area from Fort Lauderdale a day before he was expected. He had

insisted in a letter to a longtime Ohio friend who wintered in Miami that there be no public function or parties of any kind during his brief visit.[10] To accommodate Harding's wishes, the City of Miami limited itself to a small flotilla delivering a formal welcome in mid-bay when he arrived aboard New Jersey Senator Joseph Frelinghuysen's yacht. From that point on, Fisher appeared to dominate Harding's visit. American Automobile Association executive David Jameson, who was wintering in Miami, described the Fisher triumph in a letter to a friend addressed only as Batch—a copy of which was sent to Fisher:

Everybody is laughing at the way Fisher put it over Miami," he wrote. "Miami had made great preparations for the entertainment of the President-elect, had gone so far as to procure guides and arrange all the essentials. When Mr. Harding got in sight of Miami and the highly decorated boats, ladies, etc., he shied off to the east. He never stopped shieing until he had landed at the Lincoln Hotel. Mayor Smith [Miami Mayor William Pruden Smith] did succeed in delivering some sort of an address of welcome on the way to the Beach, and the Senator [Harding] did come over and have dinner at the Royal Palm in the evening. He is now down at Cocolobo, the guest of Fisher, Allison and

President-elect Warren G. Harding strikes the typical politician-child pose while playing golf in Miami Beach during his 1921 visit. (Matlack; HASF)

Thompson [fishing guide Charlie Thompson], just the same as you were when you were down here. They may slip him over to Bimini to get him a drink, but if they do, Miami will never know it.[11]

This indignity certainly was not lost on Mayor Smith or on other members of the welcoming party, particularly Miami Chamber of Commerce President Ev Sewell who, a few years later, was to engage in a bitter rivalry with Fisher over a future seaport and other matters.

Harding's boat tied up at the Flamingo Hotel docks and the president-elect and his party were whisked to the Lincoln Hotel for lunch with Fisher, then across the street to the golf course for 18 holes of play. After dinner at the Royal Palm Hotel in Miami, he and his party spent the night in cottages at the Flamingo Hotel.[12] The following day, Fisher personally picked up Harding and gave him a driving tour of Miami Beach, including visits to his buddy Allison's new aquarium and to Star Island. He then got him over to his Roman Pools where the president-elect bathed both in the pool and in the ocean.[13] While there, Harding spoke to the press the words Fisher wanted to hear: "Because of the attractiveness of Miami and Miami Beach, I hope to come here again. This beach is wonderful. It is developing like magic."[14] There was no amount of paid advertising that Fisher could have placed in the nation's newspapers that would have been as effective as a president-elect telling the country that Fisher's beach was wonderful and that he would like to return. (Harding returned for a night in 1923.) Fisher wasn't finished; he still had Harding in his clutches. That afternoon, the president-elect boarded Fisher's cruiser *Shadow VI* for the 38-mile ride down bay to the Cocolobo Club on the north bank of Caesar's Creek, where they fished for two days.[15]

While much attention was being heaped upon the Flamingo Hotel, life was continuing at a rapid pace elsewhere in Miami Beach. Before 1919 came to a close, nearly $2 million in improvements had been recorded in the young city. With the war ended, and work resumed on the new causeway, $450,000 was expended for an electric power plant, cold storage and street car line that was to cross the causeway. Fisher started a $120,000 addition to his Lincoln Hotel. Other projects included a Western Union Cable office on Fifth Street, a concrete water tower on Star Island and hundreds of new residences and store buildings.

As early as 1915, shortly after Miami Beach's incorporation, its growing number of residents called for a public school on the peninsula.[16] Thirty children of school age already lived there. They had to be sent by boat and bus across the bay to attend classes. While the Dade school board expressed sympathy with the Beach residents, it let years pass without acting. In June 1919, with Miami Beach's population burgeoning, Dade school superintendent Joe Hall was asked to appear before the Miami Beach City Council to discuss the issue. Hall told the council that the school board favored two schools for Miami Beach but wanted them near park lands that could be used as playgrounds for the students. He suggested one school be built on the Lummus Park grounds and another on the Collins Park grounds.[17] Hall then added that if someone could finance a school building immediately, one could be built in time for the 1919-20 winter season and the cost of the school would be included in the next county bond issue which, when passed, would reimburse the original investor. Thomas Pancoast wrote to Fisher who was in Indianapolis for the summer. Fisher responded that he would finance the public school building at six per cent interest "and they can build just as good a one as they want—and I think they should do so quickly."[18]

The site chosen for the school was on the west side of Washington Avenue, between 13th and 14th Streets. Miami Beach's first public school, six classrooms and an auditorium capable of seating 400 persons and designed by Fisher's preferred architect, H. George Fink, was let to bid in August 1919[19] and opened in 1920. This was not the first school on the Beach, however. A private school, run by Mrs. Eunice Martin during the winter seasons, opened on Lincoln Road in 1919.

Miami Beach Elementary School, the city's first, opened in 1920 on Washington Avenue between 13th and 14th Streets. (MB)

Miami Beach Community Church, on Lincoln Road, held its first services on March 14, 1920. (Matlack; HASF)

Things happened rapidly in 1920. Before the year ended, in addition to opening the Flamingo and having a public school, Miami Beach had its first church, the new causeway opened and trolley cars brought residents and tourists back and forth to the peninsula. Motion pictures were being filmed amid the coconut trees of the young city and seaplanes carrying tourists were a regular sight flying overhead and landing in the ocean at the Breakers Hotel. The residents of Miami Beach did not have any organized religious program until 1917. The first effort was the gathering of 14 adults and 21 children on May 27, 1917 for a Sunday School at Smith's Casino.[20] Four different Christian denominations were represented at the organizational meeting but the records of the Sunday School indicate that it came to an end in June 1918 when attendance dropped to zero.[21] In February 1919, Rev. Luman H. Royce, secretary of the Church Building Society of the Congregational Churches of America, came to Miami Beach from New York and on February 2, 1919 met with nine residents with the idea of organizing a church. A week later, 17 persons assembled to confirm that desire and the Congregational Sunday School of Miami Beach came into being.[22] With no home of its own, church members—attendance had grown to 38 by January 1920—met anywhere they could. Rev. Royce induced Carl Fisher to donate three lots on

Lincoln Road at Drexel Avenue for a permanent church building, the mother church's Board of Home Missions loaned $40,000 and the community pitched in $28,000 for building costs.[23] Jane Fisher told it differently:

One evening Carl and I were walking up Lincoln Road in the oleander-scented dusk," she wrote. " 'We need a church, Carl,' I said to him. I could see him scowl. 'Nobody on the Beach has time to go to church. We're building a city, honey.' 'But no city can be the right kind of a city without a church,' I persisted. Carl started one of the outbursts of profanity that revealed his inner nervousness. Then he stopped. 'Where in hell do you want your church?' I was meekly submissive. 'Anywhere you say, darling.' Carl was carrying a stick. He leaned over and pushed it into the ground. 'This is as good a place as any. Here's your land. Now go ahead and build your gee-dee church.' The beautiful little church on the most valuable corner of Lincoln Road is still irreverently, but affectionately, known in Miami Beach as the 'gee-dee church.' Carl gave the land and fifty thousand dollars toward its building."[24]

Although the Walter DeGarmo designed, mission–style church was still under construction,

Trolley cars of the Miami Beach Electric Company stand in their barn area on the County Causeway. (Williams; SPA)
Below: Construction on the County Causeway, begun before America's entry into WW I, was halted during the war. This photo of the County Causeway (now MacArthur) was taken on Nov. 30, 1918, and shows the fill upon which the causeway would be built. Note that none of the Venetian, Palm and Hibiscus Islands had been created yet. Fisher Island (center) was not filled in as much as it is today and the Dodge Islands (Dade County's seaport) had not yet been created out of fill pulled up when the shipping channel was deepened. (Parks)

first services were held there on March 14, 1920, with Rev. Royce officiating. In April 1920, Fisher formally deeded the 160 by 200 feet of land to the church and made a cash contribution of $10,000.[25] First named the Miami Beach Congregational Church, it was changed early in 1921 to Miami Beach Community Church as a desire to serve people of most denominations. The completed church, Miami Beach's only church at the time, was formally dedicated on Palm Sunday, March 20, 1921.[26] There was no permanent minister, however, and visiting clergymen filled the pulpit until one could be found. The search for a minister extended all the way to San Jose, California, where Rev. Elisha A. King was preaching. He answered the call to the new frontier on the peninsula, became the church's first permanent minister in December 1921 and served until March 1940.[27]

If Miami Beach was moderately accessible via the wooden Collins Bridge, it became wide open on February 17, 1920, when the new County Causeway (renamed in 1942 in honor of World War II hero Gen. Douglas MacArthur.[28]) opened to the public. This was another of J. N. Lummus' ideas-come-true.

Originally contracted to be completed by October 1918, the causeway was delayed by war. In addition to allowing automobile traffic to reach the more populated South Beach directly rather than by the Collins Bridge—and without a toll—trolley cars carried those who did not have autos. Fisher's Miami Beach Electric Company first obtained a franchise to operate trolley cars in Miami Beach, then obtained a 30-year franchise to operate a line across the causeway.[29] Construction of the single-track trolley line, however, lagged behind work on the causeway proper and was not completed until December. Fisher ordered ten cars for the new service. He built a barn to

Pete Chase and his family. (Matlack; HASF)

house the cars on Alma Island, the nub of land near the west side of the causeway. Fisher already had a power plant for his electric company there, which now is the site of a Coast Guard Station and Florida Power & Light plant, as well as the dock for the Fisher Island ferry. At 2 p.m. on February 17, automobiles lined up at either end of the two and one-half miles of causeway. The *Metropolis*, in attempting to get an automotive headcount, reported that "during the few minutes it took to open and close the drawbridge at the eastern end about 5 o'clock in the afternoon, 49 cars east-bound and 54 westbound congregated."[30] Total price of the new causeway: $625,000.[31] The first trolley cars that roamed Miami Beach in December stayed there; it would be another 10 days before work was completed to allow them to cross the causeway to Miami.[32] On the Beach, the line operated in a loop that ran from the end of the causeway at Fifth Street north to Dade Boulevard and back to Fifth Street.[33] Over the years, another track was added to the cross-bay line but the trolley line did not last two decades. (In 1939, trolley operations to Miami Beach ceased and were replaced by buses.[34])

Several months after the trolley cars began running in Miami Beach, a man who was to play a critical role in the development of Miami Beach began riding in them. Carl Fisher brought C. W. (Pete) Chase to Miami Beach in March 1921 from Key West and promptly forgot why he hired him. Faced with finding a workplace for Chase, Fisher dispatched him to the trolley barns where the boss there assigned him the task of being a spotter. Not only was his job to prevent people from riding free, but he was to keep an eye on the conductor as well. In a 1968 interview, Chase explained his duties: "The spotter gets on the street car, sits on the back seat, watches the conductor to see if he rings up the fares. If he doesn't ring up the fares, then you report him. That was my first job [for Fisher], the nastiest, dirtiest, stinkingest job you absolutely think of."[35]

Chase was destined for things better than sitting in the back of the trolley to see who paid and who did not. What attracted Fisher to him in the first place was Pete's pluck. He was born to theatrical parents in Kansas City in 1886 and, for a while, was a child actor. He spent his early adult years as a teacher in New Hampshire and as a salesman in New York City. In 1910, Chase joined his father and brother at Sugarloaf Key near Key West to establish the Florida Keys Sponge and Fruit Company— farming sponges and making a vain attempt to grow fruit.[36] When World War I broke out, the Chase family's English investors ceased their financial sponsorship and the business soured. Pete took a brief fling at cigar making in Key West but quit when he realized he didn't know a thing about making cigars. It was then that he established Key West's first Chevrolet agency. The war ultimately caught

Auto traffic jams up around a trolley car at the opening of the County Causeway in 1920. (Matlack; HASF)

up with Chase and he went off to service. Upon his return, in the summer of 1919, he found employment with a firm that imported molasses from Cuba.[37] Chase's active participation with Key West's Rotary Club led to his luring Fisher to the island city to conduct a boat race. That's when Fisher hired him, at twice the salary he was making in the molasses business. When Chase asked Fisher what his duties would be, he said Fisher told him: "Well, if we're planting houses, you plant the houses. [sic] If we're planting grass, you plant the grass. If we're entertaining visitors, you entertain the visitors. And if a mule dies, you bury the mule."[38]

Following his stint riding Miami Beach's trolleys, Chase claimed he invented his next job by creating the Miami Beach Chamber of Commerce in the summer of 1921. What is known for certain is that Chase, along with Thomas Pancoast, Lambert Rook, A. J. Zoller and Line Harger met at Joe's Restaurant on July 13, 1921 to plan its organization.[39] Catalyst to this was a growing breach between the

Founders of the Miami Beach Chamber of Commerce pose for posterity. (Pancoast Family) **Below:** *Early Miami Beach Chamber of Commerce building was alongside the Fifth Street terminus of the County Causeway.* (SPA)

very wealthy people living north of Lincoln Road and those of more ordinary means living south of it. For a fledgling community attempting to attract investors, residents and tourists, such widely-divergent factions were detrimental. The Chamber was formed and its by-laws written on June 22, 1921, with its headquarters at the offices of Carl Fisher at the corner of Washington Avenue and Lincoln Road. Fisher's Alton Beach company offered a percentage of Chase's time to serve as secretary treasurer. There were 38 charter members. Less than three weeks later, the chamber's rolls had grown to 228.[40] Pete had elevated himself to sales manager for Fisher. Over a period of nearly two decades, Chase was to be a close ally and spokesman for Carl and his properties.

The sudden departure from the scene of J. N. Lummus was surprising. On July 21, 1919, he abruptly resigned from the Miami Beach City Council and announced that he was leaving for Alabama to enter the oil business.[41] One only can guess at Lummus' reasoning, as he barely mentions his departure in his book, saying only that he "went west." Unquestionably the initiator of much of the earliest development on the beach, Lummus' contribution was overshadowed by Fisher's showmanship. Lummus created in his mind a mercurial relationship with Fisher, who was his partner in much of the venture. Lummus wasn't making any money, and while Fisher may not have been either, Carl's pockets were much deeper. Years later, Lummus claimed that neither he

nor his brother earned one dime from any development of the beach but that they paid back every cent they owed, either with cash or land.[42] A year prior to his resignation from the council, Lummus, for reasons unknown, apparently waged political war on Fisher, threatening to "burn Fisher in taxes."[43] In 1918 Miami Beach, Lummus as mayor was not a voting member of the city council. The council met in special session on July 29, 1918 as the Board of Equalization and voted a new method of tax assessment for the city that cost Fisher more for his properties. Ironically Pancoast, Fisher's partner in development, voted in favor of the raise, as did his son, J. Arthur Pancoast, who also sat on the council.[44] Lummus, technically a figurehead mayor, was not part of the deliberation or vote, or even officially present. Yet documents in the Fisher Collection at the Historical Association of Southern Florida do not mention the Pancoasts but do pin the pressure to raise Fisher's taxes on Lummus' influence. George Kline, an attorney who represented Fisher and was a member of the Miami Beach City Council wrote in a letter to Fisher, that he had not been notified of the special meeting. Fisher replied that he did not "know just what Mr. Lummus expects to gain by 'burning us in taxes'—except possibly to satisfy a personal grudge."[45]

Despite Lummus' occasional forays against Fisher, he continued to correspond with the man he saw as his rival as if they were the best of friends—

Members of the Miami Beach Women's Club stand in front of their clubhouse off Pine Tree Drive at 24th Street. (Matlack; HASF)

with the caveat that he began his letters formally: *Dear Mr. Fisher,* but signed off with *kind personal regards.*[46] As best can be ascertained, Fisher tried to avoid rancor in the relationship. He responded courteously to Lummus' letters, but also used the formal salutation: *My dear Mr. Lummus.*

There can be several other reasons why Lummus went to Alabama and, later, to Louisiana and Arkansas. One is that he was looking for a quick infusion of cash through oil discoveries to come back to Miami Beach and become a player again. Another is that he was losing control of himself to alcohol. Clues to Lummus' drinking problem can be found in a letter his brother, J. E., wrote to Fisher in 1919 and in another written to Fisher from J. N. in 1920. "I saw my brother this morning and talked with him about my conversation with you at the Beach yesterday and he requested me to ask you to drop over to see him at the Sunny Oaks Sanitarium, if you can conveniently do so," wrote J. E. "I found him pretty sick and nervous, but he is perfectly rational and said if you could find time to drop in and see him he would be glad to have you do so."[46] J. E. apparently was playing the middle man in closing whatever gaps divided the two pioneer developers. There is nothing to indicate that Fisher ever went to see Lummus but the tone of subsequent correspondence between J. N. and Fisher made it obvious that whatever grudge Lummus had with Fisher had been placed aside for the time being. Lummus, through letters, kept Fisher abreast of his new life in the oil business. Fisher even purchased 100 shares of the Lummus Investment Company at $1,000 a share.[48] Although he kept his home in Miami Beach and occasionally returned for visits, Lummus' mind was on oil. "I have been right busy this past week closing up with the boys on the Anderson and Penticost leases," he wrote Fisher in early 1920. " As soon as I can get these two other wells under way. I'm going to run home for a week or ten days as I am getting damn tired of this monotonous life out here."[49] Six months later, Lummus was back in Miami, hoping to catch on with Fisher in some manner. He wrote to Fisher in Indianapolis in August 1920, saying he was back in Miami Beach, had shut down operations in Louisiana and was not going to do anything more with oil until the following summer. "I am in the market and want to line up something I can make some money at this winter," he wrote. "I will not tie up on anything until I hear from you. I have not drunk two quarts of whiskey since last May—one year ago—Weight 180 pounds so am in pretty good trim to stand hard pounding."[50]

Fisher responded promptly but offered nothing other than congratulations for Lummus' return to Miami Beach and his improved health. "We have made no plans for the handling of real estate next winter," Fisher wrote. "I will be very glad to go over all prospects with you when I come down in the 1st of November."[51] Nevertheless, Fisher continued to involve Lummus and to recognize his role in Miami Beach history. When Fisher was developing his plan for a seaport on what later came to be called Fisher Island, he included Lummus in as a tribute to his foresight. "Enclosed please find a Stock Certificate for 100 shares in the Peninsula Terminal Company, which includes the property south of the Government Cut, approximately 200 acres," Fisher wrote Lummus. "You will remember that when we talked about the organization of this Company, that I told you at the time I would give you some of the stock for the reason that you were the first to bring the property to my attention."[52]

J. N. Lummus was not to play a major role in the further development of Miami Beach. He and his wife divorced and he moved to Miami. But the Lummus name was far from gone from the Beach scene. His son, J. N. (Newt) Lummus, later sat in Dad's old chair as mayor of Miami Beach.

Thousands stand on the shoreline of Miami Beach to celebrate Easter Sunrise services in 1927. (MB)

CHAPTER EIGHT

'A REGULAR AMERICAN OF THE APPROVED TYPE'

While millionaires basked in the privacy of restricted clubs in more northern sections of Miami Beach, less prosperous vacationers and residents did their ocean bathing at South Beach. (Matlack; HASF)

Jim Allison, who withdrew from the Flamingo Hotel project to satisfy an ambition to build a major aquarium and marine science laboratory, realized that dream at the beginning of 1921. As did Carl Fisher, Allison counted John LaGorce among his close friends. He named LaGorce treasurer of the Miami Aquarium Association, and Fisher, vice president. Allison's $200,000 aquarium on the north side of the Beach end of the County Causeway was the morning-after to Fisher's extravagant New Year's Eve unveiling of the Flamingo. The aquarium opened just hours after the Flamingo party. It had 50 glass–front tanks, each with a visible area of four by six feet, and a number of larger display tanks.[1]

Constructing the aquarium was not without its problems. In July 1920, one of the 32-foot-high glass tanks shattered, spilling sharks, grouper, barracuda and other species onto the floor. Since workers were on the scene when it occurred, they were able to rescue the struggling fish and get them into other tanks.[2] As construction continued, skylights were placed so that the sun shone into the tanks and not the corridors. This emphasized the coloring of the specimens. Allison hoped a biological laboratory he created would take the aquarium out of the realm of simply a tourist attraction and onto a more highly-regarded plane.

Unique about the Allison aquarium was that at the end of each season, the specimens were released back into the sea. A January 28, 1923, *Miami Herald* article reported that boats set out at the onset of the

Jim Allison built an aquarium at the end of the County Causeway in 1921. Despite an enormous publicity boost by John LaGorce in National Geographic Magazine, the aquarium failed in 1925.(Matlack; HASF)

winter season using several methods of bringing in specimens—methods novel in those days but routine today. "Besides the familiar method of rod and reel," the *Herald* story said, "great wire traps baited with crawfish [Florida lobster] are sunk in places known to be popular with the finny tribe. . . . A novel method of capture is the use of a sort of dredge arrangement which is dragged behind the boat on the ocean bottom in shallow waters, catching many small fish which bask among the seaweed and are caught entangled in its meshes." Allison's aquarium had a short life, failing in 1925[3] despite a huge boost on the eve of its opening by LaGorce and his *National Geographic Magazine*.

LaGorce was associate editor of *National Geographic Magazine* at the time and later ascended, briefly, to editor of the distinguished publication.

LaGorce, symbolic of many highly-placed people of the day, was a bigot. He also used his office to help his friends and, indirectly, his own pocketbook. LaGorce's specialty at *National Geographic* was marketing and advertising, but he occasionally wrote articles for his publication. He wrote a lengthy promotional piece on behalf of the aquarium for the January 1921 issue of *National Geographic*.

It was not the first time LaGorce used his position and prestige to help his chums in Miami Beach, nor would it be the last. And it was Fisher's practice to keep LaGorce happy, with free automobiles, lodgings in Miami Beach and other gifts. (Fisher even named his private Miami Beach golf club in LaGorce's honor.) In 1918, LaGorce wrote and published a pamphlet containing mostly flowery language about Fisher's development. Called *A Little Journey to Altonia*, another name for Fisher's Alton Beach project, Fisher used LaGorce's pamphlet for mailings to prospective customers. LaGorce closed out his effort:

> Although my quill were dipped in liquid rhetoric, I could not do justice to this wonder-spot, so come see for yourself; and having seen it, there is no doubt in my mind as to your captivation—that is, if you are a regular American of the approved type, who loves out-of-door sports in a land of blue sky and golden sunset, overrunning with all the creature comforts to fall back on when hospitality is to be offered or accepted.

Carl Fisher (left) and his close friend, John Oliver LaGorce. The differences in their views about minorities were shaded in nuance. Years after his death, the National Geographic Society expressed embarrassment over LaGorce's bigotry.(MN)

The reference in that closing paragraph to "a regular American of the approved type" is most tell-tale. In his days, LaGorce was highly respected world-wide, and an invaluable booster for Miami Beach. Neither cars nor cash could buy the kind of favorable publicity he provided. However, as seen by today's standards, LaGorce was a first-class sexist, bigot and racist. The National Geographic Society's own 1987 volume commemorating its Centennial attested to that and, seemingly, apologized for LaGorce's personal characteristics in his 52 years with the society. "It was only through reading his correspondence and memos," it reported, "that one becomes aware that, unless they kept their place, JOL [John Oliver LaGorce] did not like women, blacks, or Jews—though not necessarily in that order."[4]

When Fisher sought LaGorce's help in locating a Japanese to whom he sent money to come over and become his gardener, LaGorce replied, in part:

Haven't you got a snapshot or some sort of a picture of this Jap that I can send over with the letter, for you know as well as I do that it is like looking for a nigger porter by the name of George who used to work at the Pullman Palace Car Company somewhere to find a Jap in Tokio [sic] when you haven't even got his name right and don't even know that he lives in Tokio.[5]

During his lengthy tenure at *National Geographic*, LaGorce's biases poured out. In 1926, he wrote Gilbert Grosvenor, founder and president of the *National Geographic Society*—sponsor of the magazine—of a way he hoped to keep blacks from obtaining Society membership: "securing from the N. E. A. [National Educational Association] the names of all negro schools and colleges in the Southern states, and to obtain a list of the faculties. These names should be checked against our membership list as they were all nominations, and in the mailing out of nomination letters such names could be omitted by the simple process of putting a tab on the Addressograph card that would trip it through without printing, as in the case of dues."[6] During World War II, LaGorce opposed the Society running a story on blacks in the military because "I fear it would promptly bring insistent demands from the group of educated Negro agitators who for political reasons have been encouraged and aided by a well-known source to strike now for equality in this country. . . ."[7]

His attitude toward Jews was no less obnoxious. In 1920, he wrote to Grosvenor of his opposition to the Society being involved in the distribution of films because the film industry "is known to be practically in the hands of some of the most unscrupulous men and associations in the country,—mainly Jews who have by a process of elimination and massacre absorbed or done away with the smaller fry, and their business methods have been an unpleasant odor in the commercial nostrils for a long time."[8]

Prejudices such as these were not solely in the mind of LaGorce; most white Americans seemed to share them, and Carl Fisher was among them. The difference between LaGorce's and Fisher's prejudices, however, was nuance. While LaGorce displayed contempt for all blacks and Jews, Fisher had more subtle ways of showing his prejudices: a paternalism towards blacks and a caste-system litmus test for Jews.

Contrary to popular belief, blacks were living in Miami Beach long before civil rights legislation was enacted in the 1960s. The 1920 census showed that of 702 people living in Miami Beach, 35 were black. They were either domestics in white people's homes or farm laborers. Six blacks were listed as living and working as farm laborers on the James Snowden property, site of today's Fontainebleau Hilton Hotel. The John Collins farm had four blacks, and Thomas Pancoast employed two. Of the blacks living in Miami Beach in 1920, only two, George and Leathe Baker, were registered voters.[9] The others were ineligible because they didn't pay their poll tax, or because they were Bahamians and not U.S. citizens, or because they just didn't bother to registered. George, 34, was a laborer on the Collins farm and Leathe, 22, was a housemaid there.

Many more blacks working on construction projects had to be transported back and forth daily across the Collins Bridge from Miami. Fisher saw this as costly and ineffective.

A black woman watches over a white family's children at a Miami Beach bathing casino. (Alice Wood)

A largely black work force built Miami Beach's streets and public facilities. To ease the time consumed in busing the black workers back to Miami, Carl Fisher created a short-lived black village in Miami Beach in 1920.(Matlack;HASF)

"Something must be done and done at once!" Fisher demanded in a letter to Pancoast:

> . . . and I think it is up to the Miami Beach Improvement Company, the Schilling Company, who employ a good many laborers, and ourselves, and to immediately erect fifteen small houses suitable for negro laborers, furnish them with suitable sanitary arrangements, and surround the entire plantation with a fence that is properly built, so that the place will not be an eye-sore to the rest of the property. We should also have a small store-room so that some one of their own number can operate a store.[10]

Little more than three months later, Fisher went public with his plan. He announced that a community to house and provide services for his black laborers would be built. At first, Fisher said, it would consist of three acres but could be expanded to 15. Twelve concrete houses were to be built at once, in addition to a schoolhouse, playground, motion picture theater and church.[11] Fisher's plans were grandiose and unfulfilled. Cottages for blacks were built in the vicinity of 41st Street and Pine Tree Drive — the Collins farm area — but were torn down several years later to make room for white development. The few blacks who lived on the beach were not living independently but in servants quarters.

In addition to housing, blacks having access to the ocean was a growing dilemma. Pancoast wrote to Fisher: "We have a problem on our hands that is going to be a little difficult, I am afraid, to handle and the longer it goes the more difficult it is going to be."[12] That problem was the growing number of blacks in Miami Beach who used the ocean for bathing and swimming. Segregation laws were strictly enforced in the South in those days, and where there weren't specific laws, custom worked against blacks. As an example, blacks were not allowed to drive automobiles in Miami until just a few years before 1920.[13] But, as Pancoast noted in his letter, well-to-do tourists who came to Miami with black chauffeurs resented this so much that tourist-conscious Miami relented and opened the door to black drivers. "They go up the Beach between Snowden's property and the House of Refuge," Pancoast wrote of the newly mobile blacks, "and park the cars along Ocean Drive and go in and bathe."[14]

In 1918, wealthy black Miami pioneer D.A. Dorsey became principal owner of what then was called Terminal (now Fisher) Island.[15] His goal was to create a black resort there but the obstacles placed in front of him were too great, and the project was quickly abandoned. In seeking a place for blacks to bathe in 1920, Pancoast considered the former Dorsey property on the south side of Government Cut but abandoned that because it was necessary to take a boat to get there. Fisher advised:

> The negroes should have a place of their own to bathe, where they can get suits and bathe in the Ocean the same as white people, and if I knew where we could build such a place for them at not too prohibitive a cost, it would be to our advantage to build it. We certainly should not allow people to come over from the city without being properly clothed—nor should we allow them to dress or undress in their cars along the Beach. This business is going to be a great deal of trouble and cause us a lot of damage. . . . It is really a matter that should be handled by the City of Miami and the City of Miami Beach.[16]

Nothing really was settled, and blacks were denied access to the beaches of Miami Beach until civil rights legislation forced it four decades later.

Unlike blacks, Jews were not totally excluded from Miami Beach facilities. They were able to buy property and to rent in the areas developed by Lummus and there was no significant effort to keep them from bathing in the ocean. Hungarian-born Joe and Jennie Weiss worked as a waiter and cook, respectively, in small New York City restaurants, before seeking the warmth and fresher air of South Florida in 1913. Joe was an asthmatic and doctors told him to move to a more favorable climate.[17] Borrowing $50 from his life insurance policy, Weiss made for Miami, leaving his son Jesse and wife behind until he could call for them. Shortly after arriving, he obtained work at Smith's Casino, perhaps the first Jew to obtain employment or live in Miami Beach. The Weisses' job was to run the lunch counter at the casino. They lived on property near the casino and, with their money saved, went into business for themselves.[18] Jesse Weiss told a story that when he first came of school age, there were only three other boys on the beach, and they would travel by ferry boat to school in Miami. On the first day of the new elementary school in Miami Beach, Weiss claimed the distinction of being the first student enrolled by virtue of his friends pushing him forward when it came time to register.[19]

Jews who came to Miami Beach in later years believed Fisher was an anti-Semite, and it's difficult to argue with the charge against him. Jesse Weiss saw Fisher in both complimentary and unfavorable ways. "The best thing Carl Fisher did for Miami Beach was to come here," he once said. "He was lusty, he was gung-ho, he was compassionate—to a point. He was also prejudiced. . . . He would refer to people in ethnic terms that were very uncomplimentary."[20] By 1921, an estimated 25 Jews lived in the Lummus section of Miami Beach. This was not the case further north.

One could try to say Fisher was a selective anti-Semite but that would just be muddling the issue. Fisher's attitude toward Jews was dependent upon who they were, how much money they had in the bank and how they looked. Several correspondences give a greater insight into Fisher's thinking, which reflected the attitude of a considerable portion of the nation's non-Jews. In the spring of 1921, Fisher's bond sales for the Flamingo Hotel were not going well. While the hotel ran near capacity, he was not recouping any of the money he had invested in it and he wanted those funds for other projects. He wrote to his financial advisor Lyman Kendall in New York, "At the present time I

Carl Fisher recommended Jewish department store mogul Bernard Gimbel for membership in the Miami Beach Golf Club. (Chase Family)

GREEN  HERON

SUNNY ISLES   **NO. MIAMI BEACH**

ROBERT GALLAHER, Owner

COTTAGES - - - APARTMENTS

400 Feet of Private Beach—Life Guard

GARAGE—DAILY MAID SERVICE—EXCELLENT FOOD

TELEPHONE 2871 GOLDEN BEACH EXCHANGE
— GENTILES —

While most of the hotels and apartments north of 23rd Street advertised as being restricted—restricted that is to white non-Jewish clientele, the Green Heron was more blatant than most. (Sunday Pictorial)

have a $350,000 Bond Issue on same, but I am going to have to make some big sacrifices soon to complete my work there, and I don't want this hotel to fall into the hands of Jews."[21]

Fisher's fear of the Flamingo being bought by Jews spoke to his desire to have his properties catering to nothing less than the highest caliber of clientele. His stereotypical image of Jewish people did not fit that category, although he numbered Jews among his friends and often broke his own rules to admit Jews whom he felt met his acquired standards of social elegance. Eugene Stahl, owner of Miami's Helene apartment house, wrote to Fisher enclosing some brochures he had produced to solicit business for the 1921–22 winter season. "I am enclosing one of the booklets with the rate sheet and the 'No Hebrew' card enclosed just as I am mailing them out to my prospects," wrote Stahl. "The latter you will understand as it is my intention to make of the Helene the very best place of its sort and the most desirable among particular people to be found in the state. Jews are no more to be desired with me than they are at the Flamingo or the Lincoln Inn."[22] "

"I don't think it is necessary for you to enclose a card which states 'Hebrew Patronage is not Solicited,' " Fisher replied:

> You can usually tell by the names of the people applying for apartments and their occupation whether they are desirable or not—and I would advise if you haven't sent these cards out with the booklets that you omit them. There are some Hebrews who

are very high class people, and it does seem a shame to injure their feelings unnecessarily if it can be avoided. The average run of Hebrew trade at a Hotel is not desirable, particularly at a resort hotel, and it is quite a question of knowing just how to handle the undesirable ones best.[23]

What Fisher was telling Stahl was that butchers and garment workers with Jewish names weren't welcome but that chairmen of the board or prominent politicians with Jewish names were. Fisher wrote to the Miami Beach Golf Club asking that the club extend membership privileges to Mr. and Mrs. Bernard Gimbel.[24] Gimbel was the president of New York City's esteemed Gimbel's Department Store. In another letter, Fisher wrote his version of the "some-of-my-best-friends-are-Jews" retort. While the challenging letter is not in the Fisher Collection, it is obvious that its author—a Mr. Klein—wondered if Fisher had changed his restrictive policies when his company sold an ocean front house to Yellow Cab Company and Hertz U-Drive It-founder John Hertz in 1927. "Mr. Hertz is a very high type of man and we have several men here on the Beach who are very good friends of mine who are Jews, and they are not all necessarily rich," Fisher wrote. ". . . The late Julius Fleischmann was a very good friend of mine. . . . So I think you are mistaken in some of your viewpoints."[25] (Fleishmann, founder of the margarine company that bears his name and who, indeed, was a close friend of Fisher and possessor of a home on Miami Beach as early as 1921, may have been born

Jewish, but he wasn't buried that way. After Fleischmann died while playing in a polo match in Miami Beach in 1925, his body was taken first to New York, then to Cincinnati. On both occasions, as well as in Miami Beach, Unitarian ministers officiated at funeral services.[26])

Fisher, the rough and tumble bike racer of two decades earlier, was in with a fancier crowd now. He wanted his resorts to be places where only the gentry assembled. And he hired people to make certain that wish wasn't violated. Charles Krom, his Flamingo Hotel manager, fit the mold perfectly. Although he bickered at times with Fisher and probably thought himself of higher status, given Fisher's family upbringing and Krom's college diploma, Krom followed the boss' desires dogmatically because, in essence, they were his own as well. Krom detested conventions. They brought in a crowd he felt was disruptive to the other guests. In 1926, a group of Realtors made an attempt to bring a convention to the Flamingo Hotel.

Arguing against bringing the convention to the Flamingo during the winter season, Krom wrote, ". . . the class of people who visit the Fisher Hotels have become quite disgusted hearing so much of real estate in the past few years. At least 95 percent of our guests come down to Florida for rest, recreation and pleasure, but they have been harassed on all sides by real estate and you know more than half of the papers for the past couple of years was devoted to real estate advertising." While this attitude might sound suicidal considering that Fisher was in the real estate business, Krom knew he stood on solid ground; he knew Fisher wanted his hotels free of anything that might perturb his guests. "All convention people are naturally noisy," Krom continued. ". . . I have never yet seen a convention that didn't have some Jews in the crowd and I don't believe a bunch of Realtors are going to be different than any other." Krom left the door open for non-Jewish Realtors, saying that if he had to, he would accept part of the convention crowd, "and it should be distinctly understood that we would not have any Jews wished on us."[27] Despite Fisher's penchant for waiving his restrictions regarding Jews who were prominent or wealthy, Krom continually pressed a strict line. In 1929, he wrote to Fisher that Octavius Roy Cohen, a well-known writer of short stories, was attempting to obtain a reservation for a lengthy stay at the Flamingo. Acknowledging that the Cohens were "very nice people," Krom nevertheless cautioned Fisher that because Cohen was so well known as a writer who was Jewish, "it will be pretty well known generally where he is staying

and in view of the policy which we have always pursued, I don't think it would be policy for us to take him."[28] There is nothing to indicate that Fisher ever reacted to Krom's letter, and quite probably Cohen was refused at the Flamingo.

Paramount among Miami Beach legends is that the city once enacted a law requiring blacks to have passes to be on the streets after dark. This was not true and, yet, in practice, it was. Miami Beach did pass an ordinance in 1936 requiring special identification for all people involved in the tourist business. Conceived ostensibly for health and crime prevention reasons, the ordinance wound up including practically everyone who worked in Miami Beach. But its enforcement was applied principally to blacks. According to long-time Miami Beach residents and officials, police challenged few whites for being on the streets after dark, but regularly targeted blacks. This was the time-worn practice of selective enforcement, a discrimination as evil as any ordinance that might actually have required only blacks to have an ID card. Signed by Mayor Louis Snedigar, the ordinance required:

That from and after passage of this Ordinance, every person employed in any night-club, any place handling liquor, beer or wine in any form, places of amusement, hotels, rooming-houses, apartment houses, delivery services, restaurants, bath-clubs, bath-houses, solariums; and all caddies, newspaper delivery boys over the age of seventeen, special police officers and domestic servants, taxi-cab drivers, vending machine operators, and charter-boat operators, in the City of Miami Beach, Florida, be and they are hereby required to register within forty-eight (48) hours from the time of their employment, or after passage of this Ordinance, in a book of registration to be kept by the Chief of Police of said city, and to be also finger-printed and photographed.[29]

The words "Negro," "colored" or "black" did not appear anywhere in the ordinance. During World War II, air raid wardens also had to carry the ID card.

Despite a preponderance of Jewish residents and tourists from the '30s until recently, the tone of racial and religious exclusivity has haunted Miami Beach's history—from its beginnings with Fisher and his colleagues, to later years when blacks and Jews were excluded from other hotels, from golf and private clubs, a practice which—ever so slowly—is ebbing as the 20th Century comes to a close.

CHAPTER NINE

"EVERYWHERE CAN BE SEEN THE SIGNS OF CONSTRUCTION"

Carl Fisher's elephants were put into service to help build Miami Beach. (Matlack; HASF)

"Men who have studied seaside resorts and have seen the development of beaches are unanimous that South Beach from Sixth Street to the government [cut] is going to be the premier beach resort of the south." That was the assessment of an unnamed writer for the *Miami Metropolis* when that newspaper took note, in mid-1921, of the progress of Miami Beach through what today would be labeled a "Special Advertising Section" but then was melded into the regular news columns of the newspaper.[1] While it was not visionary enough—or intended—to anticipate the immense resort growth that would come over the years to the north of that district, the commentary properly placed South Beach's destiny as that of a popular tourist resort.

Nevertheless, the article was a valuable magnifying glass on the growth of Miami Beach on the eve of a boom that was to sweep not only that city but all of Dade County and bring enormous development throughout south and central Florida. On the page, and in a separate box, it was boasted that in mid-1921, South Beach had two bathing casinos, three hotels, eight apartment houses, two pharmacies, two garages, two restaurants, 14 lunch stands and a sundry number of shops to take care of much of the needs of most residents. The articles recognized not only the pioneer businesses but the new ones as well. Dr. W. G. Perry, who had succeeded across the bay with his Red Cross Pharmacy, opened the Causeway Pharmacy as well as the Causeway

Candy Shop at Fifth and Lenox, just east of the post office. Rebozo's Pharmacy, operated by H. E. Roseberry, "outgrew the original location in three months and is now well-rooted in the Michaelson building at the corner [Ocean Drive and 2nd Street] where all the travel of South Beach passes by."[2] The West Indies Importing Company was doing business in Hardie's Casino—as well as at Elser's Pier in Miami—selling imported West Indian items, particularly Bahamian mats, hats and curios. There even was a competitor for this speciality. The Nassau Novelty Company, just down from Hardie's Casino, also was selling island goods. Joseph Montfil opened the Miami Beach Hardware and Paint Company at 109 Atlantic Avenue, later renamed Collins Avenue; a speciality of the store was free delivery of kerosene to customers. Miami Beach's first grocery store, owned by Mr. and Mrs. Thomas Gillingham, was operating at 816 First Street. The Flamingo Bakery established itself in mid-1921, immediately next door to Joe's Restaurant where, the article said of Joe Weiss: "He can cook a neat trout, a slice of any fish, so well that one always remembers it and goes back for more."[3]

Joseph Montfil stands with his family in front of their Miami Beach Hardware and Paint Company, which opened in 1921, at what then was 109 Atlantic Avenue. The name of the street later was changed to Collins Avenue. (Matlack; HASF)

The stone crab was not yet fare but would be several years later when, according to stories filtering down through four generations of the Weiss family, a Harvard ichthyologist hired by Jim Allison to work at the aquarium suggested to Joe that the claws of the hard-shelled crabs along the shores of South Beach were edible but not the best tasting; too much iodine. Either by design or by accident, Joe first boiled the crabs, then chilled and served them to an employee. *Voila!* A new eating sensation was created and Joe's Restaurant was on its way to culinary immortality.[4]

Growth hardly was restricted to south of Fifth Street, however. What was going on north of that district was a different kind of progress. Wealthy people bought lots and built estates. Hotels, catering to a more restricted audience, were being constructed, and the Fisher and Pancoast interests continued to promote their portions of Miami Beach as a mecca for a higher social stratum than South Beach. Aviation for tourists also became a part of the scene. Long gone was Curtiss' flying school on the west side of Miami Beach, but the Bennett-Ballard Company, using Curtiss biplanes, maintained a landing field near Lincoln Road from where they took tourists on flights. Two planes, the *Skylark* and the *Bluebird*, were devoted to the tourist trade.[5] Another aviation company, Aero Limited, landed seaplanes in the ocean alongside the Breakers Hotel to pick up thrill-seekers for flights over the ocean and land. After a flight in a seaplane, F. O. Van Deren, secretary of the Alton Beach Company, proclaimed that a lifetime of walking and riding in Miami Beach would not give a true idea of the beauties of the peninsula.[6]

Even before Miami Beach barely emerged from a mangrove jungle, motion picture makers discovered the near-virgin land and proclaimed it, at times, the South Pacific; at other times part of the Arabian desert. As early as 1914, tourist films boosting the area were being made, featuring a cavalcade of automobiles coming across the Collins Bridge from Miami to Miami Beach.[7] Newly-widened Lake Pancoast became a Seminole encampment for the motion picture *Fate's Chessboard*. Collins Avenue and 29th Street turned into the South Pacific for another film and the area just north of today's Fontainebleau Hotel became a desert for a 1921 motion picture.[8] None other than the storied film maker D. W. Griffith saw prospects in the area for film making but realized it could not be accomplished without proper facilities. In a 1921 letter, Griffith observed: "Despite very crude and unpleasant handicaps picture makers have repeatedly gone to Florida, and we believe their visits would be materially increased were there adequate and reasonable studio facilities."[9] In 1921, there was much talk but limited activity in creating a huge movie studio on the mainland near Hialeah. It would have been the catalyst for many more location shootings at the beach, but promoters built only one building and the industry did not blossom in the Miami area for several decades more.

The object of Fisher's and Pancoast's efforts was not so much to disguise Miami Beach as the Arabian desert or a Pacific island but to promote it for what it was: an excellent location for both tourists and residents. By 1921, Miami Beach had more than 20 estate homes.[10] While the number of residences in South Beach was far greater, the prestige of the estates fit into the promotion plans for the area to its north.

And while sophistication may have been the preferred method of promoting their interests, a little gimmickry went a long way. Fisher received a most unusual gift in 1921 that provided him with years of free publicity for Miami Beach. "As soon as the weather moderates sufficiently to take a chance of shipping a little elephant, I am going to forward one to you by express with a man in charge," wrote Ed Ballard, an Indiana friend and a former owner of the Ringling Circus, to Fisher. "His name is Carl II. He is a great little pet and I am sure you will become attached to him."[11]

"I am going to have a lot of fun with him," Fisher wrote back to Ballard, "and I am going to get a lot of publicity out of him too. I am going to send to Ceylon for a regular trainer of elephants and I am

going to make this elephant do stunts or know why. I have already sent for the trainer who ought to arrive in two months."[12] At the same time he responded to Ballard, Fisher wrote to his friend LaGorce in Washington, D.C.,

I never saw so many possibilities for advertising. I am certain I am going to get a million dollars worth of advertising out of this elephant. One of the particular things we are going to do with him is to make him tamp down the polo fields between games, also carry trees, haul ice and work in the garden. I have sent to India for a special Mahout trainer, red cap, brass collar, camel smell and all. We are going to teach him to swim in the sea and pull gondolas, etc. [13]

Fisher was obsessed with bringing a trainer from Asia to handle Carl II but chose Aaron Yarnell from the ranks of his assistant gardeners to fill in while the new trainer was enroute. Yarnell, a black, had impressed Fisher with his handling of mules and, well, if you could handle a mule, you probably could handle a baby elephant. Despite Yarnell's success with Carl II, Fisher wanted the elephant's handler to be more intriguing. He continued his quest for a trainer from Asia and imposed upon his friendship with M. U. Salie of Ceylon, a gem miner and importer, to help locate one. Salie produced one but ran into complications, in getting not only the trainer but

Theda Bara acts out her role in a 1921 motion picture about a South Pacific island. The site actually was in Miami Beach, at 26th Street and Collins Avenue. (Matlack; HASF)

Salie, who was accompanying him into the U.S. The U.S. government considered Salie a bigamist and was delaying his entry and, with him, Sernal Isarnol, the long-awaited elephant trainer.

Using some of his well–placed friends in Washington, D.C.,[14] Fisher finally got Isarnol to Miami Beach but the elephant rejected the Indian trainer. Yarnell had been the trainer for about nine months and the elephant had grown attached to him. Carl II refused to respond to Isarnol's commands, reportedly chased him up a water tower, and was directly responsible for Fisher throwing his hands up in disgust, sending Isarnol back to Ceylon and declaring Yarnell the one and only trainer for Carl II. Fisher later changed Carl II's name to Nero and used him to haul lumber and other heavy objects as well as provide rides for children. Nero, however, turned bad and was eventually given to the Detroit Zoo.[15] But Fisher was not without an elephant. About two years after obtaining Carl II/Nero, he added a small female named Rosie to the Miami Beach promotional menagerie. Rosie was everywhere to be seen, on golf courses, at construction sites, carrying children in the specially-built cart. The elephant became a legend around which Miami Beach publicity prospered. Her publicity value ran for almost a decade—and her legend even longer. In 1932, when pressed for cash, Fisher sold Rosie to an Atlanta zoo.[16] At the time he was seeking to sell Rosie, he described her as:

Miami Beach's first mayor, J. N. Lummus, watches as Frank Katzentine, owner of radio station WKAT, presents an award to Mr. and Mrs. Kotaro Suto for their years of dedication. (MB)

kind and gentle as a Newfoundland dog . . . . [She] hauls her own food in a cart. She gives herself a bath from a hose, and she can dance the Black Bottom better than most Harlemite entertainers. She has been photographed in possibly millions of films; rotogravure pictures by the thousands of feet have been run by all the newspapers in the country.[17]

That was precisely what Fisher had in mind the moment he laid eyes on Carl II.

While Fisher's experience with the Ceylon trainer may have been lamentable, it was the opposite with Japanese gardeners. In 1916, he placed an advertisement in the local newspapers for a gardener for his ocean front home. This time, he did not have

Nero and/or Rosie were the subject of thousands of publicity photos. (HASF)

to deal with visas and beauracracy. Kotaro Suto, a Japanese national, already was in Miami. Over the decades, Suto came to be identified with the landscaping of Miami Beach. While much of the credit for the actual planting and nursing does belong to him, it should be noted that Fisher already had employed landscape architects to green the Beach. In the beginning, Suto was Carl and Jane's personal gardener. He, along with another gardener—Shige Tashiro—were among two of four Japanese who actually lived on the Fisher estate as servants.[18] Suto was a special person. Born on a farm 150 miles west of Tokyo in 1884, he emigrated to the United States in 1900 and worked for 15 years in San Francisco as a day laborer, truck farmer and gardener. He arrived in Miami in 1916 and landed a job with Fisher.[19] Suto was dedicated to greenery. It was said that as the plows tore up mangrove roots in Miami Beach, Suto followed immediately behind planting trees and shrubs in their place.

But the job of landscaping Miami Beach was a huge endeavor and not the responsibility of Suto. Fred Hoerger was superintendent of Alton Beach Realty and Miami Beach Bay Shore and served as landscape engineer for the Fisher interests. It is Hoerger who is credited with introducing new methods of planting in Miami Beach's unusual soil— a mixture of black hammock sand, which was natural to the Beach and the former bay bottom land, which was used as fill.[20] In 1920, both Suto and Tashiro returned to Japan for the express purpose of finding wives. They came back, married, in late 1921 and

resumed their landscape work.[21] Suto was a favorite with Fisher and stayed with him for 25 years. Except for six months when he returned to Japan after World War II, Suto made Miami Beach bloom, both as Fisher's personal gardener and as an independent nursery man on a plot of land Fisher gave him on Prairie Avenue.[22] After the Japanese attack on Pearl Harbor in 1941, U.S. authorities briefly detained Suto and his wife. "My trouble," he said at the time, "is I was born in the wrong country. I want to be an American,"[23] a goal he achieved after the war.

Fisher not only planted his property but told his partners what they ought to plant. "Before I leave [for the summer]," wrote Fisher to Thomas Pancoast in 1920, "I want to ask Mr. Brayton to plant the Pine Tree Road clear north to the north end of the pines and to put not less than 10 fine coconuts on every lot that we have sold in your subdivision. . . . " Fisher also suggested that:

A large number of your small and ragged avocados be replaced by coconuts, Royal Palms, Bougainvillea and other ornamental trees—particularly flowering trees like the Bougainvillea, so that people driving thru the trees will note the beautiful vista of flowers and palms.[24]

Like their predecessors, Fisher, Pancoast and Lummus planted hundreds of coconut trees to give Miami Beach a tropical look. This time, however, the rabbits were no longer there to feast on the young trees; they had been driven out by the land clearing.

Causeway island that housed trolley cars also was Carl Fisher's Miami Beach port. The first ship to dock brought Cuban polo players to Miami Beach for a 1921 tournament. (SPA)

By 1921, Miami Beach was experiencing a mini-boom. With each day, there were new announcements of record building permits, of new residents and distinguished visitors. Luring them were bathing casinos, golf courses, regattas, picnic areas and other features. "That Miami Beach's progress is steadily growing is shown by the building program for the first ten months of the present year, which has reached a total of a million and a half [dollars]," observed the *Miami Herald* on October 25, 1921. "As one result, a thousand more people can be accommodated this year. Everywhere can be seen the signs of construction which are the marks of progress. Changes seem to be made overnight."[25]

A piece of property south of Hardie's Casino on Ocean Drive was an example of the growth of land values. Real estate broker Lambert Rook purchased it for $25,000 in 1921 from two women who had bought it in 1916 for $1,400. Rook, who was J. N. Lummus' son-in-law, recalled that the lot was first offered to him in 1916 but he thought $1,400 was too high a price. Nevertheless, he told the salesman he was going to dinner and would think it over. When he returned, the salesman informed him the two women had purchased the property. "That dinner cost me $23,000," Rook grumbled.[26]

Fisher, meanwhile, continued to come up with unique ideas. Not convinced that dairies on the Miami side of the bay could provide the quality products he desired for his guests at the Flamingo Hotel, Fisher transported an entire herd of dairy cows from Wisconsin for the winter season and kept them on the Collins farm near 41st Street. His

Flamingo Hotel guests thus were assured absolutely fresh dairy products.

As early as 1920, Fisher also saw a major seaport growing on the beach side of the bay. He looked south, across the government cut to the small patch of land that, in 1905, was separated from Miami Beach by the new channel. Originally called Rabbit Island, Fisher asked the City of Miami to contribute $500,000 to expand the 33-acre island with fill, bulkhead it and build piers. In turn, he said, the island would be Miami city property and under city administration.[27] He argued that a ship should not be made to travel a long channel from the ocean to the west side of the bay. He was backed, naturally, by the new City of Miami Beach which, as early as 1919, sought to have the deep water harbor on the east side of the bay.[28] Fisher's plan was met with hostility by Miamians, particularly Ev Sewell, president of Miami's Chamber of Commerce, who one day would become Miami's mayor. Sewell and the Miami chamber wanted a new deep water port on the west side of the bay with a deep channel leading to Government Cut. The struggle between Fisher and Sewell went on for more than a decade, leading to acrimonious feeling between the two communities the men represented. "The City of Miami is determined, through their Chamber of Commerce, to extend the deep water project to the City of Miami, instead of creating their harbor nearest the ocean where it belongs, and saving several million dollars in digging a channel across the bay," Fisher complained in a letter to friend and defeated Democratic presidential candidate James Cox.[29]

Venetian Islands, looking east, in 1926. Visible are (foreground) Biscayne Island, then San Marco. Both are in Miami's city limits. Beyond them can be seen San Marino and DiLido Islands, both in Miami Beach. (Hoit; HASF)

Fisher secured a government permit to increase the size of the island—now owned by his Peninsula Terminal Company and renamed Terminal Island—by 210 acres.[30] Still unsure of how things would work out with the City of Miami, he delayed plans for the building of piers.[31]

In reflecting on those early years of the 1920s, Pete Chase recalled that land sales on the Beach were sluggish. As secretary of the Miami Beach Chamber of Commerce, but with no building to house it, Pete and his father created their own outdoor office where the new causeway spilled onto Fifth Street:

We set up planks attached to wooden horses, slapped some bunting around it, put an umbrella on top and made a sign that said "Information." That's where we operated from for about a year until a chamber building was put up on the south side of the end of the causeway.[32]

Chase's recollection of soft sales in Miami Beach in 1921 and 1922 corresponded with a significant drop in nationwide business activity in those two years. The slump was greater than that which heralded the Great Panic of 1907[33] but soon would be overshadowed by the Great Depression of the '30s. This did not deter others from gambling on new projects. As Fisher and Lummus had shown

Louis (Red) Snedigar was elected mayor of Miami Beach four times. He spoke often about his drinking and gambling problems but remained popular with Miami Beach voters. (SPA)

almost a decade earlier, where there wasn't land to sell, it could be created by dredging up bay bottom to give more prospective buyers even more waterfront property. A new development company entered the scene that wanted to create a chain of islands running alongside Collins' Bridge which, while only a decade old, was being seen as an old horse that needed to be put to sleep, particularly with the opening of the County Causeway. The Bay Biscayne Improvement Company, which included as its founders prominent Miamians J. F. Chaille, H. M. Anderson and F. C. B. LeGro, bought the bridge from the Collins and Pancoast interests and, in 1921, began construction of four islands in the bay. By August, the islands—Rivo Alto, DiLido, San Marino and San Marco—were being dredged out of bay bottom and linked with Belle Island via the Collins Bridge. LeGro boasted to prospective buyers that the islands would be a foot higher than the mainland and that the nature of the soil on these islands— sand and shell—was such that one could walk on the land almost as soon as the silt was deposited. The plan was to have all the islands, with the exception of San Marco, within the limits of the City of Miami Beach.[34] There were loftier plans in the offing for this group, more islands—some running east and west, and many more running north and south up the bay—and

Miami Beach Police Department, 1921. (MB)

visions of a new bridge to replace Collins' wooden structure. But that was to come later.

These formative years of Miami Beach brought new and enduring names to the young city. One such person was Louis F. (Red) Snedigar who, beginning in 1922, served four terms as mayor of the city, as well as one as councilman (1947-48) before being elected to the Dade County Commission. Born in Bartow, Florida in 1890, Snedigar was a star athlete at Stetson University. He was so good that, in 1913, the legendary Connie Mack, owner and manager of the Philadelphia Athletics, signed him to a contract.[35] Snedigar, an infielder, was no stranger to Miami's baseball diamonds. The year before signing with the Athletics, he played for the Miami semi-professional team but nettled a *Miami Herald* reporter. The unnamed reporter wrote that Snedigar was among the dirtiest of players and particularly noted that Snedigar, in attempting to score a run, "hurtled his 180 or 190 pounds of beef against the Key West catcher with the force of a catapult."[36] (That type of play, of course, is seen as a positive in today's baseball.) Despite his contract with Mack, Snedigar didn't make it to the major leagues. He used his 1914 law degree to return to Miami to join the firm of Shutts, Smith and Bowen. For five years, Snedigar lived in Miami. But in 1919, he looked across the bay and decided that was where he wanted to live and raise a family. Percy Cavill, an Australian long distance swimmer, owned property on the west side of Collins Avenue between 19th and 20th streets. He built a cottage from driftwood claimed from the nearby ocean. As more people began to build around him, the reclusive Cavill sold his house and a portion of the property to Snedigar, then departed for the solace of the Bahamas.[37] By then, Snedigar had left Shutts, Smith and Bowen and formed a law partnership with Francis Miller, with offices both in Miami and Miami Beach. Snedigar turned the Cavill house into a real estate office and went into that business as well. Next door, at 1912 Collins Avenue, he purchased the home of Jim Mathews who would later build the classic Washington Storage Company on Washington Avenue.[38] Certainly the voters cared for him, and so did Carl Fisher. What Red and Carl had in common was a passion for booze, outlawed but quite available. Red's second son, Jim, tells of impromptu, friendly wrestling matches between Snedigar and Fisher as the two drank until the bottle or bottles were empty. While everyone in town knew that Red was a lush, they kept voting for him because they liked the job he was doing.

Snedigar, who joined Alcoholics Anonymous in his later years, often told stories of his drunken days as mayor. His favorite was about the tourist who came to town from Sanford and got loaded. "He was

tossed into the jail late at night and immediately demanded use of the telephone," Snedigar told a 1947 meeting of Alcoholics Anonymous. " 'I'll get out of here,' he said. 'I know the mayor of this town. Just let me get him on the telephone.' So the desk sergeant said, 'Never mind the telephone, bud. The mayor is right in the next cell. Just take it up with him personally.' "[39] Snedigar had more than one such encounter with his police department. When he was caught being a public drunk, he was whisked off to jail to sleep it off; the cell door remaining open in deference to his position. On one occasion, a sympathetic policeman drove Snedigar home rather than put him in jail. Snedigar's wife met the two at the door and demanded her husband be taken straight to jail until he was sober enough to come home properly.[40] Snedigar also was fond of gambling and often bet with bookmakers. His transgressions were overlooked by the citizens and he acknowledged his problems publicly. "I have been justly accused of a weakness of character," he told a mayoral rally in 1934. "It has been a great handicap. However, I have not been accused of gunnery or murder. . . . If you don't want a freckled-faced, red-headed, bespectacled man, get another candidate."[41]

A speaker on his behalf that night added: "Red resembles Mae West. He ain't no angel."[42]

Red was elected to his fourth term in that campaign. His driving exploits were notorious, alcohol being at the root of his difficulty. Twice within six months, Snedigar flipped his old Ford coming off the new County Causeway, turning north onto Alton Road. While it might have been easy to blame the new-style shock absorbers put on his car by inventor Bob Hassler, a Fisher buddy, Snedigar's lack of sobriety was also responsible.[43] "My father wrecked more cars than Joey Chitwood," recalled his son, Jim. "He was pretty safe when he was driving around Miami Beach, but when he got on the Miami side, the cops there didn't take too kindly too him. There was a time when he plowed his car into a Biscayne Boulevard lamppost that was adorned on top with a gargoyle. The gargoyle plunged through the thin roof of his car, narrowly missing him. When the Miami police officer asked Snedigar if he was drunk, he pointed to the gargoyle and said: "You'll have to ask my friend." The cell door on the Miami side did not remain open, despite Snedigar's position in Miami Beach.[44]

The Miami Beach Snedigar came to as the 1920s were about to begin was a town largely in the shadows of the bigger city across the bay. It was ruled by Carl Fisher's dollars and penchant for promotion, with others such as J. N. Lummus and Thomas Pancoast in the wings to wield significant power of their own. Lummus and Pancoast were the town's first two mayors, followed by T. E. James (1920-22), one of five signatories to the incorporation papers of Miami Beach[45] and one of the seven original alderman. [46] James was an officer of the Southern Bank and Trust Company, run by the Lummus brothers and, thus, a continuum of the power grip of the three developers: Fisher, Lummus and Pancoast. Snedigar, although once with a law firm that represented Fisher (Shutts, Bowen, *et al*), seemed to be the first mayor not tied to Beach bosses when he was elected on October 23, 1922. But one could not preside over the fledgling city without falling under the influence of Fisher, which was not such a bad thing.

In October 1920, Rose Weiss—unrelated to Joe and Jennie—arrived. While men like Snedigar made their reputations around conference tables and in pow-wows with the Pancoasts and Fishers, Rose Weiss traveled the road of social consciousness. If Jews could be identified by the sound of their names, as Fisher had claimed,[47] then the 1920 census of Miami Beach would have you believe that Joe and Jennie Weiss were the only other Jews living in Miami Beach when Rose arrived. But, contrary to Fisher's thinking, many Jews do not have names that appear to be Jewish, so it is impossible to know if other Jews lived there because census tables do not identify by religion. In her span of many decades in Miami Beach, Rose Weiss came to be known as the

Mother of Miami Beach, and, also, the "Eighth Councilman" of the city, so frequent was her attendance as a watchdog and advocator at council meetings.[48] Weiss, an immigrant who settled in New York, suffered terribly from asthma and doctors advised her to seek a different climate. Leaving her husband Jeremiah behind while she investigated this strange new frontier, Rose sailed from New York to Jacksonville then continued her journey to Miami by train. There she was met by other Jewish women who were Miami residents. The bus she took across the new County Causeway had a flat tire enroute, which did not give her a good first impression of the area.[49] Eventually, she reached Brown's Hotel on First Street and Ocean Drive, where she rented an apartment with a kitchen. "I could breathe again, " she later boasted. "I fell in love with the place. It was a paradise."[50]

Rose quickly sealed her future to Miami Beach. She sent for her husband and children and bought the unfinished structure of what became the Royal Apartments, 221–223 Collins Avenue. But it was her civic work that brought Rose into prominence. In 1920 or 21, she recounted, Rose found a sobbing youngster with shabby hair and a torn slipper standing in front of the new Miami Beach public school. She asked the principal for permission to take him for a haircut, shoes, etc. After the transformation, she took him to his home. "I knocked. . . and a woman

Miami Beach residents plant trees on the new County Causeway. Community activist Rose Weiss, sits on top of Rosie the elephant. (MB)

Miami Beach's pioneer residents pose for posterity in this 1920s photograph. (HASF)

came to the door.," she recalled. "She didn't recognize her own child. And, she says, "hello, hello" and I smiled. And from then on, I continued to do welfare work. . . . There wasn't a child on this beach who was hungry or had nothing to wear, that I didn't supply for them."[51] So significant was her role in early Miami Beach welfare work that none other than Carl Fisher became a good and respectful friend. When Pete Chase formed Miami Beach's Chamber of Commerce in 1921, Rose not only became a charter member but the chamber's membership chairman. She personally enrolled 60 members from the South Beach area.[52] Rose Weiss went on to design the official flag of Miami Beach and, as a volunteer, ran the city's Welfare Department until a professional came on board. During World War II, she sold more than $5

million in War bonds. The immigrant mother with the asthma problem who came to Miami Beach in 1920 more than paid back the city for her health.

Miami and Miami Beach were growing fast in the early years of the second decade but could not yet be classified as boom towns. That, according to published estimates,[53] did not begin until the spring of 1923. Men such as George Merrick and N. B. T. Roney soon were to join the ranks of the Tatum brothers, Carl Fisher and J. N. Lummus as the Miami area's giants of early development. Merrick, who sold real estate from his downtown Miami office, soon was to concentrate on his own personal project, Coral Gables, and Roney, who had a portfolio of projects in Miami, soon was to move across the bay to become an epic name in Miami Beach.

CHAPTER TEN

"THE WHOLE PLACE WAS SELLING LIKE MAD"

Billboard advertisement for "America's Winter Playground." (SPA)

The prospect of oceanfront living was beginning to appeal to many when, just a few years earlier, it was almost unheard of. It all changed when John Collins built his bridge. The beach was opened to the automobile and the automobile brought people. In 1922, Miami Beach was growing rapidly. Yet, for all the estates being built, as well as apartment houses, cottages and hotels, Miami Beach still retained much of its agricultural roots. In 1922, Miami Beach claimed the largest avocado and mango grove in the world. On 160 acres just north of 23rd Street, the orchards stretched north toward the Tatum property and from the ocean west to the shores of Indian Creek. While workmen poured concrete elsewhere on the Miami Beach, 7,000 avocado and 1,000 mango trees produced tons of fruit for shipment north.[1] The trees planted by John Collins in 1907 were living up to the old man's expectations. By 1922, his star in Miami Beach development was pretty much eclipsed by that of his son-in-law Thomas Pancoast and Fisher. It is safe to assume, however, that he probably was more proud of the success of his trees than of any housing or hotel developments south of his groves.

But the march of growth could not be stemmed. The existence of mango and avocado groves would not last beyond the next few years. By mid-1922, building records were being shattered. Already additions were being built to the Flamingo and Wofford hotels. Expensive new residences were constructed for Chicago industrialist W. F. Whitman and for Wisconsin inventor and capitalist Frederick

Osius.[2] Graphic evidence of the growth of Miami Beach need not be confined to real estate numbers. The role of the dairy Carl Fisher created near 41st Street and Prairie Avenue to supply his guests at the Flamingo Hotel continued to expand as new hotels opened elsewhere in Miami Beach and as new homes continued to be built. On the eve of the 1922–23 winter season, the Miami Beach Dairy purchased another carload of milk cows from its northern supplier, bringing the stock up to 135 at the dairy, with another 140 head in an Everglades division created on the other side of the bay.[3]

But these were not the best of times for Fisher. The mild depression that struck the U.S. in 1921 created financial problems for him. He already was overextended as a result of his many projects. He sold his automobile company in Indiana, borrowed on stock he held in Globe Realty and in Speedway and forfeited his annual pledge to the Lincoln Highway Association. His wife Jane cited the expense of running houses in Indianapolis, Detroit, St. Joseph's, Michigan, and Miami Beach as reaching an overwhelming state. "The house on the beach was staffed at times by twenty people, and our grocery bills were often a thousand dollars a month," she complained, adding that she began having a tailor repair her husband's suits from the year previous rather than create new ones and that she would "scramble through my own wardrobe for geegaws to freshen up hats that were three years old!"[4]

If there was something that could bring Fisher out of his temporary doldrums, it would be the birth of a son. Carl Jr., was born in Indianapolis in the fall of 1921, thrilling his proud daddy. The euphoria was short-lived, however. The child was born with an obstruction of the stomach. The baby lived but 26 days. Carl Sr.'s father died earlier in the year and his mother was in poor health. If Fisher's obsession with his projects had not already driven a wedge between him and Jane, the death of their son did. "We had entered separate worlds, Carl and I, and neither would hold for us anything we really wanted." Jane observed. "A dear friend said later, 'How different life would have been for all of us, Jane, if that baby had lived.' "[5] Their lives changed dramatically. They rarely were seen together. "I went in for society," Jane wrote. "Carl began drinking."[6]

Prohibition had become the law of the land in 1920, but Dade County, where Miami Beach is, had voted itself dry as early as 1913.[7] Local prohibition laws were lax, however, and few who wanted a drink went without one. It was when liquor was outlawed nationally and its prohibition enforced by federal authorities that a drink became more difficult to obtain. Fisher, however, did not lack for one. As Jane noted, Carl began to drink hard during Prohibition. Some of his best friends became his suppliers and drinking buddies. When President-elect Harding stayed overnight at the Flamingo Hotel, it was reported that he had a good game of cards and a few drinks with Fisher. Jim Allison had a place in his aquarium where he was able to secret away cases of liquor. In 1921, law enforcement authorities nabbed Allison's former chauffeur entering the aquarium at an off-hour. It turned out he previously had stolen 35 cases of booze from the special Allison vault and was returning for more. The former chauffeur led police to Allison's hideaway. "The Revenue Officers came over yesterday afternoon with a diagram of the entire lay-out of where you had placed your liquor," Fisher wrote to Allison who was in Indianapolis at the time. ". . .They were very nice, very polite and completely thorough. . .John [Levi] suggests that we immediately advise you regarding the offense, which is not particularly serious—only $500 fine for the first offense. . . . The Herald treated the matter very decently this morning, I thot, [sic] considering that the Revenue Officer said this was the second largest haul they had ever made."[8]

In that same correspondence, Fisher reported to Allison that he had received a letter from LaGorce that very morning, "that if I stop off in Washington

An army of salesmen for the Tatum Brothers' Altos Del Mar stand along their oceanside property. (SPA)

Boom-time crowds pack the Roman Pools' beachfront. Of all the public casinos, the Roman Pools was considered the most posh. (SPA)

he wants me to bring him a dozen bottles of Mitchell's Imperial. He is just a little bit too late."

C. G. Fowler, who was president of the National Fowler Bank in Lafayette, Indiana, and a good friend of Fisher, wrote him in 1923 to warn that driving back to Indiana from Florida with liquor could be dangerous. "I got through with two cases of O.K. in trunks and suit cases," wrote Fowler, "but the enforcement officers are very active all over the state."[9]

As the Prohibition years progressed, Fisher became more deeply involved in illegal booze, both as a personal escape and as a supplier to his friends. The press of business, the death of his infant son and the consumption of large quantities of alcohol were putting a strain on his marriage from which Carl and Jane would not recover. The problems were mostly Fisher's own doing. He had extended himself beyond his means and reach. Elsewhere, others were faring better. Soon, the area would experience a colossal Boom, so colossal that Fisher quickly regained his financial clout and moved on to more projects.

As 1923 dawned, there were signs that the economic depression was rapidly lifting. Across the nation, business was picking up and in Miami Beach, mild sales began turning to record sales. The Tatums, who were developing Altos Del Mar in the northern portion of Miami Beach, advertised "The Boom Is On."[10] and had 30 salesmen on the job by February. While a March 30 United Realty Company advertisement in the *Miami Herald* was for land in the City of

Miami, it reflected the rapidly growing trend of the entire community: "Miami is on the brink of its first real Boom. . . . There has really never been a Boom in Miami. Rapidly increasing population and realty valuation have been due to consistent growth, but this year people who know indications declared that the city's strides will establish a new precedent for expansion."[11]

Miami Beach's winter season hit high strides in January and, with it, sales increased. Pete Chase recalled:

> . . . they began picking up very, very fast . . . The whole place was selling like mad. Same thing in '24 and '25 and part of '26. . . . People up north were making money hand over fist. Fisher had all these acquaintances up north; they began to come down here and they saw what Fisher was doing—what a great place it was and how it was being built and beautiful and everything.[12]

The social set became very much part of the Miami Beach scene. The *Miami Herald* and *Miami Metropolis* would report daily on what they called a parade of society at the bathing casino, describing in detail the costumes worn, who was wearing them and at what hotel they were staying. Miami Beach's three golf courses were jammed to capacity and famous names were checking into the hotels. "The height of the season has arrived," reported the *Miami Herald* on January 29, "and society will be led a merry whirl during the next weeks with social event crowding social event upon the calendar, with interesting sports events following each other in dizzying succession. Much entertaining was done at casinos, tea gardens, Star Island Yacht club, Cocolobo Cay club[13] and private homes during the last week, and this week the gayety [sic] promises to continue in the same if not greater degree." J. C. Penney, the merchandising giant, brought pianist Arthur Rubenstein and violinist Paul Kochanski to his Belle Isle mansion, where they entertained 250 guests with a sunset

Miami Beach's apartments and hotels were filled to capacity as the whole nation discovered South Florida. (Olive Delahunt)

"musicale" while, at the same time, the largest crowds ever—estimated at more than 10,000—jammed Miami beach's bathing casinos. "A line of cars could be noted from one end of the three mile [County] causeway to the other, passing in constant succession," reported the *Miami Herald* on January 29. The best of times had arrived. So certain were the Tatums that the leap in land values would continue to accelerate that they placed advertisements in newspapers offering to buy back every lot on Ocean Drive in Altos Del Mar subdivisions purchased before January 1, 1921, at 15 percent cash above the price originally paid, and any lot facing on Collins Avenue for a profit of 50 percent. Realtors throughout Miami Beach now were busy selling new lots or already-constructed homes. Building permits for January 1923 reached $198,000 compared to $41,000 for the same month the year before.[14]

A new player had joined the already-established land entrepreneurs of Miami Beach. His name came in four parts: Newton Baker Taylor Roney, but he preferred to be known as N. B. T. Roney. Others called him "Newton Bath Tub" Roney or "No Back Talk" Roney, even "Nothing But Trouble" Roney. His friends referred to him as "Newt."[15] When he settled permanently in Miami in 1918, Roney, a Camden, New Jersey lawyer, real estate and development entrepreneur, saw great possibilities in the young city. Shortly, however, his business interests drifted across the bay where he was to establish himself as one of the giants of Miami Beach development. By 1925, he was referred to as "the largest individual real estate dealer in Southeastern Florida" and "the greatest single builder at Miami Beach."[16] Roney first visited Miami in 1909 at a time when what was to be Miami Beach, was mostly was under cultivation by John Collins. Roney returned for another visit in 1917, then decided his future was in South Florida and moved from New Jersey the following year.[17] He immediately plunged into the real estate business. Roney's first venture was a building in Miami on Flagler Street. He then purchased Elser's Pier, an entertainment hall at the foot of Flagler Street on Biscayne Bay. He sold that within a year and purchased the Biscayne Hotel in downtown Miami, where Burdines now stands. He bought it for $210,000 and sold it in early 1925 for $1 million.[18]

Of lesser note at the time was Roney's activity in Miami Beach. In 1918, he purchased five oceanfront lots from J. N. Lummus for $16,000 and the following year bought out the interests of J. N. and his brother, J. E., in the Ocean View Company.[19] Roney's first building on Miami Beach was on the corner of Fifth Street and Collins Avenue. (He had

J. C. Penney's mansion on Belle Island, as seen on this postcard, played host to personalities such as president-elect Herbert Hoover and pianist Arthur Rubenstein. (SPA)

purchased more than four blocks fronting on Washington and Collins avenues north of Fifth Street.[20]) In addition, he was busy purchasing other lots throughout Miami Beach. Roney also helped organize the Miami Beach Bank and Trust Company in 1923. It was the second bank in Miami Beach, the first being the Miami Beach First National Bank at Lincoln and Alton roads, which opened in 1922.[21] Roney constructed his bank's building at 601 Collins Avenue and was one of its largest stockholders.[22] He also was an early financier of Miami's third newspaper, the *Miami Tribune*.[23] In the first five years of the 1920s, Roney had become a powerful force on Miami Beach. He owned buildings that contained more than 200 shops between Third and 23rd streets along Collins Avenue.[24] Next, he purchased the 600-foot long oceanfront site where Collins and Pancoast had a decade earlier advertised "special inducements and liberal terms to parties who will erect the class of hotel desired."[25]

Before building his hotel, however, Roney had another major project to deal with, the building of a Spanish colony that William Whitman envisioned in 1922.[26]. Whitman's plan called for eight or 10 houses and cottages on each of the blocks he owned on what now is Espanola Way. The property, formerly the Richard Carney tract, ran from the oceanfront west to Meridian Avenue, between 14th and 15th Streets. Whitman constructed only a few residences. In December 1924, Roney purchased 10 undeveloped blocks of Espanola Way between Washington and Jefferson Avenues[27] and had his architect, Robert Taylor, design six hotels—all on corner lots—eight apartment buildings and four other buildings.[28] Like

Whitman's, Roney's plan was not fully carried out. Instead, only two hotels were built, with 16 apartment buildings and a number of shops—all with a Spanish design.[29]

Another new player on the scene was James M. Cox, twice governor of Ohio and the Democratic Party's presidential candidate in the 1920 election won by Warren Harding.[30] Cox was a newspaper man, having started his career as a reporter in Cincinnati before the turn of the century. He owned newspapers in the Ohio cities of Dayton and Springfield. Cox met Fisher years earlier when Carl was in Dayton in relation to Fred Avery's rudimentary automobile headlight. They remained friends as Cox climbed both the publishing and political ladders and Fisher became renowned for both his Prest-O-Lite battery innovations and his development of Miami Beach. When Fisher invited him to come to Miami in 1923, Cox agreed. "Tell me now, man to man, whether it gets too warm in Miami in March," Cox wrote Fisher in January 1923. "I would like to feel I can stay until the first of April. Forget you are a southern propagandist and tell me the truth."[31]

Obviously ignoring Cox's plea not to be a propagandist, Fisher wrote back:

We always have a warm spell in March. It lasts about one week or 10 days; and it is the worst thing that ever could happen to southern Florida, for the reason that a lot of people imagine that it is warm at home and that the winter is over, and they go out of here like rats from a sinking ship. . . . The temperature, however, seldom reaches above 81 and it is NEVER—so help me God!—within thirty degrees as hot in this country as it is in Dayton or Indianapolis during July and August. . . . I am just going to have a nice gin fizz made with our Florida limes; and then I am going to the beach for a swim. And, I imagine, about the time you are

reading this cheerful information it will either be snowing or a cold drizzly rain with you.[sic][32]

"I fell completely in love with the place, confident that it would grow into a great city," wrote Cox in his biography. "Living in a hotel was always an intolerable experience to me. When I made up my mind to spend a part of each year in Miami, I realized that to find happiness there, I must get something to occupy my time."[33] Fisher suggested that the city's afternoon newspaper, the *Miami Metropolis* might be for sale, and Cox jumped at the opportunity. After a very short negotiation, Cox purchased the paper from S. Bobo Dean for cash.[34]

On that same first trip, Cox purchased land on Miami Beach and began building a house on Bay Road north of a site where Fisher was constructing his third hotel, the Nautilus. Cox also was to go into partnership with Roney in the July 1925 purchase of 115 acres of land just north of Golden Beach. Called Seminole Beach, Cox and Roney bought it for $3 million and sold it in lots shortly thereafter for $7.6 million. The lot sale took all of six and one half hours and became a prime example of the frenzied wheeling and dealing associated with salesmen known as the "binder boys," whose sales tactics blemished the Miami area's Boom days.[35]

When determining where to build his latest hotel, Fisher again chose the bay side of Miami Beach. It was his idea to build hotels in places that were unlikely to be developed. The oceanside was seen as prime land for estates. And, as part of his thinking, Fisher wanted hotels on the bay side because that was where he was conducting his huge boat races and polo matches. The Flamingo, at 15th Street, was at the southern edge of his racing courses; the Nautilus, just above 41st Street, would be on the northern leg. Also, Fisher had moved his polo fields from where they originally were located just south of Lincoln Road near Alton Road. Land in the Lincoln Road area was becoming much in demand, and Fisher found it economically smart to sell the land in lots and move his polo grounds north where land was not selling just yet. Costing $870,000—considerably less than the Flamingo—the Nautilus opened its doors on January 10, 1924.[36] As its manager, Fisher chose Charles Krom, the brother of Flamingo manager George Krom. The Nautilus was a Fisher showcase. He created two islands from bay bottom for his pool and cabana areas as well as for radio station WIOD—Wonderful Isle Of Dreams—and a cottage colony. (Called Collins Island and Johns Island, they were named for John Collins and John Levi and were linked by

N. B. T. Rooney built two hotels and 16 apartment buildings in trying to create an artists' colony on Espanola Way. (Matlack; HASF)

Artist's sketch of Nautilus Hotel, Carl Fisher's second hotel on Biscayne Bay. (SPA)

Right: *The baroque entrance to the Nautilus Hotel. (Matlack; HASF)*
Below: *Lobby of Nautilus Hotel. (Matlack; HASF)*

One of the Nautilus' Towers. (Matlack; HASF)

A panoramic photograph of construction in front of Nautilus Hotel (SPA)

short bridges to the Nautilus grounds.) The hotel offered the ultimate for wealthy guests: posh rooms, a swimming pool with cabanas, beautiful stairways and chandeliers, a gourmet dining room and, of course, the adjoining polo fields which began just north of 41st Street, with horse stables to the south of them.[37] As at his other hotels, Fisher's policy was to restrict who could stay at the Nautilus.

As the 1923–24 winter season approached, the Boom was in full bloom. Lots sold quicker than you could say N. B. T. Roney. In anticipation of the upcoming season, hotels opened earlier than the usual January date. The Wofford—now grown to 100 rooms—rolled its opening back to December 6; the Lincoln was fully opened by November 1.[38] (The usual opening date was January 1.) Miami Beach now had 21 hotels, ranging in size from 15 rooms to 250, capable of accommodating 4,000.[39] In addition to the Nautilus, another new hotel, the Pancoast, opened as a 122-room resort located on the ocean at 29th Street. It was built by J. Arthur Pancoast, grandson of John Collins. Restricted like Fisher's hotels, it catered to the wealthy and genteel. Architect Martin L. Hampton had gone to Spain specifically to study designs he might incorporate into the Spanish-themed hotel. J. Arthur Pancoast and his wife lived in an apartment on the side of the hotel. Kay Pancoast, wife of Russell Pancoast, recalled her brother-in-law's hotel also catered to the young. "We always had a young people's dance," she said. "We danced a lot to the Jerry Twitchell band. It was a charming place."[40]

South Beach, too, was experiencing a boom in new but smaller hotels. The 55-room Seabreeze at Collins and Third Street, the 30-room Marlin at Collins and Fourth Street and the 18-room Carol, also at Collins and Fourth opened that year. Roney entered the hotel business by building a small one in 1923–24, at 415 Collins Avenue.

The rush of progress in 1923 was just the tip of the Boom. What followed in 1924 and 1925 was overwhelming, not only in Miami Beach but throughout the southern half of the state. "Miami was transformed from a sleepy little town on the edge of Biscayne Bay into a Magic City of modest skyscrapers and legendary real estate profits," observed Kenneth Ballinger in *Miami Millions*, his 1936 book documenting the Boom. T. H. Weigall, an Englishman who came to America in August 1925, drifted to Boom-time Miami, lived in Miami Beach and made a bundle of money working for George Merrick's Coral Gables development. He wrote in his 1932 *Boom in Paradise:*

> The Boom began at the psychological moment when its repercussions on the rest of America was most likely to be felt. It

began at a time when there was more money in the United States than there had ever been before, at a time when the infinitely smaller Boom in California had already lost a great part of its novelty, and at a time when the almost universal adoption of the automobile had made possible a nation-wide trek unthinkable in the days of the Alaskan gold-rushes and the Booms in the Middle-West. The Florida Boom, too, had the inestimable advantage of being advertised on a scale, and with a degree of skill, which had never previously been approached in the advertising of any similar activity. And Florida, though having been to a large extent actually created out of worthless swamps and impassable bogs by the skill and capital of its engineers, had about it the additional glamour of an absolutely untested intrinsic value. Nobody knew what Florida land was actually worth, apart from Boom conditions; nobody knows even to this day.[41]

Hotels and office building were springing up in downtown Miami, sub-divisions with exotic names were spreading far west into the Everglades and south toward the Keys, while the push north was developing what were boondocks in North Dade, Broward County and beyond, up the Gold Coast of Florida. As 1923 turned into 1924, Miami Beach took on a touch of sophistication to go along with its booming land sales and construction. Tire magnate Harvey Firestone purchased the Snowden estate that ran from ocean to creek north of 44th Street, and the Snowdens, without a home of their own, took up winter residence at the Flamingo.[42] The Star Island Yacht Club, opened in 1923, debuted its second season with a formal dinner dance limited to 100 persons. As manager, the club secured the services of George B. Everart, who possessed an international reputation, having opened Maxim's in Paris, the Ritz hotels in both London and New York, the Plaza in New York and, for the past 10 years, the Beach Club in Palm Beach.[43] The Florida Art League exhibited 300 paintings at the Miami Beach Chamber of Commerce building while Cesare La Monica and the Miami Beach Casino Orchestra performed nightly at the 23rd street casino. In a fit of enthusiasm, the *Miami Beach Register*, a weekly magazine covering Miami Beach's social, recreational and commercial life, headlined in its January 16, 1924, issue: "The World's Here." It went on:

> Anyone who is the least bit inclined to be a hero-worshiper. . . can have a wonderful time at Miami Beach, just watching the world linger here long enough to escape the cold of the north, to have a bit of paradise on this

side. For in Miami Beach may be seen in the space of a season representatives of practically every nation, of practically everything worth while.

The magazine reeled off the names of celebrities visiting Miami Beach, including philosopher Dr. William Lyon Phelps, heavyweight boxing champion Jack Dempsey, golfer Gene Sarazen as well as:

> well-known manufacturers, women high in society, statesmen. . . . Some day, if the migration of celebrities continues, it won't be necessary to publish "Who's Who in America." The Miami Beach city directory will be all that's needed.[44]

The 1924 Miami Beach City Directory did reflect the growth of the city. Belle Isle, the swampy terminus of Collins' wooden bridge, now was the site of stylish homes of the wealthy. Bay Road, from 14th to 18th Streets, also was lined with homes, interrupted by the Flamingo Hotel. Fifth Street was the center of the commercial district. There were but eight groceries in Miami Beach in 1924, all of them on South Beach.[45] Other developers soon entered the picture. On the bay side of Miami Beach, a real estate syndicate composed of several members, among them the Gryzmich Brothers and Henry Levy, bought a mangrove patch called Mead Island from A. P. Warner and the Mead brothers for $250,000,[46] renamed it South Island and began its development. Just above South Island was another mangrove patch called North Island. (Existence of the two mangrove islands can be traced as far back as Bernard Romans' mid-18th century survey of the area.) The syndicate originally planned to name the development's streets after persons. But the Dade County Commission, which had control of street names, rejected the idea, and the developers decided to name the streets after French towns and provinces. Included in the new naming was a change, again, of the island's name, from South Island to Normandy Isle.[47] In 1925, the first housing, comprised of four apartment houses, was begun along with the fountain at the east end of the island. The following year, another real estate

firm built private homes but went out of business within a year. North Island was to remain in its native state until 1939 when the City of Miami Beach bought it, pumped up the land and created the Normandy Shores Municipal Golf Course.[48] Meanwhile, Biscayne Point north of Normandy Isle was being developed by the Biscayne Point Realty Company. Calling itself the "Jewel of Biscayne Bay," Biscayne Point projected 4,900 feet into Biscayne Bay with each lot fronting on water.[49] To the south, four spits of land jutted out from the west side of the Beach into the bay. Fisher owned part of those nubs, and Atlanta capitalist Stephen A. Lynch, the remainder. With the Boom in bloom, Fisher became concerned that Lynch would be competition. Officials rejected an application for bulkheading and filling and Fisher then cut a canal between the Beach proper and his share of the properties, thus turning Lynch's portion into islands, and with no bridge to get across.[50] With that, Fisher kept Lynch from participating in the Boom, but a decade later his property was developed as the Sunset Islands, linked by a bridge across to Bay Road. By 1925, Miami Beach had no fewer than 122 subdivisions.[51]

The arrival of a higher social class played very much to Jane Fisher's desires. She enjoyed attending or hosting tea parties and dances. Carl, who liked the idea of a better class of people frequenting his development, did not necessary care to rub elbows with them all the time, nor did he spend much time with Jane any more. He kept much to himself, or to his cronies. And his drinking increased to dangerous levels. When Jane decided to adopt a two-year-old child, hopefully to replace Carl Jr. in her husband's heart, it was a failure. Carl refused to be a part of the December 1922 adoption; Jane went it alone.[52] Jane missed most of the Boom. So upset was she with her relationship with Carl that she went off to Europe with her adopted son Jackie. "Carl might have no time for me," she later wrote, "but leisurely Paris gave attention to the wealthy American woman who drove through the Rue de la Paix behind a uniformed chauffeur in a Minerva town car, wearing pinned to her sables a cluster of white camelias from the garden of her villa near Paris."[53]

What Jane missed in her chosen exile from Miami Beach was the height of its Boom. People were buying and building simply on whim. Wealthy Ohio and New York Realtor J. Perry Stoltz retired from the real estate rat race and came to Miami Beach in his yacht on vacation in 1923.

Arched entrance leads into Normandy Isle. The northern island remained undeveloped until 1939 when the City of Miami Beach created a golf course there. (Matlack; HASF)

Retired Realtor J. Perry Stoltz came to Miami Beach for rest and relaxation but soon was caught up with the urge to be part of the scene. He built the Fleetwood Hotel in 1924–25 at Eighth Street and the bay. (Matlack; HASF)

Much like Cox—and Fisher more than a decade earlier—Stoltz found it difficult to frequent an area without being involved in business there. "Last year, I came down to Miami Beach only on conditions that I forget business altogether and not buy a thing, real estate or otherwise," he claimed in a 1924 newspaper interview. "I succeeded fairly well, except—when I went north in the spring, I found I was owner of 2,000 feet of bay front . . . between the bay and Alton Road." [54] Much of that property would be developed over the following 21 months to become the second major hotel built on the bay side below Lincoln Road. Stoltz arrived aboard his *Fleetwood III*, a vessel he named for his son Fleetwood. He also named his hotel after his son. The Fleetwood Hotel, located on the bay at Eighth Street, formally opened on January 15, 1925. It stood 16 stories high—the Flamingo was only 11 stories—had 350 rooms, a roof garden for dining and dancing, and a club room for yachtsmen. It was advertised as "Florida's largest fireproof hotel." [55] The hotel also was the site of radio station WMBF—for Wonderful Miami Beach Florida. From there William Jennings Bryan broadcast nationally on opening night, extolling Florida's future while highlighting the debut of the Fleetwood. [56]

Roney, meanwhile, was allowing no moss to grow under his feet. He followed his December 1924 announcement of the plan to create the Spanish village off Washington Avenue with a February 1925 notice that he would build on the site where Collins and Pancoast long had sought a world-class hotel. He announced the $2 million dollar Roney Plaza Hotel on Collins Avenue at 23rd Street. It was to be, by far, the largest hotel on the oceanfront. He chose as his architects the New York firm of Schultze and Weaver, the same group that designed Cox's Miami

News Tower and the Biltmore Hotel in Coral Gables. [57] As the Roney was under construction, one of several unexpected cataclysms struck the South Florida area. This came in the form of a railroad embargo and delayed, among many other construction projects in the district, work on Roney's hotel. The area was growing ahead of its supply lines. Railroad cars and ocean-going vessels arrived filled to their brims with building materiels, but there were not enough laborers to unload them. In August 1925, nine ships were at Miami's docks unable to unload. Miami's port, which had accepted 206,000 tons in 1922, had to deal with 1.1 million tons in the first half of 1925 alone. [58]

The Florida East Coast Railway, its Miami-area yards jammed with thousands of unloaded freight cars, called an embargo on freight coming in until the backlog subsided. [59] Construction jobs stood still, running up the cost of building and putting men out of work. In lieu of the railroad, builders took to shipping their materials to Miami via ships. This caused an even greater backup of large sailing vessels in Miami's harbor, as well as out in the ocean where they awaited their turn—sometimes for days—to come in to port.

This, along with a second cataclysmic phenomenon known as the "binder boys" brought the out-of-control land Boom back to reality. Helen Muir, in her book *Miami, USA*, described the binder boys most succinctly: "[They] took up options on

Carl and Jane Fisher pose with her adopted son Jackie for the Miami Beach Register. (MB)

land for a small sum of money [typically 10 per cent] with a first payment due usually in a month's time. The binder boys had no intention of holding on to the options but sold them over and over at a profit. This alone raised the price of property."[60] The "binder boys" descended upon Florida beginning in the spring of 1925; most came from the North. Headquarters for many of them in Miami Beach was the Fleetwood Hotel; in Miami, it was the Ponce de Leon Hotel. Kenneth Ballinger described a binder boy as:

an individual slightly under normal height, never very clean or neat, bending every effort to make a lot of money in a hurry without the slightest pretense of remaining in Florida once that was done. He was attired in golf knickers, because they didn't need pressing nor the addition of a coat, and the binder boys made the knicker a one time standard male garb in almost any gathering, even church. He spoke with a peculiar dialect, which soon had even the natives pronouncing the word "binder" to rhyme with "cinder" instead of with "kinder." He slept in hotel or rooming house halls, three and four to a single room, or wherever he could find temporary space.[61]

Ballinger was doing a verbal dance, using innuendo to avoid saying that Jews made up a large number of the binder boys. Isidor Cohen was not so gentle. The pioneer Jewish merchant of across-the-bay Miami—he arrived in February 1896—wrote in 1927:

Much of the widely heralded prejudice against the Jews—which is greatly exaggerated—has been caused by a very energetic and rather vociferous crowd of co-religionists that invaded this town during the flurry in the real estate market in the memorable years of 1925. These indiscreet fellow Jews had made themselves obnoxious to the local non-Jewish conservative realty operators, and to the rest of the community, who manifested a hostile spirit toward them which spread toward their local brethren as well as toward Jewish tourists who came the following season. However, it should be admitted that more or less prejudice prevailed prior to the hectic Boom in the form of exclusion of some co-religionists from certain hotels and golf courses at Miami Beach.[62]

An example of how binder boys ran up the price of property was manifest in Cox/Roney's Seminole Beach which, today, is Hallandale Beach. Binder boys besieged Roney's office with offers to purchase options on Seminole Beach property even before Roney put it up for public sale. The original Cox/Roney investment of $3 million sold to mostly binder boys for $7.6 million. They, in turn, sold their options at higher prices, buying already-inflated options from others and selling higher again—so much so that the resale of the original $3 million property amounted to $12 million in less than a week.[63]

The reign of the binder boys did not last more than six months, from March to August 1925.[64] But land was selling so fast and at such inflated prices everywhere throughout the state that even Fisher was beginning to worry. (Fisher never veered from his original pricing. While refusing to take part in the inflation of Miami Beach property, his companies nevertheless realized $23 million in sales in 1925.[66]) Fisher expressed his concern in a letter to Cox, adding an admonition of the press:

If you are keeping in touch with the buying of Florida property, you must know that literally millions upon millions of dollars is being shipped into Florida for the purchase of land, lots, apartments, houses, etc. Some of the property now being sold in Florida will not bring as much money in thirty years as it is selling for now. . .We are bound to have a flare-back and Miami and Miami Beach are going to suffer as a result of some of the exploiting schemes that have been carried on around Miami and further North. You have published in your paper, and so has the *Herald* and other papers, scheme after scheme which has never materialized and many people have invested thru [sic] the fact that a supposedly reliable newspaper publishes a statement of what some real estate dealer proposes to do. If you will check back thru [sic] your papers and look for statements that have not made good in the last two or three years, you will be amazed.[66]

One of those land speculators keeping to his word on Miami Beach projects was Roney. He opened his Roney Plaza Hotel in February 1926, amid the waning enthusiasm of the Boom, and misfortune in Miami's harbor. The latter was in the form of a large sailing ship, the *Prins Valdemar*, that capsized and blocked the harbor. Much of what the hotel needed was on some of those ships unable to reach port. "Deprived of many of the needed features to provide the usual gala opening," wrote *The Miami Daily News*, on February 7:

the building nevertheless stands ready to contribute its share toward the success of the present winter at Miami Beach, and forecasts greater things for the winters to come. Robbed as it temporarily was of these things that reflect the spirit of show, the great hotel

N. B. T. Rooney built the landmark hotel that bore his name on land long held out by the Collins and Pancoast interests as a site for a large hotel on the ocean. It opened in early 1926. (HASF)

stands virtually as a monument signifying triumph over obstacles as great as any ever overcome by man, even in the most remote section of the world.[67]

That the Roney managed to weather the freight embargo and the capsizing of the *Prins Valdemar* and still open within three months of its original December 1, 1925, completion date was a marvel.

The capsizing of the *Prins Valdemar*—cataclysm number three—had a bad effect on much of Greater Miami. The Shipping News column of the *Miami Daily News* on Sunday, January 10, 1926, indicated a pretty active harbor. Fourteen vessels were coming and 23 already were in port. Lumber, general cargoes and boatloads of tourists kept the port so busy that the *Prins Valdemar* was ordered from its berth to an anchorage in the bay off the Fleetwood Hotel to make room for freight vessels. The *Prins Valdemar's* journey toward the Fleetwood was to end in disaster that night, ultimately blocking Miami's harbor for 42 days. The *Prins Valdemar* was a former Danish sailing vessel that was going to be converted to a cabaret and night club. In the meantime, it was assisting in the shipment and unloading of sand ballast in the building of Municipal Pier 3, near the southern edge of today's Bicentennial Park in Miami. As the 3,100-ton, 241-foot-long barkentine neared where the U.S. Coast Guard station now is located on the MacArthur Causeway, she ran aground and eventually capsized.[68] Millions of dollars of goods went undelivered and 45 million feet of lumber stayed at anchor at the harbor's mouth while the righting and refloating of the *Prins Valdemar* dragged on.

Another of the building projects that was to suffer from the calamities that came along with the Boom was Roney's Espanola Way. Slowed by delays in building supplies, Roney nevertheless plunged ahead with his concept of an artist's colony for Miami Beach. In February 1926, the *Miami Daily News*, not recalling Whitman's 1922 plan, reported:

The idea of a Spanish Village where artists and lovers of the artistic might congregate amid congenial surroundings was first suggested to Mr. Roney when several people who had formerly lived in New York came to Miami Beach. They mentioned that with all the tropic surroundings of the Beach, there was no place where an artist would feel the same atmosphere as he would in Greenwich Village in New York or in the artist quarter in Paris.[69]

Sidewalk cafes were planned as well as craftsmen specialty shops, studies for architects,

studios for artists and several restaurants. Roney's Spanish Village was not the success as was his oceanside hotel. It never lived up to expectations and became more known as a congregating point for bookies and, later, as a site for dance studios before being resurrected in the late '80s and '90s as part of the exploding South Beach scene.

Having rebounded from the financial depths he found himself in at the beginning of the decade, Fisher was anxious to move on to bigger things. With Jane living apart from him, Carl had no pangs about spending even more time in his work. He sold his Michigan home and bought another in Long Island. This was to create another challenge within him. Having sold $6 million worth of lots in Miami Beach in 1924 and quadrupling that in 1925, he decided to create a Miami Beach of the North, on Long Island's eastern end. It was called Montauk. Fisher purchased approximately 10,000 acres in 1925, with the idea of developing Montauk Point as a summer resort and deep–water trans–Atlantic port. "We will let contracts for approximately five or six million dollars worth of hotels, club houses, stores, docks, golf courses, etc.," he wrote to a trade publication in September 1925.[70]

This was Fisher's Waterloo. His obsession with Montauk marked the start of the decline of Carl Fisher's domination of the Miami Beach scene. It did not necessarily slow his pace but Montauk now shared his already crowded mind with Miami Beach.

In opening the King Cole and Boulevard hotels in 1925, his dream for Miami Beach was coming closer to fulfillment. He, and his colleagues, had carved a city from the jungle, built streets, bridges, homes, hotels and gardens, seen it become the playground for some of the country's richest people, and brought it to the forefront of tourist attention. Along the way, he made a bundle of money— estimated at more than $50 million. What more could he accomplish? Others, such as Roney, were available to continue the miracle of Miami Beach growth; Fisher had new worlds to conquer. That ambition, along with his drinking habit, was to prove to be his downfall. Montauk eventually wiped out his bankroll.

But before that happened, other storm clouds gathered—and struck!

The fourth cataclysm to visit Miami Beach was one shared by everyone else in South Florida. It came sweeping in from the Atlantic Ocean on a September night in 1926. The Boom had long since burst but the hurricane of 1926 drove hard the nail in the coffin.

CHAPTER ELEVEN

THE HURRICANE AND OTHER STORMY MATTERS

A view of South Beach immediately after the storm and ocean waters had subsided. (Parks)

Storm flags of all sorts soon were to fly from Miami Beach—and elsewhere in the South Florida community. Financial storms: a crush of bad notices in Northern newspapers regarding land sales would cause considerable problems; the binder boys would had to be dealt with. Emotional storms: Fisher's marriage to Jane would go from bad to worse to pfft! Political storms: Miami Beach's police chief would be sent to jail for smuggling narcotics.

And the Big Blow was just around the corner.

In advance of that, however, the pace was fast, furious and exciting. Simple early social functions such as picnics and bathing at one of the seaside casinos, or bridge games at J. N. Lummus' home, had changed with the opening of the Flamingo Hotel to afternoon teas attended by those seeking a higher social stratum. When the Nautilus opened, it became an additional venue for social events. In 1922, Rev. and Mrs. Elisha King of the Community Church invited all unmarried people in Miami Beach to their home. This grew to become the Young People's Association, the first organized social club on the Beach.[1]

Wealthy Philadelphians J. Hunter and Caroline Barton bypassed the established social life of Palm Beach to visit Miami Beach in the winter, along with their son, Alfred, who was to leave an indelible mark on the Miami Beach social scene as founder of the Surf Club. Alfred, a decorated veteran of service in France during World War I, recalled in

a 1965 newspaper interview that when his family established residence in Miami Beach in 1924 "parties were given at home in those days, teas and tea dances, sometimes for 300 guests, or dinners for 30 with others coming in later and an orchestra."[2] The Bartons built a large Mediterranean-style house at Collins Avenue and 18th Street, calling it *Buen Retiro*. They paid $23,000 for the property and another $47,000 for construction of the house, which was two stories high and had five bedrooms, each with a private bath, on the second floor.[3] The house was filled with Gothic and Renaissance furniture and art. No sooner had it been complete than Mrs. Barton established her claim as the Queen of Miami

Top: *Alfred Barton, shown celebrating the Surf Club's 25th anniversary, atop a girl-laden cake.* **Center:** *Its employees were steeped in courtesy, manners and appearance.* **Below**: *The Surf Club, on the ocean at 96th Street, is one of Miami Beach's enduring institutions.* (MN; HASF)

Beach society. She opened *Buen Retiro* on Christmas Day 1924 with a tea dance in her walled garden[4] and had as early houseguests European royalty that she and her son had met immediately after the war when Alfred, still in the service, was planning and conducting lavish parties for Gen. Henry T. Allen, commander of the U.S. Army of Occupation in Germany.[5]

Palm Beach's grip on Florida society loosened a bit when the Bartons established a higher plane of social life in the new community on Biscayne Bay. Jane Fisher, of course, revelled in the luxuriant social life. Ever since she had come to Miami Beach, she lived in the shadow of Palm Beach society life. Now, her city was beginning to have one of its own, not quite on the scale of Palm Beach's but good enough for her. "Oh, Palm Beach!" she cried out in a 1967 taped interview with author Polly Redford. "They thought we were just scum. We were *nouveaux riches*, you see. New money from the Midwest, automobile money from Indiana and Michigan. They were old money from the East, bankers and railroads. You know—*Easterners*."[6]

While Fisher was his own best publicity man, he nevertheless felt a need to hire someone to beat the drums for his properties. As early as 1920, the man doing publicity for the Indianapolis 500-mile auto race, Steve Hannagan, was being recommended to him. It took a while to get the two together but when they did, the nation's newspapers were chock-jammed with the outpouring of publicity emanating from the Fisher-Hannagan team. In August 1920, Hannagan made the mistake of trying to dictate terms of winter employment to Fisher, including a salary of $75 a week with all travel expenses and lodgings in Miami Beach to be paid for by Fisher.[7] No one dictated to Carl Fisher; so, four years later, Hannagan found himself again trying to connect with Fisher. Carl played hard to get: "I just made arrangements last week for a publicity man at Miami Beach," he wrote Hannagan on September 23, 1924, "which closes the matter for this year." Nevertheless, Fisher provided a letter of recommendation to other Miami Beach interests on Hannagan's behalf, citing Steve's seven years with the Speedway and telling them that the only reason Hannagan was not working with him in Miami Beach was because Fisher already had wrapped up a publicity man.[8] It worked. Hannagan hooked on for the winter months with the Wofford Hotel, where he was living, and with the Miami Beach Casino. But, for the 1925–26 season, Hannagan was in the employ of Fisher, beginning a storybook relationship between the press agent and the City of Miami Beach. Hannagan's forte was

Although he could be considered his own best publicity man, Carl Fisher nevertheless brought in Steve Hannagan from Indianapolis to do his publicity. Hannagan put Miami Beach into the nation's newspapers and magazines with a continuing practice of providing photos of Miami Beach bathing beauties. (Olive Delahunt) **Below:** The Club Lido, now the Rod and Reel Club, on Hibiscus Island, was a popular gambling and entertainment club, although gambling was illegal. (Matlack; HASF)

Prospective buyers flock to the Sunny Isles Bath House to see the new development. (Fishbaugh; SPA)

bathing beauties and beach scenes and he foisted them onto the American public through magazines and newspapers which were willing to publish just about anything he offered up.

A number of gambling clubs, including the Palm Island, Seminole, Tee House and Lido, were operating in the area in 1925. Gambling was to have an on-off relationship with the Miami area and all of Florida throughout the years. At one point, in the 1930s, slot machines were legalized by the Florida legislature, but for the most part, casino-type gambling was something that went on in spite of laws against it. Law enforcement officials and politicians made a practice of looking the other way (when they, themselves, weren't in the casinos) and some got rich by looking the other way when they were in a position to crack down on illegal activity.

A study in 1925 of the Miami Beach central district—from Fifth Street north to Dade Boulevard and the Collins Canal—showed that 20 per cent of the buildings were hotels, 20 per cent apartment houses, 35 per cent residences, 5 per cent office buildings and the remainder public buildings such as the school and fire station.[9] Western Union built an office on Fifth Street near Alton Road through which all U.S. messages headed for South America would be relayed.[10] Among the latest arrivals in central Beach hotels, in addition to the Fleetwood, were the William Penn, a 125-room hotel at Eighth Street and Washington; the Helene—begun in 1921 but not completed until late 1924—at 15th Street near Alton Road; the George Washington at Fifth Street and Washington Ave.

Well to the north of this district, even beyond the old Lifesaving Station, Harry B. Graves purchased land, including three-quarters of a mile of oceanfront footage where he planned a huge residential and tourist development called Sunny Isles—"The Venice of America."[11] Graves widened and deepened

streams, had the many islets landscaped and hoped to cash in on the great Florida Boom. While some of the property did develop, Sunny Isles did not prosper as a section until after well after the Boom.

What might have had something to do with the slowness of Sunny Isles to develop during the Boom was the fact that people again were tinkering with the land. Miami Beach was about to become part of an island. As early as 1916, there were proposals to dig a channel from the bay to the ocean across a low-lying piece of land known as Baker's Haulover.[12] The parcel was thus named because of lore that a man named Baker, a sponge fisherman, hauled his boat from the bay to the ocean across this narrow strip, which at times was covered by a shallow sheet of water. Advocates of the cut claimed it was necessary because of the building of the County Causeway about 12 miles to the south, as well as the artificial islands that were being created in the bay. People living along the upper bay claimed that a new causeway would act as a dam and prevent tidal flushing of the upper bay, which is exactly what happened. Even before the causeway was completed, the upper bay smelled foul, fish were dying and

Claude Renshaw came from Montana to serve as Miami Beach city manager. He stayed at that post for 33 years. (MB)

mosquitoes were a plague.[13] Work on the cut began in September 1923. The bridge spanning the new channel was completed first, and on April 14, 1925, the waters of the bay and the ocean were joined at Haulover Cut[14] The only way to get to Miami Beach now was over a bridge or by boat; the last natural land link had been breached.

The political scene in Miami Beach was beginning to heat up. The city council, in Louis Snedigar's second term as mayor, tired of its police chief, C. E. Brodgen, and forced him to resign. His replacement, an Oklahoman named Damon Lewis, caused the city great embarrassment when, after just a few months, he was indicted in Kansas City for smuggling narcotics and sent off to Leavenworth for seven years.[15] One of the problems among City Council members was that all of them were businessmen; they had their own vested interests. To avoid talk of conflict of interest, they decided to bring in a more independent person—an outsider— to run the city's affairs. Claude Renshaw, former mayor of Roundup, Montana, and an engineer by trade, became Miami Beach's first city manager.[16] He proved to be an enduring administrator, serving for 33 years until he retired on March 1, 1958. (By comparison, there were 13 others who served either as city managers or as acting city managers in the 35 years after Renshaw left office.)

Throughout South Florida, action needed to be taken against the binder boys. And it was. Just which is the correct version of their demise is open to debate. There are two possibilities. In the first, Roney put binders on property adjoining his. The binder boys bought up these binders and began escalating the prices. When the second payment came due, Roney cut the prices of the lots—below what the binder boys had contracted with others to pay. The bottom fell out, the binder boys were stuck with a shrunken bankroll and payments they couldn't make. Miami Realtor J. Kenneth Roberts said: "It was one of the greatest stickups ever recorded beyond the confines of the Chicago stockyards. . . . With many a hoarse and obscene oath they packed up their extra white knickers and their other belongings and went straight back to New York, where a man can gamble as he pleases."[17] The second scenario concluded that the market simply exhausted itself. A lot that began at $7,000 and soared to $50,000 on binders simply wouldn't sell at that inflated price. The last bidder waited until the price dipped down to $25,000 before buying. Binder boys who had signed binders for higher amounts than that lost money.[18] When the binder boys fled the Miami area in late 1925, they left behind $8 million in binders.[19]

As the 1925–26 winter season concluded, mixed news flowed from Carl Fisher's offices and all of Miami Beach. Of the 3,000 lots developed by Fisher Properties, only 246 remained unsold.[20] For the just concluded season, 290 lots were sold. As Miami Beach grew, so did her needs. Among them was a public library. A group calling itself the Miami Beach Library and Art Institute Association requested that Russell Pancoast, as architect, prepare specifications for a library, art museum, and natural history museum. The association chose Pete Chase to be in charge of fund raising.[21] Enthusiasm for the project was high in 1925. Pledges reached $100,000 but much of the money went uncollected when

Boasting the largest swimming pool in Florida, the Deauville opened in early 1926 as principally a bathing and entertainment facility but with hotel rooms. (MN)

circumstances of nature and economy intervened. Until a proper library could be built, the Miami Beach Women's Club operated one of its own in the Hampton Arcade on Lincoln Road. When first organized, the library contained 947 volumes. In a short time, that number grew to 6,600.[22] Eventually, a library was built in the park property donated by John Collins years earlier to the City of Miami and later sold to Miami Beach. By then, Collins was dead and the library named in his memory.

Former Fisher land salesman Joseph Eisener built what was proclaimed as the largest swimming pool in Florida as part of the Deauville Casino, which opened at 67th Street and the ocean in early 1926. The pool was 165 feet long and 100 feet wide and located on the second floor behind the hotel rooms. Planned as an entertainment capital, the Deauville provided dining rooms, ballroom dancing, entertainers, exhibitions by champion swimmers and divers and state-of-the-art bathing facilities.[23]

So fast was Miami Beach developing that what was relatively new outlived its usefulness quickly. The Collins Bridge, the link that opened Miami Beach to development, had become a relic in just a dozen years. The Bay Biscayne Improvement Company, which was building the Venetian Islands, purchased the bridge from the Collins/Pancoast interests and announced plans to construct a new one in its place, a series of 12 concrete bridges linking the islands, the mainland and Miami Beach. In January 1925, work began on the project. By March, Collins' wooden bridge was being dismantled.[24] The Venetian Way opened on February 28, 1926. Collins, who was not present when his own bridge opened in 1913, attended the opening of Venetian Way.[25]

The Bay Biscayne Improvement Company had even more plans. In 1925, the creators of the Venetian Isles, across which the new causeway was being built, announced plans to build additional islands, running north up the bay from Venetian Way. Connecting the six islands would be a mile-long highway to be called Campanili Drive. All the islands, as well as streets, were to have Italian names—in keeping with the already platted and sold residential islands along the causeway: San Marco, DiLido and Rivo Alto. The land for the proposed islands was under seven feet of bay water.[26]

Plans for the chain of islands were controversial. Many opposed their creation, contending that the islands would destroy the beauty of Biscayne Bay. In just a dozen years, the pristine nature of the bay had been disrupted by, first, the Collins Bridge, then the dredging and filling by the Fisher and Lummus interests, the creation of Palm, Hibiscus and Star islands, the County Causeway, the building of islands running east and west across the

bay, the creation of Haulover Cut, the filling in of land in the north bay by Graves, the building of Venetian Way and the proposal to create a string of islands running north and south. The issue of the new islands was argued throughout the community, particularly within the Miami Chamber of Commerce, which finally voted in favor of it. At the time of the June 1925 vote, the plan had grown to nine islands running as far north as to be abreast of Normandy Isle and Biscayne Point. The sale of lots on the islands commenced on October 20, 1925, but the sales moved slowly. When the real estate bust came in 1926, the pilings of the southernmost island, Isola DiLolando, were the only visible sign of construction.[27] The pilings remain today, just south of the Julia Tuttle Causeway.

For every failure, there was success—although the signs were evident that the Boom was slowing down. The Boom had been so frenzied that many Northern investors drained their bank accounts to get in on the Florida land sale. This loss of financial resources created a backlash in the Northern states— one of distrust, rumor and half-truths. Northern institutions, including the press, claimed that most of the Florida land being sold was under water and made allegations that soon the Boom would bust and, thus, leave the investors holding much devalued assets. Ohio passed a law that made it illegal for certain enterprises to peddle Florida real estate in that state.[28] Miami attorney R. Freeman Burdine, son of the department store founder, went on a 10-week fact-finding tour. He found that New York newspapers, when writing about Miami, referred to nonexistent bread and milk famines. He cited one New York businessman returning from a trip to Miami and telling a newspaper that Miami dairies all were unsanitary, the milk watered and selling at 90 cents

a gallon. The result was a counter-campaign by prominent Florida businessmen and developers.

Carl Fisher was immensely disturbed by the bad publicity. He wrote to an influential friend:

The harm done to this country came from crooks and speculators from the north. They came in like a swarm of locusts and the newspapers and bankers up north never stopped to investigate the matter at all. They jumped on the State and they have caused us a great deal of trouble. My own firm is no [sic] troubled by these rumors but a great many of the other firms have been troubled by the lack of confidence of these people who have purchased property and who have now lost considerable faith in Florida.[29]

But the smell of a dying Boom was extensive. Fisher's sales manager, Pete Chase, found it necessary to write to Fisher property owners in May 1926: "Just a few authentic facts are here being sent you. From these, it's very plainly seen that this part of Florida is still going ahead faster than most any other spot in America. Too much was expected of Florida last winter. That's the real reason for most disappointments."[30]

Enclosed with the Chase letter was a chart from the Miami Realty Board that showed huge increases in local building permits, postal receipts, municipal collections, railroad tonnage received and forwarded and bank deposits.

Fisher worried because business at his Nautilus Hotel had dropped off for the 1925–26 season. Hotel manager George Krom blamed it on image. "You will appreciate the location of the Nautilus has caused us to have a clientele who desire quiet and refinement," Krom wrote Fisher. "The reason for this class of people not coming to Miami this year is due to the fact that numerous people who were in Miami last summer returned North and reported a crowded overrun condition such that it was impossible to get decent accommodations and for such accommodations that were available, were charged exorbitant rates."[31]

Krom also attributed the drop in business to the bottling up of the harbor, the freight embargo, a smallpox scare and the crowded condition of the County Causeway: "We had one family who occupied nine rooms and were paying us $255 a day who left us and went to the Royal Palm [in Miami] because they could not get back and forth over the Causeway," he wrote Fisher.[32]

Meanwhile, Jane and Carl decided to end their marriage. They maintained what appeared to be, at best, a platonic relationship. Although their social lives traveled separate paths for a number of years, Carl continued to have a fondness for her, perhaps not as a lover but more as a father. He wanted to do anything he could to make Jane's life happier. His attorney, Frank Shutts, suggested that the easiest and best way to proceed with the divorce was through French courts. Shutts contacted an attorney in New York who specialized in French divorces. Before agreeing to anything, Fisher sent Shutts' February 24, 1926, letter to Jane who was living in Port Washington, New York. At the bottom of Shutts' letter, Fisher wrote by hand: "Jane. This is best way to proceed and save much time and trouble for both of us." With the services of New York attorney Dudley Field Malone secured for $12,500,[33] Fisher even was able to avoid traveling to France for the divorce. The breakup remained amiable. "We just don't get along together as we should," he acknowledged, "and we are not having any fuss over the matter but we both will go our own way without any argument."[34]

Hardie's Casino lay in ruins following the 1926 hurricane. (SPA)

People survey the destruction on Ocean Drive following the 1926 Hurricane. Brown's Hotel is at left-center. (SPA)

The Boom was broken, so was the Marriage. And now came the Big Blow, the fourth cataclysm of Miami Beach's adolescence. Its first mention in the *Miami Daily News* was on September 15, 1926. It appeared on page 16. "Miami Warned of 3 Tropical Storms at Sea," said the three-column, three-line headline. The South Florida community was just 72 hours away from disaster in the form of a hurricane that hit land at approximately 2 a.m. on Saturday, September 18. In that first story, there was reference to a storm near Bermuda, another a short distance from Nassau and a third that had been reported northeast of St. Kitts on Monday. The weather bureau in Washington advised of the last: "This storm has attained considerable intensity." On the following day, one of the storms passed between Miami and Nassau, causing heavy rain in the Miami area. The second was blowing at the Virginia Capes and the third was reported to have passed over Cuba and to be approaching the Bahamas. The *Miami Daily News*, in its first notice, said the third storm's intensity was unknown. By Friday afternoon, things had changed. The story of the storm moved out to Page One in the lead position. "Miami Warned of Tropical Storm," said the page-wide headline. But a smaller readout below it stated: "Disturbance is Headed for Nassau, Weather Bureau Advises."

Nevertheless, Miami put up storm warnings at 11 a.m. on September 17, only 14 hours before it smashed ashore at Miami Beach into a rather surprised community. There had been forewarning in the presence of a late July hurricane, which struck north of Miami but inflicted some damage on the area. Even before that, Coconut Grove pioneer Ralph Munroe warned the local population of the danger of hurricanes. When proposals were made in the Spring of 1926 to develop a string of coral islands south of Cape Florida, he successfully testified in opposition to them, saying the further altering of the land mass—i.e., tantamount to additional damming of the bay—would cause added problems should a hurricane hit the area. Munroe pointed out that the storm surge of a hurricane would sweep away anything on those islands and the backwash of a storm, caused by the reversal of winds following the passing of the eye, would cause huge waves, possibly tidal, trying to get from the bay back to the seas.[35]

Following the relatively mild July hurricane, Munroe wrote: "We have had a beautiful time with a hurricane apparently made to order for me, blowing with just enough energy to put the fear of the Lord into the scoffers, and very possibly make them see the light."[36]

Munroe's forecast obviously did not come to fruition. The mildness of the July hurricane only further settled the population into complacency; if that's all a hurricane can do—uproot some fruit trees—then what is there to fear? The last noteworthy hurricane struck the area in 1910 when the population of Miami Beach could be counted on one, maybe two hands.

When the September hurricane struck, Miami reported sustained wind at 96 miles per hour and Miami Beach suffered gusts of 132 miles per hour.[37] Strong tides surged ashore, waters covered the narrow peninsula. To the west, rising water flooded the new city of Hialeah. Fierce winds severely damaged downtown Miami buildings and large vessels were blown onto the new Biscayne Boulevard. The great storm moved across the state to emerge into the Gulf of Mexico between Ft. Myers and Punta Gorda and aim its parting shot at the area between Pensacola and Mobile. At least 114 in the Miami area died, hundreds more were injured and thousands were left homeless. "Miami Beach was isolated from the mail and no word has been received as to the effect of the storm there," reported the *Miami Daily News* in its hastily published one-page edition of September 18. "It is feared that a monster tidal wave has swept across the entire island city."

An anonymous letter from a Miami Beach resident to his mother was published in Leo F. Reardon's 1926 *The Florida Hurricane and Disaster*. It was an eyewitness account of a family enduring the storm in Miami Beach.

By 2 o'clock [in the morning] the wind, which had steadily increased, had reached a velocity of over a hundred miles per hour and some of the awnings were being torn off the building—tile from the roof was being torn off and pieces crashed down on the steps of the entrance to the building. A window gave way with a crash, and the onrush of wind into the room above, shook the entire building, striking fear into the hearts of the children and women. . . . By 3:30 or 4 o'clock in the morning the vacuum caused by the terrific speed of the wind past the front door of the building had pulled the front door partly past the jams, and with a rope tied to the inside knob, three of us were required to keep it from being pulled and torn out entirely—another two hours would bring daylight—it seemed it would never come—seconds seemed hours, hours an eternity. It was five o'clock when we could feel relief—the roar of the storm was dying down some, and at six o'clock dawn began to break through, six-thirty daylight—most welcome I had ever seen—seven o'clock calm.

The letter writer, like so many in Miami Beach and Miami, were fooled into thinking that was the end of the storm. People ventured outside, not knowing it was the eye of the hurricane, and the second half, even fiercer, was just a short time away. In that brief respite from the winds and rain, he made further observations:

The WIOD radio towers in front of our building were broken down—the roofs were off many houses—the sisters of St. Dominick's dormitory building in which they were living was still standing, but roof partly off—(they are safe)—the furniture and beds

N. B. T. Roney pitched in and helped remove hurricane-driven sand from in front of the Roney Plaza Hotel. (Parks)

in the apartments on the north side are drenched. We tried to sweep out the water—save the bedding and clothes and survey the premises—we were thankful for our lives—we wondered about others. Wires, trees, awnings, roofs, furniture scattered everywhere was evidence of the havoc wrought—lives must have been lost. How will we feed the babies—the electricity and water are off—the wind had now changed from the north to the south. Is the storm coming back? It is back—it is on us now—why didn't we get the Sisters out of their building? The ocean is on us, "higher and higher—two feet—three feet—four-foot waves driven by the wind and sheets of white spray. . . .The water is at the floor in the hall—the winds over 150 miles per hour—the roar is louder—crash—boom—nothing can withstand this. . . .

And not much did. R. W. Gray, who was in charge of the Miami Weather Bureau at the time, later wrote: "The intensity of the storm and the wreckage that it left cannot adequately be described. The continuous roar of the wind, the crash of falling buildings, flying debris, and plate glass; the shriek of fire apparatus and ambulances that rendered assistance until the streets became impassable; the terrifically driven rain that came in sheets as dense as fog; the electric flashes from live wires have left the memory of a fearful night in the minds of the many thousands that were in the storm area."[38]

When Reardon, an executive of the *Miami Tribune*, left his own battered Coral Gables home, he toured the Greater Miami area for purposes of recording his impressions in a book. Among his observations of Miami Beach:

My first view of the storm's ravages at America's Playground brought tears to my eyes. Beautiful Belle Isle is prostrate. The homes of Lee Rumsey, J. C. Penney and 'Junior' Matthews withstood the gale but present a sorry sight with their shattered windows and ruined furniture. I am told the great pipe organ in the Penney home was damaged beyond report. All royal palms are down. The Bay front area from the causeway to Carl Fisher's Flamingo Hotel is stark naked. Commodore Stolz's 100-foot yacht [Fleetwood III] is in ruins, and partly sunk against the masonry of the causeway. The canal from Belle Isle to Meridian Avenue is half full of wreckage from the Mayflower Hotel, and the new Boulevard Hotel, of the Fisher interests, which was opened a month ago. . . . The glass dome is gone from the

Flamingo and the furniture in the lobby and ground floors damaged. . . . We proceeded through scenes of desolation to South Beach. Here is where the gale did its worst. It took the Coney Island of Miami Beach, twisted and gnarled it into an unrecognizable mass and flung it down on the sands. Hardee's [sic] and Smith's Casinos might as well have been under a barrage of heavy cannon for days. The Million Dollar Pier is damaged. The South Beach Casino is tottering. . . . Charlie's Grill is a shell. The Ritz Restaurant is no more. . . . Not an apartment block, hotel or storage on South Beach escaped the ravages of the storm. . . .[39]

What the previous cataclysms had not succeeded in doing, this one did. It would be very tough to come back from this natural disaster. John Levi, Jim Allison and Carl Fisher were not in Miami Beach when the storm struck; they were at Fisher's home in Port Washington, New York where Fisher was developing Montauk Point. First damage assessments from the Miami Ocean View Company came in the form of an unsigned telegram to Levi the day after the storm. "Storm is over. Did a great deal of damage. Much property loss. Your house damaged. Considerable roof off and windows broken. Reports are that storm is detouring tonight. Barometer dropping. Several people killed and many injured. County Causeway is out, using Venetian Causeway." For the promoters of the area, damage control with the Northern press was critical. In a wire to Allison the same day, he was advised: "Your house in pretty good condition. Hospital badly damaged. Without exception, every building on entire Beach badly damaged. We need lanterns."

Within 24 hours, City Manager Renshaw declared martial law in Miami Beach. His order required everyone to be off the streets by 6 p.m., that no food, water or other necessity be sold without first obtaining a permit from the city, no automobiles be used without a permit. He appointed persons to be in charge of sanitation and wholesale food distribution and asked "all men who can should report at the city hall to clear the wreckage and to volunteer for police duty."[40]

Fisher and others, naturally, tried to minimize the damage but when news—and photos—of what the storm had done began arriving at Northern newspapers, the truth of the storm's extent could not be minimized. Collins Avenue and Ocean Drive were covered in sand, vehicles abandoned willy-nilly. Mounds of sand filled hotel lobbies, salt water undermined pilings and structures. Coconut trees on the Pancoast Hotel property, planted by Osborn and Field 43

years earlier, came crashing down. Ahead was a massive cleanup and rebuilding.

On October 8, Fisher wrote to his friend LaGorce, assessing the losses he had experienced as a result of the storm. ". . .You might be interested to know that the total amount of our damages at the Beach, as far as our own Company was concerned, including The Bay Shore Company and the Alton Beach Company, will probably be around $400,000, of which we will collect insurance, I imagine, of about $200,000," he wrote. "Considering the wind velocity, we were probably lucky. However, a great part of all the damage was on tile roofs and awnings tore loose and beat all the windows out and the wind got under the edge of the roof and blew them off. No shingled roofs on the Beach were injured, although they were right in the path of the storm. The houses that stood best were those we purchased from Sears Roebuck."[41]

Nature was to take still another swipe at reeling Greater Miami. A third hurricane struck the area[42] less than five weeks later, on October 20, 1926, inflicting far less damage but disrupting—even setting back—the recovery from the September storm. "The ocean front north of Snowden's [north of today's 44th Street] is again washed through from ocean to Indian Creek, in five different places some of which are quite wide," reported Pete Chase. "At the Montemare School, three-fourths of the entire roof of the northwest wing has blown off, thereby causing plenty of water damage to all rooms, in that wing on both upper and lower floors. Mr. Fisher's house O.K. except for some leak stains around a few windows and a few trees partially blown down, and about fourteen inches of water in the organ motor room."[43]

Chase also reported that part of the roof of the Nautilus Hotel had blown off and that about 100 rooms at the Boulevard Hotel were partially water damaged. W. A. Kohlhepp, a director of the Carl G. Fisher Company, sent Chase's report on to Fisher in Long Island and added a few of his own observations, particularly as they pertained to repair work still in progress from the previous storm. "A great many of the temporary roofs placed at various buildings were blown off and I have today ordered all roofs of this kind to be put back with a metal strip around the edge of the roof," wrote Kohlhepp. "Some of the newly set trees were blown down due to the fact that they were not properly braced but these can easily be reset and I do not believe there is any damage to shrubbery unless the water stands on the island too long."[44]

Fisher, his fortune tied into the new Montauk Point project, was further strained with the rebuilding effort in Miami Beach. His star was beginning to dim.

CHAPTER TWELVE

SAINTS FRANCIS, PATRICK, AND VALENTINE

Irish–born Father William A. Barry was sent to Miami Beach in 1926. He struck up a friendship with Carl Fisher which, although sometimes tumultuous, resulted in the construction of St. Patrick's Church and School. Barry was later elevated to monsignor. (MH)

What Miami Beach needed to show in the wake of the hurricane was more than just repairs. It needed a sign that it was moving forward. That came in November when the $300,000 Biscayne Plaza Theater opened at Collins Avenue and Biscayne Street. The opening of a 1,500-seat motion picture theater in advance of the tourist season was a signal that Miami Beach was not just a winter tourist resort, that its permanent population was significant enough to support a large theater and that there was more to Miami Beach life than just cleaning up after the storm.

Construction resumed on the new high school at 14th Street and Drexel Avenue, which would be named Ida M. Fisher High School, in honor of Carl's mother, who died in 1925.[1] Classes would not move in until January 1927.

Fisher's friend Jim Allison, who was disappointed about the failure of his aquarium, was not so discouraged as to drop any thought of future enterprise in Miami Beach. Fisher had filled in land to create two islands and named both for his close friends. Allison Island and LaGorce Island sat at the mouth of Indian Creek, through which sailors such as Ralph Munroe took their vessels down to visit the Crocodile Hole 40 years earlier. On LaGorce Island, Fisher planned and built single family residences. On the other, Allison envisioned a state-of-the-art hospital on land Fisher donated. Ten months before the hurricane, he created what then was called Allison Hospital. The three-story Spanish-style building, designed by August Geiger and built by

With the hurricane blown past, construction resumed on Ida M. Fisher High School, named in honor of Carl Fisher's mother. It opened in January 1927. (MN; HASF)

outpaced income. Not a well man, Allison sought out both Fisher and recently-arrived Father William A. Barry for a way out of his dilemma. Through a New York intermediary, Father Barry and Fisher made contact with the nursing nuns of the Sisters of St. Francis of Allegheny, New York. They agreed to take over operation of the hospital—as St. Francis Hospital. On October 19, 1927, Mother Alice (born Catherine Henry in Ireland) set out from New York for Miami Beach along with Sisters Magdalena, Josephine Marie, Dolores, Modesta and Antoinette.[3]

John Orr at a cost of $3.5 million, opened January 1, 1926. What set Allison Hospital apart from others is that it catered to people who could afford the finest. It was said that the cost of the dining facilities at Allison Hospital exceeded the expense of the medical equipment. The hospital boasted private rooms and a magnificent kitchen, even a gourmet chef.[2]

Unfortunately, Allison opened his hospital at the same time the Boom began to spring a leak. The need for luxurious hospital care was not as great as Allison imagined. He was experiencing the same problem as he did with his aquarium: expenses far

Negotiations between the ill, cantankerous Allison and Mother Alice were strained. They battled from the start, principally because her cost-cutting plans ran against his wishes. If the hospital was to survive, it no longer could employ five men to work under the landscape gardener; the automobile used by Allison's resident manager would have to be transferred to the Sisters to be utilized as a motor pool vehicle. Electric fans in the hospital rooms were sold to purchase food, and the meals lost some of their gourmet appeal.[4] Throughout the period of transfer of authority, the wheelchair-bound Allison

In 1926, Jim Allison built a hospital at the top of Indian Creek which he named for himself. The Sisters of St. Francis took it over in 1927. (MN; HASF)

grumbled from his Star Island home, threatening to remove the Sisters from his hospital. But Mother Alice had performed a miracle in spite of his carping. The finances of the operation had improved considerably. The arguing did not end until August 3, 1928, when Allison died of pneumonia while in Indiana. The hospital was then purchased by the Franciscans.

Father Barry's role in the rescuing of the hospital was just one of two major developments in which he involved himself during this period. By 1925, there were but two churches in Miami Beach: Elisha King's Community Church on Lincoln Road and H. W. Blackburn's First Methodist Church at the corner on Sixth Street between Washington and Jefferson. In May 1926, Father William Barry arrived in Miami Beach to tend the needs of Catholics in the oceanside city. Born in County Clare, Ireland in 1886, he was ordained a Catholic priest in Baltimore in 1910.[5]

St. Patrick's Church dedication, 1929. (SPA)

Msgr. Barry and Mother Magdalena cut the cake for St. Francis Hospital's 25th Birthday. (MN; HASF)

The Barry family devoted itself to the Church. Brother Patrick was Bishop of St. Augustine, sister Mary Gerald was Superior General of the Adrian Dominican Sisters in Michigan[6] and another brother, Joseph Barry, was a parish priest in Ireland. After assignments in St. Augustine, Jacksonville and Deland, Father William Barry was one of three priests assigned by his brother to establish new parishes in the Greater Miami area. No sooner did he arrive than he befriended Carl Fisher, a non-Catholic. "Carl and Father Barry became close friends," Jane Fisher wrote in her book "They liked prize fights, motion pictures and each other. . . Father Barry urged ice cream upon Carl as a sweet substitute for scotch."[7]

Despite their friendship, business was business. Father Barry wanted Fisher to provide him lands upon which to build the first Catholic church in Miami Beach. Fisher responded by providing temporary space near the polo fields and the Nautilus Hotel at 37th Street. Father Barry's first Mass was held in a polo stable there. He also established an elementary school in other stables. By August 1927, Father Barry was growing impatient about a permanent site upon which he could build. He sought several lots on Lincoln Road. Fisher considered them too valuable to donate to the church and, instead, served up property near the polo fields. He donated six of the 12 lots on a block near 40th Street. The other six were purchased by the church for $4,233 each.[8] But Father Barry was deeply concerned that he could not continue to pay the mortgage for the lots he bought and still be able to erect a church and other buildings. What Father Barry proposed was that Fisher issue deeds to the church without further payment or obligation on the part of the church.

111

Mobster Al Capone bought this Palm Island estate in 1922 for $40,000. It included a gatehouse, house (center) and pool house. (MN; HASF)

Schoenberg's biography of Capone claims the house, which he says was characterized by the federal government as a "palatial home," was on Indian Creek Drive.[13] People were outraged, but Capone was not run out of town as he was in Los Angeles. He spent the winter and made friends with Parker Henderson Jr, son of a former mayor of Miami. Henderson and Capone were seen together at boxing matches, horse races and with celebrities. Henderson became the middle man for the transfer of money to Capone from Chicago via Western Union, signing as "Albert Acosta." In the first four months of 1928, Capone received $31,000 in that manner.[14] Another person from a prominent Miami family to link himself to Capone that first season was Jack Sewell, son of John Sewell—the man who came to Miami in advance of the railroad in 1896 and constructed Henry Flagler's landmark Royal Palm Hotel. Like Henderson, Jack Sewell's father had been an early mayor of Miami and his uncle, Ev Sewell, ran Miami's Chamber of Commerce and soon also would be mayor of Miami. In a newspaper interview, Jack Sewell boasted of his relationship with Capone:

Fisher, already reeling himself with financial problems, played hardball with Father Barry. In a response, he cited all the money the Fisher interests already had spent on behalf of the church. Father Barry and Fisher ultimately came to an accommodation on the purchase of land. Construction of St. Patrick Church and School was completed in 1928. It was dedicated in 1929.

If there was something Miami Beach—and all of Greater Miami, for that matter—did not need during the hurricane recovery days of 1927, it was notoriety. But it came rolling into town in the closing days of the year in the form of Alphonse Capone. The Chicago mobster and his family had been run out of Los Angeles in early December when they tried to vacation at the Hotel Biltmore, where he registered as "Al Brown" but was quickly recognized.[9] The Los Angeles police chief gave him 12 hours to leave town. Later that month, "Al Acosta" took the top-floor suite of the Hotel Ponce de Leon in downtown Miami [10] while his family stayed in a rented home in Miami Beach.[11] In his biography of Capone, John Kobler claimed Al spent his first Miami winter in a "furnished bungalow" on the beach, renting it for $2,500 for the season from an absent owner he referred to as "Mrs. Sterns."[12] Robert J.

Al Capone was constantly harrassed by public officials and the newspapers. Yet he managed to spread his influence over local gambling and night clubs. After returning from prison following an income tax charge, he lived out his days on Palm Island. (MN; HASF)

Henderson brought Capone into the Sewell Brothers' Store on East Flagler. Skeets Downs, a local gambler was with him. Capone bought over $1,000 worth of suits, shirts, underwear, ties by the handful, shoes and socks from Sewell—the kind of clothes that would make him look like a tourist. My father knew Capone was coming into the store, but not my uncle Ev. . . He was one of the people who was trying to run Capone out of town.[15]

When the season ended, Capone returned to Chicago to involve himself in a mayoral campaign in which his candidate ultimately lost. But he had the sand of Miami Beach in his shoes. He called Miami Beach "The garden of America, the sunny Italy of the New World."[16] With help from his friend Henderson, Capone bought an estate on Palm Island that was built in 1922 for brewing magnate Clarence Busch. At the time of sale, it was owned by James W. Popham, who took his money and moved over to Star Island. Capone paid $40,000 for the property at 93 Palm Avenue, a two-story neo-Spanish structure with a green-tiled roof and white stucco exterior walls. The property, however, was placed in Henderson's name, then deeded over to Capone's wife, Mae.[17]

While Capone is widely recognized as being behind the mass murder of competing hoodlums in a Chicago garage on St. Valentine's Day 1929, he was in Miami Beach that day with a surprisingly airtight alibi: Dade County solicitor Robert Taylor, at the request of New York's assistant district attorney, had summoned Capone to his office for questioning about an unrelated murder.[18] One would think Capone had cooked this up, but it was totally coincidental. The law, however, caught up with Capone in May 1929 when he was convicted of carrying a concealed deadly weapon and sentenced to one year in prison.

As time came for his release in March 1930—he got two months off for good behavior—Miamians became nervous about the prospect of his returning to the area. Even before Capone's release, James Cox's *Miami Daily News* began running a series of page one editorials aimed at stirring the community and state against Capone. "If any citizen has misgivings as to developments here in the last year he need only to communicate with police authorities in the county," the newspaper editorialized on its front page. "He will be told that while there is no means apparently at the moment of proving ownership, that Al Capone is interested in half of the gambling places that have been operating this winter. His brothers and his buddies have been here during the season and the impression is that they were collectors for Capone."[19]

As if to confirm the editorial, Dade County Sherrif M. P. Lehman said Capone was only one of the "dangerous characters" familiar with Miami and Miami Beach, adding: "In a raid 10 days ago, 18 men were arrested with $70,000 in a dice game in Miami Beach by deputy sheriffs. One of them had a gun. Nearly all were Italians from New York and were believed to be racketeers."[20] To further harass the Capone interests, police raided Capone's Palm Island home on March 20, 1930 and charged the occupants there at the time with possession of liquor.[21] When Capone reached Miami Beach in time for Easter in 1930, the *Miami Daily News* was irate. "The beer and brothel baron from Chicago slipped in to his island home riding in the second of three bullet-proof automobiles that met him [at the train station] at Hollywood, about the same time some 40,000 Miamians were assembled on Miami Beach for their annual Easter sunrise service," complained a page one story.[22]

But there was an hypocrisy to this complaint. While the *Miami Daily News* and other civic-minded detractors were acting sanctimonious about the "beer and brothel baron from Chicago," they, too, were guilty of illegal traffic in beer, although to a lesser degree. There is evidence enough of that. At one point, Fisher wrote to his Miami Beach security manager, concerned that Capone's presence in Miami Beach might hinder his own activity:

Before I left, we ordered some beer from Tom Harbin. This was a month before we left and the beer did not come in and I commence to feel like there was some sort of set up that might cause trouble, and as we were not there to use the beer, we don't want

James M. Cox, who owned the Miami Daily News *and who was the Democratic nominee for president in 1920, launched a strong campaign against Capone's presence, calling him the "beer and brothel baron." (MN; HASF)*

Miami Beach tourists were able to be photographed during Prohibition in front of a make-believe backdrop of a saloon. (SPA)

Youngsters at a birthday party for Capone's son in 1930. (Matlack; HASF)

to have it landed there. At the same time, we don't like to see Harbin get stuck. Dan Mahoney said he would take a few cases, Ed Romfh [a prominent banker, two-time Miami city commissioner and business associate of Fisher] would probably like a few, and I would like to have you help Harbin out on this beer situation. But I don't want any of it left in the house...You will have to handle it rather carefully so we will not get in a jam. I am afraid with the Capone situation as it is, we might get into a tough hole.[23]

(Fisher and his friends were knee-deep in illegal booze well before Capone arrived on the scene. Letters to and from Fisher in the Fisher Collection at the Historical Museum of Southern Florida show a constant movement of liquor and beer between Carl and his friends as early as 1921—including instructions on how to avoid detection. The illegal booze and beer network included newspaper publisher Cox.)

Capone set out to improve his Miami Beach image by beginning what he hoped would be a series of good-will dinners. His first was at his Palm Island home on May 28, 1930 for which 50 invitations were issued.[24] Dinner party guests were served spaghetti, steak and ginger ale; no alcohol was observed. Capone urged his guests to remove their jackets and neckties

and to make themselves at home.[25] He also introduced his mother, who reportedly told guests that she didn't raise her son to be a gangster. Among the guests identified were Capone's two Miami attorneys, Vincent Giblin and J. Fritz Gordon—both of whom went on in later years to serve as judges of Dade County's Circuit Court—as well as local weekly newspaper publisher J. F. Wendler and two unnamed representatives of Miami funeral homes.[26] "There were more than 50 others," reported the *Miami Daily News*, "none of whom were recognized as 'leading business and professional men' for whom the dinner was reported to have been arranged."[27]

Police and the *Miami Daily News* continued to hound Capone. The *Miami Herald*, while opposing Capone, was less intensive in the beginning, prompting the *Miami Daily News* to accuse its rival newspaper in an editorial of not being aggressive enough in doing its part to try to keep the mobster away.[28] Capone was arrested four times in 1930 for various reasons, even spending a night in jail.[29] Frustrated, Capone's attorney got Justice of the Peace Warren L. Newcomb to issue warrants charging Miami mayor C. H. Reeder, city commissioner John C. Knight, safety director S. D. McCreary and Cox with conspiracy to arrest Capone.[30] Although nothing ever came of the suit, it was Capone harassing his harassers back. Capone had not come to virgin territory. With or without him, South Florida was a hotbed of illegal gambling, prostitution, corruption and rum-running. Nevertheless, Fisher put his security manager, Michael Glenn, on a Capone watch of sorts while ignoring all the vice going on around him, some created by himself. Glenn was enthusiastic in his assignment, perhaps too enthusiastic. He passed on to Fisher every rumor he came across. "In my last letter to you, I told you I would try to find out how Capone was operating on the Beach, and who was taking care of him," Glenn wrote to Fisher in June 1930. "The [Palm] Island Club opened this past winter January 15th under a new management, and Capone has one-fourth interest for which he paid $25,000 to the present owners. He also had a one-fourth interest in the Floridian Hotel gambling room, in which he installed crooked gambling devices. . . He also owns the controlling interest in the South Beach dog track, and Carter's gambling house, as well as Albert Bouche's Villa Venice. He tried to muscle in at the Deauville Casino, but was refused, and after some kind of a threat, some men were brought from New York to protect [the] Deauville from Capone's crowd."[31]

Glenn's report did not stop there. He went on to name public officials whom he said were involved in corruption, none of which ever was substantiated or publicly charged. "The pay-off for gambling on the Beach this winter was as follows: Dan Chappel [sic; Chappell], our recently elected [state] representative from this district, was the collector from the Sherriff's [sic] office under the guise of attorney for his clients, and any gambling house opening in Miami Beach had to have the O.K. of our City Manager Renshaw."

(Renshaw served as Miami Beach city manager until his retirement in 1958 without any public charge of corruption although he was admonished, along with other Miami Beach officials, by the Greater Miami Crime Commission in 1949 for not cracking down on criminals in Miami Beach. Chappell also was free of public taint. He later was credited with being the founder of Florida's pari-mutuels industry while serving as a Florida state legislator and was an unsuccessful candidate for the Dade County Commission and Congress, and was city attorney of Hialeah)

Glenn also informed Fisher that when detectives raided the Roman Pools and confiscated gambling equipment there, the owner threatened to have someone in jail the next day, as he was paying $1,000 a week protection. Glenn claimed the equipment was back at the Roman Pools the next day. He listed other illegal activities in the community, including bootlegging, and concluded that "The above incidents will show you the futility of trying to rid the community of a man like Capone, with our present City and County officials."[32] The politically-connected Cox claimed he appealed to a man close to President Herbert Hoover to do something about Capone. "The Capone gang is attempting to break down the legal and moral restraints of this community. . .," he said he wrote to the aide. "We are still suffering from the results of the hurricane and the best within us must be asserted to rebuild the city. The federal government is apparently paying no attention to the situation." Cox wrote that the aide responded: "What can we do?"[33]

"The answer was 'Taxes', responded Cox. "That was the beginning of Capone's end."[34]

Whether it really was Cox who placed the idea in the minds of federal officials, it was taxes that got him back in prison. On October 17, 1931, Miami Beach got a respite from Alphonse Capone. He was convicted of income tax evasion and sent off to prison. Released to his family in November 1939, Capone made his way back to Miami Beach in March 1940. By then, the man believed to be behind the infamous St. Valentine's Day Massacre, was a much less powerful and sick man who just wanted to be left alone. He died in Miami Beach on January 25, 1947.

CAPONE'S FAILED TRY TO SILENCE THE PRESS

In his autobiography *Journey Through My Years*, newspaper publisher James. M. Cox related that while his *Miami Daily News* was waging a page one editorial campaign against Al Capone's presence in Miami Beach, a well-dressed representative of Capone came to his office and offered a certified check for $500,000 as first payment of a $5 million cash purchase of the newspaper.

Cox said he told the man "no manner of money would be tempting, that it would not be a matter of disposing of a newspaper but selling out a community which was in sore need of protection."

Years later, *Miami Daily News* general manager Dan Mahoney also claimed that when Capone's representative asked Cox how much it would cost to purchase the newspaper, the publisher responded: "Five cents, on any street corner."

CHAPTER THIRTEEN

THE CRASH RUINS FISHER, BUT NOT MIAMI BEACH

Miami Beach's social elite dress up in extravagant costumes for the 1930 Committee of 100's Venetian Ball. Left to Right: Philo Gelatt, Thomas J. Pancoast, E.S. Youmans. (Sunday Pictorial)

Al Capone apparently wasn't the only "undesirable" in Miami Beach when he arrived in late 1927.

While Jews were finding sections of Miami Beach hospitable, there remained restrictive sale, lease and hotel reservation practices by the Fisher and Pancoast interests. Certainly, the southern portion of the Beach was open to all, and always had been, beginning with J. N. Lummus' early developments. As evidence of the growing Jewish community in South Beach, Congregation Beth Jacob was chartered as Miami Beach's first synagogue in 1927, with services being conducted in the Royal Apartments at 221 Collins Avenue.[1] It would be 1929 before the Orthodox congregation had its own building at 311 Washington Avenue. As new hotels were constructed, many had no restrictive policies. Thus, Jews in greater numbers were beginning to frequent the Beach. Often, they would go to the Roman Pools opposite the Roney Plaza hotel. This is where the self-anointed upper caste of Miami Beach went as well. Many of the non-Jews became uncomfortable and began to seek a haven from the Semitic influx. The result was the founding of restricted private clubs.

The Bath Club had its beginnings in the winter of 1926 when founding members met and decided to organize. Initial membership to the Bath Club cost $1,500, annual dues, $200.[2] A board of governors

117

New York Governor Al Smith (left) and a friend stand on the Miami Beach seashore in 1929. (SPA)

met on April 12, 1927 and chose Robert Taylor as architect for the facility, which would be built on the ocean at Collins Avenue and 59th Street. (Originally called the Beach Club, its name was changed to the Bath Club as early as April, before construction was started.) Fred A. Poor served as president for many years. While the intended purpose was exclusiveness, the published membership and house rules did not

In 1927, Beth Jacob was Miami Beach's first Jewish congregation. Services were held at various locations until this synagogue was built in 1929. It is now The Jewish Museum of Florida. (MH)

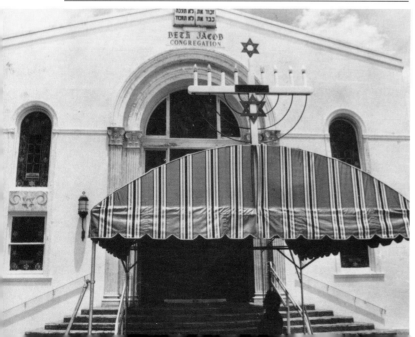

specify it. Much like Fisher and Pancoast, who did not write restrictive clauses into their deeds, the exclusion was accomplished by practice. The only reference to early Bath Club restrictive rules had to do with black employees. "Colored servants or attendants will not be permitted to enter the club except as required by members to assist them in carrying personal effects from the entrance to their cabanas," stated the 1929 Membership and House Rules booklet.[3] Even a solicitous letter to Fisher Company property owners, stockholders and investors from sales manager Pete Chase was indirect. His reference to exclusiveness was free of racial or ethnic flavor. "They [the founders] felt that many of our best families here wanted a private Casino where only members of the Club and their guests could enjoy the ocean bathing, pool swimming, social, card and lounge rooms and Club dining and dancing privileges."[4]

The club opened in time for the 1927–28 winter season. Capone wasn't invited; neither were the Weisses. Catholic members weren't encouraged either. Among the original members of this mostly Midwestern-subscribed club was Alfred Barton. He was the youngest member of the club at the time. When New York Governor Al Smith, unsuccessful candidate for president of the United States in 1928, came to Miami Beach on vacation and expressed a desire to tour the club, Barton was chosen to be his host. Smith was a Catholic and a Democrat and none of the members wanted to be seen with him. "He was charming, and so was his wife; they couldn't be nicer," Barton recalled:

It was finally arranged that I found a cabana where I could take them, but nobody would receive them. . . . Today it seems almost unbelievable that these people from the Midwest who really had nothing to boast about in particular should have been so outrageous.[5]

The Bath Club was an immediate success. The first year of operations showed a net gain of $61,500 after depreciation and a filled membership list.[6] Club rules restricted founder membership to 100 and associate membership—those voted in by founding members—to another 100.

There was no room for any more, prompting other persons desiring exclusivity to launch clubs of their own. Indian Creek Country Club, a golf-oriented private club, came into being on Indian Creek Island immediately after the Bath Club opened. The Surf Club opened at 97th Street at the ocean, the area just above the Tatums' Altos del Mar subdivisions.

Indian Creek Country Club and Golf Course, under construction. (MN; HASF)

Announcing the Opening of Indian Creek Subdivision----

RESERVATIONS BEING TAKEN FOR MIAMI BEACH'S MOST EXCLUSIVE SECTION

It has always been a policy with us to maintain our holdings until an actual shortage of adjoining property required our putting them on the market.

The great popularity and demand for Indian Creek water frontage has absorbed almost every vacant lot. We, therefore, are now taking reservations in Indian Creek Subdivision—which will be one of the most exclusive and desirable of all Miami Beach waterways.

Situated in the very center of the broadest expanse of Indian Creek, with every homesite fronting on the water, this new property has the additional advantage of being accessible by only one avenue of approach. No "thru" streets, with their attending noise and danger from automobiles and trucks. Safety—Seclusion.

For your future dwelling—or for an investment in a locality, nationally recognized as a colony of affluence and importance—we strongly recommend this, our first subdivision offering since 1925.

Conforming with our custom of many years to sell our property to original purchasers in a new tract at less than its real value, we have priced Indian Creek Subdivision at $13,500 to $15,000 for 75 foot water fronts, and $18,000 to $20,000 for 100 foot water fronts. All property depths are at least 215 feet. These are our "first offering" prices, and are subject to advancement without notice.

Terms of one-third cash, with balance in one and two years may be arranged.

Reservations taken in their order, in advance of the property being officially placed on open sale.

You will find the largest listings of homes and homesites in our office

"17 Years on Miami Beach"

CARL G. FISHER CO.

Lincoln Road at Jefferson

MIAMI BEACH

A 1930 advertisement for Indian Creek subdivision; waterfront lots sold from as little as $13,000. (Sunday Pictorial)

Wing Bohne in 1965, Barton reflected on the Miami Beach social scene of the early '30s. "At first the Bath and Surf Clubs were mostly centers of daytime activity," the story reported:

> Members served Prohibition booze to luncheon guests in the cabanas, danced the foxtrot in the shade of the palms, and women wore floppy pajamas or silk or velvet with Paris labels. People actually bathed in the sea. Gradually the hour of rendezvous got later and the club's indoor bars saw more traffic than the cabanas.[7]

Everyone, it seems, was going private—even the fishermen. In early 1929, a group of sport fishermen, headed by Pete Chase, got together and decided to form a club. Calling it the Miami Beach Rod and Reel Club, membership reached 46 by Spring and a clubhouse on Purdy Avenue on the Miami Beach end of the Venetian Causeway was built by December. Some of the area's leading sportsmen, as well as wintertime visitors, were on its roster. Unlike the others, the Rod and Reel Club put its restrictive clause in writing. Section One of the early membership rules stated: "The membership of this Club shall not exceed five hundred (500) and no

The Rod and Reel Club catered to Miami Beach's growing number of yachtsmen and game fishermen. (Matlack; HASF)

Russell Pancoast was commissioned to design the new club. Construction began in 1929 and the club opened early the next year. Around it grew the town of Surfside, which was not incorporated until 1935. None other than Alfred Barton, the social paragon of Collins Avenue, was chosen to run the Surf Club. He loved it and it loved him, so much so that he continued to run the club into the '70s. While the Bath Club kept much to itself, Barton sought publicity for the Surf Club. He was a most quotable fellow. In an interview with *Miami Herald* society writer Grace

Pretty girls make fun of a Beach or-dinance regulating bathing attire. (Romer; MDPL)

Multi-millionaires, despite the Depression, continued to winter in Miami Beach. W. K. Vanderbilt, poses with his wife aboard his yacht Ara. His luxurious mansion on Fisher Island is now the equally luxurious clubhouse for the posh Fisher Island development. (HASF)

application for membership shall be honored unless the applicant be a male Gentile of not less than twenty-one years."[8]

Of seeming concern to the community that did not have privileges at the private clubs was what one was permit-ted to wear at public beaches. The days of the cover-all bathing suit for women had all but disappeared. Miami Beach had ordinances governing bathing attire but the practical approach was to do simply what was discreet. "To expose a leg on the beach several years ago brought condemnation of a member of the fair sex in the minds of her associates," ob-served the *Miami Herald*. "Then by degrees the many yards of bathing paraphernalia have been discarded for a few ounces of wool, cotton or silk. The legs were allowed a chance to feel the sun rays. The back was given free reign as the bottom of the bathing suits became

higher and the tops became lower."[9] The newspaper article went on to say that Miami Beach authorities were going to be even more liberal in their interpretation of otherwise strict bathing attire codes. It was predicted that even straps will be dropped freely "while aristo-crats of the North become democrats in the eyes of the sun." Topless bathing also was in the works. "There are many inconspicuous places along the beach which afford bathers a modest environment where suits can be dropped to the waist, permitting the sun to penetrate the body," observed a Beach Patrol authority. "The life guards do not call attention to scanty attire unless we receive a complaint."[10]

This was in spite of a Miami Beach ordinance that expressly forbade nude bathing. But Miami Beach was supposed to be a fun place, a destination for people who wanted to let their hair—and other things—down. While rules were rules, there needed to be flexibility for the convenience of the vacationers. Thus, gambling, booze and even topless bathing were tolerated.

Not only tolerated but hailed was the cheesecake shot, a posed bathing beauty publicity photo. Steve Hannagan capitalized on it. Pete Chase credited the start of bathing beauty photos to Fisher's old seaport opponent Ev Sewell, head of Miami's Chamber of Commerce. Sewell began holding an annual bathing beauty parade and contest at the sometime around 1920.[11] But it was Hannagan who stepped in and put Miami Beach cheesecake across in newspapers around the nation. When *Life* magazine debuted in 1936, it devoted seven pages of its second-ever issue to Hannagan's success with bathing beauty photos. By then, Steve no longer was exclusively employed by Fisher but heading up the Miami Beach News Bureau, a factory churning out publicity releases and photos for all of Miami Beach. "Press agentry based on real news and hometown

Right: *Most famous for being a promoter of boxing matches, Tex Rickard, along with his toddler daughter, breaks ground for the Miami Beach Dog Track at the ocean and the southern tip of Miami Beach. South Pointe Towers now stands on the site.* (HASF) **Below:** *A few of Steve Hannagan's models ready for assignment as Miami Beach's publicity-getters.* (MN; HASF)

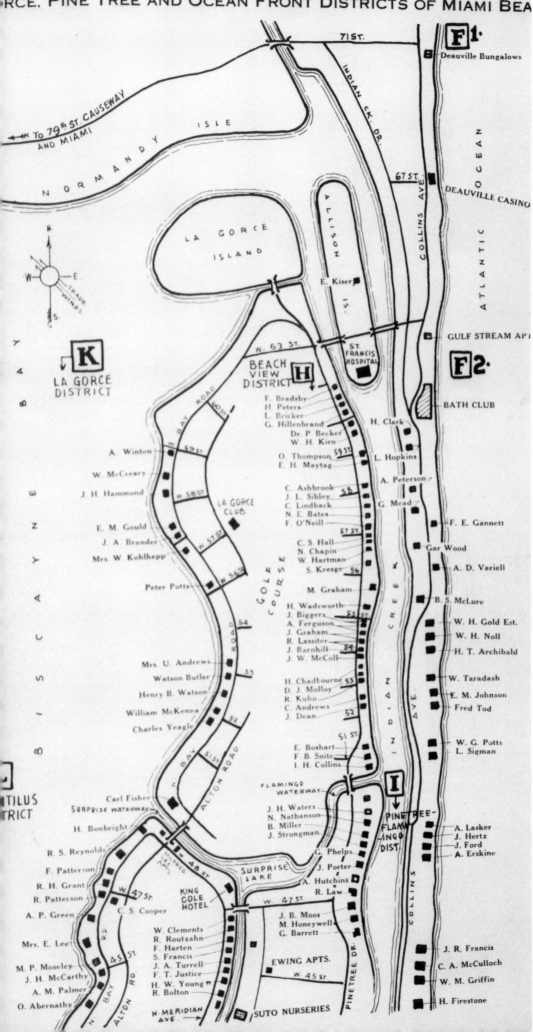

Land salesman Frank F. Stearns published a register of prominent persons' homes in 1932. This segment identified the owners of many of the residences on the narrow strip alongside the ocean as well as dozens of others on the west side of Indian Creek. (Along Greater Miami's Sun-Sea-Ara)

names is all right so far as it goes," said *Life*, "but it must go farther. To keep the Miami Beach dateline alive in the North, Steve Hannagan's men are continually cooking up preposterous excuses for photographing bathing girls. . . ."[12] Cooperating with him was Miami Beach High School, which permitted Hannagan's men to photograph its female students in bathing suits for use in publicity releases.

Fisher had a great love for sports. He built three golf courses and an indoor tennis facility on Miami Beach, a narrow strip of land where acreage was at a premium. He brought the biggest names in boat racing to Miami Beach, as well. Fueled by interest on the part of some of the richest people in the Midwest and by press releases churned out by Hannagan, events such as the annual Mid-Winter Regatta and the Miami Beach LaGorce Open golf tournament brought immeasurable publicity to Miami Beach. Significant to the creation of the LaGorce Golf Club was the naming by Fisher/Hannagan of each hole for either a sports celebrity, entertainer or business mogul. Among those so honored were heavyweight boxing champion Gene Tunney; tycoons Harvey Firestone and William Vanderbilt; humorist Will Rogers and daredevils Eddie Rickenbacker and Gar Wood. All had been visitors to Miami Beach, either as Fisher's guests or with their own money and use of their names brought broader publicity to the golf course.

But Fisher was uncomfortable when Florida's new law allowing pari-mutuels gambling reached the Miami Beach scene in 1929. It was then that sports promoter Tex Rickard opened the Miami Beach Dog Track on the southeastern tip of the Beach. It was all right to have Hialeah Race Track off in the distance; Miami Jai-Alai over in the mainland, as well, but dog racing in Miami Beach was not what Fisher envisioned as entertainment on the Beach itself. He preferred the events that appealed more to elegant participants. But Carl often swung with the tide. He first opposed any wrestling and boxing matches in Miami Beach, then turned around and tried to promote a boxing match himself.

Miami Beach lost its link to its primitive past on February 10, 1928, when John Collins, patriarch of development on the peninsula, died at the age of 90. Author Clayton Sedgwick Cooper, president of Miami Beach's Committee of 100, eulogized Collins:

In 1930, Ocean Drive had few hotels south of 15th Street. Within the next few years, however, the picture changed and hotels, which now are a key part of the Art Deco District, replaced the private hotels and filled the vacant lots. (MN)

Jesse Weiss, who succeeded his father as proprietor of Joe's Restaurant, changed its name to Joe's Stone Crab and built an international reputation for the establishment. (MH)

"There is an old Latin line that reads 'If you ask for his monument, look about you.' Miami Beach is both his monument and his eulogy. He was the awakening genius of Miami Beach."[13] Collins lived to see the mangrove jungle evolve into a tourist and residential community, as well as a winter home for some of the nation's richest people. As a farmer, he had not been enthralled with all that had happened to his old land purchase, but it was he who opened the gates to development when he agreed to build the bridge across the bay. As a businessman, he had to have been happy. He and his family prospered beyond their dreams.

Two months after Collins died, the term "Millionaires' Row" was applied to a 50-block section of Miami Beach that contained the seasonal homes of the wealthy. The homes all were on Collins Avenue, the street named for him. Property investment in 34 oceanfront homes, running from 14th Street on the south to the Bath Club on the north, was estimated at $7.6 million. The homes ranged in cost from $65,000 to $500,000.[14]

The district south of Millionaire's Row developed differently, becoming a community of apartment houses, small hotels and unpretentious residences. Frank F. Stearns, a salesman who later became assistant secretary of the Biscayne Bay Island Company, published a register of prominent residents in 1932 "whose fine homes adorn the Water Frontage of the Greater Miami area." The booklet, *Along Greater Miami's Sun-Sea-Ara*, included maps and charts. Of note was the oceanfront of southern Miami Beach which, decades later, developed into an acclaimed historic district and tourist attraction, extolled for its distinctive architecture. In 1932, however, the almost building-by-building charts by Stearns showed a district quite short on hotels but heavy with residences and apartment houses. The number of hotels fronting Lummus Park in 1932 included the Van Ness at 1390 Ocean Drive, the Shore Park at 820 Ocean Drive, the Beach Park at 600 Ocean Drive, the Mare Grande at 524 Ocean Drive and the Miami Beach Hotel at 520 Ocean Drive. Other buildings on Ocean Drive between 5th and 14th Streets included apartment houses and private homes. J. N. Lummus' former wife, Lula, lived in the house J. N. had built at 1200 Ocean Drive; city manager Claude Renshaw's home was at 844 Ocean Drive; Miami Beach mayor Val Cleary lived at 800 Ocean Drive. Apartment houses included the Casa Casuarina at 1116 Ocean Drive, the Park at 928 Ocean Drive, Casa-Grand at 834 Ocean Drive and the Standard, 760 Ocean Drive.[15]

Beach Pictorial, a season-long weekly devoted to society news and pictures, launched the 1929 winter season with photos and stories of the arrival of President-elect Herbert Hoover to spend a month vacationing at J. C. Penney's Belle Isle mansion. While Hoover kept pretty much to himself, Miami Beach society was in full bloom. "Smart society returned to Club Lido at Miami Beach [Hibiscus Island] Friday night and were [sic] feted after the exclusive fashion of the Lidos of Italy and New York," reported *Beach Pictorial*[16] Elsewhere, the magazine made liberal mention of moguls arriving in the area by private yacht to spend the winter season in Miami Beach

What made the free and open lifestyle of Miami Beach so fascinating is that it seemed to peak at a time when America's financial picture was in turmoil. Beginning with the stock market crash of October 29, 1929, and continuing for a decade, America was caught in a deep Depression. Between the day of the Crash and 1931, an estimated $50 billion in stocks was lost.[17] An indelible image was forged of big losers flinging themselves from skyscraper windows. Nevertheless, society did not ebb in Miami Beach. The outrageously rich may have lost some; maybe

Homes ranging in cost from anywhere between $65,000 and $500,000—known as "Millionaire's Row"—were built by the wealthy on a narrow patch of Miami Beach between the ocean and Indian Creek. Today, hotels and condominiums have replaced the estates. (MN)

they were now just simply rich, but their social life carried on at a frenetic pace.

Even the tourist industry held up relatively well. Shortly after the Crash, a concerned Carl Fisher wired the manager of the Flamingo Hotel inquiring as to cancellations. "The recent upset in the stock market will, I believe, affect our business a little bit this winter," responded Charles Krom, "but if the break doesn't go any further I don't think we will be hit more than ten per cent." [18] Krom's expectations held up until the second week of March 1930 when, according to Fisher, "people commenced to leave here by the thousands and we were forced to close the hotel very rapidly but at that we finished somewhat ahead on our season in spite of the stock market crash."[19]

Fisher's Montauk Point project, meanwhile, was greatly affected by the souring financial environment. When he tried to rescue it by tapping into his Miami Beach assets, his troubles became deeper. He mortgaged the polo fields for $300,000,

sold his golf course just above Lincoln Road to the City of Miami Beach, and floated bond issues on the Flamingo and Nautilus hotels. "We will be entirely out of debt within the next sixty days," he wrote New York banker Clem Keys in March 1930. "I won't have any spare cash," he continued, "but I have other assets that you might be able to use."[20] By May, Fisher was reaching rock-bottom. "Would it help to finance Montauk if a reorganization plan could be worked out to take Miami Beach properties and put them into the assets of Montauk?" he asked Keys. "My interest in these lands at Miami Beach are worth a good many million dollars, as and when the time to sell them is right, but forced on the market at this time, there is only a very limited demand for any of these properties that are destined to be very valuable."[21] He advised Keys that a group was considering purchasing Fisher's LaGorce Golf Course. Another group, Miami Beach's promotion-minded Committee of 100, was negotiating with Fisher to purchase the LaGorce club house for $25,000, which he termed a sacrifice price. "The city of Miami Beach are [sic] interested in a large piece of vacant property just south of the office building [at Lincoln Road], but they are not in a position to purchase same this year," he wrote.[22] On January 7, 1932, stockholders of the Montauk Beach Development Corporation were notified that reorganization had failed.[23] The stockholders began abandoning ship. Montauk Point Development Company defaulted on its notes in the Spring of 1932; corporate bankruptcy followed in 1934 and by the following year, Carl Fisher was in personal bankruptcy.

An aged friend, apparently unaware of Fisher's personal problems, wrote to ask if the Depression was leaving an imprint on him. "Do you know of any one it did not leave an imprint on?" he responded. "I myself lost about twenty-five million, but am still able to eat, up to this evening."[24] That was about all Carl could afford to do at that point. Stockholders such as Coca-Cola's Lindsey Hopkins, the Atlanta tycoon who also had a home in Miami Beach, moved in to assume control of what remained of Fisher's properties. Carl lost his grip on Miami Beach because he unsuccessfully tried to recreate it on a remote tip of Long Island. Jesse Weiss, who had succeeded his father in operating Joe's restaurant on the southern end of Miami Beach—renaming it Joe's Stone Crab and taking it to international fame—preferred to recall the Fisher who was on top rather than the one who lost it all. "The best thing Carl Fisher did for Miami Beach was to come here," he said "Very simply, he made the Beach; he developed the Beach. He was

and-in the summer, Montauk Manor

.... When your thoughts bend northward to lands of ever-changing seasons, another Carl G. Fisher creation beckons to you from the easternmost tip of Long Island, New York. There, beautiful MONTAUK MANOR, of early English Tudor-design, surveys nine hundred acres of playground between the waters of the Atlantic and Long Island Sound. The many forms of outdoor recreation are eclipsed by incomparable deep-sea fishing.

It is under Nautilus management.

The failure of Carl Fisher's Montauk Point development forced him into bankruptcy. (Sunday Pictorial)

also prejudiced, but I think that's something that's got nothing to do with his entire personality. . . . He did more for Miami Beach than all of our politicians put together."[25]

A depression weary nation, sought solace in Miami Beach's carefree bathing beauties that were used as fillers by the American press, courtesy of Steve Hannagan. (HASF)

CHAPTER FOURTEEN

ART DECO, BUT THEY DIDN'T KNOW IT

The Netherland Hotel, built in 1935, was one of the largest hotels on Ocean Drive. (Williams, MN; HASF)

"Inspired by the notable success of last year's special dinner dances, the Surf Club calendar for the year 1932 is imposing in its list of events," a socially-oriented newspaper reported. "There will be gala dances that promise to be as lovely as the shimmering 'Gold and Silver Ball' or the romantic 'Smarkand Festival' of yesteryear. Again Mr. Alfred Barton's artistry will be the guiding genius."[1] It is obvious that the Depression was not hitting hard at Miami Beach society, nor was it damaging tourism that much either. There still were many people who could afford Miami Beach vacations. Carl Fisher's financial problems were not born of Miami Beach but of elsewhere. "I am sorry that this year [1933] I cannot be with you in donations," Fisher wrote Dr. Elisha King, minister of the Community Church on Lincoln Road. "I need a new pair of shoes myself, and I am not joking either."[2]

Conversely, the Lincoln Road that Fisher forged out of a mangrove jungle less than two decades earlier continued to grow in stature as a premier shopping district. At the time of the 1926 hurricane, quality shops were beginning to appear on the street. Amid the many real estate offices were posh automobile dealerships, architects' offices, ladies and men's wear shops and a Bonwit Teller & Co. store at 824–28 Lincoln Road.[3] However, by 1931, Bonwit Teller had gone from the scene and a new, more renowned major retailer established. Saks Fifth Avenue of New York opened at 830 Lincoln Road. It was to become a landmark until the decline of Lincoln Road four decades later. "One of the big

Nunnally's, at 1014 Lincoln Road, was a popular place to relax after a day of shopping. (MN; HASF)

things... was to promenade on Lincoln Road," Jesse Weiss reminisced about those halcyon days.

You'd see these men there in white flannel pants, white shoes, a double-breasted blazer, a tie, starched collar, straw hats, a cane, momma on his arm—not a Jewish momma. This was all coming out of the Congregational Church. And walking by, window shopping, every morning. They'd get out of their chauffeur-driven cars at Collins Avenue and walk down one side and walk back the other. Then they'd go sit around the pools at their private clubs in bathing suits that looked like pajamas and get boozed up, and do what people do.[4]

For the architects, interesting times were ahead. The growth of Miami Beach, both as a vacation destination and as a place to live, created the need for more buildings. While the Depression took its toll on Miami, where booming construction of the Twenties slowed to a snail's pace, and while George Merrick, who created Coral Gables in the boomtime years, lost his empire to the inertia of the Thirties, Miami Beach—joined since 1928 to the mainland by a third causeway, successively called the Everglades Avenue, North Bay, Treasure Island, 79th Street and John F. Kennedy Causeway—did not appear to

suffer. Nightly during the winter season, the wealthy and near-wealthy could be seen dining at Oreste Gatti's restaurant at 1427 West Avenue. Opened in 1925, it and Joe's Stone Crab were among the leading places to dine—when the winter visitors didn't take dinner at their hotels or at the Surf and Bath clubs.

By July 1936, at the depth of the Depression, Miami Beach building permits soared to near a monthly average of $1 million.[5] In September 1936, three new schools—their construction costs ($700,000) paid for by a Public Works Administration loan and grant—opened in Miami Beach. A new high school, Ida M. Fisher, opened at 1420 Drexel Avenue; South Beach Elementary opened at Lenox Avenue between Third and Fourth Streets; North Beach Elementary was completed at 41st Street between Prairie and Chase avenues.[6]

Between 1934 and 1940, hundreds of new hotels and apartment buildings, large and small, were built—most designed by relatively unknown architects who would remain obscure until they were posthumously discovered in the late 1970s. On the periphery of that group, also, were already recognized Florida architects such as August Geiger and Russell Pancoast, both of whom maintained offices on Lincoln Road. (Much of Geiger's work preceded the Moderne movement. A resident of Dade County since 1905, Geiger built Carl Fisher's oceanfront home on Lincoln Road, the Lincoln Hotel and various stores and offices along Lincoln Road.)

What developed from the new breed of architect was a variety of styles that have come to become known, generically, as Art Deco. The full range included Zig Zag, Moderne, Streamline and Depression Moderne.[7] Hundreds of buildings that still stand in Miami Beach, including most apartment houses and hotels south of Lincoln Road and a few north of it, came from those schools of architecture. At the forefront of the new movements were men such as Roy France, Henry Hohauser, L. Murray Dixon. France came to Miami in 1932 from Chicago. His first noteworthy Miami Beach project was the Cavalier Hotel at 1320 Ocean Drive. Construction of the 55-room building took place in 1936. He would be responsible for at least four other Streamline hotels in Miami Beach.[8] Hohauser also came to Miami in 1932 but from New York. His firm is credited with designing more than 300 buildings in the Miami area.[9] Dixon, like Hohauser, was tremendously prolific. Born in Live Oak, Florida, Dixon is credited with at least 11 significant Miami Beach works.[10]

At the time they were built, and for decades thereafter, the hotels were as unnoticed as the men who designed them; or the men who built them, such as Russian immigrant Irving Miller, who owned the Cardozo, Carlyle, Hadden Hall, Claremont and Richmond Hotels. As recently as 1971, when Polly Redford wrote her *Billion Dollar Sandbar* biography of Miami Beach, the buildings were not held in high regard. Reflecting on the Thirties architecture of Miami Beach, Redford wrote:

> In tune with a new, less affluent era, these buildings were no longer Spanish baroque, for even the cheapest imitation loggias, balconies, tiled roofs, and plaster gargoyles use up extra money and space; they followed instead the then 'modern' architecture of the day, a style whose angular lines, flat sundecks, and staring windows suggested a series of stranded ferry boats parsimoniously cut up and converted into hotels.[11]

As recently as 1992, Kay Pancoast, who earned a degree in architecture from Cornell University and became a renowned designer, spoke disparagingly of the 1930s designs. "I'm appalled that they became so prominent," the widow of Russell Pancoast said in the last year of her life. (She died in April 1993.) "They were built cheaply, before a building code. Today, they would not be allowed to be built. My husband didn't know anything about Art Deco."[12] Indeed, Pancoast's best known Miami Beach projects, while important, are not attributed to the generic Art Deco style. Among his Miami Beach designs is the John Collins Memorial Library, now the Bass Art Museum (1930) at Collins Avenue and 22nd Street. Regardless of the detractors, history and reality were to deal more kindly with the modern movement.

Above: *Architect Henry Hohauser, whose firm designed more than 300 Miami area buildings, is generally credited with being the originator of modernism in Miami Beach.* (HASF) **Right:** *Abraham "Al" Galbut moved his family to Miami Beach from Monticello, New York, in the early Thirties and bought a 24-hour restaurant at Fifth Street and Washington Avenue. Today, the fourth generation of the Galbut family in Miami Beach operates a large condominium conversion company.* (Galbut Family)

Socialite Sally Hopkins, daughter of Coca-Cola magnate Lindsey Hopkins, married Robert Ludwig in Miami Beach in 1935. With the exception of the Word War II years, the twice widowed Sally has lived there ever since. (Sunday Pictorial)

Columnist Helen Muir and husband Bill enjoy an evening at the Surf Club. Bill Muir was Carl Fisher's attorney and Helen covered the social set for the Miami Daily News, *and later* The Miami Herald. *(Helen Muir)*

While the Depression brought difficult economic times, people continued to come to Miami Beach, as tourists, as developers or residents. Within those groups, there was a diversity of thought, roots and financial status. Russian-born Abraham Galbut, who owned a vegetable farm in Monticello, New York, was one example of the new Miami Beachite. Each winter, as the cold and snow made it impossible to grow crops, Al—as he preferred to be called— would put wife Bessie and children Paul, Hyman and Miriam in his 1926 Dodge and head south to Miami Beach. They would stay the season at an apartment house on Meridian and Fourth Street—the Martha Apartments—for $300 for six months. Galbut enrolled his children in Miami Beach public schools while he stayed out the winter. Meanwhile, the Depression was eating away at his farm, so much so that the bank took it over. He reasoned that if he had to start over, why not go where harsh winters did not close down your business? In 1934, the Galbuts came to Miami Beach and invested their few remaining dollars in a restaurant on a corner of Fifth Street and Washington Avenue. Al's Restaurant had no doors and was open 24 hours a day. Already familiar with the Miami Beach scene as a result of their earlier winter visits, the Galbuts fit in easily with the growing Jewish community of South Beach and reached prominence and prosperity through four generations.[13]

Helen Lennahan was a different kind of person for Miami Beach. She was a big-city woman: erudite and single. She had worked on newspapers in the New York area and, in 1934, came down to do publicity for the Roney Plaza Hotel. She did not expect to stay long in Miami Beach, just a seasonal job. But then she met William Muir, Carl Fisher's relatively new, young lawyer who worked with him on real estate matters. (Despite Fisher's seeming financial failure, he still maintained property and had a steady stream of income from various companies he had originated.) They married and set up house on Palm Island, just a few doors from Al Capone. By then Helen Muir was working for the *Miami Daily News* as a society columnist. In that role, she got an opportunity to see the side of Miami Beach that Al Galbut could not. "The galas that Alfred Barton had at the Surf Club were humorous," she recalled:

> If you came from the big city, as I did, it was ludicrous. There was one woman whose husband made a fortune in dairies; we called her The Milkmaid. Another woman—she was always wearing those glittering dresses— was married to a man who made his money in trucks. They were showy.[14]

Sally Hopkins, the daughter of Lindsey Hopkins, came from Southern affluence. She had

been coming to Miami Beach from Atlanta with her family ever since she was a little girl in the Twenties. She recalls spending her entire first grade in Miami Beach, under the aegis of a private tutor. Her father, a highly successful capitalist who earned a fortune with Coca-Cola and in automobile sales in Atlanta, was deeply involved with the Carl Fisher companies and, as Fisher's empire collapsed, was in position to gain control of it. Sally met Robert Ludwig in Atlanta, where he worked at Rich's Department Store. But when the two decided to be married in 1935, it happened in Miami Beach. "Father had insisted on it," she recalled. "He said he was a citizen of Florida." While the couple returned to Atlanta, they were destined to become residents of Miami Beach. Ludwig shortly was back, having received a boost from his father-in-law and training in New York City with Metals. Forming the Ludman Corporation with Max Hoffman, whom he met at the Reynolds school, Ludwig sold Reynolds Metals products out of the Shoreland Arcade in Miami and did well. He and Sally started with a house at 621 West 44th Street in Miami Beach and worked their way up to bigger and better. Widowed twice, she now lives on LaGorce Island. "We joined all the clubs," she recalled. "I remember, however, when my father tried to take Bernard Baruch to lunch at the Bath Club. [Baruch, a Jew, was a self-made financier who was an adviser to presidents from Woodrow Wilson to John Kennedy.] He was told that he could not do that, so father quit and joined the Surf Club. I don't know if Baruch could have had lunch there, either. I stayed in the Bath Club, however, because there were more young people there. We were going to dances, having fun; we just didn't notice the restrictions."[15]

Pauline Lux, who prefers Polly, is the daughter of a Pittsburgh glass blower. She traversed from an Earl Carroll and Ziegfeld Follies girl to her own lingerie shop on New York's Broadway to the Trianon Apartments at 702–06 13th Street in Miami Beach during the Depression. Polly used $6,000 she got from selling her lingerie shop to move with her mother and brother to Florida and to purchase the Trianon, which she described in a 1986 newspaper interview

as a broken down, 46-unit apartment house. She rented repair equipment and proceeded to renovate the Trianon. Her rooms went to people other hotels would not accept — salesmen, musical-comedy acts and families with children. From there, she bought and fixed-up more hotels in Miami Beach, including the Majestic and Imperial on Ocean Drive and the Royal on Washington Avenue.[16]

The man she was to marry in 1951, Baron de Hirsch Meyer, was not really a Baron; it was the name his father gave him. Baron came to Miami Beach in 1924 armed with a law degree from Harvard. At a party, he met another recent arrival, Leonard Abess, a CPA who recently had graduated New York University and was making only $25 a week in New York. Meyer and Abess struck it off immediately and began what was a lifetime business and personal relationship. With money borrowed from Baron's father, a Prairie du Chien, Wisconsin, general grocer, they purchased

The Floridian Hotel had name artists performing in their supper club. On its uppermost floor, a gambling casino operated for invited guests. (Chase Family)

SOPHIE TUCKER
World's Foremost Character Song-bird
Will appear at

The Floridian Supper Club

New Year's
Evening

FREDDY HAMM
and His
Recording Orchestra

The HOTEL
FLORIDIAN
MIAMI BEACH FLORIDA

DINNER · . . . BREAKFAST
DANCING

Entertainment . . . Favors

Make Reservations
At Floridian Hotel

Ten Dollars Per Person

After a short period of legalization, Floridians voted against a continuance of slot machines. Police confiscated those that did not adhere to the prohibition. (HASF)

The uppermost floor of the 10-story hotel was transformed into a difficult-to-access casino, somehow immune to the wishes of the city council and police department. The hotel elevators did not go past the ninth floor and invited gamblers had to climb the last flight.[21] Following Childers' days as a hotel manager and city councilman, he further identified himself with casino gambling by operating the notorious Royal Palm Club in Miami and, after the Navy took over his building in World War II, opened another club in Miami as the Little Palm Club. Fisher's original Miami Beach estate, at the foot of Lincoln Road at the ocean, was turned into the Beach and Tennis Club,[22] a casino that catered to the upper crust of Miami Beach society and the wealthy without social position. Because it was not a haven for hoodlums, authorities tolerated it more than places such as the Floridian casino. In his 1955 book *Moon Over Miami*, Jack Kofoed—a long time *Miami Herald* columnist—claimed one manufacturer lost $165,000 there in a single night.

The urge to gamble escalated, so much so that in 1935, the Florida Legislature passed a local option bill permitting slot machines.[23] Dade was one of the counties that opted for slot machines. Almost overnight, the area—including Miami Beach—was swamped with the devices. All that was needed to place one on the premises was $500 for a license from the county and an additional $250 to the city in which each machine was placed.[24] And they were placed practically everywhere, in storefront doorways, lobbies, theaters. Kassewitz, who said he represented one of the biggest license holders of slot machines, recalled that when a building in Miami Beach was put up for sale, the first question prospective purchasers asked was how many slot machines did it have. By the Fall of 1936, heat was being applied to both illegal gambling and the relatively new slot machines. In voting on November 3, 1936, most of the Florida counties that had opted in favor of slots voted to rescind their local option.[25]

Just days earlier, the Miami Beach Association, a group of prominent citizens including newspaper publisher Frank Gannett, hotelier and developer N. B. T. Roney, Bath Club president Fred Poor and Rev. William Barry, launched a drive to rid the city of illegal gambling. The Association said its initiative was "not a moral crusade, but a program against illegal gambling to insure the stability of property

an apartment house on Pennsylvania Avenue and Ninth Street. As Polly Lux was to achieve a short time later, one success led to another. The men founded the Miami Beach Federal Savings and Loan Association. Meyer was quickly to figure in Miami Beach politics, serving on the city council from 1930 until World War II.[17]

Like Abess and Meyer, Harold Kassewitz came to Miami Beach in the mid-Twenties and became prominent in the hectic Thirties. With a law degree, Kassewitz arrived from Fitzgerald, Georgia and began his practice in Miami but moved his offices to the Beach in 1930. He lived in an apartment at Euclid and Tenth Street. His law practice centered on representing backers of gambling. And there was enough going on to keep him busy.[18] One of many gambling sites was the Floridian Hotel on West Avenue at Sixth Street. When gambler Bert Moss came to Florida from Detroit in the early Thirties, he set up a night club and gambling casino in the Floridian.[19] The hotel was managed by Arthur Childers, who also was a member of the Miami Beach City Council. Moss' casino entertainment bill featured stars such as Eddie Cantor, Jack Benny, Sophie Tucker and the dance team of Cesar Romero and Nitza Bernelle. Childers was caught in the middle. He savored the income of a successful casino in his hotel but was pressured by fellow council members and the police to do something about the wide open gambling.[20] With Childers' vote, Moss' club was shut down, but that did not put a stop to the gambling.

values and to protect the legitimate investments of Miami Beach."[26] Getting rid of illegal gambling in Miami Beach would prove to be not as easy as voting to rescind the legalization of slot machines. Illegal gambling, crime and corruption were to have a long, profitable association with the city. When FBI chief J. Edgar Hoover, on vacation at the Flamingo Hotel in 1939, announced that his agents were investigating crime and corruption in the Miami area,[27] Miami Beach politicians were quick to react. "We know there are hoodlums here, as in every other city," Mayor John Levi was quoted. "What we want is someone, not to criticize us, but to tell us what to do."[28]

Socialite Alfred Barton, reflecting upon Miami Beach in the Thirties, told author Polly Redford:

[The] *real* Miami Beach . . . was certainly the theatrical, gangster, middle-class, New York-Chicago people . . . . They made the hotels and they created an atmosphere here which certainly was quite different from any other town in Florida. The gangster element was so predominant here during [those] years that Twenty-third Street was the hangout for every known gangster in America.[29]

Likely, Barton was exaggerating; he was, after all, a producer of extravaganzas. But he was correct in that the Miami Beach of the Thirties was being built and populated by middle-class folks. A considerable number of them were Jews: the Galbuts, the Abesses, the Kassewitzes, both Weiss families. In the most southern section of Miami Beach, this appeared to be no problem, either to the landlords or to the people already there. But elsewhere in Miami Beach, it was. The concerns of 1920 Fisher-built Miami Beach extended into the Thirties. Fisher and his colleagues feared the community would take on a Jewish image that would tarnish the ambience he and they sought to create. A brochure published for the 1935–36 winter season, and endorsed by the Miami Beach Chamber of Commerce, contained advertisements for restricted apartment houses and hotels.[30] The restrictions were boldly stated. The Indian Creek Apartments at 3300 Collins Avenue said it catered to "Gentiles exclusively." The Ansonia at 318 Twenty-First Street advertised "Exclusive Gentile Clientele." The Venetian Apartments at 1623 Lenox Avenue also mentioned "Gentiles exclusively."[31] Restrictive notices were not limited to small print in brochures. Signs posted on hotels and apartment houses also made those declarations. A photograph surviving to this day shows school children in a playground that abuts an Espanola Way apartment house, with "Gentiles Only" painted atop the building. Another such sign was uncovered in 1985 when workers peeling off old paint on another Espanola Way apartment house discovered the words "Gentiles Only" painted on the structure.[32] The most

Discrimination was no secret in earlier Miami Beach. The owner of this Espanola Way apartment house painted his restrictive policy on the outside of the building. (MN)

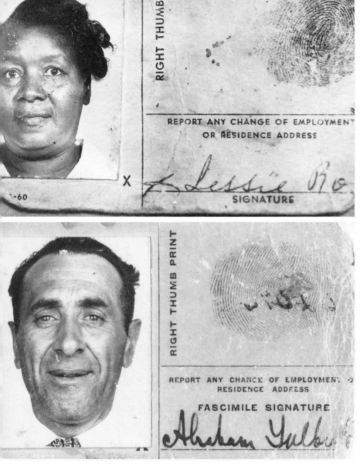

Contrary to popular belief today, Miami Beach identification cards were necessary to whites as well as blacks. All persons working in tourist-oriented fields were required to carry the cards. (MH; Galbut Family)

enduring story of anti-Semitism in Miami Beach is about a sign, ostensibly hung from an apartment house or hotel, that stated: "No dogs or Jews allowed." In her 1971 Miami Beach history, Polly Redford quotes Miami Beach activist Burnett Roth as recalling that there was an apartment hotel near Forty-Third Street that had a sign that said: "Gentiles Only. No Dogs." Roth, who was at the forefront of founding a chapter of the Anti-Defamation League in Miami Beach, said he protested the juxtaposition of the verbiage to city manager Renshaw, who convinced the proprietor of the apartment house to change it. The words "No Dogs" were removed from the sign.[33] In January 1994, Roth confirmed his recollection of the incident. He said he has never seen a sign that said, specifically, "No Jews or Dogs."[34]

Meanwhile, the years of adventure, big business and heavy drinking were taking their toll on Carl Fisher. Never a healthy man, he suffered from any number of ailments, not the least of which was damage to his liver from alcohol excess. By mid-1938, he was running out of money, steam and time. Periodically, he had to be drained of excess fluids, sometimes as much as 21 pounds at a time. His girth so swelled and shrunk during

these episodes that he took to having his suit jackets designed with two sets of buttons—one set for the corpulent Carl Fisher, and the other set for those times just after draining.[36] His second wife (and former secretary), Margaret, whom he married in June 1927, was living apart from Carl, she in New York, he in Miami Beach. Carl's friend and longtime financial associate Fred Humpage wrote Margaret in August 1938 to apprise her of Fisher's condition. "He seems more languid and more willing to remain at home and in bed . . . .," Humpage wrote, "I asked [the doctors] particularly if they could give me any idea as to what, if anything might happen and when. Their answer is that there is no way to determine it. . . ."[37]

Several months later, Fisher still was seeking new sources to cure his ailment. So desperate was he that he inquired about a veterinarian who specialized in livers and lights, the latter a term referring to the lungs of animals.[38] Carl hung on into July 1939. On the occasion of the Miami Beach Chamber of Commerce's 19th anniversary, fellow pioneer Thomas Pancoast invited Fisher to join him and some friends for a commemorative luncheon July 13, 1939 at the Pancoast Hotel.[39] "You fellows at these luncheon parties live too high for me," Fisher wrote back. "I am on a diet, mostly of pretzels and bird seed, and some of these I have to take with a high pressure gun; so, I couldn't possibly enjoy the luncheon and I know you wouldn't have any fun out of me—but, just the same, you have all my best wishes." He concluded the letter with a post script that showed he had not lost his zest for life or food: "P.S.—If you are going to sneak in any young lobster (which I know is out of season), save me a piece and I will get it at the office later in the afternoon."[40] Despite writing that he would not attend, Fisher did show up at the luncheon. The day after, Pancoast wrote him: "Of all the people who attended the birthday luncheon yesterday at the Pancoast Hotel, I felt more honored by having you present than anyone else. I know as a rule you shy away from functions of this kind and that is why I feel so deeply appreciative of your presence."[41]

Carl never saw the letter. It was received at Fisher's office the next morning, just after he was rushed to St. Francis Hospital with a gastric hemorrhage. Late that July 15 afternoon, Fisher died—with Fred Humpage, Dan Mahoney, Frank Katzentine and Dr. Frank Vorhis at his bedside; his wife Margaret was in New York.[42] Carl Fisher was 65 years old. The *Miami Daily News* wrote a succinct epitaph in the story of his death: "Carl G. Fisher, who looked at a piece of swampland and visualized the nation's greatest winter playground, died at 4:52 p.m. Saturday in the city of his fulfilled dream."[43]

. . .the city of his fulfilled dream.

CHAPTER FIFTEEN

THE TORCH IS PASSED

Memorial to Carl Fisher at Alton Road and 50th Street. The original plan was to bury Fisher there but his wife insisted that his remains be interred in the family mausoleum in Indianapolis. (HASF)

W. H. Combs Funeral Home dressed Carl Fisher's body in a tuxedo—a rose in his lapel—and placed his horn-rimmed glasses on his face. His open casket first lay at the funeral home, then was moved to the Collins Memorial Library for services.[1] Miami Beach Mayor John Levi, the man who first enticed Fisher to come to Miami, ordered all flags at half staff. Even across the bay in Miami, where Fisher's longtime nemesis Ev Sewell was mayor, a proclamation was issued calling upon all stores and business houses to close during the time of Carl's funeral as tribute to the man. Immediately, plans were made to turn a park that Fisher had donated to the City of Miami Beach—at 51st Street facing Alton Road—into a memorial and final resting place for him. If it had happened, Carl Fisher would have been the first person documented to be buried in Miami Beach.[2]

At simple services at the library, his friends LaGorce and now-Monsignor Barry were principal speakers. Fittingly, the sound of a rivet gun on a nearby construction job permeated the air as Fisher's services were held. "Laborers on the construction job," reported the *Miami Herald* of the funeral, "kept on working, making more quarters for the tourists who will come here next winter, the tourists for whom Fisher first built to attract to this land of sun and sea."[3]

Fisher's body was taken across the Venetian Causeway to a mausoleum at Woodlawn Cemetery in Miami to await final arrangements. His burial in the city he developed was not to be. His widow, second wife Margaret Fisher, instead preferred that he be cremated and his remains taken to the family vault in Indianapolis. Two weeks after his death, it was proposed that Alton Road be renamed in honor of Fisher. Prominent Miami Beach clubwoman Mrs. S. B. Rohrer was behind the move, saying that her group actually had wanted to change the name of the street while Fisher still was alive. Levi retorted: "If you had tried to, he probably would have sent his attorney down and gotten out an injunction against you."[4]

At a time, when the assessed value of the city with which he had so much to do in creating, reached $65 million, Fisher's estate totaled but $52,198.[5] His worth once was estimated at $20 million.

His friends proceeded with their plan for a memorial to him despite the fact that they could not inter his remains in it. On April 10, 1941, the Carl Fisher Memorial was dedicated in the park. Again, John LaGorce and Monsignor Barry stood to honor their friend, as did James Cox. In his remarks, Barry said: "We are here to honor a man who never sought an honor, a great man who never thought he was great. Simple and humble he was, more than the greatest man in this community; he was greater than the community. Today we give him our gratitude for what he did."[6] Cox described Fisher as the "man who made Miami Beach the great human drydock of America, to which the multitudes come for health and happiness."[7]

Another of Miami Beach's pioneer developers also died in 1939. Irving Collins, son of John Collins, and a partner of Fisher in several Miami Beach projects as well as the Montauk Point disaster, preceded Fisher in death by but two months.[8] He and Fisher were the same age. Irving Collins was the strict business man of his family. It was he who ran his father's businesses back in New Jersey. He also was one who insisted his father agree to build a bridge from the beach to Miami before they gave him money to build his canal. When Fisher and the Collins family became partners in the Miami Beach Bay Shore Company in 1919, Irving Collins was the family representative and was credited with keeping Fisher from being too flamboyant with the company's money. At the time of his death, Collins was an officer in six Miami Beach corporations, a director of the Miami Beach First National Bank and a participant in Miami Beach social functions that Fisher long ago stopped attending.[9] In contrast to Fisher's estate of $52,198, Irving Collins left $1,128,408.[10]

John Collins was gone; so were Carl Fisher and Irving Collins. J. N. Lummus no longer lived in Miami Beach and Thomas Pancoast was to die in 1941. The original cast that created Miami Beach

from a jungle had moved on, but new leadership and capital were in place to continue the job. The more southerly section of Miami Beach, those properties initiated by Lummus without legal or habitual restrictions on who may live there, were fast becoming a tourist and residential haven for Jewish people, most of whom were arriving from New York. By 1940, most of the residences south of Lincoln Road were inhabited by Jews. Jewish-owned and run businesses dominated lower Collins and Washington avenues. One could walk next door from the Miami Beach Kosher Meat Market at Third and Collins Avenue to Goldstein and Meltzer's Grocery and just a few doors down to Joe Reisman's Meat Market, or a block south to Ed Weinstein's Grocery and Lou Schulman's Delicatessen. A block to the west, on Washington Avenue, and a few further north, Adolph Daum had still another kosher meat market. Herman Popkin ran a small restaurant and Hyman Sacks sold cigars from the same address at 756 Washington Avenue.[11] The Jewish dominance reached almost but not quite to Fisher's Lincoln Road. Two blocks south of it, an office building at 1456 Washington Avenue was occupied by people with last names

Jack and Rose Samet came to Miami Beach from Atlanta in 1924. In 1932, they opened Samet's Kosher Delicatessen at 737 Washington Avenue in a narrow, three-table storefront. Jack Samet is behind the counter. Standing in front are Rose, who did all the baking, and their son Jerry. (Alvin Samet)

such as Cohen, Schwartz, Blum and Epstein while closer to the famed boulevard at 1512 Washington Avenue—within what was considered Fisher territory—people with names such as Gallagher, Kaiser, Mitchell, Beatty and Clifford lived in the Haliburt Apartments.[12]

While the conceived line against Jews held fairly well to the north of Lincoln Road, it followed the same prescription laid out by Fisher years earlier. If you were a wealthy Jew, and if you didn't carry yourself in what others perceived as a stereotypical manner, you could live anywhere you pleased.

Such was the case with Mitchell Wolfson, who had his residence at 5464 Pine Tree Drive. Key West-born Wolfson, along with business partner Stanley Meyer, established themselves more than a decade earlier, founding a chain of motion picture theaters—Wometco Theaters—which included the Lincoln Theater on Lincoln Road. His business

presence, plus the growing number of Jews living in Miami Beach and help from Carl Fisher, led to his election to the Miami Beach City Council in 1939. (Several months later, Wolfson was an honorary pallbearer at Fisher's funeral.) Wolfson was reelected twice more. After his third election, in 1943, he was unanimously elected mayor by fellow councilmen, the first Jew to be so positioned in Miami Beach.[13] In later years, Wolfson recounted how Fisher, in his declining days, assisted his 1939 campaign, thus further muddling the charge that Carl was an anti-Semite. "He [Fisher] found there were others on the Beach who were his contemporaries. . . who were very much opposed to me because they didn't think they'd want a Jewish member on the council." Wolfson recalled:

Mr. Fisher had quite a fallout with some of them as a result of supporting me, but I would think that I probably owe my election more to Carl Fisher than to almost anyone else. . . At the time there were not sufficient Jewish votes on Miami Beach to elect someone like myself. . . . Without Carl Fisher's support, I would have had a difficult time receiving sufficient votes from the Gentile community to have been elected.[14]

(Wolfson saying there were not enough Jewish votes on Miami Beach to elect him is puzzling, as Baron De Hirsch Meyer, a Jew, was elected to the city council nine years earlier.)

While the political torch had been passed, there was no "takeover" mentality in Wolfson. He understood the way things had been, and were, and while not condoning some of the practices of Miami Beach Realtors, developers, club boards and others, was too sensible to foment a "we-they" situation. "I think that most resorts, whether they were originally in the Catskills or whether they were at Saratoga, or whether they were here in Miami Beach or Palm Beach, tried to have a snob appeal to wealthy people," Wolfson told an interviewer in 1970. "The Jews weren't so wealthy at the time."[15]

Wolfson recalled a time when even newspaper advertisements carried "Gentiles Only" constraints, and of the role he played in bringing it to a stop. The Anti Defamation League asked Wolfson to talk with the two major Miami newspapers about eliminating the "Gentiles Only" tagline on hotel and apartment advertisements.

I had a good friend, Dan Mahoney, who ran the *Miami Daily News*[16] at that time. I went to see him and asked him to eliminate these ads which were offensive to the Jewish people. Mahoney said: "Mitchell, I'm the second newspaper in town. The

Mitchell Wolfson's City Council campaign headquarters was on Washington Avenue. Elected to the council in 1939, with help from Carl Fisher, Wolfson became Miami Beach's first Jewish mayor in 1943. (HASF)

Miami Herald is the big newspaper, and I agree with you. My advertising manager says we'll lose all the ads we have for these hotels, which are essential to our economic well-being, but if the *Herald* eliminates them, we'll eliminate them.[17]

Wolfson sought out John S. Knight, an Ohio newspaper publisher who bought the *Miami Herald* in October 1937. Some of Knight's key people remained in favor of the practice because they felt that since Knight's presence in town was relatively new, people might perceive banning the ads as a "Yankee" gesture. Wolfson said Knight reacted by saying he didn't care what the community thought, that the ads were seen as offensive by part of the population, and that he wanted them out of his newspaper.[18]

The election and subsequent elevation of Mitchell Wolfson was not the end of the restrictive nature of Miami Beach. It was to continue against Jews and, to a far greater degree, against blacks. By the late 1930s, the Sunset Isles, their development physically blocked by Fisher in the Boom years, were being developed by the Lynch family, but with restricted policies. Those barriers remained on one of the islands—Sunset 2—until as late as 1972.[19] To the north, the last patch of unimproved or undeveloped land in the City of Miami Beach was about to become available, but it took action by President Franklin Roosevelt in 1940 to do it. Known since 1924 as the Harding Townsite—named for President Harding—the land was largely that of the old coastal rescue station first erected in 1876. It lay between the ocean and the bay, from today's 73rd to

*Sunset Islands, ready for development. **Inset:** S. A. Lynch, president of Paramount Pictures, developed the Sunset Islands. (Andrea Lynch Cole)*

75th streets, running against the town of Surfside to the north. Due to a lack of patent, the property was homesteaded in 1920 by Lewis G. Norton, a clerk in the office of the Dade County tax assessor. He built a five-room bungalow on the site.[20] As president in 1923, Harding ruled that since real estate values of the neighboring properties had appreciated considerably, the undeveloped land was not eligible to be homesteaded. The U.S. Department of Interior cut the property into 133 lots and held an auction on February 22, 1924. The auctioneer sold 128 of the lots for $386,400—against an appraisal of $56,550! Norton continued to stay on the land, driving off purchasers with a shotgun and thwarting development.[21]

Then the Depression hit. While many lot purchasers kept up with their payments, many did not. The purchasers also contended that the original costs of the lots, for which they bid at auction, was inflated. The battle for Miami Beach's last undeveloped section now was being fought on two fronts—unsuccessfully by the family of a persistent homesteader who died in 1936, and more significantly between the federal government and delinquent lot purchasers. Both the U.S. House and the U.S. Senate passed a bill relieving the obligations of those who did not pay their full costs, but President Roosevelt vetoed it on March 15, 1940.

"While it is true that some of the purchasers have not made full payment for their lots contracted to pay more than their value as indicated by the 1936 appraisal," Roosevelt said in his veto message:

a substantial majority of the purchasers who still owe balances on their lots will, according to the same appraisal, have a value greater than the contract price, even though the

full amount is paid. In some instances the appraised value is three or four times greater than the contract price. No good reason appears for relieving purchasers of the obligation which they assumed many years ago.[22]

With the homesteader gone and the president's veto, the issue was settled. Those who could, paid their balances. Those who couldn't, sold their land to those who could. Its development stymied for almost two decades, the path was opened in the spring of 1940 to fill in the last gap on the ocean peninsula.

At the high school, 174 seniors graduated in June 1940. That year's *Typhoon*, the Miami Beach High School yearbook, listed each senior by the place he or she was born. Only six of the graduates were born in Miami or Miami Beach; three others were born throughout the entire state of Florida. But 57 of the seniors were born in New York City. The Midwestern flavor introduced by Fisher and his friends several decades earlier was swinging to a New York twang. While World War II was enveloping Europe, the growth and gayety of Miami Beach continued unbroken as 1941 headed toward December.

One of the more popular night spots in Miami Beach was Kitty Davis' Airliner at 16th Street and Alton Road. The interiors were designed around an airplane theme with waitresses dressed as stewardesses. (Parks)

International songstress Hildegarde was singing the already nostalgic *A Nightingale Sang in Berkeley Square* and *The Last Time I Saw Paris* at the Brook Club in Surfside; Bill Jordan's Bar of Music was a popular late night spot at 22nd Street facing the Collins Canal; and Walter Feldkamp and his orchestra were providing dinner dance music at the nearby Club Continental, which featured "Cuisine by Curley." The Cromwell Hotel on Collins and 20th Street was selling special $1 dinners but if you wanted to swim, dine and dance, that could be done for $1.50. The Fu Manchu Chinese restaurant established itself at 41st Street but eventually would move to 71st Street where it has remained for more than a half-century. At Baker's Haulover, Chase's seafood restaurant opened against the roar of the tide crashing against the Haulover Cut. Kitty Davis' Airliner Club and the Macfadden-Deauville Hotel restaurant were stressing a relatively new arrival in Miami Beach: air conditioning. This creature comfort was to play a colossal role in the success of Miami Beach as a resort city.

Figures released in April 1941 showed Miami Beach to be second in the nation among smaller cities in population increase the previous decade. (Hobbs, New Mexico was first.) Between 1930 and 1940, Miami Beach's population increased by 61,535—a growth of 331.4 per cent.[23] (Across the bay, Miami led the nation in population increase for cities over 100,000.) The 1940 census placed Miami Beach's permanent population at 28,012 with an equal number of persons coming as tourists. Hardly a day passed without an announcement in the local newspapers that a new hotel, apartment building or restaurant was being constructed. Miami Beach's fame even spread to motion pictures. In June 1941, *Moon Over Miami*, a musical starring Betty Grable and Don Ameche opened in movie houses across the country. While the title may have extolled the moon over Miami, the locale was entirely Miami Beach, even though the film was made on a Hollywood back lot. If anything, *Moon Over Miami* painted an exotic picture about the warm climate and good life prevailing in what had become "America's Playground."

By November 1941, it was evident that Miami Beach was a runaway success; perhaps not the way Carl Fisher or Thomas Pancoast planned it, but successful it was. In 1936, Miami Beach had 100 hotels and other accommodations for about 40,000 people. By late 1941, there were more than 300 hotels in the city, capable of accommodating 85,000 people.[24] That availability of rooms would prove to be a tremendous resource in the days just ahead—when America was plunged into World War II.

Above: Versailles Hotel under construction (MN; HASF)
Below: The Clevelander hotel, built by the Ratner family, was designed by Albert Anis. It opened in 1939 at 10th and Ocean Drive. (Ratner Family)

CHAPTER SIXTEEN

HOTELS, APARTMENTS JOIN THE WAR EFFORT

During WW II, soldiers replaced the tourists in 70,000 Miami Beach hotel rooms. (MN)

At first, it was believed that America's entry into the war following the Japanese attack on Pearl Harbor would spell doom for Miami Beach's tourist industry. It turned out otherwise. During the 1941-42 winter season, with the full impact of the war on the economy or consumers still in the future, people who planned their seasonal visits followed through. Helen Muir, a columnist for the *Miami Herald* in those days, wrote that after the initial shock of Pearl Harbor wore off "the predictions of pessimists that Miami would become a deserted playground for the duration were lost in the ring of the cash register, the beat of the rhumba, and the splash of the surf off Miami Beach."[1]

By assignment, Muir's range of vision was focused on the celebrities, rich capitalists and European gentry who, despite the war, continued to visit or live in Miami Beach. "At the Surf Club when tired millionaires gathered, the word was out to soft-pedal lavish parties as being in 'bad taste' during wartime," wrote Muir. "It never occurred to anybody to spit that taste right out of their mouths. Playing was the area's prime business and some tourists sold themselves on the idea that it was 'patriotic to keep fit' by continuing the practice of vacationing in winter."[2]

However, there was another, more dominant scene about to overwhelm Miami Beach. Rather than multitudes of tourists in flamboyant attire, these visitors wore khaki. Word of a major military presence in Miami Beach came in February 1942 when the Army Air Corps announced that 4,000 men, in training to become administrative officers, soon would arrive in Miami Beach.[3] Lt. Col. James S. Stowell was transferred from Randolph Field in San Antonio to command the new operation. The first contingent, 500 soldier-students, began classes on February 23, 1942. Officers moved into the Boulevard Hotel, the first hotel to be taken over by the Army.[4] The Miami Beach City Council leased out the municipal golf course—now known as Bayshore Golf Course—for $1 a year as the school's headquarters and drill grounds. By February 23, the Army had taken over six hotels and, with the city commission's approval, closed off certain streets in the vicinity of the school and training course, the *Miami Daily News* observed on March 1. "Ten days ago [Dade Boulevard] bordered the Miami Beach golf course. . . Now all that is changed. The golf course is a drill field, many of the adjacent hotels are barracks, and the clubhouse is the administration building of the U.S. Army Air Corps Officer Candidate School."[5]

At the high school, patriotism ran high—and shortly many students would become soldiers and sailors. Civil defense became a school project. When the call went out for male students to serve as volunteer stretcher bearers and air raid workers in case of attack, many answered enthusiastically.[6] The war even affected the County Causeway. The *Miami Daily News*, seeking to honor Gen. Douglas MacArthur, whose troops were battling vainly against superior forces in the Philippines, called for the renaming of the County Causeway in his honor. On March 3, 1942, the Dade County Commission unanimously voted in favor of the change.

Few realized the war would get closer to Miami Beach than just troops training on a golf course, or a causeway named for a general. In early February, the Germans sent U-boats to interrupt shipping lanes along the Florida coast. On February 19, they scored their first hit, the tanker *Pan Massachusetts* off the coast of Cape Canaveral. Although it was almost 200 miles north of Miami Beach, it was a sobering event. For miles around, Floridians could see the fires of war as thousands of gallons of gasoline and kerosene that were being carried as cargo went up in flames. Immediately, partial and full blackouts went into effect along the coast. The same U-boats that

The Bayshore Municipal Golf Course became a military training center as recruits by the thousands went through their calisthenics. (MN)

Mexican tanker Potrero del Llano *drifts and burns off Miami Beach on May 14, 1942. For the people of Miami Beach, it appeared the war had come to their front steps.* (MN)

could torpedo at sea also could train their guns on coastal targets. The brutality of World War II reached Miami Beach early in the morning hours of May 14. The 7,500-ton Mexican tanker *Potrero del Llano*, a neutral ship, was struck by German torpedoes eight miles off Virginia Key, just south of Miami Beach. For hours—well into the daylight—the *Potrero del Llano* drifted north the length of Miami Beach as horrified residents came out of their homes or hotels to see the sight of the vessel, with a cargo of crude oil burning out of control.[7] Thirteen Mexicans were killed in the attack and injured survivors were rushed to Miami's Jackson Memorial Hospital. Indeed the war had come to Miami Beach.[8]

Soldiers train amidst the palms of Miami Beach—with eerie similarity to the real war raging in the Pacific. (MN)

Within 24 hours of the announcement that troops would be coming to Miami Beach, a group of women met at the home of Zoe P. Renshaw, wife of Miami Beach's city manager, to consider recreation possibilities for the arriving military personnel.[9] Things can happen quite rapidly when the wife of the city manager or other prominent members of the community, such as Kay Pancoast, are involved. By early March, the Miami Beach City Council donated the use of what then was called the Municipal Pier to the recreation-minded group and granted $500 for repairs and $50 a month for maintenance. That hardly was enough to do the work necessary to create a major recreation facility for the troops but it was well-intended seed money.

With the pier in their possession, the mostly women organizers of the recreation program for servicemen began holding meetings with Army and Navy officials. And, natural to the times, an advisory board of men was formed. The first organizational breakfast was held at the Cromwell Hotel on March 25 with 300 representatives from civic clubs, churches, schools, newspapers and interested individuals from both civilian and military life. By the beginning of April, a money raising effort reached $2,661.20 and the group was chartered as the Miami Beach Pier Association.[10] Kay Pancoast was elected its first and only president. So dynamic and dedicated was her leadership that she was re-elected president each year the Serviceman's Pier was in existence. The pier opened to servicemen on April 15, 1942 with Brig. Gen. Ralph H. Wooten, commander of the Army Air Corps Training Center, officiating at the dedication. Only 417 servicemen came through it that day.[11] But their numbers grew to 1,350 the following day. By the end of the first month, 50,000 servicemen passed through its doors and by its first birthday, the count rose to 235,000.[12]

A study of the short but highly successful life of the Servicemen's Pier described the driving force of the volunteer group:

> The original roster of 300 volunteers quickly mushroomed to a thousand as each enthusiast became a one-woman recruiting station. Women who had never thought much about it before suddenly were conscious of a fierce civic pride in handling this job of providing healthy play places for the men in service. . . . Women took the active leadership. The Executive Board carried no names for lustre alone.[13]

What the women of the Pier Association accomplished was astonishing. The number of volunteers who served from April 1942 to December 1945 reached 18,000. Kay Pancoast fondly recalled some of the celebrities who visited the Servicemen's

Kay Pancoast accepts award from an army general for her work at the Servicemen's Pier. (Pancoast Family)

Pier, either as entertainers or just to mingle with the troops; among them Bob Hope, Rita Hayworth and Orson Welles.[14] More than U.S. service men were guests at the Servicemen's Pier, Pancoast recalled:

There was a swimming department where the boys could rent suits. Later on in the war, the Russians started coming to Miami Beach and to the Pier. They didn't trust anybody and they would bring their own stuff. They wouldn't let the women in that department take care of their stuff. They would put it on the floor and leave a man to guard it. I remember that there were abandon ship drills down at the end of the pier for a while. One day there was a man who didn't want to jump and was admonished by his

instructor for it. When pressed by the instructor, he told him that he already had jumped three times—from the decks of burning ships—and just didn't want to do it again. Teachers who would teach all day would come down to the Pier at night and do the same thing with these boys; I thought it was wonderful. One class was art and another was basic English. We had no translators but most of the foreign soldiers spoke English. We had a lot of Britons who came in from the Bahamas. We had French paratroopers. The Chinese were the best dancers. There also were some black soldiers. But it was not the way it is now. There was no rule against blacks using the Servicemen's Pier but I don't remember any being there. The Navy had black seamen here and had a hard time finding a place for them to swim, so they opened Virginia Beach on Virginia Key.[15]

Flora Brewster, a pioneer in Miami Beach library work, chaired the library at the Pier. It was well stocked, recalled Pancoast. Upstairs was a dance hall as well as the theater where movies were shown and live entertainment provided. So successful was the Serviceman's Pier, and so dense the population of military personnel, that seven branches were established in less than a year—in various parts of Dade County, but mostly in Miami Beach.[16] The study of the Serviceman's Pier boasted that "The history of the Miami Beach Pier Association is the story of how one American town of 30,000, backed by a county whose population reached no more than a half-million, met its part of the national crisis. Its adjustments and its transformation write the wartime saga of Miami Beach. This small resort city, smiling under the tropical Florida sun became, almost overnight, the site of the great Army commands where ultimately a quarter of all the officers and a fifth of all the enlisted men of the entire Army Air Forces of World War II were trained."[17]

Indeed, Miami Beach was taken over by Army Air Corps personnel. By August 1943, no fewer than 188 Miami Beach hotels had been "appropriated" by the government. In addition to that, the government requisitioned 109 apartment houses and 18 private homes.[18] It also took over each and every one of the Carl Fisher–built

Hup, two-three-four; a regular daily sight was of platoons of troops marching in front of Collins Avenue hotels. (MN)

THE MIAMI BEACH MUNICIPAL PIER

The Miami Beach Municipal Pier had a very checkered history. The earliest proposal to construct an amusements pier at the southeastern tip of Miami Beach was made in 1925 when a group headed by Dr. W.B. Davis and F.D. Rainey sought approval of plans for a $3 million dollar pier. By early 1926, however, George R.K. Carter, an Ohioan who came to Miami Beach shortly before the Boom and prospered initially in the real estate business, not only had entered the pier picture but already had begun construction. Beginning with permits for $620,000 worth of work,[1] the pier was well on its way when the 1926 hurricane struck, damaging its concrete pilings and some of the superstructure work atop it where a theater, among other buildings, was being constructed. Already known as the Million Dollar Pier, work began anew after the storm. Once again, a hurricane did significant damage. In 1928, a hurricane which caused relatively little devastation elsewhere on the Beach, drove a tug boat into the pilings and steel framework of the pier. Desperate for money to complete the job, Carter interested New York sports promoter Tex Rickard in the project. Rickard not only went in with him on the pier but, along with O.P. Smith, built the Miami Beach Kennel Club just south of the pier, where Government Cut spilled out into the ocean.[2] But Rickard died unexpectedly, leaving Carter alone with his project. The L-shaped pier[3] eventually was built but to nowhere near Carter's grandiose expectations. The theater Carter was building on the pier was not completed on his watch. Carter was notorious for his gambling activities. As early as 1919, Carter bought a South Beach building from J. N. Lummus and converted the second floor into an illegal gambling casino. He did the same with the pier. In concert with Jules Levitt and Sam Cohen, who later were to form the nucleus of the S & G Syndicate, Carter conducted crap games and roulette openly. When his pier was completed, Carter operated a restaurant and stage show but, in another section of the building, ran a gambling casino.[4] Eventually, Minsky's Burlesque took over the pier building and Carter moved on to other venues, including another illegal gambling house in Miami Beach and a failed 1952 attempt to promote a World's Fair along the Dade-Broward county line.[5] In 1940 the City of Miami Beach purchased the pier for $65,000, and the adjacent tract from Mrs. Rita Geist, on which stood Hardie's Casino, for $75,000 for the purpose of building a park.[6] Unknowingly, the acquisition set the stage for the development of the Servicemen's Pier in early 1942.

hotels. Had the armed forces never come to Miami Beach, it is questionable whether the mass of hotels could have survived, as travel restrictions were becoming severe. Fred Humpage, who had assumed the presidency of the Carl Fisher Corporation, wrote to stockholders in 1942:

> Although the bookings and reservations at the Flamingo Hotel at the beginning of the 1941–42 winter season indicated a most satisfactory operating season, the December 7, 1941 attack on Pearl Harbor caused a cancellation of the majority of the immediate and prospective business; consequently, we, together with all other seasonally operated hotel properties in this area, were seriously affected . . . . At the request of the United States Army Air Forces, we agreed to lease the facilities of the Flamingo Hotel for the duration; therefore, these properties are completely and unreservedly in the service of our country.[19]

Prophetically, Humpage ended his message: "The charm of Miami Beach will, in normal times, bring many of [the troops] back to us, either as guests or citizens . . . ."

The Nautilus became a military hospital and never again served as a hotel; its total lifespan as a hotel was but 18 years. Immediately after the war, it became a veteran's hospital but was left empty when the Veteran's Administration hospital moved to the Biltmore Hotel in Coral Gables. Eventually, the Nautilus, where religious restrictions were imposed in admitting guests, became Mt. Sinai Hospital, a non-sectarian institution organized and financed by Jews.[20]

For persons who spent only the winter months in their Miami Beach homes, giving them up to the government or leasing them to military personnel was not a great inconvenience. But others, such as Sally Hopkins Ludwig, were torn by the situation. Sally's husband was determined to get into the war and became a Marine. She followed him to his first assignment in Alexandria, Virginia, but when he shipped out to the Pacific and, eventually, to Guadalcanal, she returned to her family home in Atlanta. She always planned, however, to return to Miami Beach. "The house at 5577 LaGorce sat vacant during the war years," she recalled. "I wouldn't rent it to military personnel because I wanted to come home. Some saw it as unpatriotic but I couldn't help it. I kept seeing myself coming home any minute."[21]

For movie and sports fans, the plethora of movie stars and athletes in military training in Miami Beach was a wonderful opportunity for star-gazing and

Picture post cards sent nationwide by troops training in Miami Beach boasted of the wonderful climate. (Larry Wiggins)

Movie idol Clark Gable gets his mustache shaved away after arriving in Miami Beach to begin training in the Army Air Corps officer's school. (MN)

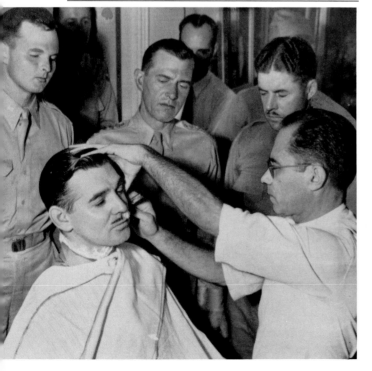

autograph seeking. Clark Gable's presence set female hearts aflutter although Gable kept strictly to his military routine. For youngsters such as Dick Kumble, now a stockbroker, it was an opportunity to seek out baseball heroes. "I stood for hours in front of the hotel Danny Murtaugh [then of the Philadelphia Phillies] was assigned to, just waiting to grab him for an autograph," he recalled a half-century later.

For the men stationed in Miami Beach, it was no vacation. Despite the ambiance and the climate, these men were in training for war. In March 1943, Private R. C. Bolton wrote an article for the Army publication *Yank* in which he reported on life in Miami Beach. It said, in part:

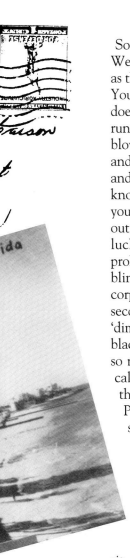

So you'd like to spend the winter in Florida? Well, brother, just join the army. It's as easy as that. But don't say I didn't warn you.... Your idea of life in a Miami Beach hotel doesn't include the jeep CQ[22] who comes running through the corridors at 5:30 a.m. blowing his lungs out on a little tin whistle and, when he has the breath, yelling, 'Rise and shine. Up and at 'em men!'... Want to know what it's like to be here? OK, I'll tell you. When the old whistle blows you tumble out of bed and snap on your lights—if you're lucky enough to have lights. They are prohibited in some hotels. But be sure your blinds are tightly closed unless you want the corporal of the guard on your back in 30 seconds flat. They have what they call a 'dimout' here, but it's the nearest thing to a blackout this side of London. OK, you're up, so now . . . you 'decide' to fall out for roll call—and I do mean fall out. This is one of the most hazardous jobs in the army here. Practically all of these hotels have front steps. These are very attractive in the daylight and make excellent places for the boys to sit during their off moments, if any. However, at 5:30 a.m., you can't see these steps even while you are falling down them, which is what usually happens. You have about 15 minutes now in which to sit and meditate, or you can make your bed . . . . You think hospital corners are difficult on a G.I. cot, try making them while you juggle an innerspring mattress that is eight inches thick.... (it's now about 6:45). You have a half hour to get shaved and clean your room. You learn for the first time why those Venetian blinds are on your windows. They're there so you can dust them every morning, and on both sides. You probably never stopped to figure that those innocent looking gadgets have about 40 slats and each one must be treated individually. Now you can understand why, with five jeeps in the room, one is assigned to that task alone . . . . Our days outside the hotel are like that at most any camp. A beautiful golf course is our drill

field, and the famous beach is the scene of our calisthenics. But our every waking moment is haunted by thoughts of our rooms and the inspection by the hotel sergeant. Many of our evenings are spent indoors. When we do get out we rush to a recently opened PX where 16 ounces of beer are handed out for a dime, and the chief topic of conversation is how swell it must be to live in a tent. But the daily average temperature here is 78. Sun shines all day. Maybe we'd better stay here at that.[23]

When Pvt. Bolton wrote that days outside the hotel were just like any day at any camp, he was almost right. What made days in Miami Beach different than days, say, at Fort Bragg or Fort Bliss was that at "Fort Miami Beach," the rifle range was on the edge of the ocean. A strip of beach between Collins Avenue and the ocean in today's Bal Harbour was the site of the rifle practice range. Troops stood on the avenue side and fired at targets on an embankment just ashore of the ocean. Bullets flew in just one direction: seaward.[24]

By 1943, much of the offshore Nazi U-boat activity had been curtailed through the work of Gulf Sea Frontier, an anti–sub fighting force headquartered in the Dupont Building in Miami. Its role was to chase German subs from the Gulf of Mexico and the nearby Atlantic Ocean. One of the great puzzles of 1942, according to the Gulf Sea Frontier, was why

Rifle practice was staged in Bal Harbour as troops fired across the beaches and toward targets on the shoreline. (MN)

the Germans did not take full advantage of the situation that year when the area was so unprepared to meet the German challenge. "Why a submarine commander cruising off the shores of Miami Beach," said a release from the Seventh Naval District in 1945, "did not elect to let loose with a five-inch deck gun and blast away at the hotels full of Army Air Corps officer candidates still remains a mystery."

Even Miami Beach's mayor went off to war. Unanimously chosen mayor by the city council in June 1943, Mitchell Wolfson resigned in September to accept commission as a major in the Army specialist reserve.[25] During his absence, his term was served first by vice mayor Herbert Frink, then by John Levi.[26]

Overshadowed by the huge military presence, the civilians of Miami Beach moved on with their lives. Of note was the 1943 installation of Irving Lehrman as rabbi of the Miami Beach Jewish Community Center at 1415 Euclid Avenue.[27] Rabbi Lehrman became a Miami Beach institution—serving his Conservative congregants for a half century—and the Jewish Community Center, first called the Jacob Joseph Congregation, later renamed itself Temple Emanuel and moved to a landmark home on the corner of Washington Avenue and 17th Street.

One year later, Rabbi Leon Kronish arrived to establish Miami Beach's first Reform congregation, Temple Beth Sholom on Chase Avenue near 41st Street. Rabbi Kronish served his congregation for 41 years until he retired in ill health in 1985.

For the teenagers of wartime Miami Beach, bonding was the order of the day, for the next day might find them in combat fatigues in a far away place. Fraternities popped up and membership usually ran along the lines of interests. Jim Snedigar, son of the former mayor of Miami Beach, co-founded the

Satans in 1941. The common bond between them was that they were athletes. The changing times of Miami Beach were reflected in the inscription by classmate Hal Lobree in Jim's senior yearbook in 1943:

Remember the sand dunes across from your house where we had sea grape fights? There sure as hell were no hotels north of 14th Street then . . . . We'll never forget the picnics and sleighrides, mid-winter hay rides and the game we beat K.O.A., 32-6 . . . . But it would take a helluva lot more pages than this book has to tell of the terrific times we've had together. . . . you, me and Schmidt [Bob Levitt] have been the Three Musketeers ever since the 7th [grade] and our friendship has been something I wouldn't change for all the money in the world . . . . Here's hoping you have all the luck in the world in winnin' those silver wings. I know you have the stuff to do it. I know we three will have a reunion after the war and be just as great pals as ever.

The "Three Musketeers" did go off to war. Lobree fought in the Battle of the Bulge and won a Bronze Star; Snedigar, amazingly, received his initial Air Corps training while billeted about a mile from his house at the Croydon Arms Hotel at 37th and Collins, got bombardier's wings and flew six missions over Japan in B-29s; Levitt, who was called "Schmidt" because he resembled another school's football player by that name, went into the Navy and was in the battle of Okinawa. All three men remain close friends today.[28]

Wartime Miami Beach was a wonder. Entertainment columnist Louis Sobol of the *New*

Miami Beach High School athletes, several of whom soon would go off to war, formed a fraternity in 1941. Calling themselves the Satans, they are, Left to right, front row seated: Bert Oschins, Bob Leavitt, Hal Lobree (co-founder), David Beeching, Jim Snedigar, (first president), George Kunde; second row standing: John Fuller, Jerry Blank, ...Peritzman, Bobby Browner, Howard Senior, Al Givot, Allen Kessler; third row standing: Bob Bonwit and Barry Bonwit. (Jim Snedigar)

Army Air Corps police patrolled Miami Beach streets. (MN; HASF)

York Journal-American wrote an open letter to a friend in the service after coming to Miami Beach to participate in a coast-to-coast War Bonds Drive radio hookup:

> Well, as you can see from the postmark, I've been down at our old playground, Miami Beach—and I want to tell you I wouldn't have missed the great bang I get out of seeing these boys training to be fliers and ground men for all the gold in Mussolini's upper and lower crockery . . . . We sold $3,500,950 worth of bonds just to the people around the Roney-Plaza. . . . The city of Miami Beach favored us, too, with a $100,000 purchase. Al Jolson went serious—so serious, as he told of the guys in the fox-holes, that he had most of the women tearful . . . . We thought Danny Kaye would get here in time, but his plane almost crashed and he didn't arrive until three in the morning. What a pale-looking ghost he was, too. . . . Most of the old clubs and restaurants are back doing business here—and what business! To get into the Park Avenue[29] takes a special letter from your senator, a hand-shaking acquaintance with your hotel doorman, and a sure-thing tip on a winning nag to the man at the ropes. Joey Adams and Tony Canzoneri are at the Beachcomber,[30] surrounded by a flock of pretty dolls wearing costumes which I seem to recall decorated the eyefuls at the Copa back in New York . . . . And, of course, there's still Joe's—and the famous stone crabs—and usually, when he's down here, J. Edgar Hoover and his sidekick, too—Clyde Tolson. . . .[31]

Although the government took over many of Miami Beach's hotels and apartment houses, property sales reached a record pace in 1944. Sales for the first seven months of the year were higher than for an entire 12 months of any other recorded year.[32] During July alone, property sales reached $7.7 million. By then, it was obvious that the war was going well for the Allies. The government released some of the hotels and apartment houses as the need for new Air Corps recruits decreased. By November 1944, the number of government-occupied hotels shrunk from the 188 in 1942 to 68; apartment houses from 109 to 11.

But the war was not yet over. In fact, German soldiers—believe it or not—opened a new front: harassing Miami Beach women. Prisoners of war, many captured during the North African campaign, had been brought to several camps in the Miami area to work at public labor jobs. In the spring of 1945, the complaints of harassment began to be heard. *Miami Daily News* reporter Grace Wing, who later, as Grace Wing Bohne, joined the *Miami Herald* for a long career as that newspaper's society editor, was sent to check out rumors that German POWs working as laborers on the streets of Miami Beach were amusing themselves "by cat-calling at women and school girls who pass by on the street."[33] She soon discovered it was not just a rumor. A female student at Miami Beach High School, daughter of a hotel owner, said that when she and her girlfriends would walk past the army garage on Alton Road after classes they were "greeted by whistles, flirtatious looks and muttered remarks in English or German,

presumably the *Hitlerjugend* equivalent of 'Hiya, Kiddo!' "

The reporter then went to a beauty salon in the 1600 block of Alton Road where several women complained of having to run a gauntlet of wisecracking, flirtatious German POWs. One of the women claimed that she saw a POW step in front of an elderly woman one day and say something loudly in German. The woman slammed the German in his head with her purse and screamed at him, also in German, until a nearby military policeman broke things up.[34]

Soon, however, everyone would be going home: the American soldiers in the hotels and apartments and the German POWs. The war was grinding down. On August 15, 1945, the day after the Japanese surrender, the Servicemen's Pier and some of the branches held huge parties. One by one, the branches began closing down. On December 1, 1945, the Servicemen's Pier closed forever.

For Miami Beach, the war finally had concluded.

Servicemen at the Nautilus-turned-hospital celebrate Allied victory in 1945. (MN; HASF)

CHAPTER SEVENTEEN

SAND IN THEIR SHOES

Ladies and gentlemen, I came to Miami for a
vacation.
But where do I live? At the railroad station!
Now for ten weeks or more
I've knocked on every door,
From every roof to the cellar floor.
And every answer I've had was: NO!
NO, WE HAVE NO APARTMENT-
WE HAVE NO APARTMENT TODAY.

So sang Beth Challis at Bill Jordan's Bar of Music nightly in early 1945.[1] Even before the war ended, it became obvious that a boom similar to that which thrust Miami Beach onto the national scene in the early Twenties could happen again. Soldiers and sailors were bringing their families to the area where they received their military training but many could not find either hotel accommodations or living quarters. Because of a freeze on construction during the war years, prices for existing structures shot up sharply. A small cottage in Surfside, which was priced at $8,000 in 1942, sold for $16,500 in 1944. The three-story Croton Hotel at 7326 Collins Avenue sold three times in 1944. The first sale was for $95,000; the third was at $142,500.[2] *Life* magazine, in a five-page spread in its February 12, 1945 edition, noted that "soldiers, sailors, war workers and tourists were all looking in vain for places to stay. The only empty hotel rooms were in Miami Beach, in the luxury hotels, where a $15-a-day room was considered a give-away."

When the government accelerated its return of hotels to private management, the room situation eased. Meanwhile, over in Miami, where land was plentiful, homes and apartment houses sprang up practically overnight. Within the city limits of Miami Beach, much of the land already was occupied. The area south of Lincoln Road was high in density and most of what remained as wide open spaces were parks, golf courses and the large estates north of 41st Street. Nevertheless, construction reached record-

The Martinique goes through the final stages of its construction en route to being 1964's "Hotel of the Year." (SPA)

Marker honors Robert Graham, who invested in what became Bal Harbour but waited until after World War II to develop the exclusive community. (MN; HASF)

breaking totals. By mid-1947, building permits totalled $6.9 million, headed for $35 million for the year. It doubled Miami Beach's record 1925 Boomtime numbers.[3]

To the north, above Surfside, an old idea—simmering since the 1930s—came to fruition. During the war, what now is Bal Harbour was the site of an Army Air Corps rifle range as well as that of a prisoner of war camp for Germans. With the war over, it was time to move ahead with the long dormant project. In 1946, Robert Cabel Graham, a Detroit truck manufacturer and wealthy farmer who was part of the original group of investors in the area, hired the firm of Harland Bartholomew and Associates to design a new residential community. What they designed conformed with the original plan of almost two decades earlier: an exclusive residential area with limited commercial activity. They broke ground in April 1946. In original deeds—no longer followed—there was a covenant that no lot be "sold, conveyed, or leased to anyone not a member of the Caucasian race, nor to anyone having more than one-quarter Hebrew or Syrian blood."[4] The Kenilworth Hotel that opened in 1946 adhered to

the same restrictive policies that governed homeowner deeds. Unlike Bal Harbour, the City of Miami Beach, its population increasingly Jewish and incensed by "Gentiles Only" or "Restricted Clientele" signs posted on buildings, unanimously enacted an ordinance on April 17, 1947, which banned such signs as being discriminatory.[5] No longer could signs within the city proclaim a discriminatory policy. It still would be all right to discriminate in actual rentals but signs could not be put up saying so.

Miami Beach may have been the cradle of unique ordinances. One, an anti-noise ordinance, practically stymied the post-war boom. In deference to its seasonal visitors, the city council passed an ordinance prohibiting work at any time within 50 feet of an adjacent hotel or apartment from November 15 to April 1. This nearly half-year-long ban on construction noise became a major issue when the owners of the National Hotel objected to the construction, in the seasonal months, of the Delano Hotel next door. Enforcing the ordinance and complaint from the National, Miami Beach police swept through the Delano construction site on February 4, 1948, arresting all the workmen. The city council, suddenly aware of the power of its own doing, met in emergency session and amended the ordinance to read "50 yards" instead of "50 feet." That really didn't solve the problem or the $500,000 suit by the Delano against the city as an entity, as well as against individual council members. The issue dragged through the courts with injunctions being issued by some judges and countermanded by others.[6] Ultimately, the ban was rescinded and construction permitted year round.

Hill York introduced air conditioning to Miami Beach hotels after the war. (Bob Lafferty)

With new hotels going up, the great growth in tourism soon followed. Two significant accomplishments spurred it: A snowballing commercial aviation industry and the implementation of air conditioning. While several trains a day ran from the Northeast and Midwest to Miami's grimy old railroad station near the county courthouse, the airplane brought tourists from the North down in just a few hours where the train took more than 24. Thwarted by travel restrictions during the war, the airlines now were free to expand, create package tours and promotions. The men and women who did military time in Miami Beach had promised to return some day and that day was at hand. Locals said that once you got the sands of Miami Beach in your shoes, you were forever affected.

Former soldiers, sailors and airmen who packed up their families and headed south used their G.I. Bill of Rights to buy homes on the mainland, and to get a college education at the University of Miami. Still, Miami Beach's lifestyle remained seasonal. Many of the hotels and restaurants continued to close for the summer months and homeowners either returned to their northern homes or went to the mountains of North Carolina until the summer heat and mosquitoes subsided in the Miami area. A summer drive along Highway A1A from

Hollywood Beach down to Miami Beach found the beaches practically left to the land crabs. But a way to beat the summer heat, first conceived in the 1850s by Apalachicola, Florida, doctor John Gorrie,[7] was coming to Miami and, eventually, to the hotels of Miami Beach; it would be revolutionary to the tourist industry. Commercial air conditioning actually arrived in the 1930s when Everett Carroll and Ren Nitzsche founded the Hill York Company in Miami. But it was not until after the war that Miami Beach hotels recognized the need for it or could afford it.

Above: Mitzee Green and Rudy Vallee entertain night clubbers at the Beachcomber on Dade Boulevard just east of Venetian Causeway. (SPA) Below: Kenneth Laurence, just starting a career as a publicity and celebrity photographer-about-town, is besieged by show girls in a turnabout gimmick photo at the Copa City night club on Dade Boulevard. Laurence went on to open a historical documents and manuscripts gallery on Kane Concourse. (Kenneth Laurence)

Between 1946 and 1955, every major hotel in Miami Beach converted to air conditioning. One could roast on the sand for an hour or two, then escape to the comfort of air conditioning in a hotel room, movie theater or restaurant: the best of both worlds. By 1948, the term "Air Conditioned" became an integral expression in many advertisements. Pickin' Chicken at 22nd Street and Collins made certain those words appeared along with the $1.65 announcement for Southern Fried Chicken. The Albion Hotel dining room at 311 Lincoln Road stressed its "air conditioned dining room and patio" as did Joe's Broadway Delicatessen and Restaurant at 1417 Washington Avenue where the Friday special was either fried shrimp and tartar sauce or the ethnic preference: gefilte fish and horseradish, $1.25.[8]

Miami Beach was back at center stage as "America's Playground." The Miami Beach publicity mill tempted Northern publications simply by sending

Hotel Row along Collins Avenue was well known by 1948. It was to be overshadowed five years later when the area north of it was rezoned for larger hotels. (MBNB)

bathing beauty photos during the months when their readers were freezing. George Bourke, who was the *Miami Herald's* entertainment columnist, wrote an article for the *New York Herald Tribune* that alleged, in the third person, how he spent New Year's eve.

Greeted 1947 in the air-conditioned Latin Quarter," attired in a tropical-weight dinner jacket, sporting a gardenia plucked from his own garden. . . started for home at 3 a.m. along Venetian Way, a moon lighting up hedges of blooming oleander and hibiscus; the scent of night-blooming jasmine slipping past the windshield fins as his convertible—top down—rolled through the night.[9]

This was the sort of mush that sold Miami Beach. It perpetuated the vision left by the pre-war movie *Moon Over Miami*. There was a near-obligation for usually-objective South Florida journalists to turn into propaganda tools on behalf of the tourist industry, and Bourke's you're-freezing-we're-frolicking piece was meant to appeal to New Yorkers, to make them itch to race down to Miami Beach, even though George overstated the situation almost criminally. Jumping into the Miami Beach story again was *Life* magazine. Its December 29, 1947 issue carried no less than 12 pages of color photos and text, plus the cover, extolling the start of another season. (Not coincidentally, Jane Fisher managed to work herself into one of the color photos—at a time when her book on Carl's life was being published.) *Life* referred to Miami Beach as the crown jewel of the Miami area. "Each winter it becomes the mecca for stage stars, songwriters, playboys, labor leaders, big-money

executives and big-money gamblers," wrote *Life*. "Miami Beach residents breakfast, lunch and sometimes dine on terraces edging their pools. They read there, doze there, and sun-bathe there. They play gin rummy, drink *aperitifs* and gossip alongside their pools. Sometimes they even swim in them." Surely *Life* had made a mistake. Surely it meant "tourists" rather than "residents." But, no, the next paragraph went on to talk about the tourists in the hotels. So inebriated with the propaganda image of Miami Beach were its proponents that the writers absorbed the average working persons who inhabited so many of the apartments south of Lincoln Road—those who waited on tables, drove cabs, ran lunch rooms or kosher butcher shops, who had trouble paying their bills, making ends meet—into a generic elitist mass and made them appear to be sun-bathing *aperitif* imbibers rather than day and night workers, overwhelmed mothers and struggling school students.

The *Life* article may have been promoted to offset the bad press created by the hurricane that struck Miami Beach in September 1947. Miami Beach was by far the hardest hit community of what was the first of two hurricanes and a tropical storm to strike the Miami area between September 17 and October 12—leaving terrible flooding on the mainland. Damage on the Beach was estimated at $4 million. The *Miami Daily News* claimed that "the brunt of the damage was to many of the resort's 332 hotels, but there also was widespread damage to homes, apartments and other buildings which took a lacing from high water and flying debris."[10] Rebounding was—and remains—a functional activity in Miami Beach. The best way to rebound is to clean up quickly, salt the press with positive stories and put on a glitzy show to prove that all is all right. (Characteristic of that persistent attitude was a Miami Beach mayor of 25 years later. When Miami Beach ran into a drinking water problem in the early 1970s, Mayor Chuck Hall called a press conference, announced there was nothing tainted about Miami Beach's drinking water and proceeded to gulp down a glass of it for photographers.)

The Miami Beach City Council election of 1947 was a landmark in that it closed the public life of John Levi. Retiring after 26 years as a city councilman, including three terms as mayor, Levi left his colleagues by saying that the "only thing I miss is the salary, but I can borrow it from these

Bookmaking was a wide-open operation beginning with the war years and continuing to 1950, when the Kefauver Committee came to Miami Beach to expose it. (MN; HASF)

boys," waving a hand at the council. Levi, who sent the telegram that first brought Carl Fisher to Miami Beach, died six months later, on January 26, 1948.

Life away from the night clubs and hotels continued at its slow pace. The Miami Beach that wasn't entertaining tourists was a small, closely knit city. Its youth congregated at drive-ins and ice cream parlors much as did Miami youths across the bay. Russian immigrants Henry and Hannah Kumble took over a Dolly Madison ice cream parlor on Espanola Way near the high school and converted it to simply "Dolly's." It became a premier hangout for the kids. Down on Fifth Street, Herb Frink ran the Pig Trail Inn, another popular kids' hangout.

"THE PINOCHLE OF MY CAREER"

Marcie Liberman was to Miami Beach what Yogi Berra was to baseball: A master of the malaprop. When Liberman was chosen Mayor of Miami Beach on June 6, 1947, it is claimed he responded by saying it was "the pinochle of my career." Unfortunately, neither the stories in the *Miami Herald* nor the *Miami Daily News* at the time carry that quote; perhaps he said it in private. But it became one of the most widely-recalled quotes in Miami Beach history.

Liberman, a native New Yorker, came to Miami Beach in 1931 and took over his father's Mercantile National Bank in 1937. In 1943 he was chosen to the Miami Beach City Council to make up for the vacancy left by the departure of Mitchell Wolfson for World War II. As mayor in 1947, Liberman became the center of attraction due to his malapropisms, his jocular association with a St. Patrick's Day parade up Washington Avenue—the hub of Miami Beach's Jewish community—and his voting independence.

He is credited with telling fellow councilmen, "I move we abdicate for the day. I got work to do." Liberman sensed the good public relations with his malapropisms and later admitted to making some of them up for effect.

Rooms 372-73 of the Mercantile National Bank building, owned by Miami Beach Mayor Marcie Liberman, was home of the notorious S & G Syndicate, which was listed in the City Directory as "S&G Service, concessionaires." (MN; HASF)

As the 1940s came to a close, Miami Beach found itself on the verge of a hotel boom that was, at the time, to take the tourist industry by storm. And about to take his turn at bat was a young man from New York, who in the years to follow, was to do as much as, if not more, than Steve Hannagan ever did to promote Miami Beach. Eighteen-year-old Hank Meyer came to Miami Beach in 1938 with practically no money. He stayed at a $3-a-week hotel on Collins Avenue and attended the University of Miami. Meyer worked his way through college via the school's publicity department. When he was offered the opportunity to attend law school, he dove at it but gave it up after six months, admitting to himself that public relations had caught him. "They offered me my p.r. job back," Meyer reflected years later, "but at only $40 a week. I also took a job as a bus boy at the King's Cafeteria [1121 Washington Avenue]."[11]

The war came around and Hank went off to the Navy, returning in 1946 to go into the advertising agency business. But Hank decided that advertising and public relations were not the same. In 1949, Miami Beach decided to separate its publicity department from its convention bureau and hired Meyer for the job. It was the start of a beautiful marriage. Hank stayed on the job for 27 years and sculpted Miami Beach's image throughout the world. But before he was successful in that, he had to endure a series of damaging investigations into the city's crime activities by both the media and a U.S. Senate committee.

Gamblers and racketeers also got sand in their shoes. Illegal gambling was almost a lifeblood of Miami Beach. The tourist-driven city most often looked the other way in the face of high-stakes card games, bookmakers, roulette wheels and craps. A tourist, or a resident, could get a bet down on a horse race with comparative ease. Gambling was a tourist attraction. Nevertheless, well-intending citizens saw it as the wrong way to attract and do business. They were intent on selling the sun and sand, not the dank back rooms of a bookie joint, or the smoke-filled chambers of an illicit gambling casino.

The war had not done much damage to the area's criminal underbelly. In fact, it was during the war years that the S. & G. Syndicate, a local cartel of bookmakers, was formed. In 1944, five Miami Beach bookmakers agreed to eliminate competition among themselves and make the finances of other bookmakers their business. By 1948, this business, according to its own books, controlled concessions at 200 hotels and grossed over $26,500,000 in bets. Harold Salvey, Jules Levitt, Charles Friedman, Sam Cohen and Edward Rosenbaum were identified as the founders of the syndicate that controlled bookmaking in the area.[12] The name—S. & G.—supposedly stood for Stop and Go, a designation that played off the fact that sometimes the heat was on, and the syndicate had to lay low, and sometimes there was no heat at all. In addition to the local syndicate, big-time racketeers made their headquarters in Miami Beach. Gambling flourished almost everywhere in South Florida: Sunny Isles, Miami, Surfside and Hallandale.

Frank Katzentine, mayor of Miami Beach in 1932 and owner of radio station WKAT in 1948, called a meeting of representatives of the area's newspapers and radio stations—there was no TV in the Miami area yet—and sought their assistance.[13] With him was Daniel Sullivan, a former FBI agent who had recently been appointed head of the Greater Miami Crime Commission. Sullivan displayed photos and other evidence that not only locals but mobsters from elsewhere had moved to the area, bought expensive homes and yachts and were proceeding to establish themselves. In a rare display of media unity, the newspapers and radio stations pledged to concentrate on making life uncomfortable for the underworld. The *Miami Herald*, in March 1948, began

Kefauver and Katzentine. (MN; HASF)

a series of articles written by Wilson McGee designed to spotlight the local syndicate of bookmakers by exposing its accounting, collection and security systems, the inner workings of its offices, its espionage and politics.[14] For 10 consecutive days, McGee hammered away at the S. & G. Syndicate. While it named the operators of the S. & G. Syndicate, and even located its offices—curiously in former mayor Marcie Liberman's Mercantile Bank Building annex at 1618 Washington Avenue, although Liberman never was identified with gambling interests—the series was devoid of other names. While it was more than implied that public officials worked with the syndicate, none was identified.

As the Kefauver Committee found when it came to Miami Beach, the city was corrupt—from politicians to police officers to bureaucrats. The *Special Committee to Investigate Organized Crime in Interstate Commerce*, a committee better known as the Kefauver Committee, compiled mounds of damaging testimony when it came to Miami in the Spring of 1950. Chaired by Sen. Estes Kefauver of Tennessee, who was building a crime-fighter reputation en route to two failed runs at the Democratic nomination for the presidency, the committee flushed out both racketeers and public officials. Among the anti-crime crusaders was Miami Beach city councilman Melvin Richard. He testified that, shortly after his election in 1947, he was offered a share in the profits of the punchboard games in the area, if he would refrain from interfering with the operation.[15] Richard also provided the committee with a recorded telephone conversation between himself and Miami Beach police lieutenant Phil Short, a former chief of police in the city, in which Short acknowledged having been instructed some years previously not to interfere with a certain card game at one of the gambling clubs. When Richard asked Short who gave him such orders, Short responded: "Chief of Police."[16]

In his testimony, Short said, "When I was inaugurated as chief of police, I made up my mind I didn't want to get involved with anything pertaining to horse bookmaking. I had nothing to with it. I called Pat Perdue [his one-man vice squad] in and said that 'you understand what these fellows are doing, just carry on, I don't want to know anything about the bookmaking or how they run it.' " Kefauver then asked, "Mr. Short, why didn't you want to know about bookmaking, if you were chief of police? Wasn't that your job?" Short responded, "I have been an officer for better than 20 years and I knew what 'hot potatoes' were."[17]

In its report, the Kefauver Committee said that Frank Erickson and his associates made their headquarters at the Wofford Hotel, which then was operated by former New York lawyer Abe Allenberg, who was "brought to Florida to represent Erickson in his race-track interests, and set up in the hotel business with money provided by Erickson. Allenberg's partners in this venture included the notorious gangsters Anthony Carfano from New York and John Angersola from Cleveland."[18]

The Kefauver Committee report stated, "It was also apparent that the S. & G. Syndicate members enjoyed cordial relationships with members of the city government and law enforcement agencies.

The testimony at the executive hearings established substantially that large numbers of known gangsters and racketeers from New York City, Philadelphia, Detroit, Cleveland, Chicago and other cities gathered together in Miami Beach and consorted at certain meeting places, including the Wofford Hotel, the Boulevard Hotel, the Sands Hotel, the Grand Hotel, and others. These gangsters and racketeers operated at the Colonial Inn, the Greenacres gambling casino, the Club Boheme in Broward County, and the Island Club and Club Collins in Dade County.[19]

The report went on to detail how, in 1949, a former Capone associate from Chicago, Harry Russell, muscled in on the S. & G. Syndicate and forced them out of business.

Kefauver certainly was not the first in the public arena to expose the corruption. In fact, his report referred to 1944 and 1947 Dade County grand juries that found evidence of gambling operations. It then quoted the 1949 Grand Jury report:

We could not see any purpose in repeating the work of our predecessor juries to discover officially and at great length that crime and corruption do exist here. Conditions have apparently not changed since the writing of the 1944 grand jury report. There is present in our community a large number of individuals of unsavory reputation. These persons are criminals of national stature. All forms of gambling are flourishing, the 1949 jury found, and there appeared to be little effort to curb them, although they were being carried on right under the eyes of the police.[20]

It took five years more for justice to be meted out in the S. & G. case, and it is questionable as to whether it really was justice. Jules Levitt, one of only two original S. & G. founders, and Sam Friedman, brother of deceased founder Charles Friedman, stood before judge Emett Choate in a Miami courtroom to await sentencing after admitting guilt to income tax evasion. Their lawyer, Ben Cohen, argued that both men were the victims of a local government policy which countenanced gambling.[21] Cohen told the judge that Miami Beach government, in the S. & G. heyday, based its budget on the returns in fines and forfeitures from the gambling syndicate. Cohen said Levitt looked upon the gambling as a quasi-legal enterprise. "The business of bookmaking has largely flourished in some sections of South Florida," Judge Choate said. "It wrongfully flourished, but nevertheless, it was encouraged." Listening to Cohen's appeal that Levitt had sent his children to college and had been an asset to the community, Judge Choate fined Levitt $5,000 and Friedman $4,000 and suspended two-year prison sentences for both, placing them on probation for three years."[22]

For people wanting to vacation in Miami Beach, or to move there, the revelations of the Kefauver Committee, newspapers and grand juries, had little impact. Miami and Miami Beach were great places to live, to raise kids. The men of World War II, many with sand still in their shoes, kept coming down the highways, railroad tracks and airways to South Florida.

Nevertheless, there was consternation on the part of those already living here: what was the place turning into with all those crooks? For Hank Meyer, fresh on the job, representing that part of the public that sought a squeaky clean resort community catering to the family trade, an image-cleansing job lay ahead. He was up to the task. He had plenty of material. It came in the form of a Russian-born architect, a phenomenon called the Hotel of the Year and, later, a red-headed uekelele player.

CHAPTER EIGHTEEN

NOVACK, LAPIDUS AND THE FONTAINEBLEAU

Architect Morris Lapidus left his mark on Miami Beach.
(MN; HASF)

When Morris Lapidus, born in Russia in 1902, was an immigrant boy living in the Williamsburg section of Brooklyn, his Uncle Harry came by one Sunday morning to take him on a rare trip outside the *shtetl* in which the Lapidus family lived. Uncle Harry walked young Morris onto the new Williamsburg Bridge spanning the East River to Manhattan. At the center of the span, Harry lifted the boy in his arms and turned him toward the city. "Look at it, *Moishele*, the Singer Building, the tallest building in the world, twenty-five stories high. Maybe one day when you grow up, you will build a skyscraper, maybe one higher than the Singer Building. Anything is possible here in America."[1]

Morris Lapidus' contribution to the American scene is not so much measured in height as it is in sweeping curves, in poles disappearing into so-called "cheese holes" in the ceiling, in the hotels, stores and malls he created internationally. And his most indelible mark is on Miami Beach. In 1949, Lapidus—by now an architect—was little known outside New York City, where he earned a living designing stores. His ambition was to create a building of his own, to do what his Uncle Harry had visualized. It was then that a client introduced Morris to Ben Novack, a hotel owner in Miami Beach, who also had come out of Brooklyn's neighborhoods. Novack, the son of a New York Catskills Mountains hotel owner, came to Miami Beach in 1940 and in less than a decade operated the Monroe Towers, Cornell and Atlantis Hotels. He became a colorful and quite quotable Miami Beach figure. (Reporters and story tellers liked to say that Novack mispronounced words and murdered the English language, but what they didn't admit was that most of them misspelled his name as much as they spelled it correctly. Lapidus, himself, consistently and erroneously spelled it "Novak" in his 1980 autobiography: *An Architecture of Joy.*) Now Novack had an idea for a new hotel. He hired an architect for the building but was interested in engaging Lapidus to design the interior. The meeting between Lapidus and Novack was to begin a spectacular love-hate relationship, highlighted by the construction of several landmark buildings— most particularly the Fontainebleau Hotel. In his autobiography, Lapidus recalled their first meeting— a dinner with friends—as being insubstantial. "I didn't bother to mention that once I had designed a hotel years ago in which I had forgotten to put bathrooms in each guest room," he recalled.[2]

Over a short period of time, Novack and his partners, Harry Mufson and Harry Toffel, maneuvered Lapidus into taking over the entire project— including finishing off the design of the exterior of the Sans Souci Hotel. The original architect had become obstinate in his dealings with Novack and Lapidus. Lapidus was, in effect, mopping up on the previous architect's work. But it was a start, and it was not a store in a shopping center. Throughout, the extroverted Novack dominated the relationship. When the Sans Souci Hotel opened at 3101 Collins Avenue in December 1949, Lapidus' role was almost unrecognized. A newspaper story about the hotel's debut didn't even mention him. Instead, it reported that "The opening climaxes a 20-year dream for Novack, a veteran Miami Beach hotelman. He constructed the hotel from plans and notes compiled during a score of years."[3]

What Novack could not eclipse was Lapidus' interior design. The lobby and interior decoration of the Sans Souci was distinctly Morris Lapidus. He originally intended to have bird cages suspended on rods, or what were called "bean poles" that went from ceiling to floor. The idea of live birds failed and plants were put into the cages instead. In describing the Sans Souci lobby, Lapidus said "the carpet is shaped like a 'woggle' and the columns disappear into 'cheese holes.' "[4] It was far different from more conventional hotels that began appearing in Miami Beach shortly after the war, such as the Martinique, Kenilworth, Sea Gull and Saxony. And the Sans Souci was only a start. As Lapidus dreamed of some day designing his own hotel from the ground up, Novack was working on a dream of his own. It was in the vicinity of an historic—almost sacred—property on Miami Beach known as the Firestone estate.

Tire magnate Harvey Firestone, who, in 1924, bought the large estate north of 44th Street built by

Morris Lapidus' first venture into Miami Beach architecture was to design the interior of the Sans Souci Hotel. (MN; HASF)

oilman James Snowden, died in 1938. The property went to his family, principally son Harvey Firestone, Jr. As the war years began, the family lost interest in the estate as a home but saw great prospects for the land, if it were rezoned, to become the site for a hotel or apartment house. During the war, the Army Air Corps took the home as a training installation.[5] As early as 1943, the Firestone heirs sought to rezone the property but ran into significant opposition from existing hotel interests. Following lengthy battles at lower levels, the case worked its way to the Florida Supreme Court.[6] Behind the opposition was strong sentiment that Miami Beach already was overbuilt with hotels. Realtor Bernard Feiner argued:

More hotels competing with the 350 we now have, would obviously wreck existing values, spread havoc and disaster, and destroy our local hotel-housing industry. We have more than enough hotels and apartments to last us for some time, or until we catch up with those that have been constructed in recent years at great cost.[7]

To the north, Miami Beach already was faced with the threat of competition for hotel guests and apartment dwellers. Another Russian immigrant, Shepard Broad, had created a new community—Bay Harbor Islands—out of two islands in 1945, seen it incorporated into a municipality in 1947 and, through his leadership, passed a bond issue to build yet another causeway across Biscayne Bay. If the Collins Bridge opened the way to the development of Miami Beach, the soon-to-be-named Broad Causeway would have the same effect on Bay Harbor Islands, Bal Harbour, Surfside, Sunny Isles and Golden Beach. The north end of the narrow peninsula no longer was accessible primarily from the north; it now was within easier reach from mainland Miami.

But the courts doomed the battle to hold down the growing number of rooms. When the Firestones won their case in early March 1950, it led the way to a series of continuing rezoning cases for much of the land north of the Firestone estate. Over the next decade, there were significant rezoning changes— some politically questionable—as the previously guarded properties opened up to development. The early Midwest dollars that helped create an ambiance of new wealth in Carl Fisher's Miami Beach were going elsewhere. The city now was increasingly in the hands of New Yorkers and other Easterners, and the Jewish presence was becoming dominant. In the summer of 1952, with the rezoning approval safely tucked into their pockets, the Firestones sold their estate for $2.3 million to a syndicate headed by Novack.[8] Although the Miami Beach City Council opposed rezoning the estate, Mayor D. Lee Powell described the sale as "a great tribute to Miami Beach."

With the Firestone property in his hands, Novack announced plans to build a luxury 500–room hotel on the site. It came as a surprise to his partners in the Sans Souci and to other Miami Beach hoteliers. They believed that Novack purchased the property to shelve it as a potential competitor to existing Miami Beach hotels. On January 1, 1953, five stockholders of Novack's Sun 'N' Sea Corporation, which owned the Sans Souci, filed suit against Novack, contending that they and Novack decided more than a year earlier to buy the estate to prevent it from being developed.[9] But, they claimed, when Novack finally made the deal on the property, he kept the purchase agreement for himself and refused to turn it over to the corporation. The stockholders said it was their plan, and Novack's, to share the cost of purchasing the property from the Firestone heirs and turn it into a park to serve as a buffer to further hotel and apartment development. A move by the city council to condemn the land for park purposes was voted down 4–2 in February 1953.[10]

One-by-one, estate property owners used the courts to win their battle for rezoning until the Miami Beach Council caved in and permitted rezoning, at raised land values, for some of the parcels.[11] A *Miami Herald* story announcing the granting of the permit to construct the Fontainebleau Hotel, again failed to use Lapidus' name, describing the curves and designs of the future hotel without mentioning their author.[12]

The Firestone estate became the headquarters for Ben Novack while the Fontainebleau Hotel was built around it. (SPA)

Ben Novack and his wife dine with television personality Steve Allen and his wife, Jayne Meadows, while Allen was doing the "Tonight" show in 1957 from the Fontainebleau's La Ronde Room. (MN; HASF)

Within days of issuance of the permit, construction began. By mid-January 1954, bulldozers and drag lines were ripping into the site. Novack took offices in the Firestone mansion which was to remain esentially intact throughout the construction of the hotel.[13] When, on February 21, 1954, *Miami Herald* Real Estate and Business Editor Fred T. Bill did a 28-paragraph story on the hotel, expressly detailing its unique interior and exterior design, Lapidus' name did not appear until the 25th paragraph, and then only as shared billing with Novack in mentioning that orientation of the buildings on the site would admit sunshine to the cabana area all day.[14]

Prominence continued to avoid Lapidus. His contributions, much like those of the architects of the Moderne and Streamline hotels of the 1930s and early 1940s, would achieve esteem in retrospect. Shortly after the Sans Souci opened, other Miami Beach builders hired Lapidus, but not as architect and designer from the ground up. Four hotel jobs followed the Sans Souci. But on the new Nautilus, DiLido, Biltmore Terrace and Algiers, Lapidus was the relief pitcher again for builders who were not fully satisfied with their original architects or designers. "In short," observed Lapidus, "I still had never been commissioned to design a hotel from the very beginning."[15]

When Novack announced his plans to build a world-class hotel on the Firestone site, he told reporters that Morris Lapidus would be his architect. When Lapidus, in New York, got word of this, he immediately contacted Novack and inquired if, first, it was true and, second, why Novack didn't talk (and negotiate) with him before telling reporters. Lapidus claimed that Novack told him his name was the first that entered his mind when reporters asked about an architect but that he wasn't going to get the main job because he wasn't prominent enough. Instead,

Novack offered him an associate architect's job.[16] This was too much for Lapidus. He came back at Novack, demanding an opportunity to do the main job. Novack saw it as an opportunity to get an architect cheaply. "A minimum fee for a hotel such as this would be at least four percent of the cost," noted Lapidus:

> The cost was approximately $12 million, and at four percent, the fee should have been $480,000. When I finally succeeded in getting Ben to let me be his architect, I had to agree to carry out the entire assignment, including engineering and interior design, for a miserable fee of $80,000.[17]

One can argue forever as to whose idea it was to curve the Fontainebleau Hotel building. Lapidus contends he submitted 26 drawings and not one showed the building as a rectangle. But Novack felt he designed the hotel. Lapidus wrote that he let Novack believe that because once he was convinced he had, Novack approved the Lapidus design.[18]

Perhaps "love–hate" is not the best way to describe the relationship between Novack and Lapidus. Perhaps "cat and mouse" would be more accurate. The architect recognized much of Novack's ability as an innovator and as a shrewd hotel operator but when Ben began trying to design Morris' building, an imaginary line had been crossed. Lapidus refered to his relationship with Novack as three years of acting, brain–washing and deception:

> But who was brainwashing whom? As I look back, I realize that we were brain-washing each other. . . As we jockeyed the design, it was his taste, the taste of his clients, that won out in the end. It was my task to interpret these likes and, at the same time, carry out my own theories of design so that I could create a hotel—interiors and exterior—that was a product of my talent and ability, albeit under Ben's direction.

Lapidus resolved that he would not use straight lines in his hotel, just as he had avoided them in his stores. "Did I tell him [Novack] that I had been trying to get him to accept a curved building all along?" Lapidus contemplated. "What for? I had gotten what I wanted. Let him go on believing that it was his own brilliant idea."[19]

Harold Gardner, who was Novack's public relations director for the better part of 24 years, beginning in July 1954 and interrupted only temporarily when he did work for the Eden Roc and Diplomat Hotels, confirms the Lapidus version of how he got Novack to accept his ideas but adds that Novack continually insisted the idea of the curved building was his. "I saw some of the [Lapidus] drawings," said Gardner, "and some of them did not have the curve. They did have a graceful sweep to them but I couldn't call it the curve we have in the completed Fontainebleau."[20]

For lack of a name at the beginning, the hotel was called, internally, the Estate after the Firestone estate. But Novack, on a European trip with his wife, whisked past the Fontainebleau Palace, liked the name and bestowed it upon his hotel. This was not exactly pleasing to Lapidus who had designed a contemporary building that now had the name of old French royalty. Upon hearing that Novack had publicly announced that the interior design of the hotel would be French Provincial, Lapidus considered resigning. "I had devoted my entire career to modern architecture, twentieth-century architecture," he complained. . . . Now to go back to corny traditional? This was a disaster."[21] He mulled his options and decided compromise was best for all. Lapidus presented Novack with illustrations of French Provincial interiors, although he considered them preposterous for the hotel. "I wouldn't have these old-fashioned interiors on a bet," Novack told Lapidus. "I want that modern kind of French Provincial." Flabbergasted, Lapidus invented Modern French Provincial. Instead of traditional French Provincial columns, he created oval columns; he created a feeling of luxury by using marble trimmed with thin rods of gold metal.[22] Out of his creativity emerged Miami Beach's most favored, most adored, most panned, most reviled hotel.

The stairs leading from the lobby to the mezzanine in the Fontainebleau were more for design than function; there was very little on the mezzanine. However, guests rode the elevator to the mezzanine and descended the grand staircase much as would have Scarlet O'Hara. (MN; HASF)

In October, with construction of the Fontainebleau just two months from completion, Novack moved out of the Firestone estate and consigned it to the wrecking ball. It was one of the first mansions of Miami Beach to go down as rubble, to be replaced by the formal gardens that would help make the new hotel famous. The gardens recreated those of the French kings at Fontainebleau and Versailles.[23] By mid-December, with opening just a few weeks away, reporters were allowed on the premises and laden with press kits filled with trivial pieces of information. "If all the piping in the Fontainebleau were stretched out," observed a *Miami Herald* reporter, "it would reach to Fort Pierce, more than 100 miles away."[24] The $15 million, 565-room hotel opened on December 20, 1954, with pomp and ceremony, including the presence of the mayor of the City of Fontainebleau, France.[25] Sixteen hundred invited guests stormed the hotel for a $50-a-plate charity dinner to benefit St. Francis and Mt. Sinai Hospitals. "Everything was French, including the confusion," reported *Miami Herald* writer Nancy Woodward. "Millionaires in their elegant, glamorous attire lost some of their dignity as they scrambled for tables. One couldn't enter the banquet room without the precious table number."[26] One guest remarked, "You can't get in, you can't get a drink, you can't get anything, but isn't this the grandest hotel you ever saw?"[27]

Lapidus related the story of a conversation he had that night with Hubert Pajot, the mayor of Fontainebleau:

> In one conversation in my halting French, I asked him what he thought of the hotel named after his city. "*C'est une bouillabaisse.*" (It's a bouillabaisse—a soup in which shrimp and lobster and squid and clams and seven varieties of fish and an endless variety of vegetables and spices are blended.) I didn't know whether this was a compliment or a devastating criticism of the kettle of soup I had kicked up. "*Aimez-vous la bouillabaisse, monsieur?*" I wanted to know. Yes, he liked bouillabaisse, but only once in a while. Well, that wasn't too bad. After all, no one would want a steady diet of an indefinite vacation at the Fontainebleau. Once in a while, O.K., that's what it was designed for.[28]

On Christmas Eve, the hotel's soon-to-be-famous LaRonde Room opened with Vaughn Monroe and his orchestra. In the years to follow, the LaRonde Room was to host performers such as Frank Sinatra, Dean Martin and Jerry Lewis, Liberace and a constant flow of other headline entertainers. The Fontainebleau Hotel achieved immediate worldwide

An early Miami Beach landmark, the Firestone estate was leveled once the Fontainebleau Hotel began to take shape in 1954. Its site became a formal garden on the hotel grounds. It was the first of the grand estates in "Millionaire's Row" to be demolished. (MN; HASF)

status. It became Miami Beach's signature building and remains so to this day. So well known was the Fontainebleau that until Steve Muss and the Hilton people took over the hotel in 1977, there was not even a sign in front showing its name.

Lapidus' anonymity quickly evaporated. Fellow architects took note of his accomplishment. Many of them condemned him. He had broken the mold of the traditional, he eliminated straight lines and 90-degree angles. He even created an interior design that was French Provincial but was not. One architectural publication derisively described the hotel as "Miami Beach French." It would not be the last controversy in Morris Lapidus' career, which has carried him past 90 years. He endured the brunt of traditionalists criticisms, even by Frank Lloyd Wright, who, in 1956, described the Fontainebleau as looking "like an anthill." To this Lapidus responded: "I wish I could have explained that I am flattered. I *built* it for ants."[29] Lapidus voiced his own opinions, told his critics "to go to hell" and, like the obscure Moderne and Streamline architects of years earlier, endured to be exonerated, extolled and practically deified.

The relationship with Novack, tolerable though tenuous, was to fall apart a short time later when Lapidus agreed to design the Eden Roc Hotel immediately north of the Fontainebleau. Novack considered it a traitorous act because the Eden Roc was being built by his former—and estranged—partner Harry Mufson. Novack was so upset that he swore never again to speak to Lapidus or to allow him to enter the Fontainbleau. When Novack built a 14-story *rectangular* annex north of the curved building, Mufson charged that it was done with the sole purpose of casting a huge daylong shadow on the Eden Roc's pool and cabana areas. With Mufson, Lapidus ran into another strong–willed builder. Harry wanted luxury and glitz to top the Fontainebleau next door. The architect suggested Italian Renaissance but Mufson was against the use of heavy ornamentation. "You mean the Baroque influence, Harry?" Lapidus asked. "I don't care if it's Baroque or Brooklyn, just get me plenty of glamour and make sure it screams luxury."[30]

Mufson turned out to be easier to deal with than Novack; he and Lapidus got along and even

The Eden Roc is immediately north of the Fontainebleau. Its construction so enraged Novack that he built a 14-story addition to his hotel that blocked much of the sun from the Eden Roc's cabana area. (MN; HASF)

The lobby of the Eden Roc, like other Lapidus creations, included columns. (MN; HASF)

Lapidus' contribution to Bal Harbour's scene was the Tisch brothers Americana Hotel, later renamed the Sheraton Bal Harbour. (MN; HASF)

went on a buying trip to Europe together. Brothers Larry and Bob Tisch contacted Lapidus about designing a hotel in Bal Harbour even before the Eden Roc opened in 1955. Lapidus surely was on top of the architectural world: three major hotels in three years! In his past were the days of designing shoe stores, of being an assistant architect, of pleading for a chance to design a building of his own. Now, people were beating a path to his door for his services. He remained controversial, not only for his elements of design, but for what he said. By 1955, some of his thinking had changed. He pronounced modern architecture to be out of date: "too stark, too severe, too functional."[31] He scorned some of the very elements he used in his earlier designs: windows, glass walls, indirect lighting and chairs with pipestem legs. His penchant for controversy was equalled by the criticism that stormed around him, particularly after the completion of the Tisch brothers' Americana

Hotel (now the Sheraton Bal Harbour). At a 1963 convention of the American Institute of Architects held at the Americana Hotel, Lapidus came under criticism from heavy hitters in the industry. Taking the podium, San Francisco architect Robert Anshen said the Americana "is built of thin, cheap improbable materials. It is incompetent, uncomfortable and a monument to vulgarity."[32] This brought Lapidus out of his chair and toward the platform. Before he got there, however, *St. Louis Post–Dispatch* art critic George McCue asked the audience: "We must ask ourselves what is the function of this hotel. It obviously was not designed to provide privacy. I twice answered my phone when the ringing was in my neighbor's room and when he flushes I feel I should run for high ground." By this time, Lapidus had worked his way to the microphone. "I want to pose the question of this hotel which is not an architectural masterpiece but designed for people who come here for fun. Yes, it is a cheap hotel. There is a quality in architecture from the camera view. But there is also the quality of human emotion. People want architecture to give them pleasure. They want human comfort, satisfaction and warmth."[33]

Defiance and the conviction that he, not his critics, knew what the public wanted was the hallmark of Morris Lapidus' career, which continues today. He was judged harshly in his early days but reappraisal by critics years later, placed Lapidus on a pedestal as the man whose design techniques, particularly in interior design, met the demands of the vacationers to whom he addressed himself. "I'm not ashamed of my hotels," Lapidus responded after the *New York Times* criticized his new Atlantic City hotels as glittering, fantasy plexiglass facades. "They weren't built as monuments. They were built as hotels for people who want glamour and excitement in the vacation. Tinsel and glamour will always be the name of the game in any resort."[34]

The interior of the Americana Hotel was famous for its glassed atrium and "cheese-hole" ceiling. (MN; HASF)

CHAPTER NINETEEN

THE OLD REDHEAD

Arthur Godfrey sits in his penthouse apartment atop the Kenilworth Hotel in 1954. Godfrey, who had been coming to the Miami Beach area as a tourist since the 1930s, brought nationwide publicity to Miami Beach when he began broadcasting radio and television programs from there beginning in 1953 and continuing for more than a decade. (MN)

Hotels and motels were going up so fast that naming them became a job for creative writers. People simply were running out of names. A British writer, traveling Florida's southeast coast, referred to his arrival as being "in the stupefying Babylon of Miami Beach."[1] He was overwhelmed by the ingenuity in naming so many hotels and motels. In 1961, the Greater Miami telephone directory listed 460 hotels on the Beach and its immediate environs to the north. That didn't include motels. Some hotels were named for their owners, as in the Roney Plaza; in some places you had to look hard for the link: the Doral Beach was named for its builders Doris and Alfred Kaskel and the Carillon, for Kaskel's niece, Carol.[2] In 1964, no fewer than 16 hotels had "Plaza" as part of their name. There was a covey of hotel names copied from other cities: The Pierre and Barbizon from New York, the Edgewater Beach and Palmer House from Chicago. Presidents names were tapped: Madison, Washington, Roosevelt, Jefferson—even the White House. British names crept into the mix: Hampton Court, Chelsea, Cambridge, Devon and Essex. Later, the names became more romantic-sounding: Sorrento, Barcelona, Capri, diLido, Algiers, Fontainebleau, Eden Roc, Seville, Lucerne, Deauville—so much so that when the naming of the Americana was announced, there was near-rejoicing, even if the name did have the Latin suffix.[3]

Ironically, it was a hotel not located in Miami Beach but two municipalities north—past Surfside, in Bal Harbour—that brought immense publicity to Miami Beach. It came in the form of radio and television broadcasts by Arthur Godfrey from Tom Raffington's 1946-built Kenilworth Hotel near Baker's Haulover Cut. All this publicity did not

How did they find names for 460 hotels in the Miami Beach area, not including dozens of motels in Sunny Isles, by the 1950s and 1960s? With creativity. Miami Beach hotels were named for presidents, hotel owners and their relatives, and for other places around the world, such as the Sans Souci and the Fontainebleau. (MN)

come without controversy, however—a controversy that continues to the present. Since the Kenilworth was a restricted hotel, there was growing sentiment in the area's Jewish community that Godfrey was anti-Semitic. When he, along with two Cincinnati men, purchased the hotel in 1954 and the restrictive policy remained in force, there was even greater consternation among Jews regarding Godfrey. Don McNeil already had done his "Breakfast Club" radio shows from the beach and Walter Winchell had originated some of his Sunday night radio broadcasts from there. But city publicist Hank Meyer saw in Godfrey, whom he met in Miami Beach in the winter of 1952–53, the prospect of a vast national television audience. Meyer suggested that the popular radio and TV host originate some of his shows from Miami

Beach.[4] Godfrey liked the idea but since the coaxial cable had not yet reached South Florida, there was no way a live TV show could emanate from Miami Beach. Meyer fed on such challenges. "I got hold of a Southern Bell executive and, in time, the cable was run through to Miami Beach." (The coaxial cable actually arrived in Miami in June 1952, but was linked only to WTVJ's studios.[5] This enabled Miamians to see live TV broadcasts from the North but the potential for a remote sendup from Miami still was lacking.)

What Godfrey and Meyer had combined to put together was a first for network television. It involved shipping an entire New York technical crew and their equipment, as well as the performers and script writers—30 in all—1,200 miles to Miami

Beach. "I wanted to do something big, really big, before going into the hospital to get these hips fixed up,[6]" Godfrey said, "And the biggest thing I could think of was doing the shows right down here in Miami Beach—in bathing suits."[7] In preparation for their April 13, 1953 show—the first in a weeklong series of live radio and TV broadcasts—the Godfrey workers turned the Kenilworth Hotel inside out, and outside in. Police guards were stationed around the building to keep outsiders out, but even the insiders had a hard time getting in. Employees and hotel guests were fully checked out by security guards before being permitted on the grounds. A newspaper photographer, stopped by a guard from entering the hotel, was told: "Nobody can get in here without a pass except President Eisenhower and the Pope. You don't look like either of them."[8]

But into each life a little Murphy's Law must fall. And it did—thud. Bad weather chased the first Godfrey show indoors. Strong winds were the cause. "It's way down in the 65s, or something," Godfrey told his audience.[9]

"The weather chased Arthur Godfrey indoors at Bal Harbour today, and he retaliated by creating a cold wave," wrote Haines Colbert in the *Miami Daily News*. ". . . The temperature at the moment actually was 81, but the windswept pool deck of the hotel was no place to stage a television show."[10] If Godfrey committed a *faux pas* by lowering the local temperature by 16 degrees or so, he more than made up for it the following day. "It was freezing up North," recalled Hank Meyer. "Godfrey did his show from the Kenilworth by going offshore in a boat and jumping into the water and swimming to shore. Then he told his audience how great it was down here . . . It was a five-minute commercial for us."[11]

An estimated 54 million persons saw the show.[12] Immediately, there was local adoration of Godfrey. The Edison Center Lions Club of Miami sent telegrams to each of the Dade County commissioners asking that the 79th Street Causeway be named in his honor.[13] The Miami City Commission jumped on the bandwagon and also pushed for the Godfrey honor by a unanimous vote.[14] The petitions did not influence the State Department of Transportation; Godfrey was not thus honored.[15] At the end of Godfrey's first week of broadcasts, the Miami Beach Chamber of Commerce attributed 882 letters of inquiry about Miami Beach to the popularity of the Godfrey show.[16] "Arthur Godfrey caught hold of a dream . . . ." wrote Bill Baggs in the *Miami Daily News*. "Into close-windowed living rooms the country over came the freedom of sunny fun. With bleak winds outside, with snow and sleet and raw rain and cold outside, a turn of a dial brought the magic of clear skies, warm sands, sparkling water—and the

Just south of the Haulover Cut bridge in Bal Harbour, the Kenilworth Hotel was the site of the early Arthur Godfrey broadcasts and telecasts beginning in 1953. (MN; HASF)

carefree banter of a great guy. Godfrey made that magic. He did it because liked doing it—and liking it, he thought others would too. It was as simple as that."[17]

Despite the grumbling by some Jewish people about the hotel from which he was broadcasting, the Jewish leadership was impressed with what the ukelele-strumming Godfrey was doing in promoting the area. In January 1954, the Greater Miami Jewish Federation honored Godfrey at a dinner attended by 425 persons at the Saxony Hotel.[18] Godfrey, who was broadcasting from New York at the time, flew down for the dinner that night and returned afterward. The Federation presented Godfrey with a silver-covered Old Testament written in Hebrew, which he acknowledged, adding that he wished he "had years enough left to learn to read it."[19]

Godfrey's broadcasts from the Kenilworth and other South Florida locations continued for years. What Godfrey popularized, others began to copy. Other television shows began emanating from Miami Beach, always at the time of year when it was pleasant there and fiercely unpleasant elsewhere. Among them were Ed Sullivan, host of the CBS "Talk of the Town" Sunday night variety show, and Jack Paar, whose NBC "Tonight" show was popular. National telecasts reached their peak a decade after Godfrey began. Highlights of this peak were the appearance at the Deauville Hotel of the Beatles on the Sullivan show and the move of Jackie Gleason's comedy show from New York to Miami Beach.

By 1964, Godfrey, who was fond of referring to himself as "the Old Redhead," had survived one bout with cancer and was beginning to cut down on his activity. He continued his broadcasts from Miami Beach but they were on radio rather than TV. In February 1964, the same month the Beatles appeared in Miami Beach, Godfrey began his 11th year of broadcasting from the area by doing a show from the Miami Beach Convention Hall.[20] The Miami Beach Chamber of Commerce hosted a luncheon in his honor and the city renamed 41st Street for him.

The love affair between Miami Beach and Godfrey, however, underwent a severe test in 1967. That year, the Old Redhead was doing his radio broadcasts from the Diplomat Hotel in Hollywood. Following the completion of the taping of his show, Godfrey entertained a press reception. One reporter asked Godfrey: "What do you think of some of the expressions of opposition to our Vietnam position that have been voiced in this country?" Godfrey's response touched off a firestorm in the area's Jewish community. "I think it's a crying shame," said Godfrey. "Over 6,000 of our boys killed and the rest of the country still goes on like we are not at war. I think we should have total mobilization. The cream of the bloody crop is dying over there and we are still having our *bas mitzvahs* here."[21]

The storm was heavy and immediate. Why, Jewish people wanted to know, did Godfrey single

Despite a prevailing opinion among many Miami Beach Jews that Arthur Godfrey was anti-Semitic, the Greater Miami Jewish Federation honored the entertainer in 1954 when its president, Carl Weinkle, presented him with an Israeli-produced Old Testament written in Hebrew. (MN; HASF)

out a Jewish occasion as the example of America's distaste or disregard for the events taking place in Vietnam? Hank Meyer insists the charge of anti-Semitism against Godfrey was erroneous. "One rap Godfrey feared was that of anti-Semitism," Meyer said. "Godfrey wrote to me that he was not and never had been an anti-Semite and predicted that the day he died, they will take down the signs on Arthur Godfrey Road."[22] Also defending Godfrey was Larry King, then a radio talk show host in Miami Beach and a part-time columnist for the *Miami Beach Sun*. He was present at the controversial press reception. In his column of Jan. 27, 1967, King acknowledged that the quote in the *Miami Herald* was correct but said that it had been misunderstood. King explained that Godfrey had attended a *bas mitzvah* of a friend's daughter the night before he held the press reception and he used that expression only because the *bas mitzvah* was fresh in his mind. "I'm sure if he had gone to a christening party the night before, he would have said that word . . . ," wrote King. "Arthur Godfrey doesn't need me to defend him. He is one of God's good people and prejudice never made a move inside his mind . . . . It is indeed a tragedy when anyone is falsely accused because of an idle remark that is completely within the realm of understanding."

While the grumbling about Godfrey continued—his Kenilworth association never satisfactorily explained—the Greater Miami Chapter of the National Conference of Christians and Jews did not share in it. At its annual Brotherhood Awards dinner at the Fontainebleau Hotel in 1972, Godfrey received one of the Conference's three medallions awarded that year.[23] Speaking from the podium after receiving his award, Godfrey addressed the very thing of which some people accused him. "We'd better get rid of our prejudice and bigotry and hatreds," he said, "because if we're going to lick this thing and give these kids a chance, we're going to have to get along together."[24]

Despite those words, the anti-Semitism charge continued to have a life of its own. There are people in Miami Beach today who would like Godfrey's name stripped from 41st Street signposts, citing anti-Semitism as the reason. When cancer finally claimed Godfrey in 1983, Miami Beach Mayor Norman Ciment spoke glowingly of the man but with a caveat. "Although he was sometimes controversial," the mayor said, "his value to Miami Beach as a personality entertaining from this area was incalculable . . . . He was a friend to Miami Beach, a charitable amiable man . . . ."[25] Whatever may be said of Godfrey could not alter the fact that he set the table for a flood of national telecasts to emanate from Miami Beach and nearby. He was part of an era when Miami Beach was reaching the pinnacle of status as an entertainment center.

CHAPTER TWENTY

ARROZ CON POLLO MIXES WITH BAGELS AND LOX

Miami Beach's famed hotel row in the midst of the 1959-60 season. (MN)

On January 1, 1959, Cuba's Fulgencio Batista fled Havana ahead of a popular advancing rebel army headed by Fidel Castro, who, once in power, declared himself to be a Marxist. What followed dramatically altered the demographics of South Florida, including Miami Beach. Many of Cuba's professional people became the first to seek sanctuary in South Florida. In those earliest years of the Cuban Diaspora, the refugee influx had a stronger impact in Miami than in Miami Beach, which continued its romance with tourists from the North—although several thousand affluent Cuban professionals, mostly Jews, took up exile by the seashore.[1] Cubans, both as tourists and as exiles, have an extended history in Miami Beach. As early as 1933, former Cuban president General Mario Menocal took up temporary residence there. Exiled from Cuba by President Gerardo Machado, Menocal came to Miami with his family and later moved to Miami Beach. Menocal's house at the southwest corner of Lincoln Road and Collins Avenue was a center for exile political activity. At that time, the Cuban exile community living in Miami Beach and Miami numbered in the hundreds.[2] When Machado fell two years later, Menocal and most of his countrymen returned to Cuba. As they left, the *Miami Herald* lauded the exile community and left an open invitation to return. "Miami was glad to extend her hospitality to the [Cuban] exiles and will be sorry to lose them," editorialized the *Herald* on Aug. 17,

1933. "but appreciates their desire to bask again in Cuban sunshine. . . . Miami's gates will ever remain open to Cubans, as well as to men and women from every country and clime and state."

In January 1959, former Cuban president Carlos Prío Socarrás,—exiled twice by a Batista— was living in a Beach hotel with his family. After Castro took control, Socarrás returned to Cuba for two years until he realized Castro was a communist. He returned to Miami Beach and lived in a home on Alton Road the rest of his life.

Greater Miami not only was a haven for early Cuban political exiles, but for tourists from that country as well. In 1947, it was reported that more than 6,500 Cubans were vacationing in the area each week, arriving either by plane or by steamship from Havana. A survey of arriving passengers on the S. S. Florida in June 1947 revealed that nine out of 10 Cuban women tourists wanted to shop on Lincoln Road, or on Miami's Flagler Street for "smart American clothes," and that the men were looking forward to staying at a large beachside hotel, going to sporting events and movie theaters.[3]

The general manager of the steamship line reported that bookings of Cubans coming to Miami on the S. S. Florida were so strong that there was a waiting list. "Most of the Cubans are flush and get a gleam in their eye the minute the modern skyline of Miami and the Beach comes into view," he observed.[4]

Over the next dozen years, Cubans continued to find Miami Beach a fun place to visit just as Americans did Havana. But, as 1959 wore on, the Cubans coming to South Florida were not vacationers; they were fleeing a tightly-gripped communist dictatorship. Rather than a short stay for shopping and entertainment, they were coming until such time that Castro's socialist government collapsed or was overthrown. Most thought the exile would last a year or so, and they would go home.

The Miami Beach that the first wave of refugees from Castro found in late 1959 and in 1960 was, like the rest of the country, just coming out of a national recession begun in 1957. For some Miami Beach businesses, times were good. For others, not so good. City tourism officials reported that 128,900 convention tourists came to Miami Beach in 1959, spending nearly $23 million. These tourists stayed an average of five and one-half days.[5]

Even the summer months were doing well. In June 1960 alone, the national conventions of the Kiwanis, Rotary and American Medical Association brought 75,000 visitors into the area.[6] The first Miss Universe contest to be held in Miami Beach took place in July 1960. After eight years in Long Beach, California, it was lured to the Miami Beach Convention Hall—again by Hank Meyer. While the relationship between the Miss Universe promoters and Miami Beach were to be stormy over the years, the event brought worldwide publicity to the city. Nevertheless, several hotels were in bankruptcy, but the area at large was the healthiest ever, according to Meyer, who believed that the few hotels had fallen victim to "shoddy financing" more than anything else.[7]

In spite of some failures, Miami Beach was flourishing as a tourist center when the first Cuban exiles began arriving. So successful was tourism that few in that field took note of the presence of growing numbers of Cubans. Beginning with the opening of the Fontainebleau in 1954, the new hotels included plush night clubs in their plans and lured top stars there. In a short time, it proved to be a death blow to the independent, stand-alone night club. However, for a time, both flourished in an air of excitement and in direct competition with the night clubs of then-adolescent Las Vegas.

As 1959 turned into 1960, among the choices available to entertainment-conscious tourists on the winter season night club scene were flamenco dancer Jose Greco and singer Georgia Gibbs at the Americana's Bal Masque Room; singer Johnny Mathis in the Mona Lisa Room of the Eden Roc; the zany

Exiled Cuban President Carlos Prío Socarrás lived in Miami Beach for many years. (MN; HASF)

Ritz Brothers and a young singer named Connie Francis at the Deauville's Casanova Room; Lou Walters' lavish production of *Follies Francaise* at the Carillon; Tony Bennett in the Fontainebleau's La Ronde Room; Martha Raye at Copa City, Murray Franklin's night club, on the site of the old Roman Pools, was launching the careers of singer Roberta Sherwood and caustic comic Don Rickles, while the Club Chalet at the Lucerne was unknowingly featuring a preview of the area's future: a Havana Mardi Gras, starring Diosa Costello and a full cast of Latin-American entertainers.

Miami Beach south of Lincoln Road had a history of catering to moderate-to-lower income people and continued to do so, not so much impacted by the Cubans, but by retired people who had come south, principally from New York, to live out their days in sunshine and warmth. The unique hotels on Ocean Drive, designed by the new wave of architects in the 1930s, had been taken over by the elderly. On any day, from the 1950s to the 1980s, the sight of hundreds of retirees sitting on webbed chairs on the porches of these hotels was a familiar one. Derisively, the younger generation referred to those hotel porches as "God's Waiting Room."

The Lincoln Road Mall where young Ramon Mestré cavorted still was new and vibrant in 1961. Ramon, then not yet eight years old, had just arrived in Miami Beach with his mother and four siblings from Havana, part of the relatively small vanguard of Cubans that came to Miami Beach via regularly scheduled flights but which would swell in 1980 with the Mariel Boatlift. His father was a political prisoner who would spent 19 years in Castro's jails, emerging finally in 1979.[8] The family, like most Cuban exiles arriving in Miami Beach in the early 1960s, was not without means. For the Mestres, their help came from Ramon's grandfather. While the family was not wealthy any more, it got along. With no direct support from the imprisoned father, the dollars were watched closely. Ramon's mother, born in Cuba of Mexican and American parents, was an American citizen. When Ramon arrived, he was fearful of what reaction Americans would have toward Cubans. He came from an environment overseen by a nanny, but in America, he had no nanny. He did not find the physical environment of Miami Beach any different than that of Havana. As a child, he was just as rambunctious and mischievous as the other kids. Mestre was in the forefront of a growing cadre of exile youths who became overachievers. After receiving degrees in Washington and in Scotland, he went to work for Radio Marti in Washington but returned to Miami in 1989 when he became a member of the *Miami Herald*'s editorial board.[9]

The lifestyles of Cuban exiles living in Miami and those living in Miami Beach were disparate. The Cubans of Miami Beach were not as exposed to the condensed exile world of Miami. They also had more disposable income than did their fellow exiles in Miami.

For Bernardo Benes, who stepped off a plane from Havana with his wife and child in November 1960, the flight was yet another chapter of a family odyssey. In 1923, to escape the pograms aimed at Jews in Russia, his father fled to Cuba. Why Cuba? Because that's where the boat went, and Jews fleeing persecution were not fussy about where they went.[10] Besides, Cuba was right next door to the United States and that's where his father ultimately set his sights. Faced with growing communism in Cuba, the Benes family fled to the United States. Bernardo and his wife had vacationed often in Miami Beach when he took time off from his profession as a lawyer in Havana. He also was of legal counsel to the Treasury Department of Cuba. When he realized that he had to take his wife and 18-months-old son out of Cuba, it was an easy decision to choose the familiar Miami Beach.

Experienced in financial affairs, Benes landed a job as an auditor of tellers at Washington Federal Savings and Loan on Washington Avenue. His salary in 1960 was $65 a week. The exiled family, which included six adults: his parents, a sister and brother–in–law, and the Benes child, crammed into a two and one-half bedroom apartment on 14th Place and Euclid Avenue for the first year, after which his parents moved to Charlotte, N. C., his sister and her

Tony Bennett, singing at the Americana Hotel's Bal Masque Room, was one of many top-flight entertainers who performed at Miami Beach. (SPA)

husband to Washington. What remained of the Miami Beach Beneses then took up living at 15th Terrace between West Avenue and Bay Road before eventually moving to a waterfront home of their own on Normandy Isle. To obtain such a home, Benes worked for 15 years at Washington Federal, while also starting up a bank of his own: Continental, the first Cuban-run bank in the U. S.[11]

A majority of the Cuban Jews fleeing in 1960, '61 and '62—it is estimated to be in the vicinity of 6,000—settled in Miami Beach for logical reasons: it already had a Jewish touch. Benes estimated that about 70 percent of the Cuban Jews settled in South Beach and the remainder in Normandy Isles. For the older Cuban Jews, assimilation was most difficult. Many of them didn't have the capacity to learn English. They seemed lost, both spiritually and culturally. To help alleviate the problem, younger Cuban Jews rented an office in the Mercantile Bank Building to serve the needs of their seniors. And for 10 years, starting in 1962, Washington Federal Savings let the Cuban Jews use their auditorium for High Holy Day services. With a rabbi who had emigrated from Cuba—a Polish-Jew who had survived the Holocaust—the growing Cuban Jewish community of Miami Beach rented space for the High Holy Days in the DiLido Hotel before finally

Bernardo Benes, who emigrated from Cuba in 1960, quickly assimilated into the Miami community. (MH)

building a synagogue of their own on 17th Street and Michigan Ave.: the Cuban Hebrew Congregation—Temple Beth Shmuel.[12]

For Benes, his was a quick assimilation into the total community. He crossed ethnic lines comfortably, started the Public Health Trust at Jackson Memorial Hospital but reached a controversial pinnacle when he began a dialogue with the Castro regime in anticipation of the release of thousands of Castro's political prisoners. Despite it being done in cooperation and compliance with the U.S. State Department, Benes came under attack, along with others of the dialogue, by more conservative elements of the Cuban exile community. Benes stayed the course and obtained the release of the prisoners in November 1978, including Ramon Mestre's father.[13]

Miami Beach that Cubans began coming to as exiles in the early '60s was going through dramatic change—not only ethnically, but in other ways. Hoteliers such as Ben Novack, Harry Mufson and Morris Lansburgh pretty much forced lifelong independent club operators such as Albert (Papa) Bouche and Lou Walters, father of TV's Barbara Walters, to either be drawn into the hotel club circuit or to retire from the game. Both men, who at times had operated classy night clubs on Palm Island and who turned the other way when gambling thrived there as well, were victims of the changing times. In 1959, at the age of 78, Bouche gave up show business. "It costs too much money to run it the way I want to—the best way," he said. I'm getting old."[14] His *forte* had been in presenting lovely women in as little clothing as possible, but acting classy. Walters, who staged similarly brilliant French revues in Miami Beach, lost his independence and drifted into putting on shows at hotels and even at Miami's Marine Stadium. "Blame it on high taxes. . . and television and the American Plan," he complained in 1965.[15]

Morris Lansburgh, who had been in the hotel business in Miami Beach since 1940, is credited, or discredited, with bringing the American Plan to Miami Beach in the 1950s. The American Plan offered a tourist many options, including breakfast and dinner in the hotel. The idea was not new, as the Borscht Belt hotels for years had plans which included as many as three meals a day. But Lansburgh, who by the '60s either owned or operated a flock of hotels, including the Sans Souci, Casablanca, Eden Roc, Sherry Frontenac and Deauville—he later was to spread his wings to the Bahamas and Las Vegas—added other twists. If he had a premiere show at the Deauville, he would include that in a package he sold guests who were staying at another of his hotels. In doing so, he made all of his hotels self-contained

Reputed mobster Meyer Lansky lived out his days in Miami Beach, dying in 1983. (MN; HASF)

as places for guests to take their meals and get their entertainment.[16]

Lansburgh's silent partner was Sam Cohen, who was linked to the notorious Meyer Lansky. Lansky never admitted to anything other than being a bootlegger. But he was suspected of being much, much more—including being a partner of Bugsy Siegel, of controlling the gambling casinos of Havana and Las Vegas—and of being the boss of South Florida crime, operating from residences he had over the years in Hollywood, Hallandale and Miami Beach. Lansky and Siegel reportedly formed the Bugs and Meyer Mob in 1921 New York, hijacking cars and guarding bootleg shipments of illegal booze for other mobsters.[17] Lansky was charged with the attempted homicide of another mobster in 1928 but when the victim did not show up to testify against him, was released. A Jew among the principally Sicilian-bred members of The Mob, he nevertheless was accepted. A raid by police on a Chicago apartment in 1932 found Lansky with Lucky Luciano, one of the most notorious racketeers in America. Hank Messick, a crime reporter with the *Miami Herald*, wrote that Lansky's headquarters were in the Singapore Hotel on 96th and Collins, north of the city limits of Miami Beach.[18] (Another version places Lansky's center of operations at the Carlsbad Motel opposite the Diplomat in Hollywood Beach. Lansky often went to the Singapore for lunch, and met many of his friends there. Business might or might not have taken place at those lunches.) An investigative report in the *Miami Herald* indirectly linked Ben Novack, his Fontainebleau Hotel, the land under it, Lansky and Minneapolis mobsters.[19] The story caused a furor at Miami Beach city hall, quoting Mayor Elliott Roosevelt—FDR's son—as saying, "The mob doesn't

run this town. The mob owns it."[20] Almost two weeks later, under siege from Miami Beach hotel and tourist interests—the quote had been picked up by *Newsweek* magazine—Roosevelt denied saying it to three *Miami Herald* reporters, while admitting that he did tell them "many former members of the underworld from Chicago, Detroit, Cleveland and New York are domiciled in the Greater Miami area." Novack sued the *Herald* for libel. More than a year later, with the case coming close to trial, the newspaper ran a two-paragraph, front page story, in which neither the words "retract" or "apologize" were used. But it said: "We are of the opinion that the Fontainebleau Hotel is not owned or controlled by any gangsters or underworld characters. Concurrently with the publication of this statement by The *Miami Herald*, the Fontainebleau Hotel Corp., owned by Mr. Novack, is dismissing its lawsuit against the *Miami Herald*."[21]

Lansky continued to have brushes with the law until his death, of lung cancer, in 1983. For a while, he lived in Israel but was forced to leave that country. He returned to South Florida. No one ever really pinned anything on Lansky, particularly in his late years when he continued to avoid trials because of his failing health. He lived the last years of his life at the Imperial House at Collins Avenue and 52nd Street. When he died, some of the law enforcement people who unsuccessfully tried to jail him over the years admitted to having a bit of respect for Lansky. "He was probably one of my more favorite hoodlums," recalled Ralph Hill, a former Miami FBI supervisor. "Of all the hoodlums, he was the only one who added a touch of personal class."[22]

In 1971, Lansburgh was indicted along with Cohen and Lansky on tax evasion charges built around a case that had them skimming profits off their Las Vegas casino. Lansburgh and Cohen were found guilty and sentenced to one year each in federal prison, in addition to fines of $20,000 each.[23] Lansky didn't come to trial, using open heart surgery and doctor's claims that he was too ill to stand trial. Lansburgh served four and one-half months. The prison term was a terrible blow to his ego. He had risen to prominence in both Miami Beach and Las Vegas, had been a founder member of Mount Sinai Hospital, and an original member of the Miami Beach Tourist Development Authority. While his American Plan and other promotions were condemned by some as being the ruination of independent businesses in Miami Beach, his package tours nevertheless brought thousands upon thousands of tourists to Miami Beach who otherwise could not afford the visit. On February 10, 1977, while talking on the telephone in his home, he collapsed and died at the age of 60. "I remember him as being one of the greatest promoters of resort travel in the world," Ted Hankoff, manager of the Eden Roc was quoted upon Lansburgh's death. "He did everything he could to promote this town. He will be remembered for his charity and friendliness—he did many good things but didn't do them publicly."[24]

It would appear that Lansburgh's American Plan did not hurt Miami Beach restaurants as deeply as it did the night clubs because many survived the years. Wolfie Cohen, who had come to Miami Beach from waiting tables in New York State's Catskill Mountains, opened a sandwich shop called "Wolfie's" at the corner of Collins Avenue and 20th Street in 1943.[25] Celebrities such as Al Jolson and Milton Berle soon discovered the place and its reputation grew quickly. Years later, Cohen sold the restaurant and, in 1954, bought "Mammy's," another sandwich-type restaurant opposite the Deauville. He wanted to call it "Mr. Momzer," a Yiddish word for "bastard," but when the Greater Miami Rabbinical Association objected, changed it to "Mr. Mazik," another Yiddish word meaning a malicious child.[26] Because of the intermingling of both "momser" and "mazik" in daily Yiddish expressionism, the rabbis again objected. Cohen tried again by naming the restaurant for a popular cartoon character, Mr. Pumpernickel.[27] He called the restaurant "Pumpernik's" and ran into no further difficulties with the rabbis. The first of several "Pumpernik's" restaurants in the South Florida area, it was the site of some of the earliest Larry King radio interview broadcasts.[28] Under different ownership, "Wolfie's" original sandwich shop on Collins Avenue remains a Miami Beach landmark.

Restaurants appealing to upscale diners pretty much held their ground until Lansburgh made his move with the American Plan. Several of these were in the immediate vicinity of "Wolfie's". They were Chandlers, the Park Avenue, and the Embers. Picciolo's on South Beach was a favorite as was Parham's on 73rd and Collins and Curry's a block away. Pickin' Chicken at 22nd and Collins was a favorite of families with young children. Joe's Stone Crab and Gatti's continued as Miami Beach eatery landmarks. And, irony of ironies, Carl Fisher's first Miami Beach house, built in the 1914 at the foot of Lincoln Road, became Ed Mendelsohn's kosher Lincoln Manor Restaurant in 1949[29], and later the first Hebrew Academy before it fell under the wrecker's ball in 1961, first for a parking lot and later for an apartment house.[30]

Not only did the new hotels cut into the night club and restaurant trade, but by opening shops inside the hotels, they hurt the retail business. Lincoln Road, once a jewel of stylish shops, was feeling the impact. To counter the slipping business, the merchants of Lincoln Road banded together in the late 1950s and convinced the City of Miami Beach to float a half-million dollar bond issue—guaranteed by the shop owners—to re-do Lincoln Road into a pedestrian mall. Morris Lapidus was commissioned to create its layout. He designed an island of pink sidewalks, with archways, fountains, walkways and display units in a setting of hundreds of trees, shrubs and flowers.[31] But automobiles were out; they were no longer to cruise Lincoln Road, although they were able to cross it. Proponents of the mall envisioned the long promenade filled with affluent shoppers, returning Lincoln Road to its past glory. The few first-class stores that were still there during the switchover in 1960, including the much-coveted Saks Fifth Avenue left in the ensuing years. The

Wreckers dismantle Carl Fisher's first Miami Beach home, at the foot of Lincoln Road on the ocean. In its last years, the building was used as a kosher restaurant and a Jewish school. (MB)

Before Lincoln Road was turned into a pedestrian mall in 1960, automobile traffic was allowed to drive up and down the famed street. (HASF)

Once Miami Beach's grandest hotel, the Roney Plaza was razed in 1968, replaced by an apartment house of the same name. (MN)

pedestrian mall has had perhaps the most controversial life of any project in Miami Beach.

After years in the deep doldrums, Lincoln Road, inspired by the snowballing Art Deco movement, made a comeback. Where smart shops once existed, sidewalk restaurants and art galleries now function. However, it is rare that a year passes without a new plan for Lincoln Road, many calling for the restoration of automobile traffic on the street. In mid-1994, plans were being considered for a major renovation of the mall, including landscaping, repaving, and a new theater and shopping complex— and still no autos.[32]

"Transformation" is a prevailing word in the Miami Beach lexicon. The icons of early Miami Beach have come down, replaced by the new: Not necessarily better, but new. N. B. T. Roney's magnificent hotel and Smith's Casino were demolished for apartment houses; even Joe's Stone Crab knocked down the Weiss family's original house for parking space alongside the newer restaurant and living quarters. Like targets in a shooting gallery, early hotels such as the Flamingo, Fleetwood, Pancoast, Whitman-Robert Richter were knocked off in the name of progress. Almost miraculously,

(because the Art Deco movement had not yet begun), the small hotels of Ocean Drive remained relatively intact, awaiting their Renaissance.

Fisher's Nautilus had a gradual, if not distinguished, phasing out. In 1949, a group led by Max Orovitz[33] and organized as the Mount Sinai Hospital of Greater Miami, Inc., purchased the Nautilus from the City of Miami Beach.[34] The group bought the 55-bed Alton Road Hospital in South Beach in 1947 but longed for a major Jewish hospital. With the formerly restricted Nautilus in their hands, they proceeded to convert it from a hotel to a hospital. On December 4, 1949, Mount Sinai Hospital opened with 258 beds. The plan was to take down the old Nautilus one day and replace it with a modern building, or buildings. With the Nautilus still standing and functioning, construction began on a 417-bed adjacent building in 1957. It was completed in December 1959. In 1968, as Mount Sinai continued to grow as a major state-of-the-art hospital with new buildings and pavilions in other areas of the property, including bay bottom filled in by Carl Fisher, the Nautilus was torn down to make room for still more additions to the medical center.[35]

The signature of Carl Fisher was quickly disappearing. The golf course he had built immediately north of Lincoln Road changed into a civic complex that included parking facilities, an auditorium designed by Lapidus, the convention center and, eventually, a new city hall. The auditorium, transformed several times to become the Jackie Gleason Theater of Performing Arts, had its first fame as the site of boxing matches every Tuesday night. Under the auspices of veteran fight promoter Chris Dundee, boxing became a major attraction in Miami Beach. Along with his brother Angelo, who eventually was to train 11 world boxing champions including Cassius Clay/Muhammad Ali, Dundee created the Fifth Street Gym on a floor above a drug store and lunch counter at the corner of Washington Avenue and Fifth Street. It became a mecca for fighters in training, highlighted by young Cassius Clay. The Convention Center, far smaller than it is today, hosted a bevy of championship fights in the 1960s as Miami Beach was at the height of its glory as a center for boxing matches. It also hosted Miami's first professional basketball team: the American Basketball Association's Miami Floridians had a lifespan from 1968 to 1972.

But the dominant change of Miami Beach in the 1960s was in its demographics. The pungent fragrance of stuffed cabbage cooking on the stove was giving way to that of *arroz con pollo*. It would not be long before a second wave of Cubans came to Miami Beach, in greater numbers and with a reputation entirely different than that of the first wave.

CHAPTER TWENTY-ONE

"AND AWAY WE GO…"

Jackie Gleason brought his popular CBS television program to Miami Beach in 1964. (MN)

Mark 1964 as a momentous year for Miami Beach. Were they still alive, Carl Fisher and Steve Hannagan would have been ecstatic. In a period of about 10 days, three events brought to Miami Beach a wave of high visibility publicity in the fields of sports and entertainment. First, the Beatles flew in to do the Ed Sullivan television show at the Deauville Hotel, prompting mobs of excited teenagers in the streets and a media print riot that included a bevy of British journalists experiencing Miami Beach for the first time. Just two days later, Jackie Gleason and CBS announced that Gleason's television show was moving to Miami Beach and that Gleason would become a resident of Miami. Unlike Godfrey's occasional broadcasts, the Gleason show was to be weekly and permanent. This was followed by the Cassius Clay/Muhammad Ali victory over heavyweight champion Sonny Liston that brought Miami Beach datelines to newspapers all over the world.

When the Beatles arrived, the excitement which gripped the area, particularly among young people and the media, was nothing short of electrifying. Crowd control became a problem. Miami Beach publicist Hank Meyer, who when informed the Beatles were coming said he didn't know who they were, quickly learned. He publicly chastised Sullivan for not better preparing the authorities for what was expected[1]—although Beatlemania seemed to be known everywhere else. "At the race track one day," recalled Meyer, "I ran into Sullivan and apologized for my public outburst. He told me to forget about it." Miami Beach Police

The Beatles came to Miami Beach in 1964 to do the Ed Sullivan Show at the Deauville Hotel. (MH)

Chief Rocky Pomerance blamed many of the crowd problems on two radio stations that he claimed encouraged teenagers to play hooky on a schoolday to greet the Beatles. "I'm going to write the FCC about the way WQAM and WFUN stirred up those kids," complained Pomerance.[2] There is no evidence that he did. For all the griping by authorities, the Beatles' visit to Miami Beach was worth millions of dollars in free publicity to the tourist-oriented city. When the Beatles flew into Miami's International Airport on February 13, about 7,000 teenagers—mostly girls, according to the *Miami Herald*—packed the terminal and observation decks to catch a glimpse of the singing group. It was them against 127 Dade County cops. The kids won. "Outshrieking a jet, Miami teenagers smashed a plate glass door, broke 21 jalousies and tore up 12 chairs at the airport to greet England's cultural gift to America, the Beatles," wrote *Miami Herald* reporter Gene Miller.[3] Two limousines accompanied by a motorcycle escort took

John, Ringo, Paul and George to the Deauville Hotel. But they did not hide in their hotel rooms during their stay. The singers with the then-unusual moptop haircuts went nightclubbing, visited the trendy Peppermint Lounge, then up to Sunny Isles and the Castaways Motel's Wreck Bar. They also went yachting, speedboating and fishing.[4]

At the same time the Beatles were making headlines from Miami Beach, so was a young, boastful boxer who was soon to became a controversial national figure. Cassius Clay was in training at Miami Beach's Fifth Street Gym for his upcoming bout with Liston when all four Beatles—accompanied by a horde of reporters from Britain and the U.S.—paid him a visit. Clay, as good a showman as the Beatles, upstaged them from the beginning by arriving 18 minutes late. "Let's get out of here," seethed Beatle Paul McCartney during the wait. Realizing the publicity value of the moment, they chose to stay. When Clay finally arrived, he proclaimed that he was a Beatle, then lifted Ringo Starr into the air. "Yeah, Yeah, Yeah," harmonized the Beatles, using their trademark chant as they faked a menacing move toward the boxer. "No! No! No!" responded Clay pretending fear.[5] The Beatles climbed into the ring and promptly dropped to the canvas—feigning knockouts—in front of Clay as flashbulbs popped, publicists grinned and legitimate newsmen grimaced.

The insanity that surrounded the Beatles followed them right into the Napoleon Room of the Deauville for the live telecast of the Sullivan show. An estimated 1,000 persons holding tickets to the telecast—4,000 were distributed—could not get into the room although hotel publicist Gene Hogan said there were still 200 empty seats when the doors were closed five minutes before airtime.[6] Hank Meyer took the blame for the mess, saying his office and the hotel were in complete charge of ticket distribution.[7] Reporters observed that there were more older people in the audience than there were teenagers. About 4,000 youngsters had attended a dress rehearsal during the afternoon and police and ushers said the youngsters behaved better than did the adults at night. A Boston woman fainted on the way in to the telecast. When she recovered, she told reporters: "You don't know what's going on out there. You'd think it was life or death."[8]

The Beatles were supposed to be in Miami Beach for 84 hours but, on the day after the telecast, their road manager called the Miami Beach detective assigned to their security to tell him that the boys loved Miami Beach and wanted to stay the rest of the week.[9] Detective Jack Dresner called his boss, Chief Pomerance with the news and Rocky extended Dresner's assignment as security overseer for the Beatles. In the remaining days, the Beatles kept popping up for photo opportunities, thereby providing Miami Beach even more international publicity.

Clay competed for the photographers' and reporters' attention. An Olympic boxing gold medal winner from Louisville, Kentucky, Clay was sent to Miami by the group of investors—known as the Louisville Sponsoring Group—to train under Angelo Dundee, the brother of boxing promoter Chris Dundee. Angelo had a great reputation, especially one for being patient—not trying to hurry a fighter along too soon. He also was seen as a settling influence on the youngster who was given to

outbursts of energy—particularly verbal—that, at times, could not be harnessed. In 1960, young Clay arrived in still-segregated Miami and was put up in a hotel room at the Mary Elizabeth Hotel in the then-called "colored section" of Miami known as Overtown. His training, however, took place at the Fifth Street Gym, which was quickly becoming known as a mecca for top-flight boxers. Clay, as he still was known then, became an instant celebrity. He certainly helped things along with his antics, which included shouting matches, writing poetry and making wild predictions. By the time he signed to fight Liston in Miami Beach for the heavyweight championship, Clay had 19 professional fights—all victories—of which five had taken place in Miami Beach.

Unknown to most at the time, Clay became influenced by the Nation of Islam. First interested in the Muslim faith in 1961, Clay attended an assembly

As Cassius Clay, the future boxing great trained at Miami Beach's Fifth Street gym. He took the name Muhammed Ali shortly before his 1964 heavyweight championship fight at Miami Beach with Sonny Liston. (MMC)

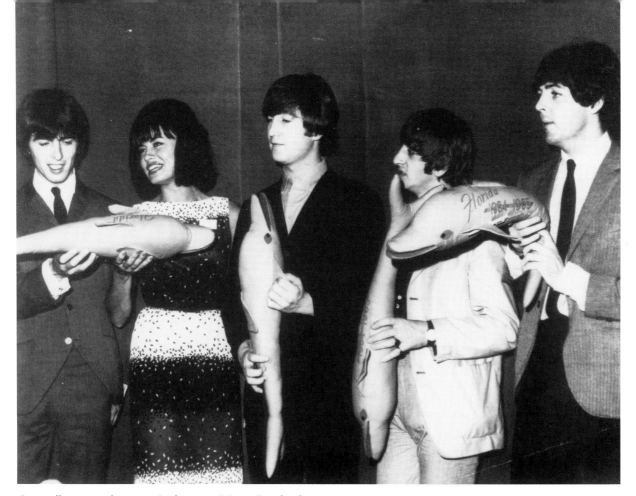

Originally expected to stay 84 hours in Miami Beach, the Beatles expanded their visit to a full week, acting much the part of tourists. (MN)

in Miami's Moslem mosque. As the time neared for the Liston fight, Clay already had become a member of the Nation of Islam, whose leader, Elijah Muhammed, bestowed a new name on the young man: Muhammed Ali, which means "worthy of respect and beloved of Allah."[10] On the eve of the fight, *Miami Herald* sports editor Edwin Pope wrote that Cassius Clay had become a Black Muslim, seen by whites as a menacing sect. Before this, Clay was more popular than the heavyweight champion. Liston was a surly sort, menacing, in with the wrong company. Clay was flighty, funny, a kid. Now things changed. The backer of the fight, Bill McDonald, threatened to cancel it. Among those concerned was Ferdie Pacheco, who had become Clay's doctor and a part of the corner team. Pacheco had an office in Overtown and a love for boxing. He stayed with the fighter most of his career. "Cassius Clay had worked so hard to get this chance at the title," wrote Pacheco years later, "yet he was prepared to risk it all for his religion. Clay was on the bus, ready to go home, when word came that the fight would go on. The world was about to see a fighter named Muhammad Ali."[11]

Clay/Ali was given little chance to wrest the title from the more experienced Liston; the odds

against him were 6-1. Liston was unable to answer the bell for the seventh round. The dancing, jabbing, cajoling challenger, despite near-blinded eyes, stung him too often in too many places. When the referee raised Muhammad Ali's arm as the new heavyweight champion, the former Cassius Clay climbed on the ring ropes and shouted continuously: "I told you—I am the greatest." [12] As if this wasn't sensational news enough emanating from the hordes of reporters and columnists in the Miami Beach Convention Hall that night, Ali's conversion and his outspoken tenacity about his relatively new religion and the transgressions he said whites had committed upon blacks were enough to keep the Miami Beach dateline on the front pages of newspapers for days to come.

Amid the flood of coverage about the Beatles in Miami Beach and while publicity still was building for the Clay-Liston bout a week later, long-standing rumors were settled when television star Jackie Gleason announced he was moving his New York-based show to Miami Beach. How much more good publicity could the city stand—and all in such a condensed period of time? Weekly TV series originated only from New York and Los Angeles prior to the time the Gleason show began broadcasting from Miami Beach.[13] Meyer may not have known the Beatles until they came to Miami Beach but he was quite aware of Gleason, a longtime entertainer and popular TV star. He read one day in Earl Wilson's syndicated column that Gleason had tired of the New York winters. Meyer called Wilson, got Gleason's home number and offered the year-round summer of Miami Beach, where Jackie could play golf and do his TV shows.[14] This got Gleason's attention. He sent people down to look over the situation and later called Hank to say that it was a great idea. There were conditions, however. Gleason required a first-rate TV origination studio and that would take money. He needed a stage, rehearsal, and absolutely cold air conditioning. Everything he said he needed, recalled Meyer, he said in a jocular tone. There also would have to be between $300,000 and $400,000 expended for new cameras. He called Mitchell Wolfson, who was chairman of Wometco Enterprises, parent company of Miami's CBS affiliate WTVJ, and explained the situation. "Wolfson said that in order to expend such money, there needed to be an assurance that the Gleason program would continue to originate from Miami Beach for several years," said Meyer.[15] Gleason spoke with CBS about it, Wolfson agreed to fund part of the needs and hoped CBS would come up with some as well. At first, CBS resisted. Ultimately, the network came around. "Give him what he wants," CBS boss William S. Paley said.[16] Gleason's career with CBS had its ups and downs. His *Honeymooner* series hit the jackpot but its popularly declined several years later. Then he rebounded with *Jackie Gleason and His American Scene Magazine*. With Meyer providing the charm and aggressiveness, the City of Miami Beach, Gleason and CBS officials met. Miami Beach approved $250,000 for the installation of technical facilities in the 3,500-seat Miami Beach Auditorium to bring it up to network studio standards.[17] While Gleason's staff wanted three days a week of exclusive use of the auditorium, the city bargained them to two, leaving room for other attractions to be booked. It was agreed to do all of the 38 projected Gleason shows for the 1964–65 season in videotape because of the high cost of live transmission. Meyer, at the apex of whatever mountains public relations people climb, called enticing the Gleason show "of tremendous importance, promotionally, to this area." W. J. Weatherby wondered aloud in his biography of Jackie: "What made Jackie Gleason decide on such a change of life—to uproot himself and his team from the New York where he had grown up, made his name, and found such favorite refuges as Toots Shor's?"[18] Was

Gleason more interested in golf than in his career, he asked. In attempting to answer his own questions, Weatherby surmised that Gleason, a superstitious man, had always listened to his instincts and that his instincts now were telling him to begin a new phase of his life. The days of Ralph Kramden and the *Honeymooners* were in the past. His Hollywood career, he thought, was limited. He wanted something new, something more relaxed than the chaos of New York. Some said he also wanted to be in a state that had easier divorce laws than did New York City. His marriage to Genevieve Halford was long-dead; they separated in 1954. Gleason was spending his time with Honey Merrill, his executive secretary since 1956. Jackie wanted to divorce Genevieve and marry Honey but the New York divorce laws were not going to be kind to Jackie. Becoming a citizen of Florida would put him under the jurisdiction of a gentler divorce law.[19] Gleason's good friend, restaurateur Toots Shor boldly predicted "That bum will be back in a week. He'll never stand Florida for long. Too sunny, too sleepy."[20] Toots was wrong. Florida would be Gleason's home for the next 25 years.

On Saturday nights, beginning in September 1964, Jackie's show would open with a fast moving scene across the waters of Biscayne Bay toward the

Jackie Gleason hams it up with publicist Hank Meyer, the man who brought the television star and his troupe to Miami Beach. (MN)

hotel-filled skyline of Miami Beach, with a voice-over proclaiming that the show was coming "from the sun and fun capital of the world, Miami Beach!" Along with Jackie Gleason came high living, publicity stunts and booze by the barrel. Jackie made the trip to Florida on a chartered train. Gleason's trademark expressions "And awaaaay we go!" and "How sweet it is!" were piped through bullhorns on the trip. Traveling with him were 97 passengers, including 40 columnists and other journalists and a Dixieland band. There were six bars for a 36-hour binge that cost CBS $250,000.[21] Mayor Melvin Richard, who was part of the negotiating team, welcomed Gleason much as Carl Fisher had welcomed president-elect Harding in 1920. But as mayor of a city that now boasted a major television program, Richard said his government lifestyle changed. In crediting Gleason with doing a lot for Miami Beach, Richard said that, as mayor, "I had a big black limousine with an armed chauffeur. I entertained royalty and presidents and kings. Everybody came to Miami Beach."[22]

While his show came from Miami Beach, Jackie had a $100,000 home built for himself alongside a golf course in Miami. In time, he moved to a $2 million house in neighboring Broward County's Inverrary, also on a golf course. He played regularly— at golf and other things. He remarried, divorced and remarried again. His show, which debuted from Miami Beach on September 26, 1964, stayed in the top 25 for seven years. No relationship between a public body, especially one as mercurial as Miami Beach's Tourist Development Authority, and a person with a large ego such as Jackie Gleason had, can stay smooth in perpetuity. A rift developed when the TDA decided to stop funding $15,000 weekly to the Gleason show, purportedly because the show was on a downslide. When Lou Price, executive director of Miami's tourist bureau, heard of it, he offered Gleason $25,000 a show to relocate to the other side of the bay.[23] Gleason moved to a reconditioned,

classic, 1926-built downtown movie theater, the Olympia, renamed the Maurice Gusman Theater of Performing Arts. Instead of the former introduction of racing over the water to Miami Beach while the announcer called Miami Beach "the fun and sun capital of the world," the Gleason show now opened with Jackie singing "Moon Over Miami." But the truth of the matter was that the Gleason show was beginning to slip. CBS cancelled it in 1970, but Gleason continued to live in and praise South Florida. The career which he feared was not in his future, was very much so. Periodically, Jackie would travel to California or to locations elsewhere to appear in motion pictures. He is credited with six motion pictures after the cancellation of his TV show, including the *Smokey and the Bandit* series of three. He also appeared in a Broadway show, *The Sly Fox*, and continued as a constant on television with reruns of his *Honeymooners* series. There can be no value placed on the positive publicity Gleason generated for Miami Beach, Miami and other South Florida locations. When he was on his deathbed in 1987, Gleason requested that he be buried in Miami Beach.[24] Not even founder Carl Fisher was buried in Miami Beach. It was considered bad business to have a graveyard in "the sun and fun capital of the world." Jackie died at the age of 71 of liver and lung cancer. He was buried at Our Lady of Mercy Cemetery in Miami. As a token replacement for his original wish for a burial site, the City of Miami Beach renamed the auditorium from which Gleason's Miami Beach shows originated in his honor. It now is known as the Jackie Gleason Theater of Performing Arts. In unanimously approving this change, the Miami Beach City Commission, for once in its tumultuous existence, spoke as one: "Jackie Gleason, who spent a lifetime making people laugh, and who did so much to publicize our city to the world, will always be remembered here, as a larger-than-life talent, who graced us with his magnificent presence."[25]

CHAPTER TWENTY-TWO

"DOUBLE, DOUBLE TOIL AND TROUBLE"

—*Macbeth, IV*

Curiosity-seekers circle around peaceful protesters outside Convention Hall during the 1972 Democratic National Convention. (MN)

One of the reasons given why the Republicans chose Miami Beach for their August 1968 national presidential nominating convention was that, because it was an island, there was a greater opportunity for crowd control—especially as it regarded Vietnam war protesters.[1] The assassinations of Martin Luther King in April and Bobby Kennedy in June also added concern for the safety of public figures. Security guards, working under the Secret Service, inspected bags and briefcases of spectators and journalists entering the Convention Hall. Reporters complained of sometimes having to go through no fewer than five checkpoints. Military helicopters flew above Collins Avenue when leading candidates left their hotels. Armed guards were posted atop some buildings and a few women reported that special police looked into their bags when they entered Burdines department store several blocks from the Convention Hall.[2]

It was at that time that the legend of Police Chief Rocky Pomerance was born. A burly, gregarious 300-pounder, Rocky let it be known that he had a plan if any groups of protesters began marching on Miami Beach. Since all but two of the bridges leading to Miami Beach were drawbridges,[3] he said he would raise those drawbridges to seal off the island. There were other reports of what Pomerance planned. One was that any protesters who became unruly would be put on a bus, driven out to Andytown, on the bug-infested edges of the

Police Chief Rocky Pomerance let leak some plans he said he had for protesters at the conventions but later admitted most were psychological plays. (HASF)

Everglades and let out, thus effectively removing them from the site of the convention. "Actually that was kind of a psychological ploy, it was not a plan at all," Pomerance admitted years later. "In modern American society, how are you going to say you can go to that city for the political convention and you, fella, you can't?"[4] As it turned out, Rocky's ploys weren't needed in 1968. But to the west of Miami Beach, six miles away, racial violence broke out the night of August 7.[5] The violence had little or nothing to do with the nominations of Richard Nixon and Spiro Agnew as the Republican ticket. While basketball star Wilt Chamberlain was running the hospitality suite at the Plaza Hilton Hotel on Collins Avenue and promoting Nixon, other blacks across the bay were rioting over what was sometimes claimed as having been started by a police confrontation, other times called an argument gone nasty between a black resident and a newsman. Rioting resumed the next day. Three blacks died by gunfire in the Liberty City section, part of which is in the City of Miami and part in unincorporated Dade County. Clearly, with such a crowd of newsmen in town for the Republican National Convention, the events taking place in Miami nearly overshadowed the convention. The few protesters at the Convention Hall area went practically unnoticed as attention was diverted to the racial unrest. Florida's Republican

governor, Claude Kirk, supposed to bask in the glory of having his party's national convention in his state, ended up in Liberty City, making appeals for peace. Civil rights leader Rev. Ralph Abernathy, who had come to Miami Beach in an attempt to influence a liberal civil rights agenda on the GOP platform for 1968, joined Kirk there.[6]

The Democratic National Convention that followed several weeks later in Chicago became a model for violent confrontation between protesters and the police. It set the stage for encounters at the 1972 political conventions, both of which were held in Miami Beach. In 1968 Chicago, demonstrators were met with brute force on the orders of Mayor Richard J. Daley. Police charged into Lincoln Park where the demonstrators were camped and forced them out with tear gas and night sticks. For the remaining four days of the convention, the confrontations between demonstrators, police and National Guard troops were awesome in their ferocity. Television cameras recorded dozens of scenes of police clubbing demonstrators.[7] With the experience of Chicago 1968, Miami Beach hoped to avoid a similar confrontation in 1972. The Democrats were hoping to field a candidate to unseat Nixon. George McGovern, through primaries and a frenetic delegate seating battle, emerged as a shoo-in for the nomination, thereby setting up an election confrontation between Nixon the conservative and McGovern the liberal. Despite McGovern's very public posture opposed to U. S. participation in the Vietnam War, anti-war demonstrators continued to dramatize their position both outside and inside the Convention Hall. On the third day of the convention, demonstrators built a 60-foot "dike" in front of the Convention Hall. Using sand and dirt, they created a wall to look like the dikes on the Tonkin Plain in Vietnam, where they said bombs by the U.S. could kill millions. In addition to that, a group of Vietnam Veterans Against the War obtained tickets to enter the hall during prime time, claiming they received the passes from McGovern's camp. At the Doral Beach Hotel, which was McGovern's headquarters, more than 200 protesters filled the lobby for six hours. McGovern spoke with the demonstrators.[8] When the convention ended on the night of the 13th, it was judged to have been considerably peaceful compared to what had happened in Chicago. With 3,000 National Guardsmen and 2,500 Army and Marine Corps troops deployed for hostile action that never occurred, they closed down their camps and returned to their home bases. Many so-called non-delegates who had camped out in Miami Beach's Flamingo Park prepared to pack up and leave as well. Die-hard Zippies, however, held a late demonstration in front of Convention Hall, burning a 4 x 8 feet picture of Lyndon Johnson and performing an "Eat the Rich" guerrilla theater.[9] Overall, despite fears for the worst, the convention was relatively peaceful—outside the Convention Hall. Inside, as in so many Democratic conventions, the delegates ate each other for lunch.

In August, however, what was feared came to pass. The Republican Convention drew a diverse group of protesters—from Yippies and Zippies to Nazis and KKK members. If ever there was bedlam this was it. It was only a matter of time before things turned violent. On the night of August 20, about 500 protesters—allegedly led by Students for a Democratic Society (SDS) youths—charged a $500-a-plate Republican dinner at the Fontainebleau Hotel. Earlier in the day, 22 American Nazis crashed an anti-war protest in Flamingo Park. The battle lasted 15 minutes with seven Nazis and two CBS cameramen being injured. The Vietnam Veterans Against the War intervened against the Nazis and destroyed a collection of arms before turning the owner over to police. Even Jane Fonda got into the act, arriving at Flamingo Park to join anti-war demonstrators. An estimated 250 Yippies and Zippies showed up at the Convention Hall to take part in mass urination performance.[10] The following night, things were a little calmer, dampened by intermittent but heavy rain showers. Nevertheless, a confrontation developed between thousands of anti-war demonstrators and thousands of Cubans marching against communism. Despite well-laid plans and heavy security, the two sides could not be restrained.

For a short while, the two factions went about chasing each other through the streets.[11] Things escalated. On the night of August 22, anti-war protesters shattered windows, burned an American flag, jostled delegates and dented automobiles in front of the Convention Hall; 212 were arrested. "We decided to make arrests when they began to assault delegates and citizens who were entering the hall," Chief Pomerance said.[12] Throughout Miami Beach, flareups were reported, as well as in the vicinity of Nixon's Key Biscayne vacation home. From Flamingo Park, a march that included groups ranging from the Vietnam Veterans Against the War to the Gay Liberation Front, headed toward the Convention Hall. An estimated 200 painted their faces ashen white while others wore Nixon masks smeared with blood-red paint. A small group of protesters-turned-vandals kicked in the window of the Gayety Theater on Collins Avenue and 21st Street.[13]

Events reached a violent peak on the night of August 24 when many among the 3,000 protesters slashed the tires on buses and accosted delegates trying to enter the Convention Hall. Police arrested more than 800 during the night, which saw law enforcement people showering tear gas into the crowds and clubbing people in the streets.[14] (In later years, Miami Beach police officials became enraged when a motion picture portrayed the city's policemen as having done the clubbing. They denied it emphatically, pointing out that there were many other uniformed agencies working the mobs of protesters.) *Miami News* photographer John Peelle

Zippies cavort in the lobby of the Doral Beach Hotel during the 1972 Democratic National Convention. Nominee George McGovern used that hotel as his headquarters. (MN; HASF)

was clubbed in the head while he photographed a police sweep on August 22. He claimed his assailant was a Florida Highway Patrol officer. A subsequent investigation by the FHP resulted in them clearing themselves. Pomerance, taken aback by the very violent turn of events, said, "I cannot understand why these people who are for peace in Vietnam are not for peace in Miami Beach."[15] At least 33 persons were injured enough to seek hospital treatment after the street fighting, while an estimated 100 others had their wounds treated at mobile stations. The tear gas took its toll as well, going so far as to seep into the Convention Hall to sear the eyes of delegates in their seats and many of the hundreds of media people in the press areas. During the hours of combat, about 2,000 lawmen saw action. The 5,500 Marines, paratroopers and National Guard troops, in reserve at stations away from Miami Beach, stayed away.[16]

Nevertheless, scenes of Miami Beach street violence filled the pages of the nation's newspapers and the screens of television sets much as the violence of Chicago had in 1968. It wasn't what Pomerance wanted. He insisted that something outside his purview had gone awry but never really found someone else upon whom to fix the blame—if there was any blame to be fixed. Throughout the turbulent events of August 1968, Rocky continued to enjoy a good reputation among delegates and protesters as well, so much so that he became a private security consultant at subsequent political conventions. The protesters respected him because he met with them. If there can be anything humorous about the 1972 GOP situation, it was a story that Pomerance told years later, on the eve of the 1988 Democratic Convention in Atlanta, where he again handled security. Pomerance revealed that during a meeting with anti-war, absurd-theater potentates Jerry Rubin and Abbie Hoffman during the 1972 GOP convention, they threatened to lead 10,000 naked protesters in a march down Collins Avenue, then on to the convention site. Pomerance said he turned to Rubin and responded, "If you can get 10,000 people to walk naked down the asphalt on a hot [August] day, I'll lead the parade. And wait until you see what I use for a baton."[17]

The march never took place.

Cuban-Americans voice their feelings outside the 1972 Republican National Convention. They later got into a confrontation with anti-war protesters. Former Cuban president Carlos Prío Socarrás is in the left foreground. (MH)

CHAPTER TWENTY-THREE

TO BE ELECTED, JUST TELL THEM WHERE YOU WERE BAR MITZVAH'D

Miami Beach's elderly population became a strong political force. (MH)

harles Whited, a highly-respected columnist for the *Miami Herald*, wrote in 1983 that Miami Beach politics was "no place for the squeamish, the thin-skinned or the seeker of longevity in public office, especially the mayor's job. Nowhere. . . is there a more contentious and fickle electorate than in this seven-mile long city of 96,000 people, most of them older than 65."[1] His counter-part, Jack Roberts of the *Miami News*, offered his opinion of Miami Beach politics four years earlier: "When I joined this paper many years ago, the city editor punished young reporters by making them cover Miami Beach City Commission meetings. It was something like joining the French Foreign Legion for the day. When you kissed your wife goodbye early in the morning, you didn't know when you would see her again. It was nothing for a meeting to last 12 hours while citizens berated each other, the commissioners, and City Manager Claude Renshaw, who never answered criticism."[2] Scott Ross, a former political consultant to Beach campaigns said, "In Miami Beach, they don't sling mud, they sling nuclear weapons. They don't play to win. They play to kill and maim."[3]

Since the end of World War II, Miami Beach politics—and its activist constituency—has been viewed with alarm and disgust, with amusement and ridicule, with shock and scorn. Is it all deserved, is

Miami Beach unique? Or is it more likely that Miami Beach politics is just like any other city's, but that it plays out as a different style of theater: the difference, say, between Ziegfeld's Follies and Yiddish vaudeville? As usual, the truth lies somewhere in between. When Carl Fisher and his associates were running Miami Beach, there did not seem to be the kind of antics that followed his reign. While there were occasional spurts of independence, Fisher and his people seemed quite in control. There was no sort of spitball war between the constituents and the politicians, as there was following World War II. The *Florida Municipal Record*, in its November 1946 issue, cited the Miami Beach City Council as being harmonious, competent, capable and conscientious. How, then, did the nastiness get started? There can be two explanations. The first has to do with the arrival of cannibalistic campaigning, a style not unique to Miami Beach but a style that nevertheless was somewhat alien to early local politicians. The second symptom was the continuing arrival of senior citizens to Miami Beach. They were retired, had time on their hands and an urge to dip into provincial tiffs that grew out of proportion to a point where council meetings degenerated to the citizens laying siege to the politicians. Lurking in the background were suspicions of dishonesty at the highest levels, of the purchasing of zoning changes and other forms of graft. Yet, it was not until the 1990s and the term of Mayor Alex Daoud that a Miami Beach politician actually was indicted and convicted.

When did this now-chronic melee start? If it cannot be located earlier, it at least can be traced to the 1949 city council race in which 21 candidates sought five council seats. In elections then, the five highest vote-getters were elected; there was no head-to-head competition. The mayor's chair was awarded to the person with the highest number of votes. A candidate who often used an alias and who was on the payroll of the Island Club, a gambling casino operated by the S & G Syndicate, targeted incumbent councilman Herbert Frink, a former mayor.[4] Frink was running for another term on the city council when Meyer Golub, who also went by the name of Mike Faust, accused Frink of being a past member of the Ku Klux Klan. In a community that had become predominately Jewish, this was a formidable charge. Frink denied the claim and demanded Faust/Golub produce evidence. A citizen's committee—which included Rabbi Irving Lehrman—looked into the accusation, tried unsuccessfully to get Faust/Golub to document his claim and eventually determined the charges were not supported.[5] Frink purchased an advertisement in the *Miami Beach Sun* headlined: ". . . Please, Help Me Clear My Name!"[6], and filed a $100,000 slander suit against his accuser.[7]

On the eve of the election, Frink had Faust/Golub arrested on a criminal libel charge.[8] Once the mud is flung, however, it often sticks to its target. It happened to Frink. He finished seventh in the total vote and lost his seat on the city council. Faust/Golub finished farther down. In that race, newcomer reformer Melvin Richard was elected and Harold Turk, the high vote-getter, was chosen mayor.

Gerald Schwartz is a campaign architect with a long—and sometimes controversial—history in Miami Beach. His first campaign was an unsuccesful one for Harold Shapiro in 1951. Two years later, he represented Shapiro again. Schwartz rented three rowboats, put Shapiro signs on them, and anchored them along the MacArthur Causeway. He called them "Shapiro's Navy." Several days before the election, Schwartz paid the owners to sink the boats during the night. Then he went to the newspapers and claimed his candidate had been victimized.[9] Schwartz said he didn't think he did anything unethical: "Sinking your own navy isn't a dirty trick. That's just cute."[10]

Shapiro collected enough votes to lead the pack and become mayor. That same campaign was noted for another political caper, this one involving Richard, still crusading against illegal gambling. On the eve of the 1953 election, someone pasted Richard campaign stickers on the windshields of automobiles in Normandy Isles and South Beach. The stickers were so placed as to impair a driver's line of vision. Richard, upon learning of it election morning, immediately offered a $100 reward to anyone finding the perpetrators.[11] Richard finished out of the money in the election. "This fiasco cost me more than 1,000 votes," Richard claimed the day after his loss. "They plastered the city with these things and when I tried to talk to people to explain that it was a trick pulled by my enemies, the people laughed at me. I couldn't talk to anyone. They wouldn't listen."[12]

In addition to dirty tricks, Miami Beach candidates found an illusory formula for gathering votes from the growing number of mostly-Jewish senior citizens. Beverlye Keusch Weinberger, who came onto the Miami Beach scene in the early '60s as a campaign coordinator for many politicians, says running for office came down to a script-like formula: "You told them where you were bar mitzvah'd, then told them you were going to give them help with Medicare and Social Security."[13] She recalled that when one candidate was running for Justice of the Peace in Miami Beach, he told voters he would get them more Medicare money. Although a Justice of the Peace has nothing to do with Medicare, the audience of senior citizens cheered him. He was elected. A firm voting bloc was established south of Lincoln Road among predominately Jewish, elderly

City Clerk C. W. Tomlinson (left) swears in the Miami Beach City Council in June 1943. They are: (left to right) D. Lee Powell, Val C. Cleary, Ralph C. Poole, John H. Levi and Mitchell Wolfson, who was chosen mayor. (MB)

and retired former union workers from the North. They were sufficient in numbers to effect the outcome. Miami Beach political candidates had to stand muster with the leadership of this bloc, for once they proclaimed a candidate as approved, the bloc voters fell in line. Often, candidates felt compelled to buy advertisements—and, thus, receive endorsements —in publications invented by the special interest groups just for the election, never to be seen again until the next election. In later years, individual condominiums and high-rise apartment house dwellers took to voting in blocs, depending on what it was they were seeking from a candidate. Miami Beach elections are steered by special interests: Medicare, Social Security, Israel, rent control, zoning. With each election, newspaper reporters referred to that year's campaign as "one of the most bitter in Miami Beach history." It was getting to be old hat. The 1957 "bitter campaign" evolved around incumbents Harold Shapiro and Hal Spaet being accused of being part of a financial deal on re-zoning. Another incumbent, Bernard Frank, was being accused of being on the payrolls of hotels opposing competition which other new hotels would bring.[14] Despite the rancor, all three were elected, while Kenneth Oka—who was accused of nothing—pulled in the most votes and became mayor.

The 1959 municipal election brought more than discord among the candidates. This was the election where voters had to decide whether to take automobile traffic off Lincoln Road. After a boisterous debate among supporters and detractors, the voters had their turn and approved changing Lincoln Road into a pedestrian mall by a 2-1 margin. (The wisdom of that vote was to be challenged for decades to

come.) Meanwhile restaurateur Wolfie Cohen joined the Miami Beach City Council amid a nasty campaign that even involved nationally-syndicated columnist and radio commentator Drew Pearson. Somehow, Pearson got Wolfie Cohen confused with Ben Cohen, who was representing the Teamsters Union. In his broadcast two nights before the election, Pearson endorsed crime-fighter Melvin Richard and said Cohen was tied in with the union, then held in great disrepute. Wolfie immediately blamed the Pearson broadcast on Richard, and the words flew. Both men finished with enough votes to be on the council but refused to shake hands afterwards—until coaxed to by others.[15]

Richard, finally achieved the mayor's seat in 1963 but two years later was faced with defending his post when Miami Beach changed its election pattern to one-on-one races. The new face Richard had to compete with was that of Elliott Roosevelt. The son of FDR came to Miami Beach in 1963 and went into the consulting business. But his name held great appeal, especially among the fiercely Democratic New Deal-era retired unionists living in Miami Beach. He was approached to run for the mayor's seat. Already elected as a Democratic National Committeeman, Roosevelt agreed to run for mayor.[16] Richard was in a tough spot. He had a good record and had served as a tough-spirited mayor. But running against a Roosevelt required something more. Despite having the backing of the hotel and restaurant interests, Richard had to go after Roosevelt personally. Elliott's wife, Patty, later wrote that Richard countered Roosevelt's candidacy by saying that his father may not have been president of the United States but he was a respected resident of

Miami Beach since 1924. Recalling that he did not come from a rich family, Richard said he dug ditches to lay city water pipes for 35 cents an hour. He talked about his work in bringing the Kefauver Committee to town, to breaking up the S & G Syndicate and made a point of telling voters that he had been married to the same woman for 24 years.[17] Roosevelt was on his fifth marriage.

There are stories that some voters actually thought Elliott was his father, dead since 1945. And the Roosevelt name still was magic with most Jewish people. Elliott piled up a record number of votes in defeating Richard. On the morning after Roosevelt's election, the *Miami News* wrote about a new look Roosevelt might bring to Miami Beach. "Roosevelt as mayor says he'll restore dignity and decorum to the Miami Beach City Hall—often a place where councilmen produce pastrami sandwiches and kosher dills and munch them in front of spectators."[18]

Today, that could be seen as an ethnic slur but yesterday isn't today. Roosevelt's wife also made a point of describing the pickles as kosher rather than plain dill or something else not so specific. "Fist fights have erupted in the council chambers; people hurled sandwiches and bits of Kosher pickle. On occasion, the police had to be called in to restore order," she wrote.[19] Ironically, Weinberger, who directed Roosevelt's campaign, years later said the sandwiches and pickles in the council chamber were explainable. She said agendas were heavy and that often there was no time for lunch. With Wolfie Cohen sitting on the council, he sent over to his restaurant for the sandwiches so that the council could continue its work.[20]

Roosevelt's one term as mayor was not particularly distinguished, nor was it a failure. He was in the forefront of advocating redevelopment of South Beach, although no specific plan had yet originated. He also harped on government inefficiency, but that was much like spitting into the wind. His popularity waned. And waiting to take advantage was the president of the Miami Beach Bar Association, Jay Dermer. It quickly became obvious that Roosevelt had a formidable opponent in Dermer. The young lawyer mounted a campaign that claimed "The Roosevelt name is no longer magic" and

Elliott Roosevelt was popular with Miami Beach voters, many of whom were strong supporters of his father, FDR. (MN; HASF)

Interested parties, including Hank Meyer (in striped tie) crowd Miami Beach Commission chambers during contentious rent control debates in 1949. (MH)

continued with charges that Roosevelt was a "wild man," a waster of taxpayer money.[21] Dermer forced Roosevelt into a runoff—with Richard finishing third. Timing may have played a major role then. One day before the runoff election, the Six-Day War broke out in the Middle East. Observers saw that as a bonanza for Dermer, whose wife was Israeli-born. The emotion of the day—the feeling of isolation Jews had as Israel fought for its existence—may have bonded together those people who ultimately decided that they had to have a Jew as mayor so that Miami Beach's strong support for the Jewish state would continue. (Not lost on them was that part of Dermer's campaign which charged that Roosevelt was soft on Arabs. Dermer supporters also reminded Jewish voters that it was Elliott's father who, in 1939, refused to allow the S. S. St. Louis, carrying more than 900 desperate Jewish refugees from Nazi Germany, to release its human cargo in a U.S. port, thus sending them back to Europe and, for many of them, death in the camps.[22])

The 37-year-old Dermer, backed by strong pro-Jewish feelings of the moment and political heavyweights Richard and Mal Englander, defeated Roosevelt by 2,065 votes. Roosevelt did not leave the public sector immediately. He became executive director of the Tourist Development Authority. Six months after losing to Dermer, Roosevelt suggested

that a section of South Beach be converted into a Latin Quarter and that an annual Pan-American Fiesta Week be held.[23] The idea fell upon deaf ears in Miami Beach but not across the bay in Miami, where the large Cuban exile population convinced Miami politicians to create a Latin Quarter there.[24]

In June 1951, City Clerk C.W. Tomlinson, swears in new Mayor D. Lee Powell, left, with Commissioners (left to right) Burnett Roth, William Burbridge, Harold Turk, Melvin J. Richard, Bernard Frank and Marcie Liberman. (Susan Powell)

As mayor, Dermer was a man on a mission. He wanted the city's eroded beaches restored and he wanted the public's right to use and walk those beaches—even behind major hotels—to be upheld. Dermer's continued insistence for the latter always was voted down by the council but not until the issue was aired thoroughly and publicly, thus drawing attention to the situation.

(The crusade did not end with the conclusion of Dermer's mayoralty. It continued unabated, but was led by civic activist Harry Plissner, one of a cadre of civic activists who, through lawsuits, appearances at council meetings and actually entering political campaigns, gave the members of the council gray hairs years before they were due. *Miami Herald Tropic Magazine* editor Bill Rose recalled those days in the 1970s when he was sent to cover a Miami Beach council meeting and first saw Plissner in action. "He was there for a minor item—something about some obscure bond issue," wrote Rose. "Yet, I sensed electricity in that room. And respect—the sort of respect you might have for a rattlesnake."[25] Rose recounted Plissner's wars: Going to court to stop oceanfront hotels from building past the high water mark; getting doctors placed on Miami Beach rescue vehicles; a near successful attempt to throw Florida Power and Light out of Miami Beach and begin a municipal utility . . .[26] Plissner was not alone. He was part of a long line of peoples' advocates who came to challenge the city's government.)

Attorney Ellis Rubin took a run at Dermer in the 1969 election on a platform of secession from Dade County and creation of a Miami Beach County. (This was not a new issue in Miami Beach. Secession supporters had tried unsuccessfully to get the State Legislature to cut Miami Beach away from Dade County twice previously, and would continue their effort into the '70s.[27]) Dermer countered that the argument was a front for casino gambling interests and won the election. In 1971, Dermer chose to give up his seat for a quixotic run against Congressman Claude Pepper. Before leaving city hall, however, he continued to joust—both temperately and intemperately—against the windmills of special interest that still whirled on Miami Beach.[28]

D. Lee Powell, at six-feet, four-inches tall, did his best to keep his head above the rising bog. Except for the charge by Dermer in the waning days of his mayoralty that Powell was part of an unholy alliance that catered to the hotel interests, the native Virginian completed a 29-year career as a Miami Beach councilman and mayor in 1971 with his dignity still intact.[29] In an interview in 1980, he recalled taking the mayor's chair. "The first time I was mayor was in 1951," he said. "I didn't seek the mayorship. There was a different law then. The highest man in

the commission race went in as mayor. I said 'Give me time to think it over.' But they didn't give me time. Bing, bang, I'm in as mayor. . . By the third time, I was a victim and couldn't do anything about it."[30]

Powell, a non-Jew, was in the forefront of fighting restrictive policies in Miami Beach—and elsewhere in Florida—including the "No Jews" signs that were posted. Later, he took on the Ku Klux Klan by drafting a bill that would outlaw the racist organization. Powell appeared before the Florida House and Senate Judiciary committees to argue in favor of his bill in 1951. "Next to me was the head of the KKK," recalled Powell. "We nearly got into a fist fight. I called him everything in the world."[31]

In 1971, Powell stepped down from politics, saying he wanted to spend more time with his family and his real estate business. Powell might have been in trouble during the next campaign, anyway. He lost a long battle to transfer the city's fire department to Dade County control and also had been accused by Dermer of being part of an unholy alliance and of "trying to dip into the public till" under a new pension proposal for city employees.[32] Powell termed Dermer's charges as not being worthy of comment but the pain had to be felt. He commented anyway. "The man [Dermer] with the gavel totes 200 pounds around on his carcass but he doesn't have one pound of integrity."[33] Meanwhile, the press ran with Dermer's charges. In an interview with the *Miami Herald* following a series of statements he made on the subject, Dermer expanded on his claim of an unholy alliance. He said it was "an alliance between certain special interests and the city councilmen they support financially which leads these councilmen very often to cast votes of influence rather than votes of conscience on matters of public interest."[34] Dermer was at his accusatory best. He divided the special interest groups into three categories: the owners of some of the large hotels; highrise owners and developers; and people trying to bring casino gambling to Miami Beach "under the guise of tourism." Dermer went after practically everyone in Miami Beach: Novack, Morris Lansburgh, Herb Robins, Robert Turchin, Steve Muss, Burnett Roth. . . He was particularly harsh on Powell and councilman Leonard Weinstein who he said were "tied lock, stock and barrel to the special interests."[35] Novack responded the he didn't "think there was a more irresponsible mayor in the history of Miami Beach."[36]

When Dermer unsuccessfully challenged Pepper, the Miami Beach mayoral field was left open to the popular, and wealthy, Chuck Hall. He was no political lightweight. Hall already had been mayor of Metropolitan Dade County and a Democratic primary

Miami Beach honored Hank Meyer by naming 17th Street, Hank Meyer Boulevard. (left to right) Mayor Malcolm Fromberg, Hal Hertz, Hank Meyer, Alex Daoud, Sidney Weisburd. (MB)

gubernatorial candidate. Miami Beach was calling Hall to its mayor's chair. His election was a mandate—he received 87.5 per cent of the vote. If there was anything that was particularly distinguished about Hall's years as mayor of Miami Beach is that he was distinguished. He carried himself regally and made a perfect representative/greeter for the city. He was reelected in 1973. As his second term was coming to a close, he was planning to run for Metropolitan Dade County's mayoralty again. Just before qualifying, in August 1974, Hall died of a heart attack. Vice Mayor Harold Rosen spent the next 15 months filling out Hall's unexpired term, then was elected on his own in 1975.

For 10 years, there would be no two-term mayor—Dr. Leonard Haber, Murray Meyerson, Norman Ciment and Malcolm Fromberg serving only one term each. When Fromberg was elected in 1983, his campaign strategist, Gerald Schwartz, sought the city's $20,000-a-year public relations contract.[37] Only coucilman Alex Daoud voted to give the contract to Schwartz. Rebuffed by Fromberg, an outraged Schwartz walked up to Daoud and told him: "Congratulations, Mr. Mayor."[38] If ever a challenge was thrown, this was it. Schwartz convinced Daoud to run against Fromberg in the fall of 1985. For a considerable time during the campaign, it looked more like the race was between Fromberg and

Schwartz. The two exchanged charges on a regular basis. While Schwartz denied the campaign had gone dirty, Fromberg's publicity man, Scot Ross, countered, "At street level, it's as nasty as ever. The whispering, the smears on the streets, the ripping out of campaign posters, the fliers that are reproduced with false charges."[39]

Rather than Schwartz, it may have been Daoud's personality that did in Fromberg. While Daoud pronounced his name "Dowd", his detractors pronounced it "dah-OOD," stressing his Lebanese ancestry. Daoud overcame that by romancing Jewish voters with his practiced Yiddish phrases. When the votes were in, so was Daoud. He won 23 of 28 precincts where seniors held the majority.[40]

But the elderly Jewish population on South Beach was declining. So Daoud nurtured the influx of Hispanics. Schwartz called it a new Miami Beach coalition, although there is no evidence that elderly Miami Beach Jews and the wave of Hispanics ever coalesced on anything. Daoud was a throwback to the old days: kissing babies, charming old ladies, showing up a bar mitzvahs, weddings and funerals. He participated in boxing matches for charity, not afraid to get his nose bopped if it was for a good cause. It got him reelected in 1987 and, again, in 1989, the first person ever elected to three consecutive terms in Miami Beach mayorality history. He had a routine, and he stuck to it as it was a guaranteed formula for success in Miami Beach.

But there was a dark side to Daoud that was not revealed until he was in his third term. Daoud could be bribed. And he could be caught at it. In 1990, police charged Daoud with accepting a $10,000 payment from boxing promoter Gilberto (Willy) Martinez. He was found guilty, but more charges were being heaped upon him. He was on controversial banker David Paul's payroll, prosecutors said, he cheated on his income taxes by not reporting $160,000 in income for 1988, he prodded his secretaries to lie on the witness stand, to alter his appointment books and to reveal to him what they gave as testimony to a grand jury. And he was charged with laundering a payoff from a subsidiary of Paul's CenTrust bank by purchasing a certificate of deposit.[41]

The battle waged for several years, with Daoud insisting on his innocence. Most stimulating of the charges was that Daoud took the payoff from Paul in return for influencing a city zoning decision to permit Paul to enlarge a boathouse at his waterfront home.[42] On June 30, 1993, Daoud changed his tune and pleaded guilty to four counts—bribery, money laundering, tax fraud and obstruction of justice—before U.S. District Judge James Lawrence King. Nine weeks later, King sentenced Daoud to five years in federal prison. As he left the courthouse, Daoud told reporters: "I'm only human. I made a big mistake."[43]

Off he went to jail, and in his place, Miami Beach voters elected an exact opposite of Daoud: a reserved, deep-thinking, highly-regarded former assistant state attorney and juvenile court judge, Seymour Gelber. Despite Gelber's dignified credentials, and those of his opponent, former State Senator Barry Kutun, the race wound up with familiar overtones. In a stunt similar to the old Melvin Richard auto windshield sticker trick, computerized wake-up calls began coming on election morning between 3 and 4 a.m., to sleepy recipients, ending with a reminder to vote for Gelber.[44] Gelber said the calls were part of a trick to incense voters into casting a ballot against him. Kutun's camp denied it had anything to do with it. Kutun had other problems on election morning.

Above: Governor Bob Graham, (center) joins Miami Beach Commissioners (left to right) Bruce Singer, Stanley Arkin, Ben Grenald, Mayor Malcolm Fromberg, Sidney Weisburd, Alex Daoud, and Billy Shockett and public for 1984 dedication of new Ocean Promenade, at 23-46th Streets. (MB) *Below:* The third Miami Beach City Hall was dedicated in 1977. The first was at 609 Collins Avenue, and the second at 1130 Washington Avenue. (MH)

Upon hearing that his sister was being hassled by rivals at a precinct polling place, he drove there with a .22 caliber pistol in his belt. Police were called in to disarm the mayoral candidate. Kutun spent twice the money as did Gelber in the campaign but Gelber wound up receiving twice as many votes as did Kutun. Upon receiving Kutun's concession of defeat, Gelber remarked, "There is a mandate for change."

The jury is still out.

CHAPTER TWENTY-FOUR

A WAR OVER SOUTH SHORE

Steve Muss, who built apartment houses and rescued the Fontainebleau Hotel, ran into stiff opposition when he tried to implement a controversial plan for South Shore. (MH)

When the halcyon 1960s began turning into the 1970s, it was becoming evident that Miami Beach was beginning to show its age, both in population and in structures—particularly south of Lincoln Road. There had been warning signals as early as April 2, 1965 when a *Time* magazine article—in a forerunner to its infamous "Paradise Lost" article of 1980—published a quote attributed to Doral Beach Hotel publicist Jerry Dobrin that Miami Beach was a "predominately Jewish resort." With 50,000 Baptists due in Miami Beach for a convention that summer—in addition to the Miss Universe pageant—this was not an image Beach publicist Hank Meyer wanted to promote. Although the magazine article was generally positive about Miami Beach as a vacation stop, Meyer saw the "Jewish resort" portion as being harmful to luring tourists from all walks of life. "For years I've been dedicated to the concept of Miami Beach as an All-American resort and [it] is contrary to the best interests of our nation, our citizens and our community to identify any area with an ethnic tag."[1]

In addition to the ethnic identity, Miami Beach had an old-age identity; so much so that a Committee To Keep Greater Miami Beach Young formed in 1967 to attract younger people to live there. The Miami Beach City Council aided the committee with some money to help defray the cost of making a film about young families in Miami Beach.[2] The committee met with some success in luring 23 families in the first six months, but the "senior citizen" image held firm.

The area called the "South Shore" of Miami Beach was populated by a last generation of foreign-born elderly Jews. A study of the social and economic conditions in the area recommended that urban planners wait before doing anything about South Shore, because the existing population soon would die off—enabling a fresh look at the situation without the need for significant social concerns.[3] It is apparent that the study had little impact on those planning Miami Beach's destiny. Before a decade had passed, an overwhelming plan for South Shore had been drawn requiring a relocation of the older residents until new apartments could be constructed. It came in the form of the South Shore Redevelopment Authority, created in 1976[4] but contrived well before that. It also brought to center stage a New York transplant named Steve Muss who already had left his mark on Miami Beach in the hotel and apartment field but now was on a collision course with urban redevelopment and the social upheaval it sometimes brings. As the years moved along, Muss came to have an impact on Miami Beach greater than anyone since Carl Fisher.

Muss, who was handling the family's New York projects while his father built in Florida, came to Miami Beach in 1961 in a role swap with his father. Alexander Muss & Sons was building homes, apartments and shopping centers in New York as early as 1952. Alexander Muss came to Miami Beach in 1961, built the first Seacoast Towers, then turned the Florida operation over to Steve.[5] Tall and overbearing, Muss quickly established himself in Miami Beach, particularly when he and a group he headed, rescued the Fontainebleau Hotel from bankruptcy. Ben Novack filed for personal bankruptcy in 1977 after it became known that he owed his hotel $3.3 million. While Novack tried desperately to save his world-famous hotel, as well as other properties—the Sorrento Hotel and 400 acres of land west of Miami International Airport—the odds kept stacking up against him. In August 1977, Novack owed $7.4 million to creditors who did not hold mortgages or liens on the hotel. Novack also needed to find someone who would finance a $35 million second mortgage.[6] The creditors agreed to give Novack 30 days to come up with the money before the hotel was auctioned on the courthouse steps. Novack, however, was broke and on Dec. 2, 1977, his heart was broken as well. That's when the Muss team purchased the Fontainebleau in bankruptcy court for between $26.8 and $27.8 million.[7]

In 1964, senior citizens filled the porches and rooms of South Beach hotels that later would be recognized as "Art Deco." Those living south of Sixth Street feared the relocation factor of South Shore Redevelopment. (MN)

At that point, Muss embarked on a major renovation of the hotel and began a management deal with Hilton Hotels. Novack's Fontainebleau became the Fontainebleau-Hilton. For the first time since the hotel opened in 1954, there was a sign out front displaying the name. When Muss rescued the Fontainebleau, he already was in the midst of a huge controversy about the city's future. South Shore Redevelopment had become a factor in Miami Beach politics, and Muss was vice chairman of the redevelopment agency. What many saw in redevelopment, they did not like. There were no parades down lower Collins Avenue when Muss put his money into the Fontainebleau and kept its doors open. Residents saw him as a power broker, a man whose money could influence elections.

Novack, meanwhile, could not accept the fact that the hotel was not his. He remained bitter and insisted that he be called "Mr. Fontainebleau" so that Muss could not adopt the title—if ever he wanted to.[8] In 1983, Novack auctioned off crates of artifacts he had remaining after his debts had been satisfied.

When a reporter asked if this final sale left him sad, he replied, "The courts took all the sentiment out of me. The only things I feel bad about is what happened in general. These, these are things. Just things. Why should I be sad?"[9] Novack died on April 5 at the age of 78, following a stroke.

What Novack and Muss had in common, in addition to their desire to accumulate and possess, was a contempt for the media, particularly the *Miami Herald*. Novack often boasted that he made the *Herald* apologize for its 1967 claim of mobsters running the Fontainebleau, but the word "apologize" never appeared in the story the newspaper ran about the settlement of Novack's libel suit. Muss, too, was seeing himself victimized by the press. He was Darth Vador before there was a Darth Vador.[10] Muss was at the forefront of the South Shore Redevelopment Agency. When the Miami Beach City Commision gave the ad hoc committee on South Shore redevelopment the power of an Authority, it conferred the jurisdiction to condemn land, issue bonds and enter into contracts.[11] Muss was a member of the ad hoc committee and became vice chairman of the Authority. The chairman was Jim McDonnell, an executive with Andy Frain Services, a security and ushering service. Within two years, the Miami Beach City Commission purged McDonnell and appointed Muss chairman.[12] As early as July 1976, with McDonnell as the helm, the less-than-six-

months-old Authority had settled on a plan for its section of Miami Beach, which ran from ocean to bay and from Sixth Street to Government Cut. It was designed by Steve Siskind, brought in from San Francisco by Muss to be the full-time director of the agency. Siskind's proposal was stunning: a series of waterways or canals weaving through the entire district, with 2,100 new apartments on both sides of Fifth Street for people of all incomes—a proposal the agency later tried to disavow—several large hotels, smaller hotels and motels, tennis, restaurant and shopping facilities. The cost would be about $400 million with about $270 million coming from private developers.[13] The uproar could be heard all the way to Disney World. Environmentalists complained about the waterways, public officials fretted about the cost, senior citizens were traumatized over the fact that they would have to be relocated, property owners were stunned at the likelihood of a building and repair moratorium on their land and everyone seemed shocked that the plan called for razing every building south of Sixth Street, with a few exceptions such as Joe's Stone Crab.

It all came at a time of an already-existing conflict between landlords and their tenants as a result of city-imposed rent controls. In 1974, the city had agreed to rent controls which dictated that the "legal maximum rent of an apartment is that rent which had been in effect on the freeze date of October

The demolition of Smith's Casino and the Beach End Hotel in 1964, marked the end of the place where much of Miami Beach's early history was made. It was also the birthplace of the infamous S & G Syndicate. (MN)

16, 1974.[14] The act said landlords could apply for increases in rent only if there was mutual agreement between the landlord and tenant; or if there had been a major capital improvement in the property since October 16, 1973; or if there were unique circumstances prevailing at the time of the rent freeze, such as substantially lower than usual rents. With no increases in their income, landlords were hesitant— sometimes financially unable—to keep up their properties. That utopian situation for the renter came to a close in 1977 when the Miami Beach City Council voted down a proposal to extend the moratorium beyond its expiration date.[15] Up went the rents, as one would expect. And, at the same time, plans were made to uproot the population of South Shore in phases. For some, even what they could afford, they no longer could have. Muss, as a protagonist of the redevelopment plan, became a bogey man to many. Residents mounted emotional appeals through newspapers and at city council meetings to not be thrown out of their homes. A condominium apartment at 221 Washington Avenue, built in 1971, five years later was scheduled for demolition under the redevelopment plan.[16]

Trying to ride out the storm, Authority members listened, apologized, but continued with the plan—and altered it. The placement of 750 low-cost rental units among the 2,100 new apartments was in the original announcement in 1976[17] but, in 1977, some Authority members were balking at honoring that promise. Max Serchuk, a 76-year-old member of the Authority, threatened to hold up the entire project until the 750 low-cost units were authorized. By a 3-2 vote, the Authority reluctantly agreed to build the units. Voting against was chairman McDonnell, which may have been one reason that he lost his post. Also voting against it was Irwin Sawitz, married at the time to Jesse Weiss' daughter Jo Ann, and operator of Joe's Stone Crab. "I am not

objecting to taking care of the people who are here now," Sawitz said, "but I'm opposed to creating a permanent burden on this city to take care of people who don't live here now—who may not even be born yet."[18] Muss, citing political pressure, voted in favor of the low-cost housing, as did the remaining two Authority members, Serchuk and David Klevens.[19]

The saga of South Shore moved on to the next stage in July 1978 when the South Florida Regional Planning Council gave its approval to the project after the Authority agreed to redesign the proposed canalway to prevent water stagnation and decrease the prospect of hurricane damage. Construction was prohibited within 50 feet of the beach erosion line; residential units would be built for the people to be relocated. Additionally, the school board agreed to build a new elementary school in the district.[20] More than a dozen of the biggest developers signed up by the August 1978 deadline to build all or part of the project.[21] The Worsham Brothers of Atlanta won the contract.

There was no letup in the assault on the redevelopment plan, nor was there any letup by Muss and the Authority in trying to implement it. Environmental groups continued to challenge the concept of canals, and in November 1979, the scales appeared to tip against the entire project when two opponents of redevelopment, Murray Meyerson and Mel Mendelson, won city commission seats— Meyerson as the mayor. Mendelson owned a business in the South Shore district, one that would have to be uprooted if the plan progressed. While the Authority was bringing Worsham into the project as a partner, based on a preliminary handshake, Meyerson sought a referendum on redevelopment, while allowing existing plans for the bayfront to proceed. There was not much give elsewhere. Commissioner Alex Daoud, who was in favor of

Model of South Shore Redevelopment plan called for almost complete razing of the area and a network of man-made canals (MN)

Café Cubano and guayberas added a new element to the continuing transformation of Miami Beach. Large numbers of Cuban refugees arrived there in 1980. (MH)

redevelopment, was facing a recall campaign as opponents bought full-page ads calling for his ouster. And former city attorney Joe Wanick was preparing a lawsuit on behalf of the Taxpayers, Homeowners and Tenents Protective Association that would challenge even the bayside compromise allowed by Meyerson in his call for a referendum.[22]

As the calendar turned to mid-1980, there was an unexpected tidal wave of new people arriving in Miami Beach. They weren't particularly welcome. They were Mariel refugees. Most of them simply were fleeing communism but with them came a good number of criminals whom Fidel Castro released from jail to send to the U.S. With South Beach in a decaying situation (the building moratorium was in effect) many previous residents had moved out and were replaced by the refugees, many of whom were settled there by public agencies.

Between the arrival of the Mariel refugees, who were seen by many as inferior to the first wave of Cuban refugees, and the outbreak of a riot across the bay in Liberty City, the entire area was taking a terrible pounding in the press. That's when *Time* magazine dropped its bomb on Greater Miami's image with its "Paradise Lost" cover story. For people planning a revitalization of Miami Beach, the bad press coupled with a rising crime rate on South Beach, particularly muggings of older people, did not help with luring investors to the project.

In 1981, Miami Beach Commissioner Simon Wikler proposed the abolishment of the redevelopment agency, with the city taking over the project and scaling it down considerably, This came just as the agency was planning a $15 million bond sale to begin the first phase of construction, South Shore Marina.[23] The continuing debate and challenges to redevelopment wore Muss down; he threw up his hands in frustration and retreated to his hotel, declaring that he was through with public ventures. He wanted to be left alone, particularly by the press. "I don't call the press the Fourth Estate," he said, "I call it the Fifth Column."[24] The death knell for the South Shore plan came on December 13, 1982, when the Authority admitted that redevelopment, as envisioned by its planners, never would take place. "This is probably the end of redevelopment as we hoped it would be for the last seven years," commented acting agency chairman Marwin Cassel.[25] "This is just what I expected," said Mayor Norman Ciment. "We don't need an agency for redevelopment. We can have redevelopment in South Beach through a rezoning plan and private enterprise."[26] Within the week, the city commission voted to lift the building moratorium. The battle had ended but the battlefield reflected the clashes of the previous eight years. Buildings were in an unrepaired state, vacant lots were overgrown with weeds, the population had changed dramatically.

Meanwhile, Muss had become the largest property holder in Miami Beach, as well as the biggest taxpayer. He had placed the Fontainebleau-Hilton back atop the pedestal of world-class hotels, and now was appealing to tourist-oriented businessmen with what he believed to be an overhaul of South Beach that would bring tourists back to the area by the millions. Despite his detractors, the Miami Beach Chamber of Commerce honored Muss in 1979 as the Miami Beach Chamber of Commerce's "Man of the Year." One of those who did not speak on Muss' behalf was Mayor Jay Dermer. "I think he has control of the commission," Dermer gruffed. "Anything Muss wants, Muss gets."[27]

Muss insisted his goal "was to make a statement for Miami Beach that will be heard around the world and to recreate Miami Beach as a world-class resort, the Fontainebleau-Hilton making an immediate statement and redevelopment making a somewhat longer-range statement."[28] Much of Muss' woes could be blamed on his gruffness, his insistence on having it all his way. He was discredited for what people did not like about him but rarely credited for what good he did for the community, as a developer, a taxpayer and as a civic activist. Dr. Leonard Haber, a psychologist who also was on the City Commission and was previously mayor, assessed the years of Muss' public activity: "We rarely get a glimpse of a man like Steve Muss, yet with Muss we've had three full-length movies. . . . He's made himself available to public scrutiny, whether it be denigration or respect, and he's certainly ignited the gamut of feelings in people, from the most positive to the most negative. He's afforded the public an unusual long view into the personality and ambition and workings of a very immense figure, normally a very private figure."[29]

To keep pace with the rest of the country, the Miami Beach Convention Hall expanded in the '80s. The city commission honored Muss by renaming the building for him: The Stephen Muss Convention Center. It was to honor the man for his lobbying efforts with the state to permit a local tax to pay for

The Hilton Plaza Hotel, opened in 1967, is credited with being the last major hotel built in Miami Beach. Now essentially a condominium, it is on its seventh different name: the Castle Beach Club. (MN; HASF)

the center's expansion, and also to provide the City of Miami with funds to build a sports arena.[30] The decision was reached without a public hearing. Mussphobia was ressurected. A petition to restore the original name was signed by more than 6,500 Miami Beach residents. Shortly before a referendum vote was to be taken in 1989, Mayor Alex Daoud reported that Muss had contacted him and requested that his name be removed from the building.[31]

Demographics, lifestyles, fortunes and names were changing elsewhere in Miami Beach. For one, the era of the "Hotel of the Year" had come to an end. When the Hilton Plaza opened in December 1967, few expected that it would be the last major Miami Beach hotel built for decades to come but that is what it turned out to be. (Some may argue that the Alexander, which opened as a hotel in 1983, was the last but the Alexander was built in 1963—as the Seacoast Towers North Apartments. Muss converted the apartments to a hotel with a $35 million renovation.) Not only were there no new hotels, but many apartment house owners began converting their buildings to condominiums at a time—the late '70s—when renters in South Beach were seeking new rentals in order to vacate the decaying district. At a state legislative hearing held in Miami Beach in 1979 regarding condo conversion, State Representative Hal Spaet, a former member of the city commission, testified that Miami Beach residents over the age of 65 had the highest suicide rate in the U.S. He blamed it on "loneliness, isolation, the tensions of living on a fixed income and the feat of being uprooted from their homes."[32] The soaring rental rates north of Lincoln Road, the prevalence of recently-arrived Cuban refugees in the southern portion, the conversion of existing apartment houses to condos and the decline of major hotels contributed to tough years for Miami Beach.

So much was tentative. A case in point was the odyssey of what started out as the Hilton Plaza Hotel at 54th Street and Collins Avenue in 1967. After the first year of the hotel's existence, the owners ended their franchise agreement with Hilton and changed the name to the Hotel Plaza. Behind that name was a cost-savings effort to retain the same initials, as all the dishes, cups and towels were inscribed with the initials "HP." In August 1970, the hotel was sold to Hugh Hefner, who renamed it the Playboy Plaza. Hefner held on to it for three years, then sold it to Harold Konover, who brought in Hyatt to manage it as the Hyatt Konover. Within a year, Konover ended the relationship with Hyatt and modified the name to the "Konover." After becoming ill, Konover sold the hotel to Miami Beach Commissioner Abe Hirschfeld, who brought in the Premier hotel chain to run it as the Castle Hotel.

The relationship between Hirschfeld and the Premier was just as brief as other relationships regarding the hotel. Hirschfeld—whose reign as owner of the hotel was just as stormy as was his time as a Miami Beach City Commissioner and as, briefly, publisher of the New York Post—sold the Castle to Crescent Heights, Inc., a condo conversion specialist outfit run by Russell Galbut and Sonny Kahn. The hotel was renamed the Castle Beach Club and converted into a condominium, with a hotel component remaining but under the ownership of HI Development Corp.[33]

The advent of condominium living in Miami Beach began with the Carriage House in the 1960s and spread like wildfire. Hotel owners were caught unaware of the danger. Condominiums took away winter guests from their hotels. Rather than fly to Miami Beach for a few weeks in a hotel, they purchased condos and spent time there whenever they cared to, getting the same view and the same beach. In addition, many Northern businessmen were able to write off much of their Miami Beach condo costs by sending business prospects to their condos and charging it off on their taxes as a business expense. Just prior to the condo explosion, business at Miami Beach hotels was excellent. "When business is good," commented Stu Blumberg, president of the Miami Beach Hotel Resort Association, "you don't see what's coming up from behind you. By 1972, you could see there was a softening of the hotel business."[34] An expansion of the Convention Center for the national political conventions of 1972 brought other conventions to Miami Beach. But the world was getting smaller. Jet airliners now made it easier to go elsewhere. New competitive markets were opening: the Bahamas, the Caribbean. A New Yorker could fly to San Juan, with its different culture, for not much more than it cost to fly to Miami Beach—and San Juan was not subject to an occasional cool front in the winter as was Miami Beach. To counter that, tourist industry people created package tours that made it cheaper and more convenient for the Northern tourist to go to Miami Beach. Then Disney World came to Orlando.

The odds were stacking up against Miami Beach. By the late '70s, the Convention Hall again was seen as too small compared to convention centers in competing cities, the hotel product was becoming old, and when Novack went bankrupt, it appeared the bottom was dropping out. Also, crime became an issue in Miami Beach. Statistics showed that in-season tourism was down 10 percent from 1982 to 1983 and 25 per cent from 1981 and that only 35 percent of available hotels rooms were taken during the 1983 summer months.[35] Mayor Norman Ciment blamed the Visitor and Convention Authority for not doing its job well and Bob Dickinson, chairman of the VCA, countered by laying the blame on "the provincialism and parochialism of people like Mayor Ciment."[36] The hotel industry blamed the decline on a drop in business from Great Britain and Latin America and a domestic tourist market that did not recover from the publicity of Liberty City and Mariel. "It's the worst I've ever seen," Leonard (Doc) Baker, president of the Miami Beach Chamber of Commerce, was quoted. "Our hotel people are desperate."[37] The Sea Isle closed down, the Sea Gull closed for the summer for the first time in a decade, the Barcelona shut down temporarily. "It's like a cemetery," complained Max Berger of the Welworth Hotel.[38]

South Beach tenements housed what was perceived by many to be the breeding ground of crimes perpetrated by Mariel refugees. Police answered 57 calls and made 36 arrests in a five-months period at just one apartment house on Jefferson Avenue.[39] In the neighborhoods of South Beach, the elderly became terrorized, practically every time they heard someone speaking in Spanish. Dickinson's condemnation of the soon-to-be one-term Ciment being provincial and parochial had come on the heels of a plan by the mayor to put up roadblocks to keep Mariel refugees out of Miami Beach. "The city attorney tells me that as long as we stop every car on the causeways, we do it legally."[40] Ciment's proposed ordinance got nowhere. The idea was universally ridiculed as being as being even more detrimental to Miami Beach's image. Crime, indeed,

Right: One of the few successes of the South Shore Redevelopment plan was the mandated new South Pointe Elementary School. (MH) *Below:* South Pointe Towers, built on the site of the Miami Beach Dog Track, stands as a singular beacon in the promising but yet unfulfilled South Shore. (MH)

was prevalent, but looking for a scapegoat was not going to cure it. The fear Ciment, and most people in Miami Beach, had about the Mariel refugees was not necessarily unfounded but out of proportion. Of the 1,307 Hispanics arrested in Miami Beach for crimes such as homicide, rape, aggravated assault, burglary, theft and arson during 1981 and 1982—the period when many *Marielitos* were released from jail and came to the Beach—only 144 were Mariel refugees.[41]

But the pereception persisted, both locally and internationally. Just when it was thought that Miami Beach was buried, it arose from the ashes from a direction no one ever expected. It had its beginnings in the fierce dedication of a woman named Barbara Capitman.

At the time, she had no idea what she was starting.

CHAPTER TWENTY-FIVE

MIAMI BEACH'S FUTURE IS FOUND IN ITS PAST

Barbara Capitman, whose tenacity led to the famous Art Deco District, sits at her mother's period desk in 1982. (MH)

She had an interesting childhood. The daughter of an industrial designer and sculptor, Barbara Baer Capitman has been to France and England as early as 1929, when she was only nine years old. She was exposed to writers and artists, to the more esoteric aspects of life. Like her mother, Barbara was not going to spend her days as a housewife. She wanted a career. She chose journalism, specializing in the design industry. She became a member of the American Society of Interior Designers. With such a background, it was only a matter of time, and circumstance, that would bring this woman into contact with the Miami Beach buildings designed in the 1930s and early 1940s by still relatively unknown architects.

Early in her New York professional career, she edited a magazine on prefabricated houses,[1] then became a reporter for an Atlantic City newspaper. Between 1948 and 1960, she wrote 17 books in the "how to" category. Covering Henry Wallace's 1948 third party campaign against Harry Truman and Thomas Dewey, she met United Press International reporter William Capitman and eventually married him. They moved to Martha's Vineyard in Massachusetts. In 1973, William accepted a position as a marketing professor at Florida International University in Miami. Just two years later, William died and Barbara faced a new life. She continued with her journalism career, as Southern editor of *The Designer* magazine, but she felt another calling.

"As a relative newcomer to Miami, surviving the stunning blow of my husband's death, I gravitated to the American Society of Interior Designers' (ASID) meetings for companionship," she wrote in her 1988 book *Deco Delights*, "and there I found others who were not that happy about the new buildings, like the huge Omni, just beginning to be built along the bay [in Miami]. At a cocktail party, Leonard Horowitz, a young designer, and I decided to form a new association that would present alternative ideas about what designers might find valuable in Miami."[2]

One June afternoon, a group of five designers founded the Miami Design Preservation League (MDPL) and by December 1976, they discovered Art Deco, the design style they believed best represented Miami. The first to take note of Capitman was Jo Werne, a *Miami Herald* home and design writer, who reported in 1976 that the then relatively-unknown woman was calling a community forum to discuss growth limitations, preservation of old buildings and Art Deco.[3]

Her small MDPL group embarked on a project to locate hotels that, in their opinion, were well designed. "There are 334 hotels on Miami Beach and we estimate that 150 of them would come into the category of good design," Capitman said. She spoke with foresight: "We believe that tourism would benefit if some of these old hotels which are real treasures were restored. Most seasoned travelers prefer to stay in a hotel that has some history or attractive design to recommend it." She emphasized that even modern-day hotels could qualify, but her accent was on the old. "Instead of tearing down the old hotels," she challenged, "why not put money into interior improvements, paint, landscaping, promenades? Why not use some of the small hotels primarily as restaurants, some as dormitories for older people?"[4]

With those words, and through subsequent actions and rallies, Barbara Capitman led a revolution in Miami Beach that led to the nation's first 20th Century historic district. "Art Deco" became a stock term among travel agents and tourists. It had its roots in a 1966 retrospective at the *Musée des Arts Décoratifs* in Paris. The term did not find its way into the English lexicon until 1968, when it appeared as the title name of a book by Bevis Hiller[5] Art Deco is an umbrella name encompassing several categories of design dating back to the 1920s. In 1963, not only was Art Deco a non-existent term, but the myriad designs that came to be known by that name were so lightly regarded that a booklet published that year by the South Florida Chapter of the American Institute of Architects ran photographs of 80 examples of architecture in the Greater Miami area—and not one of them portrayed any of the buildings that later would be lumped together as Art Deco.[6]

In January 1977, a group met on Ocean Drive, divided into teams and walked throughout the district, noting the styles of the hotels and small apartment houses. The group was led by Carl Weinhardt Jr., director of Villa Viscaya [a palatial home and formal gardens built by James Deering in Miami in 1916] and Frederick Bland, a young architect. When they regrouped, Weinhardt took up everyone's notes and maps and proclaimed: "The area definitely is Deco."[7]

Leonard Horowitz joined Barbara Capitman to form the Miami Design Preservation League, a group dedicated to seeking valuable architectural design in the Miami area. They discovered Miami Beach Art Deco. (MN)

That encouraged members of MDPL, an association that included designers, museum directors and editors, to attend city commission meetings as a lobbyist group of distinguished citizens. In 1978, the MDPL reported to the city that it had identified a section of Miami Beach as a collection of historic, yet still 20th Century, buildings. It was, roughly, the first outline of the Art Deco historic district. "We were experiencing the excitement of an archaeological dig," Capitman wrote.[8]

The *Herald*'s Werne accepted an invitation from Horowitz to tour the old hotels on Ocean Drive. She recalled that when he pointed out the porthole windows, the decorative screen doors and floors, she was impressed. The hotels were in deplorable condition but she could see how, with some restoration work, they could be quite inviting. Shortly thereafter, the *Herald* did a picture layout of some of the buildings in the target district. Werne also recalled how ambitious Capitman was to get publicity. "One day, I stepped off the *Herald* elevator to find Barbara at the reception desk, going down a list of reporters' names with the receptionist to find one that would see her," said Werne. "Barbara was always looking to get stories in paper, so much so that some of us began trying to avoid her. Even though we were sympathetic with her cause, she overdid her calling on us."[9]

To some, Capitman's quavering voice caused a reaction much like running a fingernail down a blackboard. But, by 1978, she had the attention of many— including those who wanted her to go away. She lobbied against the demolition of two buildings, the Hotel Rex at 618 Euclid Avenue, and a one-story house at 750 Michigan Avenue.[10] Both were declared unsafe by city building inspectors, but just as naturalist Marjory Stoneman Douglas of Everglades repute found beauty even in a vulture, Capitman saw charm in buildings where others didn't. "They're spoiling a thing of great beauty," Capitman complained. ". . . Anytime you take down a building like that, it's like taking down a building in Charleston, Savannah or New Orleans."[11]

She presented a treatise that the buildings from the southern edge of Miami Beach to 21st Street were of historical importance. Nonsense, countered the owners of the properties, they are just plain buildings. Capitman didn't win many battles early in her campaign, but as she spoke out and marshalled her forces, trying to tear down a building in that district was becoming more difficult. By December 1978, MDPL had grown to 1,000 members and had become a significant lobbying force. Lined up against them were about 2,500 property owners who didn't like the idea of being told what they could or could not do with their property.

The battle was being fought on several fronts, as South Shore Redevelopment was active at the time. Capitman drew her lines immediately north of the redevelopment district. At a hearing in December 1978, a state review board heard Capitman's plea proposing a historic preservation district in South Miami Beach for roughly 12,000 buildings. The district was bordered on the east by the ocean, on the south by Sixth Street, on the west by a line slightly east of Alton Road and by Washington Avenue north of Lincoln Road, and on the north roughly by the Collins Canal and 23rd Street.[12] The meeting turned out to be an Art Deco love-in. It opened with a City of Miami Beach proclamation honoring Capitman, then settled down as government officials, businessmen and architectural and artistic types praised Art Deco. But Capitman still had a battle on her hands. A month later, with a week to go before the state rendered a decision, the Miami Beach Board of Realtors and the Miami Beach Resort Hotel Association came out in opposition to the district, which encompassed about one-seventh of the entire city. Then the Miami Beach Apartment Association joined in.[13] What seemed to set off the opposition was the size of the district. Miami Beach's city manager, Gavin O'Brien, advised the state that city officials were concerned because there remained many questions to be answered. "We've been talking about this district for two and one-half years," a stunned Capitman reacted. "We've spoken at meetings and in the papers. The *New York Daily News* wrote about the district last weekend. Paul Goldberger of the *New York Times* is doing a story now. We've had a headquarters for information on the Beach for about a year. How can people say they don't know the answers?"[14]

On May 15, a photo of Barbara Capitman appeared in the *Miami Herald*. It showed her jubilant, with her face turned toward the heavens and her arms raised in joy. Behind her was the 1939 Henry Hohauser-designed Cardozo Hotel on Ocean Drive. Despite the powerful opposition, she had won. The National Register of Historic Places designated the neighborhood as "Old Miami Beach."[15] "No one in their right mind just walks around and looks at old buildings," said Miami Beach Resort Hotel Association executive director Murray Gold. "They want to see glassblowers and cobblers. These people (MDPL) are only for preservation. They don't care about investments, business and the future."[16]

There was, and is, an irony about all this. The old guard of Miami Beach wanted to think new, while the new force preferred to think old. The designation of the special district meant a lot of things. It made it more difficult, but not impossible, to demolish a building in the district. It also meant tax advantages to property owners who restored their buildings. The designation also brought with it low-interest federal loans for restoration work and forbade the demolition of any of the buildings by any government-funded projects.

Capitman's experience with "how to" magazines came in handy when the MDPL published a 32-page guide explaining what Art Deco was and how to care for it. MDPL originally planned to do a book but found that it took several years to get a book published. The League was driven to publish quickly for fear that property owners would restore their buildings improperly, or even destroy them.[17]

This was, and remains, a constant fear of Art Deco *afficionados*; that people who owned the buildings would not know, or care to know, just how to restore them. Immediately, MDPL set out to create a master plan for the district.[18] At issue: Should Ocean Drive be closed to cars, as was Lincoln Road? How can restoration proceed without disenfranchising what remained of the elderly and poor? What can be done to prevent demolition of buildings? Before any master plan could be developed, however, there still were wars to fight. In January 1980, the owner of a Spanish-style home on Euclid Avenue applied for a permit to tear it down in order to construct a five-story condominium. And a city engineer determined the cupola of the Waldorf Towers at 860 Ocean Drive was unsafe. So the owner tore it down. "These are two very bad developments for Art Deco," complained Capitman. "The terrible thing is they can demolish a building in a day. We have no legal sanction. We need a municipal ordinance to save the buildings."[19] She identified other buildings which she said were being threatened. Abe Resnick, a part-owner of two of the hotels she cited, said what Capitman was proposing was unconstitutional.[20] The Miami Beach City Commission was caught in the middle, and waffled. "There's a problem because we want to protect the concept of Art Deco, which is a good one," said commissioner Daoud, "At the same time, we have to protect the land owners." Mayor Murray Meyerson said he was concerned about long-term moratoriums; "I'm not firm on my position yet."[21]

As debate continued, so did demolition. The Boulevard Hotel, built in 1925 by Carl Fisher, became a retirement hotel in the 1950s and was bought in 1974 by Resnick and his associates for $1.1 million. Located on Dade Boulevard adjacent to the Bayshore Golf Course, it closed on April 15, 1980. Resnick's son, Jim, said the building would be demolished and a 16-story, 180-condominium building put up in its place.[22] Capitman called the Boulevard exactly the type of building that was being renovated elsewhere

When the Boulevard Hotel was demolished in 1980, the last of Carl Fisher's grand hotels fell to the wrecking ball. (MH)

around the country. "It's a civic responsibility to see that these things aren't destroyed," she complained.[23]

The Boulevard did come down—and nothing was put up in its place. Today, it is a vacant lot.

Times weren't very good for MDPL. Funding from various sources, from federal to local levels, was drying up. Like a locomotive engineer stripping all the wood from his railroad cars to feed the furnace and keep the train going, MDPL began giving up its fixtures one by one to meet its 1630 Euclid Avenue office bills. Out went the air conditioning, out went the copying machine, eight desks, two filing cabinets—piece by piece, until there was little but bare walls. Capitman remained optimistic: "We'll get help. We've been in this situation a couple of times before."[24] She and her son, Andrew, made a personal investment in the new district, purchasing the Victor Hotel at 1144 Ocean Drive and beginning a $75,000 restoration project in September 1980. The Victor, designed by L. Murray Dixon in 1937, reopened in December, with guests adorned in 1930s attire setting a style mood that was to become standard in the district.[25]

The euphoria of that opening night, and of the Art Deco Moon Ball that accompanied it, was soon to be shattered by yet another assault on a building in the district. Again Resnick was the antagonist. This time it was the New Yorker Hotel on the ocean at 1611 Collins Avenue. Built in 1940 and designed by Hohauser, the building was on the National Register of Historic Places but not protected by any law. As wreckers prepared to demolish the building, a *Miami Herald* reporter caught a confrontation in the hotel's parking lot between a demolitionist and Mitchell Wolfson, Jr., co-chairman of MDPL and son of the former mayor of Miami Beach and chairman of Wometco Enterprises. Wolfson had been sent to try to stop the demolition. The exchange between Wolfson and demolitionist Dan Feldman captured

Pro-Deco supporter Teresa Gordon exchanges words with an anti-Deco group in front of the doomed New Yorker Hotel in 1981. (MN)

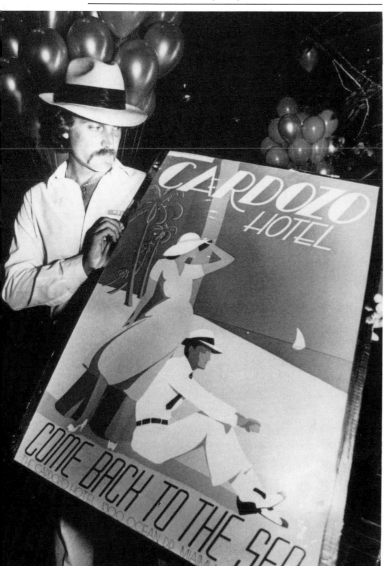

Artist Woody Vondracek displays a poster he created for the Cardozo Hotel. His posters quickly became identified with Miami Beach Art Deco. (MN)

the essence of the tug of war between developers and preservationists:

"There's a special spirit, a special vocabulary to the building," pleaded Wolfson. "There's spirit, distinction, beauty."

Feldman snapped back: "The molding is warped. The windows are warped. This building is falling down."

Wolfson came back at him: "Just look up at this building, the curving angles. The distinction lies in the form, the architecture. You can see it all around you."

Feldman: "What are you going to do when a wall collapses and kills somebody? Where will your league be then?"[26]

As they talked, workmen removed the furnishings from the hotel and razed the cabanas. Pickets appeared. Let us talk, both sides reasoned. Resnick agreed to delay further demolition until MDPL personnel removed pieces of the building they considered to be of historic value.[27] Then the demolition continued until the New Yorker was no more.

Like so many others, *Miami Herald* columnist Charles Whited was torn between both sides. While he expressed disappointment in the possible demise of the building, he held that its owner had a right to

Biscaya Hotel, formerly the Floridian, is imploded after being condemned by the Unsafe Structures Board—thus ending a losing campaign by preservationists. (MN)

incredible color and flair," that could be a strong tourist draw.[29]

Resnick and his partner, aware of the dark image cast upon them by pickets and the ensuing publicity, came upon an idea. Rezone the property from high-density residential to commercial, permit them to tie three buildings—the New Yorker and the neighboring Sands Hotel and Georgian Condominiums—into a combination of shops, condos and perhaps hotel rooms, and they would not tear down the New Yorker; at least not the facade.[30] Capitman was ecstatic. "I feel absolute, utter, sheer delight," she said. "This is the first time in recent history that a demolition has been stopped and the whole process reversed. This is really going to be a turning point of the city."[31]

Her enthusiasm soon turned to horror. Three months later, the wrecking ball began bludgeoning the New Yorker. Resnick and his partner, Dov Dunaevsky, who commissioned an architectural plan for the three buildings, turned it down. Through a spokesman, the developers said the plan was a boondoggle and, instead, they would produce something that would serve as an economic stimulator "rather than a financial fiasco."[32]

There were two other significant losses dealt preservationists, not including Capitman's dead-last finish in a five-person city commission race in 1983. One was the Biscaya Hotel on the north side of the foot of the MacArthur Causeway. Formerly the Floridian Hotel, it occupied the site of Jim Allison's aquarium. The hotel was closed since 1977, its decaying structure a home for stray cats. Owner Harvey Goodman, last of a long string of owners of

do with it as he wanted.[28] A week later, Whited was back on the subject of Art Deco but, this time, solidly in the movement's corner. He was chagrined that the Miami Beach City Commission ignored a plea by MDPL for a three-month moratorium on demolitions within the district, which would have allowed the group time to present a plan for developing the district. He saw in it what Capitman had visualized earlier: "A unique district in Miami Beach, harking back to that Depression decade's

Barbara Capitman (left) with Mattie Bower, was the burning force behind the movement to save the Senator Hotel. Her campaign failed. (MN)

Tony Goldman, New Yorker, restored two Art Deco hotels and figured prominently in the re-birth of South Beach. (MH)

the property, claimed he had plans to restore the building but was stymied by the long moratorium on buildings south of Sixth Street. When the city ordered the building razed, preservationists took up the fight, but to no avail.[33] The Biscaya came down in March 1987. Nothing replaced it.

Perhaps the most bitter loss sustained by Capitman and MDPL was the Senator Hotel at 1201 Collins Avenue. Capitman made the Senator her most momentous project. When her book *Deco Delights* was published in 1988, the frontspiece photo was that of the Senator. The caption overline: *The Senator—Symbol of the Deco District*, verified that she considered this a watershed battle. The Senator was scheduled for demolition in March to be replaced by a multi-story parking garage by the Royale Group, a company owning a number of buildings in the district. The Royale Group contended that by sacrificing this one building, other of their properties such as the Cardozo, Tides, Carlyle, Leslie and Cavalier Hotels would be better served by additional parking spaces.[34] When preservationists, buoyed by sympathetic media exposure, managed to delay the demolition, Capitman felt she had won the day. Again, her joy was hasty. The razing of the Senator began on October 12, 1988, just after a balky Capitman was led away from the site by Miami Beach police.[35]

For every defeat, however, there were victories; colossal victories. Investors began recognizing the district after positive newspaper articles appeared. When Gerry Sanchez sold the Clevelander Hotel at a profit in 1984, it stimulated other investors to come in.[36] When unconventional artist Christo came

to Biscayne Bay to wrap many of its undeveloped islands in pink, he was accompanied by an international press corps that stayed at the Carlyle Hotel. In addition to Christo's remarkable accomplishment, those writers also raved about the Art Deco District. Throughout the district, the sound of saws and drills, the smell of fresh paint became the norm. One by one, renovated hotels began reopening, particularly on Ocean Drive, where it was becoming the "in" place to be. To the west, on Washington Avenue, where cherished old restaurants such as "The Famous" used to draw largely the Jewish trade, trendy new restaurants took their place. Some stayed, some didn't; the hazard of being trendy.

By 1985, Ocean Drive was becoming a mecca for the young and stylish. The *Miami Herald* credited the Carlyle Bar and Grill as the birthplace of Ocean Drive night life, followed by the Waldorf Towers. Gerry Sanchez, who was a pioneer investor in the new Ocean Drive, restored two hotels—the Breakwater and the Edison—and opened restuarants in them. Tony Goldman, a New York restaurateur, bought two hotels, the Park Central and the Imperial, and opened them to night life.[37] South Beach became a destination not only for stateside tourists and for locals, but for the European crowd as well. Brash and loud, SoBe—as many call it—also was sophisticated. Movie stars and celebrities from the music world frequented the bistros, while tourists and young Miamians filled the street-level bars and restaurants along Ocean Drive and Washington Avenue. These were not necessarily days of sheer delight for Capitman, however. Fortunes were being spent, and lost, on restoring the hotels. Her son, Andrew, was one who lost money on trying to restore and run some hotels. Sanchez did not find the district to be the cash cow his Clevelander Hotel sale augured earlier.

And Capitman was not satisfied that Miami Beach had passed strict laws protecting the buildings. She saw a trend away from devout adherence to the rules of historic preservation. The soft pastel original colors of the buildings were giving way to brighter, more decorative design. In writing a glowing report of the success story of the Art Deco district, particularly Ocean Drive, *Miami Herald* architecture writer Beth Dunlop warned: "Ocean Drive is at a critical juncture these days, endangered by its own success, threatened by those who would make it too glitzy—or too common—without any real understanding of its architecture or its history."[38]

For purists, that can be alarming. What was originally created by the pioneering architects was being desecrated, in places, by gaudy paint and T-shirt shops. For the Grand Dame of Art Deco, the days were troubling—and running out. Suffering from heart problems, Capitman's health began to deteriorate. She died on March 29, 1990, at the age of 69. A week short of her passing, she gave her final interview. Terribly ill, she nevertheless kept up her battle for Art Deco. "I have this awful feeling, from experience," she said. "I sense this mood to relax and compromise, this mood of self-complacency. It's such a scary thing. I can see the whole Art Deco District being gone in two years."[39]

The two years passed but Capitman's deathbed fear did not come to pass. People who worked closely with Capitman, such as her successor Nancy Liebman, later kept a firm grip on the controls but learned, and practiced, one thing Barbara Capitman could not: compromise. Capitman took on all roles within the MDPL, felt no one else could do them. She also would not back down from a position. It was to be the way she wanted, or not at all. Liebman said the City of Miami Beach would have passed stronger preservation laws earlier if only Capitman had been able to compromise on some issues. When the MDPL convinced the city to create a Historic Preservation Board, Capitman was noticeably ignored when it came to being named to the board. When opposition to her dogmatic positions arose within the MDPL, Capitman sought to dissolve the league. She wanted to run it her way, or not have it exist at all. That became the end of her tenure as executive director of the MDPL. Members got together to put the group's purpose into focus and recognized that saving the district was a bigger issue than Barbara Capitman.[40] "Barbara was her own worst enemy, but the best friend the district could ever have because of her persistence and fanaticism," Liebman observed.[41]

With each loss of a property, the newly-focused MDPL exacted a repayment: stronger preservation laws. "Our theory was that it was better to go forward and get something than be rejected because we wanted the whole thing," Liebman observed after she left the league and became a Miami Beach City Commissioner in 1993.[42]

The Art Deco District became a backdrop for all manner of photos—from professional commercials to happy tourists. (MH)

Even Liebman, admittedly, had fears about the Art Deco District being taken over by T-shirt shops. That fear lessened as vogue houses, such as Armani, also discovered the district. Miami Beach is always evolving. Today, South Beach is being billed by many as "Europe in America"—a sophisticated yet rakish tropical place to play, wine and dine. By daylight, rollerblade fanatics, some dressed in barely detectable swim suits, swirl in and out of traffic, or around the cameras and lighting equipment of a fashion shoot, while some of the few remaining senior citizens look on in bewilderment. By moonlight, the district is alive with neon, dining, Beautiful People, Beautiful People wannabes, and music—perhaps too much music, or music too loud, as working-class neighbors growl about loss of sleep.

On any given night along Ocean Drive, automobile traffic is in gridlock, pedestrian traffickers rub up against each other in a too-tight, two-way flow of parading gawkers and cruisers, and lines form beyond midnight to get into the in-rage restaurants and discos on Collins and Washington Avenues. The former Amsterdam Hotel, a 1930 Mediterranean 16th century-design building unlike any of the others on Ocean Drive (it even has a rooftop observatory) was transformed, with millions of dollars and the loss of a building behind it, into the showcase—yet private—home of Italian designer Gianni Versace. The purchase price in 1992 was $2.9 million, the extensive restoration work was on top of that. Gloria and Emilio Estefan recognized the ambiance and diversity of South Beach and bought the Cardozo Hotel. Just to the north, portions of Lincoln Road were recreated as trendy art galleries and restaurants. South Beach became such an important draw for tourists and residents alike that to do anything to destroy it would be seen as communal suicide, even by those who originally opposed the district.

Nevertheless, while South Beach became a great lure for dining, drinking and dancing, the capacity of its hotel rooms was not enough to host a major convention. Miami Beach was losing ground in the national competition for large conventions. Where hoteliers first looked at the Historic District area as a place where someday a large hotel might rise, historic preservationists had circled the wagons. The need for a convention hotel became acute. With millions of dollars expended on expanding and modernizing the Miami Beach Convention Center, there was not a single hotel within walking distance of the center that could house any substantial number of delegates. What's more, many of them were getting a bad press for the condition of their rooms and service. Geography and politics placed the Historic District in close proximity to the convention center. If any major hotel was going to be built, there was

bound to be a clash. With Nancy Liebman succeeding Capitman in 1987 as the leader of the MDPL forces, she faced pressure from the city to work with the big hotel proponents. That's where the art of compromise came in. Preservationists told the city they would support a convention hall in the Historic District if the city supported expanding the locally-designated Historic District to match that of the national designation. The deal was worked out.

The City of Miami Beach purchased empty lots upon which once stood the New Yorker, Sands and Poinciana hotels as well as the adjacent St. Moritz, still standing. Out of those four properties will be carved an 830-room hotel in time for the winter season of 1998—with the St. Moritz, in some form, restored. The nearby Royal Palm and Shorecrest are not owned by the city, nor are the Bancroft and Jefferson hotels, all of which are expected to be redeveloped into an upscale retail center and condomininiums in theme with the new hotel as a Historic Convention Village. In early 1994, a private developer purchased the Bancroft $6.3 million. He pledged to build 100 condominiums and 40,000 to 70,000 feet of retail space and parking while saving the Bancroft's facade.[43]

With each day, there were new announcements, new openings, new demographics for Miami Beach. The city was on a path that took it from being what had become a senior citizen community to being one of diversity, youth and vibrancy. The old people of South Beach were disappearing rapidly, either victims of mortality, raised rents or crime and fear of crime. The Hispanic population, which grew to be half the total population of the city, also began to decline as rental prices advanced beyond their reach. Meanwhile, young people who could afford them were moving into the apartment houses that lined Biscayne Bay from Eighth Street to Lincoln Road, and also in the areas near Flamingo Park, where old apartment buildings were being restored as part of the Historic District. Tourist-less hotels were being converted to condominiums as were apartment houses that fronted on the Atlantic Ocean. Ironically, many of the people buying condos in those former hotels and apartment buildings were South Florida residents seeking a second home. Seventy percent of the buyers of condos in the Castle Beach Club were South Floridians.[44]

This is ironic because most of J. N. Lummus' first customers back between 1914 and 1919 also were South Floridians, buying up cottages near the foot of Miami Beach as weekend and summer homes by the seashore.

Miami Beach seemed to be at another crossroads: Was it going to regain its form as a center of tourism, or simply become a bedroom community?

Galbut and Kahn—Crescent Heights, Inc.—put their money behind condo conversions. By mid-1992, they converted four apartment buildings and two hotels into 2,339 condominiums. Miami Beach was in need of more, not fewer, hotel rooms. Crescent Heights was seen by some as being destructive of Miami Beach's tourist capability as well as its existing residents. Stories were whispered—some published—that Crescent Heights played hardball with residents of the buildings it had purchased. The stories broadcast images of elderly people forced out of their previously rental apartments by the high cost of the same apartment as a condominium.[45] Galbut and company, obviously, saw things in a different light. They saw it as rescuing failing hotels and apartment houses, refurbishing them with millions of dollars of work and providing affordable condominium living.

Despite its internecine warfare, Miami Beach was surviving. Throughout the world, it was being linked to the *chic* destinations of the rich and famous, utilized as a fashion-photo center by international houses and publications, and as a prime location for motion pictures and television shows. Miami Beach was seen as a city driven by powerful people, not always powerful as in "rich," but powerful nonetheless. The book remains open on Miami Beach. She has been romanced and succored by many, jilted and left at the altar by many others. Each day brings new self-proclaimed messiahs to Miami Beach, some who follow through on their promises—people such as Tony Goldman who picked up Barbara Capitman's challenge and, in his own way, became a big player and restorer in South Beach. At present, German-born Thomas Kramer, who has been soaking up South Beach properties, is in the headlines. What the South Shore Redevelopment Agency hoped but failed to accomplish in the 1970s, Kramer is claiming he will do—his way—in the 1990s. Within a year of his first visit to Miami Beach in 1992, Kramer purchased more than $30 million worth of property south of Sixth Street.[46]

In early 1994, Kramer was saying he would do over the most southerly portion of South Beach to to be much like the Italian Riviera's Portofino. But that's another chapter in the history of Miami Beach— yet to be documented or written.

When John Collins stood at the abandoned coconut plantation shortly after the turn of the century and wondered what to do about all the property he had obtained, he believed the answer was in avocados. At the time, he was right. What evolved from that, in such a relatively short time of the planet's history, would have stunned him to his Quaker roots.

ON THE FRONT LINE OF THE ART DECO MOVEMENT

Commissioned by Gerry Sanchez, a mural by Maita Pita, originally in the lobby of the Breakwater Hotel, depicts those in the forefront of the Art Deco movement and the members of the Miami Beach City Commission and staff at the time of the district's inception. They are (not in order): M. Kinerk, E. Martin, L. Horowitz, A. Rauzin, M. Rebozo, N. Liebman, N. Kasdin, M. Pelierin, S. Cook, A. Holtz, B. Singer, L. Beilinson, G. Sanchez, A. Suarez, A. Daoud, S. Weisburd, B. Grenald, J. Marder, R. Hoberman, B. Capitman, S. Arkin, A. Resnick, W. Shockett, J. Kurlancheek, R. Parkins, S. Kogel, G. Vitale, R. Foesman. (MB)

REFLECTIONS

EPILOGUE

The Sterling Building, 1946. (SPA)

Perhaps this book should have been published in a loose leaf binder. In that way, there would be an opportunity to place *addenda* to the story of Miami Beach. As I churned through the last pages of the manuscript, it was quite evident that the promises, dreams and hopes I had closed with soon would turn into actuality, or smoke. All histories are antiquated beginning with the day after the last sentence is written but at the pace with which things are occurring in Miami Beach, I'm not certain you can make it through the first 24 hours without dramatic change.

Too close to deadline did the Miami Beach City Commission choose Loew's Hotels/Forest City Ratner as their unanimous first choice for negotiations to build the long-awaited 830-room convention hotel. At the same time, they also agreed to negotiations with an African–American/Sheraton Hotel partnership to build another hotel alongside as promised in the agreement to end a black tourism boycott. Both proposals included restoration of the historic Art Deco hotels on the site—a far cry from traditional Miami Beach political thinking.

A week later, the commission selected Cobb Theaters/Lincoln Road Development Group as their first choice to build a major league–sized motion picture theater, a small legitimate theater, artist housing and a retail area behind Lincoln Road at Lenox Avenue.

Almost anonymously, Pacific International Equities—originally a Canadian-based company—is in the midst of constructing condominiums, townhouses and apartments at three Miami Beach locations.

Pending are petition initiatives that could place casino gambling in Miami Beach. Other major incentives—giant apartment houses—are on the drawing boards, or being floated as trial balloons in the pages of the community's daily and weekly newspapers.

It all lends itself to an initial feeling of tentativeness, but that is far from the truth.

There is a remarkable amount of permanence to Miami Beach. Evidence, please, that two rabbis served their Miami Beach congregations for almost a half-century each, that the venerable Lincoln and Colony theaters continue to serve the cultural needs of the community, that Wolfie's still is dishing up corned beef sandwiches and that many of the hotels constructed during the Depression not only still exist but now are an indispensable part of the city's lure as a tourist center.

One can lament that the Fifth Street Gym was torn down, as was the Senator Hotel, but there remains permanence in people and institutions.

Judy Drucker, the Sol Hurok of Miami Beach, has led the Concert Association of Florida at the top of the city's cultural calendar since 1966. The Bass Art Museum stands as a significant repository of art and the Holocaust Memorial is an ominous reminder of a tragedy. Mitchell Wolfson progeny Mickey Wolfson's Wolfsonian Museum on Washington Avenue, when it opens in 1995, will be a unique museum of Decorative and Propaganda Arts.

Saks Fifth Avenue may not be on Lincoln Road any more, but the street, *sans* automobiles, remains a modified constant: old ice cream parlors replaced with trendy cafes; shoe stores and ladies better dresses supplanted by an explosion of art and design galleries. It has also become a major street of culture including the studios of the world-renowned Miami City Ballet and headquarters of the New World Symphony. On tap is a $12 million renovation of the 1960s Morris Lapidus designed mall, including sidewalks, sewers, drainage and foliage. Further north, the 41st Street Merchant's Association is working on plans to make that area more pedestrian friendly. North Beach, too, is undergoing a planning study.

What years ago was a Miami Beach cafeteria specializing in chicken soup and pot roast now is a *chic* night spot where the party-goers first start lining up for admission close to midnight. The mom and pop sandwich shops of yesterday's South Beach may now specialize in *lechón asado, piccadillo* and *café con leché*, but the doors remain open and the customers come as they have for decades.

Above all, a more mature city leadership—including the politicians—has come to recognize that the varied elements of Miami Beach need each other to form the whole. Whereas, not that long ago, the big hotel interests and the preservationists would tear at each other as though survival depended upon the other's demise, they have realized that one complements the other—that the ambiance of exciting nights on South Beach goes hand-in-hand with a convention of business-types who will meet by day in coat and tie at a large convention hotel, then metamorphose by night to vogue attire, slicked-back hairdos and pendulous jewelry for a nocturnal fling at another world.

As with any other city, there have been dark days and bright days for Miami Beach.

I am reminded of what Carl Fisher's old ally, Pete Chase, once said of when pioneer John Collins first arrived at the abandoned coconut plantation and saw the desolation around him:

"With utter failure staring him in the face, he made one last effort, and this one last effort brought glittering success."

That same attitude, that drive to make another effort, is what still prevails among the people who live on the old sandbar.

APPENDIX

MIAMI BEACH MAYORS

Jan. 16, 1917 .... J.N. Lummus
Oct. 28, 1918 .... Thomas J. Pancoast
Oct. 25, 1920 .... T. E. James
Oct. 23, 1922 .... Louis F. Snedigar
Dec. 17, 1924 .... Louis F. Snedigar
Dec. 21, 1926 .... J. N. Lummus, Jr.
Dec. 18, 1928 .... Louis F. Snedigar
Dec. 16, 1930 .... Val C. Cleary
Dec. 20, 1932 .... Frank Katzentine
Dec. 18, 1934 .... Louis F. Snedigar
June 1, 1937 .... John H. Levi
June 6, 1939 .... John H. Levi
June 3, 1941 .... Val C. Cleary
June 1, 1943 .... Mitchell Wolfson*
                                    John H. Levi
June 5, 1945 .... Herbert A. Frink
June 3, 1947 .... Marcie Liberman
June 7, 1949 .... Harold Turk
June 5, 1951 .... D. Lee Powell
June 2, 1953 .... Harold Shapiro
June 7, 1955 .... D. Lee Powell
June 4, 1957 .... Kenneth Oka
June 2, 1959 .... D. Lee Powell
June 6, 1961 .... Kenneth Oka
June 4, 1963 .... Melvin Richard
June 1, 1965 .... Elliott Roosevelt
June 6, 1967 .... Jay Dermer
Nov. 18, 1969 .... Jay Dermer
Nov. 16, 1971 .... Chuck Hall
Nov. 6, 1973 .... Chuck Hall
Aug. 21, 1974 .... Harold Rosen**
Nov. 4, 1975 .... Harold Rosen
Nov. 1, 1977 .... Dr. Leonard Haber
Nov. 6, 1979 .... Murray Meyerson
Nov. 3, 1981 .... Norman Ciment
Nov. 1, 1983 .... Malcolm Fromberg
Nov. 6, 1985 .... Alex Daoud
Nov. 3, 1987 .... Alex Daoud
Nov. 7, 1989 .... Alex Daoud
Nov. 19, 1991 .... Seymour Gelber

*   Mitchell Wolfson left office in October 1943 for military service. John H. Levi was chosen to complete Wolfson's term.
**   Harold Rosen was elected to fill the unexpired term of Chuck Hall, who died in office.

J. N. Lummus, Miami Beach's first mayor, and Jane Fisher, display the Miami Beach flag, designed by Rose Weiss. (SPA)

ENDNOTES

CHAPTER ONE

1 William Gerrard DeBrahm, *The Atlantic Pilot* (London: T. Spilsbury, 1772), chart entitled "The Ancient Tegesta, now Promontory of East Florida," facsimile edition introduced by Louis de Vorsey Jr. (Gainesville, Fla.: University Presses of Florida, 1974).

2 P. Lee Phillips, *Notes on the Life and Works of Bernard Romans* (Deland, Fla.: Florida State Historical Society, 1924), chart entitled "Part of East Florida," facsimile edition introduced by John D. Ware (Gainesville, Fla.: University Presses of Florida, 1975).

3 John Kunkel Small, *From Eden To Sahara: Florida's Tragedy* (Lancaster, Pa.: The Science Press, 1929), 95.

4 Vernon Lamme, *Florida Lore Not Found in the History Books* (Boynton Beach, Fla.: Star Publishing Co., 1973), 82.

5 Don d'Escalante Fontenada, *Memoir of Don d'Escalante Fontenada Respecting Florida,* translated from the original, c1575, by Buckingham Smith (Washington, D.C.: 1854), edited by David O. True (Coral Gables, Fla.: Glade House, 1945), 25–26.

6 Arva Moore Parks, *Where the River Found the Bay* (Tallahassee: Florida Division of Archives, History and Records Management for the City of Miami, 1979), 51.

7 Parks, *River,* 54.

8 Letter, Bishop Geronimo Valdes of Cuba to Spanish Crown, Dec. 9, 1711, as cited in *River,* 52.

9 Letter, Governor of Cuba to the Spanish King, July 26, 1743, as cited in *River,* 53.

10 *Royal Gazette,* 1817, as cited by Arva Parks, *Miami: The Magic City* (Tulsa, Okla.: Continental Heritage Press, 1981), 22.

11 Roland Chardon, "Norris Cut," *Tequesta,* Vol. XXXVII (1977), 57-58.

12 Roland Chardon, "Cartographgic Analysis of Coastal Change: Natural and Urban," *Geoscience and Man,* Vol. XVIII (Baton Rouge, La.: Louisiana State University, School of Geoscience, 1977), 261–263.

13 Thelma Peters, *Biscayne Country* (Miami, Fla.: Banyan Books, 1981), 50.

14 Rose Wagner Richards, "Reminiscences of the Early Days of Miami," *Miami Morning News,* 1903; see Agnew Welsh Notebook XXXVI, Miami-Dade Public Library.

15 Jefferson Brown, *Key West, The Old and the New* (St. Augustine, Fla.: The Record Company, 1912), 15.

16 Harry Gardner Cutler, *History of Florida, past and present, historical and biographical* (Chicago and New York: Lewis Publishers, 1923), Vol. III, 348.

17 William Curry Harlee, *Kinfolks, A Genealogical & Biographical Record, Vol. III* (New Orleans, La.: Searcy and Pfaff Ltd.), 934.

18 On Bremon Landing usage, see Henry J. Wagner, "Early Pioneers of South Florida," *Tequesta* Vol. IX (1949), 65. On Brama Landing usage, see Ralph Middleton Munroe and Vincent Gilpin, *The Commodore's Story* (Ives Washburn, 1930, reprinted by Historical Association of Southern Florida, Northberth, Pa.: Livingston, 1966), 121. On Brahman Landing usage, see Charles Edgar Nash, *The Magic of Miami Beach* (Philadelphia: David McKay Co., 1938), 69.

19 Charles Peacock, proprietor of Bay View House in Coconut Grove.

20 History of Biscayne Bay House of Refuge, MS, National Archives, Records of the United States Coast Guard, RG26.

21 *Ibid.*

22 Peters, *Biscayne Country,* 51.

23 The other houses of refuge on the southeast coast were located four miles north of New River Inlet, at Gilbert's Bar on Hutchinson Island east of Stuart and at Bethel Creek 13 miles north of Indian River Inlet.

24 Thelma Peters, "The Log of the Biscayne House of Refuge," *Tequesta,* Vol. XXXVIII (1978), 45.

25 Munroe and Gilpin, *The Commodore's Story,* 96.

26 Peters, "Biscayne House of Refuge," 45.

27 *Ibid.,* 46.

28 Munroe and Gilpin, *The Commodore's Story,* 192.

29 *Ibid.*

30 Peters, "Biscayne House of Refuge," 48–49.

CHAPTER TWO

1 William Theobald, palm registration specialist, Florida Department of Agriculture and Consumer Services, Forestry Division.

2 Subsequent historians followed Nash's narrative. Unfortunately, Nash put no footnotes, bibliography or acknowledgments in *The Magic of Miami Beach;* therefore there is no accessible source of his information. Nash died in 1982 and his widow, living in Maryland, says she has no knowledge of the whereabouts of his notes. She does have, however, correspondence from Effie Lum praising Nash's completed book. If it was Effie Lum who transmitted the original information to Nash, then it should be considered credible but not primary until 1886, which is when she came to South Florida.

3 Nash, *The Magic of Miami Beach,* 69.

4 Theobold interview.

5 Munroe and Gilpin, *The Commodore's Story,* 120.

6 Letter from Henry Lum to E. G. Gerison, Dec. 26, 1882, Vol. IX, Miscellaneous Letters to Surveyor General, 1883 [sic], Department of Natural Resources, Tallahassee, Fla.

7 Letter from Henry Lum to unspecified person, Jan. 30, 1883, Vol. IX, Miscellaneous Letters to Surveyor General, 1883, Department of Natural Resources, Tallahassee, Fla.

8 Monmouth County, N.J., Census, 1880.

9 *Ibid.*

10 Florida State Land Records, Department of Natural Resources.

11 Deeds Books A–Z, Dade County Records Library.

12 *Ibid.*

13 Charles W. Pierce, *Pioneer Life in Southeast Florida,* edited by Donald Walter Curl (Coral Gables, Fla.: University of Miami Press, 1970), 171.

14 *Ibid.,* 169.

15 *Ibid.,* 170–171.

16 *Ibid.,* 171.

17 *Ibid.*

18 Nash, *The Magic of Miami Beach,* 72.

19 "May We Present: Capt. Richard Carney," *Miami Herald,* Aug. 3, 1936.

20 Nash, *The Magic of Miami Beach,* 76.

21 "Meet the Man Who Once Owned All of Miami Beach," *Miami Daily News,* Dec. 24, 1933.

22 Munroe and Gilpin, *The Commodore's Story,* 183.

When Carney died, the *Miami Herald* reported in his June 22, 1941, obituary that, following the Spanish-American War, Carney purchased and operated the steamer *Lake Worth* and ran mail and passengers between Fort Lauderdale, Miami and Coconut Grove. In 1904, he signed on as yacht captain for wealthy industrialist W. L. Mellon of Pittsburgh. He stayed with the Mellons, captaining four different yachts named *Vagabondia* until his retirement in 1930. In his later years, he was assistant Miami dockmaster.

23 Charles W. Pierce, "Pioneer Life in South Florida," MS, Historical Society of Palm Beach County.

24 *Ibid.*

25 Dade County Deeds Books A–Z.

26 "Father and Daughter Dead," Red Bank, N.J., Register, May 29, 1895.

CHAPTER THREE

1 W. T. Cash, *The Story of Florida, Vol. II* (New York: The American Historical Society, 1938), 749.

2 Letter from John Wescott to Col. Coryell, Jan. 14, 1882, transcribed by Dr. Joe Knetsch, Division of State Lands, July 28, 1992, Florida Collection, Florida State Library, Tallahassee.

3 Nelson M. Blake, *Land into Water—Water into Land* (Tallahassee, Fla.: University Presses of Florida, 1980), 85.

4 *Minutes,* Board of Trustees of Internal Improvement Fund of the State of Florida (3:234-35), as cited in Blake, *Land into Water—Water into Land,* 85.

5 Edward N. Akin, *Flagler: Rockefeller Partner & Florida Baron* (Kent, Ohio: Kent State University Press, 1988), 177.

6 Blake, *Land Into Water,* 87.

7 "Man First to Develop Miami Beach, Now 85, Here Enjoying Fairyland," *Miami Herald,* Oct. 15, 1922.

8 Records Department, Division of State Lands, Florida Department of Natural Resources.

9 Linehan, Mary Collar, *Early Lantana, Her Neighbors and More* (St. Petersburg, Fla.: Byron Kennedy, ca 1971), 40

10 As cited in Linehan, Early Lantana, 40.

11 *National Cyclopaedia of American Biography,* Vol. XXI (New York: James T. White & Co., 1931), 192.

12 *Ibid.*

13 Taped interview with Russell T. Pancoast Jr. by Polly Redford, March 30, 1967, Special Archives, University of Miami.

14 *Ibid.*

15 Miami Beach Improvement Co., "The Bridge" (Miami, Fla.: Miami Beach Improvement Co., 1915); Miami Beach Public Library and Art Centre, John S. Collins Memorial" (Miami Beach, Fla.: Miami Beach Public Library and Art Centre, 1938).

16 Nash, *The Magic of Miami Beach,* 88.

17 E. V. Blackman, *Miami and Dade County, Florida* (Washington, D.C.: Victor Rainbolt, 1921), 201.

18 "Pioneer, 88, Marks Birthday With Story of Miami Beach," *Miami Daily News & Metropolis,* Dec. 29, 1925.

19 Nash, *The Magic of Miami Beach,* 88.

20 "Miami Beach History Related by Pioneer" *Miami Herald,* Nov. 25, 1926.

21 *Ibid.*

22 *Ibid.*

23 *Ibid.*

24 *Ibid.*

25 "Many Improvements Will Be Made by the Ferry Company at the Beach," *Miami Metropolis,* May 25, 1907.

26 "Miami Beach History Related by Pioneer," *Miami Herald,* Nov. 25, 1926.

27 John Sewell, *Miami Memoirs* (Miami, Fla.: The Franklin Press, 1933), republished by Arva Moore Parks (Miami, Fla.: Arva Parks & Co. with Tulsa, Okla.: Lion & Thorne, Ltd., 1987), 185.

28 *Ibid.*

29 "Some Reasons Why the Magic City Celebrates," *Miami Evening Record,* July 28, 1902.

30 Sewell, *Miami Memoirs,* 189.

31 *Ibid.* (Neither Brossier's 1930 recollection nor the March 15, 1905 edition of the Miami Evening Record reports how so many people found sufficient transportation to make the six-mile journey across the bay from Miami. Microfilm records of the *Miami Metropolis* do not contain that day's newspaper.)

32 "The Cut Was Made to the Ocean," *Miami Evening Record,* March 15, 1905.

33 "Drowned in the New Ship Channel," *Miami Metropolis,* March 20, 1905.

34 Taped interview with Russell T. Pancoast by Polly Redford, March 30, 1967.

35 Nash, *The Magic of Miami Beach,* 89.

36 Pancoast interview.

37 *Ibid.*

38 *Ibid.*

39 *Ibid.*

40 Advertisement, *Miami Metropolis,* May 24, 1912.

41 *Ibid.*

42 "Ocean Beach Improvements Little Short of Wonderful," *Miami Herald,* Aug. 18, 1912.

43 *Ibid.*

CHAPTER FOUR

1 J. N. Lummus, *The Miracle of Miami Beach,* Miami, Fla.: The Teacher Publishing Co., 1940; Miami, Fla.: Miami Post Publishing Co., 1944) 27.

2 *Ibid.,* 29.

3 Book 2 of Plats, pp. 38, 47, 87, Records of Dade County, Fla.

4 Blackman, *Miami and Dade County,* 232.

5 Lummus, *Miracle of Miami Beach,* 29.

6 *Ibid.*

7 "Work on Bridge is Progressing Famously," *Miami Herald,* July 27, 1912.

8 "Work Will Start Tomorrow on Bridge to Cross the Bay, Connecting Miami With the New Collins Beach Resort," *Miami Herald,* July 21, 1912.

9 "Thomas Pancoast Returns to Miami to Make His Home," *Miami Herald,* Aug. 31, 1912.

10 "Improvements at Fairyland [sic] Resort," letter from Avery C. Smith, *Miami Herald,* Aug. 28, 1912.

11 Legal Notice, *Miami Metropolis,* Aug. 24, 1912.

12 Advertisement, *Miami Metropolis,* June 10, 1908.

13 "John Collins Attaches No Strings to His Donation of a Park Site on the Ocean Front to the City of Miami," *Miami Herald,* July 12, 1912.

14 "Miami Beach to Beauty [sic] Old Park," *Miami Herald,* June 11, 1919.

15 "Thomas J. Pancoast Returns to Miami to Make His Home," *Miami Herald,* Aug. 31, 1912.

16 "Will Finish Pile Driving," *Miami Herald,* Dec. 10, 1912.

17 "Four Thousand Feet of Bridge," *Miami Herald,* Feb. 11, 1913.

18 "Fisher Buys 200 Acres Ocean Beach Property Which Means Development of Entire Peninsula North of Government Cut," *Miami Metropolis,* Jan. 23, 1913, 1, 3.

19 "Automobile Crosses to Peninsula on Viaduct," *Miami Metropolis,* May 22, 1913.

20 *Ibid.*

21 "Pile Driving to Collins Bridge," *Miami Herald,* Dec. 22, 1912.

22 "Opening of Big Bridge Across Bay Celebrated," "Tolls Now Charged to Cross Bay Bridge," *Miami Metropolis,* June 13, 1913, 1–2.

23 Advertisement, *Miami Herald,* Feb. 13, 1913.

24 Lummus, *Miracle of Miami Beach,* 31–32.

25 *Ibid.,* 32.

26 Welch sometimes is credited with building the first house on the beach; at other times, the credit goes to A. J. Bendle. While the two did build on the beach in 1913, the honor of building the first house remains with Charles Lum who put up a two-story residence on the south end of the beach in 1886.

27 Lummus, *Miracle of Miami Beach,* 42–43.

28 "New Collins Bridge," *Miami Metropolis,* Dec. 28, 1912, "Work Started on Pavillion," *Miami Herald,* Dec. 12, 1928.

29 Advertisement, *Miami Metropolis,* Feb. 13, 1913.

30 Nash, *Magic of Miami Beach,* 99.

31 Advertisement, *Miami Metropolis,* Feb. 14, 1913.

32 "Another Big Day at Collins Property Sale," *Miami Metropolis,* Feb. 21, 1913.

33 Fisher, Jane, *Fabulous Hoosier* (New York: Robert M. McBride, 1947), 129–130.

34 *Ibid.,* 17–18.

35 This episode is an example of Jane Fisher's propensity for exaggeration. In her version, the *Elph* was driven ashore in a deserted area by a hurricane. In her book, she talks of days of living as beachcombers, foraging for food, and of a national press concern for the Fishers' whereabouts. Weather bureau records show no hurricane activity in December 1909. Instead, the Deep South suffered an extreme cold wave in the period between Christmas and New Year's, hardly grist for a hurricane. Levi's version is considerably more understated. He said they ran onto a sandbar, spent the night; Carl and Jane then got off the vessel, and left John to see matters through, including necessary repairs.

36 "May We Present: John Levi," *Miami Herald,* June 26, 1936; "Growth of Beach Traced to Accidental Discovery in 1912 [sic]," *Miami Daily News,* May 16, 1937.

37 *Ibid.*

CARL FISHER BEFORE FLORIDA

1 Fisher, *Fabulous Hoosier,* 37–39.

2 *Ibid.,* 39–40.

3 *Ibid.,* 47.

4 *Ibid.,* 55.

5 *Ibid.,* 56–59.

6 *The Encyclopedia of Motor Sport,* edited by G. N. Georgano. (New York: Viking Press, 1971) 95; Devaney, John and Barbara, *The Indianapolis 500,* (Chicago: Rand McNally, 1976), 6.

7 Devaney, *Indianapolis 500,* 7–8.

8 Fisher, *Fabulous Hoosier,* 97.

9 *Ibid.,* 11–12.

CHAPTER FIVE

1 Fisher, *Fabulous Hoosier,* 21.

2 Blackman, *Miami and Dade County, Florida,* 235.

3 "The Carl G. Fisher Residence Robbed of Valuable Jewelry," *Miami Herald,* Feb. 21, 1912.

4. "Robbers Get Big Haul in Fisher Home," *Miami Metropolis,* Feb. 21, 1912.

5 Fisher, *Fabulous Hoosier,* 76.

6 *Indiana: A Guide to the Hoosier State,* compiled by workers of the Writers' Program of the Work Projects Administration in the State of Indiana (New York: Oxford University Press, 1941), 349.

7 Lincoln Highway Association, *The Lincoln Highway* (New York: Dodd, Mead & Company, 1935).

8 Papers of the Lincoln Highway Association, University of Michigan Engineering and Transportation Library, Ann Arbor, Michigan, as cited by Drake Hokanson in *The Lincoln Highway: Main Street Across America* (Iowa City, Iowa: University of Iowa Press, 1988), 153.

9 Hokanson, *The Lincoln Highway,* 8–9.

10 *Ibid.,* 16–18.

11 "Fisher Buys 200 Acres Ocean Beach Which Means Development of Entire Peninsula North of Government Cut," *Miami Metropolis,* Jan. 23, 1913.

12 Fisher, *Fabulous Hoosier,* 97.

13 *Miami Metropolis,* Jan. 23, 1913.

14 *Ibid.*

15 Lummus, *The Miracle of Miami Beach,* 32–33.

16 Mortgage Book 33, page 417, Records of Dade County, Fla.

17 Mortgage Book 39, page 85, Records of Dade County, Fla.

18 Fisher was not the only person from whom the Lummuses borrowed money. They found another benefactor in Edwin B. Lent of Peekskill, N.Y. He loaned the Lummuses sums ranging between $50,000 and $150,000 from 1913 to 1916—at eight per cent interest and a bonus of $10,000 per year for each of the three times the one-year loans were renewed. The Lummuses also borrowed $120,000 from Frank Furst and R. P. Clark and $30,000 from B. F. Potter.

Lummus, in his book, called those high interest loans a good deal because he, too, made money on them.

19 "Fisher Improvements To Go Forward Under Mr. Levi's Supervision," *Miami Metropolis*, May 3, 1913.

20 Fisher, *Fabulous Hoosier*, 130.

21 *Ibid.*

22 "Casino on the Beach Be Open Next Saturday," *Miami Metropolis*, April 3, 1913, 1, 5.

23 "F. B. Shutts Acquires a Tract Across Bay," *Miami Herald*, May 7, 1913.

24 Carl Graham Fisher. Collection of Letters, Other Documents. Historical Museum of Southern Florida, Miami, Fla.

25 "Bay and Beach Required Much Dredging," *Miami Daily News*, July 26, 1925.

26 Lummus, *Miracle of Miami Beach*, 43–44.

27 *Ibid.*, 45–46.

28 Lummus' writings and claims carry extraordinary weight. Of the three principals of those early beach days, only he wrote a memoir and often included reference to legal documents. Neither Fisher nor Collins, nor even Thomas Pancoast, actually sat down to give a detailed version of the record. In subsequent years, Fisher associates and Pancoast descendants related stories about happenings in 1912, 1913 and 1914, but they either weren't there then or, if they were, were either too young or were not part of the original planning and execution. There are Jane Fisher's accounts, but her embellishments and lack of documentation raise red flags as to accuracy. Lummus does not attempt to downgrade Fisher's accomplishments as much as he tries to elevate his own. When he and Fisher cooperated on a project, he recognized it. The glamour of the Fisher name, his personality and the success of his press agents more or less brought newspaper writers and historians to shine the spotlight solely on Fisher, thus leaving an offended Lummus sulking in the shadows.

29 "Bull Isle Fill Completed in 40 Days Time," *Miami Metropolis*, Aug. 13, 1913.

30 "Miniature Railroad on Beach Being Built to Hasten Improvement," *Miami Metropolis*, Sept. 6, 1913, 6.

31 "Wilderness Transformed into Beautiful Alton Beach," *Miami Metropolis*, Dec. 10, 1913.

32 Advertisement, *Miami Metropolis*, Jan. 22, 1914.

33 "21 Houses Now Being Built on Beach," *Miami Metropolis*, June 25, 1914.

34 "32 Costly Residences Are Now Being Built on Ocean Beach Sites," *Miami Metropolis*, July 3, 1914.

35 Advertisement, *Miami Metropolis*, March 21, 1914.

36 *Ibid.*

37 Biographical manuscript by Fred Wellman, 1919, CF–HASF.

38 "Parade Vividly Portrays History of Dade County," "Official Festival Program," "Historical Parade of Particular Interest," *Miami Metropolis*, Jan. 11, 1915, 9, 14 and Jan. 13, 1915.

39 "64.2 Miles An Hour Made by the Fast Hydroplane in Teeth of Strong Gale," "Award Trophies to the Regatta Winners," *Miami Metropolis*, Jan. 17, 1915, 1–2, and Jan. 18, 1915, 2.

40 "Dixie Highway Project Has Gathered So Much Momentum," *Miami Herald*, March 31, 1915.

41 "Miami Welcomes Highway Officials, Ovation Here Eclipses All Others," *Miami Metropolis*, Oct. 25, 1915.

42 "Outline of Dixie Highway," map, *The Dixie Highway*, October 1916, 9.

43 Letter from Carl Fisher to M. M. Allison, CF–HASF.

44 "$40,000 to be Cost of C. G. Fisher Beach Home," *Miami Metropolis*, March 28, 1914; "Work to Start in Two Weeks on C. Fisher Mansion," *Miami Metropolis*, Aug. 28, 1914.

45 Fisher, *Fabulous Hoosier*, 127.

46 "Millions Invested by Famed Men Here," *Miami Metropolis*, March 28, 1914, 1.

47 Junior League interview with Russell Pancoast, conducted by George Moretz, Aug. 26, 1970, HASF.

48 J. Arthur Pancoast, "A Successful Failure," *Tropic Magazine*, Sept. 1914, 14.

49 Junior League interview.

50 Oral history interview with Jesse Weiss by Ann Bishop, 1983.

51 "Miami Beach is Now a City of Its Own," *Miami Herald*, March 27, 1915.

52 Lummus, *Miracle of Miami Beach*, 58.

53 "Miami Beach Is Now a City of Its Own," *Miami Herald*, March 27, 1915.

CHAPTER SIX

1 "Resort Hotel For Miami Beach Planned," *Miami Herald*, March 11, 1915.

2 "Build a Hotel at Ocean Beach At Once," *Miami Herald*, April 24, 1915.

3 "Ocean Beach Has Shown Wonderful Development, Lots Are in Demand," *Miami Herald*, July 26, 1915, 8.

4 George M. Chapin, *Florida 1513–1913, Past, Present and Future* (Chicago: S. J. Clarke Publishing Co., 1914), 711. City of Miami Library, Florida Room.

5 "Brown's Hotel Sold For the Second Time," *Miami Metropolis*, May 16, 1922.

6 Lummus, *Miracle of Miami Beach*, 66–67.

7 "Miami Beach to Beautify Old Park," *Miami Herald*, June 11, 1919.

8 Deed Book 112, page 88, March 19, 1914, Dade County, Fla., Records Department.

9 "Human Races," *World Book Encyclopedia*, Vol. 16, 54.

10 Nathan C. Belth, *A Promise To Keep: A Narrative of the American Encounter With Anti-Semitism* (New York: Schocken Books, 1981), 38.

11 *Ibid.*, 41.

12 "Carl Fisher Builds More at the Beach," *Miami Herald*, Oct. 15, 1916.

13 "Apartment House at the Beach Completed," *Miami Herald*, Jan. 21, 1917.

14 "Lincoln Hotel at Beach Sold," *Miami Herald*, March 16, 1940.

15 *Ibid.*

16 "Ocean View New Company Is Organized," *Miami Herald*, April 14, 1916.

17 "Carl Fisher's Plans For a Beach Windmill," *Miami Herald*, Nov. 26, 1916.

18 Cecil R. Roseberry, *Glenn Curtiss: Pioneer of Flight* (Garden City, N.Y.: Doubleday, 1972); also see Alden Hatch, Glenn Curtiss, Pioneer of Naval Aviation (New York: Julian Messner, 1942).

19 Lummus, *Miracle of Miami Beach*, 39.

20 "Miami Been Selected for Big Aviation School," *Miami Metropolis*, Nov. 11, 1916, 1.

21 Sanborn Insurance Company map, 1918, Library of Congress, Map Division.

22 "DeWald Is Better: Bennet On Field," *Miami Herald*, April 16, 1917, 3.

23 Roseberry, Glenn Curtiss.

24 Lummus, *Miracle of Miami Beach*, 82–84.

25 *Ibid.*, 83.

26 "Big Island Created by Dredge Out in the Bay," *Miami Metropolis*, July 30, 1913, 1, 8.

27 Sanborn Insurance Company map, 1918: Library of Congress, Map Division.

28 "Society Held Sway at Polo Game," *Miami Metropolis*, Feb. 21, 1919, 4.

29 "First Polo in Florida on Beach Grounds Today," *Miami Metropolis*, Feb. 20, 1919, 7.

30 "The Breakers," (advertisement), *Miami Metropolis*, Nov. 27, 1917, 4.

31 "Wofford Hotel First By Ocean," *Miami Daily News*, July 26, 1925.

32 Plat book of Greater Miami & Suburbs, Dade County Plat Books, Plate F, 1925.

33 Blackman, *Miami and Dade County*, 102.

34 Advertisement, *Miami Herald*, Jan. 5, 1919.

35 Letter from Carl Fisher to Frank Seiberling, Feb. 3, 1919, CF–HASF

36 *Ibid.*

CHAPTER SEVEN

1 Fisher, *Fabulous Hoosier*, 157.

2 Letter from Charles Rauh to Carl Fisher, July 14, 1919, CF–HASF.

3 Letter from Carl Fisher to Charles Krom, May 29, 1920, CF–HASF.

4 Letter to Charles B. Sommers from Carl Fisher, Oct. 5, 1920, CF–HASF.

5 Letter to John LaGorce from Carl Fisher, Dec. 4, 1920, CF–HASF.

6 "Naturalist Brings Flamingo to Beach," *Miami Herald*, Oct. 18, 1921.

7 "Beautiful Flamingo Is Opened Formally with New Year's Party Night," *Miami Metropolis*, Jan. 4, 1921, 9.

8 Letter from Carl Fisher to Warren G. Harding, Dec. 6, 1920, CF–HASF.

9 Letter from Warren G. Harding to Carl Fisher, Jan. 12, 1921, CF–HASF.

10 "President-Elect Harding Now At Miami Beach," *Miami Metropolis*, Jan. 29, 1921.

11 Letter from David Jameson, Jan. 31, 1921, CF–HASF.

12 "President-Elect Harding Arrives In Miami, Spending Today At the Beach," *Miami Herald*, Jan. 30, 1921.

13 "Harding Fishing Today at Cocolobo Key," *Miami Metropolis*, Noon Edition, Jan. 31, 1921.

14 "Harding Likes Florida and the Florida 'Crackers,' He Tells Metropolis Reporter," *Miami Metropolis*, Jan. 31, 1921.

15 "Harding Returns to Miami Tomorrow Night," *Miami Metropolis*, Home Edition, Jan. 31, 1921.

16 "f Children at Beach to Require School," *Miami Herald*, July 7, 1915.

17 Letter from Thomas Pancoast to Carl Fisher, June 19, 1919, CF–HASF.

18 Letter from Carl Fisher to Thomas Pancoast, June 20, 1919, CF–HASF.

19 "Contract To Put Up Beach Public School Given New Local Firm," *Miami Metropolis*, Aug. 6, 1919.

20 Rev. Elisha A. King, *Planting A Church in a National Playground, Miami Beach, Florida.* (Miami Beach, Fla.: Personal Help Library, 1942), 10.

21 *Ibid.*

22 *Ibid.*

23 50 Years (Miami Beach, Fla.: Miami Beach Community Church, pamphlet), 1971.

24 Fisher, *Fabulous Hoosier*, 140.

25 "Splendid Gift Made Miami Beach Church," *Miami Herald*, April 3, 1920.

26 King, *Planting A Church*, 13.
27 *Ibid.*, 15.
28 Minutes, Dade County Commission, March 3, 1942.
29 Minutes, Miami Beach City Council, March 19, 1919, as cited by Edward Ridolph, *Biscayne Bay Trolleys* (Forty Fort, Pa.: H. E. Cox, 1981), 16; Minutes, Dade County Commission, June 5, 1919, as cited by Ridolph, *Biscayne Bay Trolleys*, 17.
30 "Thousands at the Opening of Causeway Over the Bay," *Miami Metropolis*, Feb. 18, 1920.
31 *Ibid.*
32 "New Street Car Line Starts Operating At Miami Beach Today," *Miami Metropolis*, Dec. 8, 1920.
33 Ridolph, *Biscayne Bay Trolleys*, 17.
34 "Railway Firm Starts Beach Coach Service," *Miami Daily News*, Oct. 18, 1939.
35 Oral history interview, Polly Redford with C.W. (Pete) Chase, Dec. 10, 1968, HASF.
36 *Ibid.*
37 *Ibid.*
38 *Ibid.*
39 "Recommend C. of C. As Civic Body Name," *Miami Herald*, July 13, 1921.
40 "C. of C. Selects Its Governors and Accepts Code of By-Laws," *Miami Herald*, July 23, 1921; "C. of C. Governors to Meet Monday," *Miami Herald*, July 24, 1921; "Promise Surprise in C. of C. Campaign," *Miami Herald*, Aug. 2, 1921; "190 Members Added to Chamber Rolls," *Miami Herald*, Aug. 6, 1921.
41 "Lummus Resigns From Beach City Council, Is Going to Alabama," *Miami Metropolis*, July 22, 1919.
42 Lummus, *Miracle of Miami Beach*, 80.
43 Letter from George Kline to Carl Fisher, Aug. 7, 1918, CF–HASF.
44 Minutes, Miami Beach City Council, July 29, 1918.
45 Letter from Carl Fisher to George Kline, Aug. 12, 1918, CF–HASF.
46 Letters from J. N. Lummus to Carl Fisher, Feb. 21, 1920, Aug. 3, 1920, CF–HASF.
47 Letter from J. N. Lummus to Carl Fisher, Feb. 8, 1919, CF–HASF.
48 Report of North Louisiana oil operations, Dec. 23, 1919, CF–HASF.
49 Letter from J. N. Lummus to Carl Fisher, Feb. 21, 1920, CF–HASF.
50 Letter from J. N. Lummus to Carl Fisher, Aug. 3, 1920, CF–HASF.
51 Letter from Carl Fisher to J. N. Lummus, Aug. 7, 1920, CF–HASF.
52 Letter from Carl Fisher to J. N. Lummus, April 22, 1922, CF–HASF.

CHAPTER EIGHT

1 "Miami's Aquarium Opened to Public For First Time," *Miami Metropolis*, Jan. 1, 1921.
2 "Collapse of Huge Tank at Aquarium Sends Fish Flying Through the Air," *Miami Herald*, July 3, 1920.
3 In January 1925, Allison sold the aquarium and its grounds to developer Jerome Cheribino, who announced that he shortly would build a hotel—the Floridian—on the site.
4 C. D. B. Bryan, *National Geographic Society: 100 Years of Adventure and Discovery* (New York: Harry N. Abrams, 1987), 299-301.
5 Letter from John Oliver LaGorce to Carl Fisher, Nov. 18, 1920, CF–HASF.

6 Bryan, *National Geographic Society*, 301.
7 *Ibid.*
8 Bryan, *National Geographic Society*, 300.
9 Voter's List, Precinct 13, Miami Beach, *Miami Herald*, Oct. 30, 1920.
10 Letter from Carl Fisher to Thomas Pancoast, Feb. 25, 1919, CF–HASF.
11 "Carl Fisher to Establish Industrial Center at Beach for Colored People," *Miami Herald*, June 12, 1919.
12 Letter from Thomas Pancoast to Carl Fisher, Sept. 23, 1920, CF–HASF.
13 *Ibid.*
14 *Ibid.*
15 "Island Opposite Miami Sold For Colored Resort," *Miami Metropolis*, May 1, 1918.
16 Letter to Thomas Pancoast from Carl Fisher, Sept. 28, 1920, CF–HASF.
17 Jesse Weiss, recorded interview by Ann Bishop, 1980.
18 *Ibid.*
19 *Ibid.*
20 *Ibid.*
21 Letter from Carl Fisher to Lymnan Kendall, May 11, 1921, CF–HASF.
22 Letter from Eugene Stahl to Carl Fisher, Oct. 6, 1921, CF–HASF.
23 Letter from Carl Fisher to Eugene Stahl, Oct. 10, 1921, CF–HASF.
24 Letter from Carl Fisher to Capt. H. C. C. Tippett, Miami Beach Golf Club, Feb. 18, 1924, CF–HASF.
25 Letter to a Mr. Klein from Carl Fisher, March 19, 1927, CF–HASF.
26 "Fleischmann's Body on Way to New York," *Miami Daily News and Metropolis*, Feb. 7, 1925; "Fleischmann Rites Observed," *Miami Daily News and Metropolis*, Feb. 9, 1925; "Fleischmann's Body Carried to Cincinnati," *Miami Daily News and Metropolis*, Feb. 11, 1925.
27 Letter from Charles Krom to C. W. (Pete) Chase, Nov. 1, 1926, CF–HASF.
28 Letter from Charles Krom to Carl Fisher, Dec. 7, 1929, CF–HASF.
29 City of Miami Beach, Ordinance 457, Nov. 4, 1936.

CHAPTER NINE

1 "Development of Business at South Beach," *Miami Metropolis*, June 4, 1921.
2 *Ibid.*
3 *Ibid.*
4 "Old Joe Sure Knew His Crustaceans," *Miami News,* May 10, 1964; Jo Ann Bass and Richard Sax, *Eat at Joe's* (New York: Clarkson Potter, 1993), 18.
5 "Theatrical Stars Take Air Flights," *Miami Herald*, Jan. 24, 1920.
6 "Miami Beach News: Many Flights Made," *Miami Herald*, Jan. 3, 1920.
7 "First Pictures to Boost City Taken at Beach," *Miami Metropolis*, Nov. 2, 1914.
8 Richard Alan Nelson, *Lights! Camera! Florida!* Ninety Years of Moviemaking and Television Production in Sunshine State (Tampa: Florida Endowment for the Humanities, 1987), 43.
9 Letter from D. W. Griffith to E. G. Sewell and E. E. Brackett, July 11, 1921, CF–HASF.
10 Sanborn Insurance Company map of Miami Beach, January 1921, National Archives, Washington, D.C.
11 Letter from Ed Ballard to Carl Fisher, Feb. 28, 1921, CF–HASF.
12 Letter from Carl Fisher to Ed Ballard, Feb. 7, 1921, CF–HASF.
13 Letter from Carl Fisher to John LaGorce, Feb. 7, 1921, CF–HASF.

14 Western Union telegrams, Dec. 19, 21, 22, 23, 27, 1921, CF–HASF.
15 Memo from Carl Fisher to F. R. Humpage, April 8, 1932, CF–HASF.
16 Letter from Carl Fisher to Edward Crozer, Dec. 3, 1932, CF–HASF.
17 Letter from Carl Fisher to F. R. Humpage, April 9, 1932, CF–HASF.
18 Census, 1920.
19 Ben Frank and James Monahen, "Happy Where the Heart Is: The Inspiring Saga of Kotaro Suto," Reader's *Digest, June 1954.*
20 "Miami Beach Landscaping Has Its Special Problem: Bay Marl Proved Usable to Excellent Advantage, Says Hoerger," *Miami Daily News*, July 26, 1925.
21 "Bring Brides From Nippon to Florida," *Miami Herald*, Oct. 27, 1921.
22 "See Lincoln Road Lure" *Miami Beach Sun*, June 2–3, 1963.
23 "Born In Wrong Country, Asserts Jap At Beach," *Miami Herald*, Dec. 17, 1941.
24 Letter from Carl Fisher to Thomas Pancoast, May 11, 1920, CF–HASF.
25 "Miami Beach Calls Thousands Across Causeway to Surf," "Beautiful Miami Beach Offers Sterling Attractions for All Seekers of Pleasure," "Speaking of Building," *Miami Herald*, Oct. 25, 1921.
26 "Rook Pays $25,000 For Beach Business Lot," *Miami Herald*, June 10, 1921.
27 "New Harbor Plans Are Suggested by Carl Fisher," *Miami Herald*, Feb. 4, 1920.
28 "Miami Beach Council Says Their Town Logical Deep Water Harbor," *Miami Herald*, June 9, 1919.
29 Letter from Carl Fisher to James M. Cox, Feb. 19, 1923, CF–HASF.
30 Letter from Carl Fisher to Joseph Weisener, Oct. 18, 1922, CF–HASF.
31 On March 29, 1925, the *Miami Daily News* reported that Fisher's organization announced plans to construct a 130-foot high suspension bridge across Government Cut from Miami Beach to Terminal Island. But the continuing struggle over the location of the seaport impeded construction. Had the bridge been built, today's huge ocean liners would not have been able to clear its span on the way to sea from either the proposed Fisher port or today's Dodge Island Seaport, which lies halfway between the sites sought by Fisher and Sewell.
32 C. W. (Pete) Chase, recorded interview by Polly Redford, Oct. 5, 1966.
33 Ameritrust Company, Cleveland, Ohio, as referenced in *World Book Encylopedia*, Vol. 5, 1991, 157.
34 "Venetian Islands' Beating Contract," *Miami Herald*, Aug. 7, 1921, 12.
35 "Snedigar Signs With Athletics," *Miami Herald*, May 12, 1913.
36 "Dirtiest Ball Ever Played on the Royal Palm Grounds," *Miami Herald*, Aug. 10, 1912.
37 "Behind the Front Page," *Miami Herald*, Dec. 21, 1940.
38 Author interview with Jim Snedigar, Oct. 28, 1993.
39 "Mayor Who Slept One Off In His Own Jail Tells How He Quit Drinking," *Miami Herald*, May 9, 1947.
40 Author interview with Jim Snedigar, June 18, 1992.
41 "Snedigar Lauded For Robust Life At First Rally," *Miami Herald*, Nov. 27, 1934.
42 *Ibid.*
43 Author interview with Jim Snedigar, June 24, 1992.
44 *Ibid.*

45 The others were R. N. Wilson, J. N. Lummus, J. Arthur Pancoast, J. T. Blackman, H. H. Filer, C. H. Perry: Incorporation Papers, Town of Miami Beach, filed March 26, 1915.

46 The others were C. H. Perry, H. H. Filer, W. E. Brown, W. E. Norton, F. C. B. LeGro and Thomas J. Pancoast, Minutes Miami Beach Incorporation meeting, March 26, 1915, City Clerk's Office.

47 Letter from Carl Fisher to Eugene Stahl, Oct. 10, 1921, CF–HASF.

48 Malvina Weiss Liebman and Seymour B. Liebman, *Jewish Frontiersmen, Historical Highlights of Early South Florida Jewish Communities* (Miami Beach: Jewish Historical Society of South Florida, Inc., 1980), 42.

49 Oral history interview with Rose Weiss, HASF, Oct. 16, 1969.

50 Oral history interview with Polly Redford, April 27–28, 1967.

51 Oral history interview with Rose Weiss, HASF, Oct. 16, 1969.

52 Oral history interview with Polly Redford, April 27–28, 1967.

53 Kenneth Ballinger, in his 1936 book *Miami Millions*, quotes pioneer Realtor Kenneth Keyes: "In my opinion the real estate boom which reached its climax in 1925 began to get under way in the spring of 1923. Building permits in April, May, June and July of that year totalled $5,723,695, almost a million and a half dollars monthly."

CHAPTER TEN

1 "Largest Bearing Avocado and Mango Grove in World Now at Miami Beach," *Miami Herald*, March 23, 1922.

2 "Building Records Are Being Broken," *Miami Herald*, June 12, 1922.

3 "Buy More Milk Cows," *Miami Herald*, Nov. 14, 1922.

4 Fisher, *Fabulous Hoosier*, 152–153.

5 Ibid., 192.

6 Ibid.

7 "Dade County Is Voted Dry," *Miami Metropolis*, Oct. 30, 1913.

8 Letter from Carl Fisher to Jim Allison, April 28, 1921, CF–HASF.

9 Letter from C. G. Fowler to Carl Fisher, April 16, 1923, CF–HASF.

10 Stuart McIver, *The Greatest Sale on Earth* (Miami: E. A. Seeman, 1980), 27.

11 Ibid.

12 Taped interview of C. W. (Pete) Chase by Polly Redford, Oct. 5, 1966.

13 The Cocolobo Cay Club was built by Fisher in 1916 on Adams Key in South Biscayne Bay as a hideaway for sportsmen.

14 "$198,000 in Building Begun During Month," *Miami Herald*, Jan. 31, 1923.

15 "Roney a Man of Vision," *Miami Herald*, April 27, 1968.

16 *The Book of Florida* (Florida Editors Association, 1925), 131.

17 Kenneth Ballinger, *Miami Millions* (Miami: Franklin Press, 1936), 109.

18 Ballinger, *Miami Millions*, 109–110.

19 Lummus, *Miracle of Miami Beach*, 91.

20 Ballinger, *Miami Millions*, 110.

21 Officers of the First National Bank were Edward Romfh, chairman of the board; John Levi, president; Thomas Pancoast, vice-president; F. Lowry Wall, vice-president and cashier, Miami Beach City Directory, 1925–26.

22 Officers of the Miami Beach Bank and Trust Company were Ben Shepard, president; N. B. T. Roney, vice-president; A. H. Patten, cashier, Miami Beach City Directory, 1925–26.

23 The Miami Tribune began publication early in 1924. Editor was Clayton Sedgwick Cooper, while Leo F. Reardon was president of the publishing company. The newspaper ceased publication in August 1927 but returned as a daily tabloid, under new management, in November 1934. It was purchased in 1937 by *Miami Herald* owner John Knight and closed down.

24 Ballinger, *Miami Millions*, 110.

25 Advertisement, *Miami Metropolis*, March 21, 1914.

26 "Spend Half A Million Dollars in Development at the Beach," *Miami Metropolis*, April 18, 1922.

27 "Roney to Build Spanish Village at Miami Beach," *Miami Daily News*, Dec. 27, 1924.

28 Lummus, *Miracle of Miami Beach*, 91.

29 "Espanola Way to Offer Unique Cultural Center," *Miami Daily News*, July 26, 1925.

30 Cox's vice-presidential running mate was Franklin Delano Roosevelt.

31 Letter from James M. Cox to Carl Fisher, Jan. 26, 1923, CF–HASF.

32 Letter from Carl Fisher to James M. Cox, Jan. 30, 1923, CF–HASF.

33 James M. Cox, *Journey Through My Years* (New York: Simon and Schuster, 1946), 313.

34 Cox later changed the newspaper's name to the *Miami Daily News & Metropolis*, then dropped *Metropolis* altogether. He then built Miami's landmark building to house his newspaper. The Tower of Seville–inspired News Tower on Biscayne Boulevard later became the Freedom Tower, the place through which several hundred thousand Cuban refugees were processed in the first years after Fidel Castro's rise to power.

35 Ballinger, *Miami Millions*, 113.

36 "New Nautilus Hotel Will Open Its Doors This Evening," *Miami News and Metropolis*, Jan. 10, 1924.

37 Ibid.

38 "Miami Beach Hotels Schedule Earlier Opening This Year," *Miami News and Metropolis*, Oct. 19. 1923.

39 Ibid.

40 Author interview with Katherine Pancoast, April 8, 1992.

41 T. H. Weigall, *Boom in Paradise* (New York: Alfred H. King, 1932).

42 *Miami Beach Register*, Jan. 16, 1924, 13.

43 Ibid.

44 Ibid.

45 Atlantic Food Shops, 300 First Street; Beach Haven Groceteria, 809 Fifth Street; Flamingo Market, 125 Collins Avenue; Gillingham Grocery, 209 Fifth Street and 816 First Street; Guarantee Market & Grocery, 320 First Street; Miami Grocery Co., 1100 Lincoln Road; Samuel Soliter's Grocery, 5 Ocean Drive; 1924 Miami Beach City Directory.

46 Ballinger, *Miami Millions*, 35.

47 Normandy Isle Archives, Miami Beach City Clerk's office.

48 Ibid.

49 Advertisement, *Miami Herald*, March 20, 1925.

50 Ballinger, *Miami Millions*, 74.

51 "Beach Has 122 Subdivisions," *Miami Daily News*, July 26, 1925.

52 Fisher, *Fabulous Hoosier*, 194–195.

53 Polly Redford, in her "Billion Dollar Sandbar" refers to Carl Fisher having mistresses. She specifically cited successive Fisher secretaries Ann Rossiter and Margaret Collier but does not reveal her source for this information, although it is suspected the source was Jane Fisher. Margaret Collier became Fisher's second wife. See Polly Redford, *Billion-Dollar Sandbar* (New York: Dutton, 1970).

54 "Retired Means Little in J. P. Stoltz's Life," *Miami Herald*, Jan. 1, 1924.

55 Advertisement, *Miami Herald*, Jan. 1, 1925.

56 "Bryan Broadcasts Fleetwood Opening," *Miami Herald*, Jan. 16, 1925.

57 "Roney to Start Work on $2,000,000 Hotel," *Miami Daily News*, Feb. 1, 1925.

58 Ballinger, *Miami Millions*, 115.

59 Ibid., 119.

60 Helen Muir, *Miami U.S.A.* (Coconut Grove, Fla.: Hurricane House, 1953), 146.

61 Ballinger, *Miami Millions*, 97.

62 *Miami Herald*, April 24, 1927.

63 Ballinger, *Miami Millions*, 113.

64 Ibid., 97.

65 Carl Fisher financial files, CF–HASF.

66 Carl Fisher letter to James Cox, July 29, 1927, CF–HASF.

67 *Miami Daily News*, Feb. 7, 1926; also see "Roney Plaza Hotel Leads Construction for Beach this Year," *Miami Daily News*, July 26, 1925, 17.

68 "Double Barrier Now Blockades Harbor," *Miami Daily News*, Jan. 11, 1926.

69 "Famed Seaside Rendezvous Ready," *Miami Daily News*, Feb. 7, 1926.

70 Letter from Carl Fisher to V. H. Power, Manufacturers Record, Baltimore, Md., Sept. 26, 1925, CF–HASF.

CHAPTER ELEVEN

1 "Miami Beach Society Events Have Interesting Background": *Miami Daily News and Metropolis*, July 26, 1925.

2 "Barton Remembers When Miami Beach Was a Wilderness," *Miami Herald*, March 23, 1965.

3 Taped interviews by Polly Redford with Alfred Barton, May 12 and May 18, 1967; Richter Library, University of Miami.

4 "Alfred Barton: The King Arthur of Beach Society's Camelot Era": *Miami Herald*, Nov. 13, 1978.

5 Ibid.

6 Redford, *Million Dollar Sandbar*, 77.

7 Letter from T. E. Myers of the Indianapolis Motor Speedway to Carl Fisher, Aug. 3, 1920, CF–HASF.

8 Letter from Carl Fisher "To Whom it May Concern," Dec. 17, 1924, CF–HASF.

9 "Beach Central Section Grew Most Rapidly," *Miami Daily News and Metropolis*, Jan. 4, 1925.

10 "Nation's South American Cables Will Pass Here," *Miami Daily News and Metropolis*, Oct. 12, 1925.

11 The original purchase was land on the Miami side where Biscayne Bay came to its northern limit at Dumfoundling Bay, but in 1921, Graves purchased three-quarters of a mile of oceanfront footage from the Tatums' Ocean Park Company and built a road from his western

property over to the ocean, according to the *Miami Herald* of March 16, 1922.

12 "Permission of Owners of Land Be Needed to Make Cut at Baker's Haulover," *Miami Metropolis*, June 30, 1916.

13 Peters, *Biscayne Country*, 278.

14 "Bay, Atlantic Waters to Join with Baker's Haulover Blast," *Miami Daily News and Metropolis*, April 14, 1925.

15 Ballinger, *Miami Millions*, 126.

16 *Ibid*.

17 Stuart McIver, *The Greatest Sale on Earth: The Story of the Miami Board of Realtors, 1920-1980* (Miami: E. A. Seemann, 1980), 66–67.

18 Ballinger, *Miami Millions*, 99.

19 McIver, *Greatest Sale on Earth*, 68.

20 "3,000 Fisher Lots Sold," *Miami Herald*, April 22, 1925.

21 "Begin New Library," *Miami Herald*, April 22, 1925.

22 Undated news clippings under heading "Library", Miami Beach City Clerk's office.

23 "Largest Swimming Pool in Florida Opens Today," *Miami Daily News*, Feb. 6, 1926. The Deauville had a checkered life, eventually was sold to health faddist Bernarr McFadden and demolished in 1956 for a new Deauville Hotel.

24 "Longest Wooden Bridge Passes Into History," *Miami Daily News*, March 15, 1925.

25 "Venetian Way Goes Into Use," *Miami Daily News*, March 1, 1926.

26 "Chamber Polls Member Views on Bay Isles," *Miami Daily News*, June 2, 1925.

27 The pilings remain to the present. Easily recognizable in the bay between the Julia Tuttle and Venetian Causeways, the pilings outline what would have been the bulkheaded island. On Oct. 27, 1944, the City of Miami Beach paid $35,000 for the land inside the pilings and, over the years, glamorous ideas for the property have been presented only to fade out. It began to be called Pelican Island because of the water birds that roosted on the pilings.

28 Frank B. Sessa, Anti-Florida Propaganda and Counter-Measures during the 1920's; *Tequesta*, *t*No. XXI (1961), 41–51.

29 Letter from Carl Fisher to James Davis, May 11, 1926, CF–HASF.

30 Letter from C.W. Chase, Jr., May 17, 1926, CF–HASF.

31 Letter from George Krom to Carl Fisher, March 22, 1926, CF–HASF.

32 *Ibid*.

33 Letter from Carl Fisher to Dudley Field Malone, March 16, 1926, CF–HASF.

34 Letter to Winifred Hussey from Carl Fisher, March 12, 1926, CF–HASF.

35 Munroe and Gilpin, *The Commodore's Story*, 1930, 340.

36 *Ibid*.

37 "Some Devastating North Atlantic Hurricanes of the 20th Century"; U.S. Department of Commerce, National Oceanic and Atmospheric Administration, 1971.

38 Florida Hurricane Survey Report, State of Florida, 1965.

39 Leo F. Reardon. The Florida Hurricane and Disaster, 1926, (Miami, Fla.: Miami Publishing Co., 1926, reprinted: Coral Gables, Fla., with Tulsa, Okl.: Lion & Thorne, Ltd., 1986), 33.

40 *Ibid*., 32.

41 Letter from Carl Fisher to John LaGorce, Oct. 8, 1926, CF–HASF.

42 National Hurricane Center tracking records show that the center of the storm passed about 25 miles offshore as the hurricane traveled in a generally north, northeast direction. Sustained winds near the center were recorded at 110 miles per hour, but the weaker side of the hurricane struck Miami Beach.

43 Memo from Pete Chase to W.A. Kohlhepp, Oct. 21, 1926, CF–HASF.

44 Letter from W.A. Kohlhepp to Carl Fisher, Oct. 21, 1926, CF–HASF.

CHAPTER TWELVE

1 Ida Fisher's maiden name was Graham, yet when the Miami Beach PTA chose a name for the new high school, the name selected was Ida M. Fisher. Presumably, that was for her original middle name—lost in history—although the practice much of the time was to use a woman's maiden surname, i.e., Ida G. Fisher. In "Fabulous Hoosier," Jane Fisher writes that she pointed out the error to Carl, to which she said he responded: "What the hell is the difference?"

2 "Well Done, St. Francis, Both The Hospital And The Steak," *Miami News*, June 28, 1964.

3 Raymond P. Sloan: *On a Shoestring and a Prayer*, (Garden City, New York & Doubleday Co.,) 1964, 64.

4 *Ibid*.

5 Father William Barry was elevated to Monsignor in 1937.

6 Mother Gerald, in 1940, founded and became first president of then-Barry College for Women in Miami Shores. It now is co-educational Barry University.

7 Fisher, *Fabulous Hoosier*, 252.

8 Letter from Father William Barry to Carl Fisher, Nov. 30, 1927, CF–HASF.

9 John Kobler, *The Life and World of Al Capone* (New York: Da Capo Press, 1992), 210.

10 Robert J. Schoenberg, *Mr. Capone: The Real and Complete Story of Al Capone*, (New York: Quill, William Morrow, 1992) 194.

11 While the *Miami Daily News* and *Miami Herald* continually reported at the time that the alias was *Acosta*, Kobler and Schoenberg, in their biographies, referred to it as *Costa*.

12 Kobler, *Life and World of Al Capone*, 213.

13 Schoenberg, *Mr. Capone: The Real and Complete Story*, 194.

14 Kobler, *Life and World of Al Capone*, 214.

15 "Scarface Liked Sparring—and Silk"; *Miami Herald*, June 23, 1968.

16 Kobler, *Life and World of Al Capone*, 214.

17 *Ibid*., 216.

18 Schoenberg, *Mr. Capone: The Real and Complete Story*, 216.

19 "Miami Will Defend Herself," *Miami Daily News*, March 13, 1930.

20 "County-Wide Mop Up of Racketeers is Lehman's Plan," *Miami Daily News*, March 14, 1930.

21 "Habeas Corpus Plea of Capone Aids [sic] is Denied," *Miami Daily News*, March 21, 1930.

22 "Al Capone Slips Into Home Here as Thousands at Easter Service," *Miami Daily News*, April 21, 1930.

23 Letter from Carl Fisher to Michael J. Glenn, May 27, 1930, CF–HASF.

24 "Capone Plans First of Good Will Dinners," *Miami Daily News*, May 27, 1930.

25 "Police Patrol Outside Capone Walls as Miami Guests Feted," *Miami Daily News*, May 29, 1930.

26 *Ibid*.

27 *Ibid*.

28 "An Observation," *Miami Daily News*, May 15, 1930.

29 "Capone and 3 Friends Spend Night in Jail," *Miami Herald*, May 15, 1930.

30 "City Officials in Conspiracy, Capone Says," *Miami Herald*, June 25, 1930.

31 Letter from Michael Glenn to Carl Fisher, June 6, 1930, CF–HASF.

32 *Ibid*.

33 James M. Cox, *Journey Through My Years*, (New York: Simon and Schuster, 1946), 316.

34 *Ibid*.

CHAPTER THIRTEEN

1 "Beth Jacob Temple Never Has Closed," Edward Newman, president of Beth Jacob Congregation, Reader's Forum, *Miami Herald*, Aug. 15, 1993.

2 Letter from C. W. (Pete) Chase to Fisher Company property owners, stockholders and investors, Sept. 14, 1927, CF–HASF.

3 CF–HASF.

4 Letter from C.W. Chase Jr., Sales Manager for Carl G. Fisher Properties, to Fisher property owners, stockholders, and investors, Sept. 14, 1927, CF–HASF.

5 Tape-recorded oral history interview of Alfred Barton by Polly Redford, May 12 and 18, 1967.

6 Bath Club annual report, Feb. 9, 1929, CF–HASF.

7 "Barton Remembers When Miami Beach Was a Wilderness," *Miami Herald*, March 23, 1965.

8 Archives Division, Richter Library, University of Miami.

9 "Miami Beach Attire is Left to Discretion," *Miami Herald*, Sept. 15, 1929.

10 *Ibid*.

11 Conversation with C. W. Chase by Margaret Nedeau, Miami Beach News Bureau, April 20, 1961; Miami Beach City Archives, Miami Beach City Clerk's office.

12 "Steve Hannagan's Girls," *Life Magazine*, Nov. 30, 1936.

13 Nash, *The Magic of Miami Beach*, 139.

14 "50 Blocks of Beach Leaping Into Nation's Eye as Finest `Millionaire's Row' of All," *Miami Daily News*, April 22, 1928.

15 Frank Stearns, *Along Greater Miami's Sun-Sea-Ara*, (Miami, Fla.: F. F. Stearns, 1932), 13–15.

16 "The Lido is Open," Beach Pictorial, Jan. 27, 1929, 10.

17 World Almanac, 1993, 441.

18 Letter from C. S. Krom to Carl Fisher, Nov. 18, 1929, CF–HASF.

19 Letter from Carl Fisher to Howard Coffin, May 8, 1930, CF–HASF.

20 Letter from Carl Fisher to C. M. Keys, March 21, 1930, CF–HASF.

21 Letter from Carl Fisher to C. M. Keys, Dec. 15, 1931, CF–HASF.

22 *Ibid*.

23 Letter from Park G. Haynes, vice president of the Montauk Point Development Corporation, to stockholders, Jan. 7, 1932, CF–HASF.

24 Letter from Carl Fisher to Claude Mercer, Oct. 5, 1934, CF–HASF.

25 Taped oral history interview with Jesse Weiss by Ann Bishop, 1982.

CHAPTER FOURTEEN

1 "Surf Club Plans Gala Season," *The Sunday Pictorial*, Jan. 3, 1932.
2 Letter from Carl Fisher to Dr. Elisha King, April 17, 1933, CF–HASF.
3 Miami Beach City Directory, 1926.
4 Oral history interview with Jesse Weiss by Ann Bishop, 1982.
5 "Miami Beach Building at Rapid Pace," *Miami Herald*, July 21, 1936.
6 "New Miami Beach Schools Will Open," *Miami Herald*, Sept. 13, 1936.
7 *From Wilderness to Metropolis: the History and Architecture of Dade County, Florida, 1825-1940*, Dade County Historic Preservation Division, 1982, 130–132.
8 The St. Moritz (1939) at 1565 Collins Avenue, the Sands (1939) at 1601 Collins Avenue, the National (1940) at 1677 Collins Avenue and the Versailes (1940) at 3425 Collins Avenue.
9 Among Hohauser's Miami Beach accomplishments were the Edison Hotel (1935) at 960 Ocean Drive, the Essex House (1938) at 1001 Collins Avenue, the Century (1939) at 140 Ocean Drive, the Cardozo (1939) at 1300 Ocean Drive, the New Yorker (1940) at 1360 Collins Avenue and the Warsaw Ballroom (1940) at 1450 Collins Avenue.
10 Dixon's accomplishments include the Tides (1936) at 1220 Ocean Drive, the Victor (1937) at 1144 Ocean Drive, and five 1939 hotels, all on Collins Avenue: the Marlin at 1200 Collins Avenue, the Nash—later renamed the Senator—at 1201 Collins Avenue, the Tiffany at 801 Collins Avenue, the Tudor at 1111 Collins Avenue and the Palmer House at 1119 Collins Avenue.
11 Redford, *Billion Dollar Sandbar*, 204–205.
12 Interview with Kay Pancoast by author, April 8, 1992.
13 Interview of Hyman Galbut by author, Dec. 17, 1993.
14 Interview with Helen Muir by author, July 1, 1992.
15 Interview with Sally Hopkins Woodruff by author, Dec. 2, 1993.
16 "From Show Girl to Benefactor," *Miami Herald*, May 5, 1986.
17 Interview with Leonard Abess by author, May 13, 1992.
18 Interview with Harold Kassewitz by author, May 13, 1992.
19 The Floridian Hotel, built in 1925 on the site of the aquarium, underwent a name change to Biscaya. Demolishing it in 1987 caused major protests by preservation groups.
20 Jack Kofoed, *Moon Over Miami* (New York: Random House, 1955),182–183.
21 *Ibid.*
22 Some histories refer to the Beach and Tennis Club as the Bath and Tennis Club, but the 1931 Miami Beach City Directory lists it as the Beach and Tennis Club.
23 House Bill No. 1131, Florida Legislature, June 10, 1935.
24 *Ibid.*
25 The elimination of the machines did not occur until Oct. 1, 1937, because of the valid licenses being held by operators.
26 "Group at Beach Promises To Stop All Gaming," *Miami Daily News*, Nov. 1, 1936.
27 "G-Men Probing Crime and Civic Corruption in Miami, Chief Says," *Miami Herald*, Dec. 22, 1939.
28 "Officials Welcome G-Man Probe of Crime in Miami," *Miami Herald*, Dec. 22, 1939.
29 Oral history interview with Alfred Barton by Polly Redford, May 12, 1967.
30 Archives, Miami Beach City Clerk's Office.
31 Ironic in the 1935–36 winter season brochure was an advertisement for the Alamac Hotel at 1257 Collins Avenue. It was run by the Jacobs family— principally Albert and Walter—who advertised "delicious Hungarian cuisine and dietary laws"—which meant that the hotel's restaurant was kosher.
32 "Workers find anti-Semitic sign of the past," *Miami Herald*, July 14, 1985.
33 Redford, *Billion Dollar Sandbar*, 214.
34 Hyman Galbut—now a retired attorney— says he remembers a sign proclaiming "No Jews or Dogs" on the George Washington Hotel at 516 Washington Avenue in the 1930s. He contends he would contemptuously smack his hand against it on the way to school. Coincidentally, singing star Gloria Estefan, when interviewed for the November-December 1990 issue of Philip Morris Magazine, said that when her family came to Miami from Cuba in 1959, "I do remember, vividly, my mom getting real upset with signs all over the place that said `No Children, No Pets, No Cubans.'"
35 Minutes of Miami Beach City Council Meeting, Nov. 4, 1936; Miami Beach City Clerk's office.
36 Oral history interview with C. W. (Pete Chase) by Polly Redford, Sept. 28, 1966.
37 Letter from Fred Humpage to Margaret G. Fisher, Aug. 18, 1938, CF–HASF.
38 Letter from Carl Fisher to Lafayette Page, Jr., Nov. 7, 1938, CF–HASF.
39 Letter from Thomas Pancoast to Carl Fisher, July 7, 1939, CF–HASF.
40 Letter from Carl Fisher to Thomas Pancoast, July 10, 1939, CF–HASF.
41 Letter from Thomas Pancoast to Carl Fisher, July 14, 1939, CF–HASF.
42 "Carl G. Fisher Dies In City He Made Rise From Swamps," *Miami Daily News*, July 16, 1939.
43 *Ibid.*

CHAPTER FIFTEEN

1 "Fisher's Body May Be Buried in Beach," *Miami Herald*, July 18, 1939.
2 Historian Thelma Peters, in her 1981 book *Biscayne Country*, reports that Mary Sullivan Barnott Peden claimed— p.50—to have buried several of her children in the sand dunes near the House of Refuge where her husband was keeper from 1877 until 1883. It has not been documented.
   Long before he fell ill, Fisher had planned for his final resting place on the island across from the southern tip of Miami Beach. Called—through the years — Rabbit Island, Peninsula Terminal Island, Terminal Island (at the time of Fisher's death), later Fisher's Island and, finally, Fisher Island, Carl built a mausoleum for himself there, his name inscribed in stone atop the vault. His long-time associate Pete Chase told the *Miami Herald* ("Two Millionaires Share Tract With Uncle Sam, *Miami Herald*, June 13, 1948) and the *Miami Daily News* (Beach Has 2 Cemeteries But No One's Buried There," *Miami Daily News*, Dec. 29, 1956) that when the 1926 hurricane struck, it did a great deal of damage to the mausoleum. It never was repaired. It would not be until the 1980s, when development was underway for a deluxe residential community on the island, that the mausoleum was destroyed.
3 "Carl G. Fisher Rites Conducted On Beach," *Miami Herald*, July 19, 1939.
4 "Fisher Boulevard Proposal Opposed," *Miami Herald*, Aug. 3, 1939.
5 Fisher's estate: $42,087 worth of stock in the Carl G. Fisher Corporation, his house at 650 West 51st Terrace, appraised at $12,500, with a $6,000 mortgage, plus $341.62 in cash. His clothing, jewelry and automobile were valued at $2,165; he was holding $1,104 worth of accounts receivable. ("$52,198 Estate Is Left by Carl Fisher," *Miami Herald*, March 16, 1940).
6 "Friends Dedicate Fisher Memorial Amid Ceremonies," *Miami Daily News*, April 11, 1940.
7 *Ibid.*
8 "Collins Rites Set Tomorrow," *Miami Daily News*, May 23, 1939.
9 *Ibid.*
10 "Collins Bequeaths $1,128,408 Estate," *Miami Daily News*, Dec. 27, 1939.
11 Miami Beach City Directory, 1940.
12 *Ibid.*
13 "Wolfson Chosen Mayor by Unanimous Acclaim," *Miami Herald*, June 3, 1934.
14 Oral history interview with Mitchell Wolfson for Temple Israel by Marcia Kanner, Nov. 24, 1970.
15 *Ibid.*
16 Dan Mahoney was James Cox' son-in-law and publisher of the *Miami Daily News*.
17 Oral history interview with Mitchell Wolfson for Temple Israel by Marcia Kanner, Nov. 24, 1970.
18 *Ibid.*
19 "Sunset Island No. 2—A Picky Paradise," *Miami News*, May 5, 1972.
20 "Harding Tale Tragic," *Miami Herald*, April 21, 1940.
21 "10-Year Fight Lost by Action," *Miami Herald*, March 16, 1940.
22 "Harding Tale Tragic," *Miami Herald*, April 21, 1940.
23 "Miami Beach Second In U.S. Population Gain," *Miami Herald*, April 13, 1941.
24 "200 New Hotels Pierce Ever Changing Skyline," *Miami Herald*, Nov. 16, 1941.

CHAPTER SIXTEEN

1 Helen Muir: *Miami, U.S.A.* 221.
2 *Ibid.*
3 "Beach Gets Air School for 4,000," *Miami Daily News*, Feb. 19, 1942.
4 "500 Student Soldiers Due in City Today," *Miami Daily News*, Feb. 20, 1942.
5 "Beach Golf Links Become Drill Grounds in Jig Time," *Miami Daily News*, March 1, 1942.
6 "We Call It Patriotism," "Getting Results," *The Beach Breeze* (student newspaper) Feb. 25, 1942.
7 "Eyewitness Describes Ship Burning off Miami," *Miami Daily News*, May 15, 1942.
8 It might be argued that the terror of Nazism first visited Miami Beach in early June 1939 when the S. S. St. Louis, a German passenger vessel carrying more than 900 fleeing German-Jews, cruised off Miami Beach within sight of residents after

being refused disembarkation in Havana. Despite pleas from Jewish and other religious groups, the United States did not allow the ship to come into a U.S. port.

9 Mark A. McCloskey and Commander Thomas H. Rickman, Jr., USNR: *Professional Study of the Servicemen's Pier, Branches and Branch Services*, 1945, 95, Archives Department, Otto Richter Library, University of Miami.

10 *Ibid.*, 12, 95.

11 *Ibid.*, 95.

12 *Ibid.*, 92.

13 *Ibid.*, 12.

14 Interview with Kay Pancoast by author, April 8, 1992.

15 *Ibid.*

16 According to the McCloskey-Rickman Report, Branch No. 1 was at the White House, Charles and New Yorker Hotels in the vicinity of 14th Street and Ocean Drive and Collins Avenue. Cocktail lounges and playrooms were converted to meet the servicemen's needs. Branch No. 2 was at the Flamingo Hotel where two cottages were turned into welcome centers for servicemen. This branch was later moved to Coconut Grove to serve troops stationed in that area. Branch No. 3 was located in the Atlantis and Traymore Hotels on 24th and 25th, respectively, and Collins Avenue. In these hotels, all sorts of entertainment were offered, from dances to dart games. The Whitman Hotel at 34th and Collins served as Branch No. 4. Sunday afternoon patio dances were popular features there. Later, that branch was moved to a private home at 16th and the ocean where kitchen parties were conducted. A large home at 4223 Collins Avenue, owned by George and Goldie Reubin, was turned over to the Pier Association for use as Branch No. 5. It was dubbed the Pelican House for the pelican logo used by the association. At first Pelican House was used for Air Corps personnel, but later it was converted to the use of combat returnees and their wives. Branch No. 6 first was located at the Deauville bathing casino, then moved to the Fleetwood Hotel. Alfred Barton's Surf Club hosted Branch No. 7, where flags of the Allies lined the entranceway. Service men and women were given free reign to swim, dance and socialize at the club. In addition to the branches, an information center for service men and women was established in a cottage at 505 Lincoln Road; and a hostess service, which utilized one-third of all volunteers, was in operation at 18 hotels.

17 McCloskey and Rickman, 11.

18 Sanborn Map of Miami Beach, 1943; records maintained at Miami Beach City Clerk's office.

19 Letter from Fred Humpage to stockholders of the Carl G. Fisher Corporation, Dec. 22, 1942, CF–HASF.

20 The founders of Mt. Sinai originally planned for the hospital to be at the site of the Alton Road Hospital, a small institution at Sixth Street and Alton Road. But it was purchased by the city in 1942. It later returned to private hands and is known as South Shore Hospital and Medical Center.

21 After Robert Ludwig died, Sally married Coca-Cola chairman Robert Woodruff.

He died in 1985. Interview with Sally Woodruff by author, Dec. 2, 1993.

22 The word "jeep," which came to be the name given to a military general purpose (G.P.) vehicle and which remains today as the name of its civilian successor, originally was used, according to Webster's *New World Dictionary*, as military slang to identify personnel. Its origins were with a comic book character, Eugene the Jeep, a person who possessed extraordinary powers.

23 "A Private Tells You About Army Life In Sunny Miami Beach," Reprinted from *Yank* in the *Miami Daily News*, April 9, 1943.

24 "New Beach Soldiers Developing Marksmen's Eyes," *Miami Daily News*, July 11, 1943.

25 "Wolfson Off Thursday to Camp Custer," *Miami Herald*, Sept. 19, 1943.

26 Wolfson began his training in the school of Military Government of Occupied Territories and participated in the Allied landings in southern France in 1944. He was awarded four battle stars, the Bronze Star and the French Croix de Guerre. As the war closed out, Lt. Col. Wolfson participated in administration liaison of occupied territories, serving in Austria and the Rhineland. When he received his discharge in October 1945, he returned to his role as president of Wometco Enterprises but did not re-enter Miami Beach politics.

27 "Rabbi Lehrman To Be Installed," *Miami Daily News*, Nov. 28, 1943.

28 Interview with Jim Snedigar by author, June 24, 1992.

29 The Park Avenue restaurant was at 339 22nd Street.

30 The Beachcomber night club was at 1271 Dade Boulevard.

31 "Sobol Writes to a Pal Overseas," *New York Journal-American*, Jan. 27, 1944.

32 "Beach July Sales Highest on Record," *Miami Herald*, Aug. 6, 1944.

33 "Nazi POW 'Wolf' Tactics Anger Miami Beach Girls," *Miami Daily News*, April 22, 1945.

34 *Ibid.*

MIAMI BEACH MUNICIPAL PIER

1 Memorandum of background check of George R. K. Carter by Daniel Sullivan, Operating Director, Crime Commission of Greater Miami, Aug. 15, 1950; Miami Herald Library.

2 "Carter's Dream May Come True After Trouble," *Miami Daily News*, July 7, 1929.

3 The pier measured 570 by 50 feet on one leg and 150 by 90 feet on the other. A 110-feet ramp connected the pier with the shore, "Beach Acquires Geist Holdings on Ocean Drive" *Miami Daily News*, Aug. 25, 1940.

4 Memorandum of background check of George R. K. Carter by Daniel Sullivan, Operating Director, Crime Commission of Greater Miami, Aug. 15, 1950, *Miami Herald* Library.

5 *Ibid.*

6 "Beach Acquires Geist Holdings on Ocean Drive," *Miami Herald*, Aug. 25, 1940.

CHAPTER SEVENTEEN

1 "Miami Worries About Another Boom," *Life Magazine*, Feb. 12, 1945.

2 *Ibid.*

3 "Miami and Miami Beach Head for Building Records," *Miami Herald*, July 1, 1947.

4 Pat Morrissey, editor, *Miami's Neighborhoods*, (Miami, Fla.: The Miami News, 1982), 8–9.

5 "New Warrant Issued in 'Bias' Sign Case," *Miami Herald*, July 3, 1947.

6 "Court Order May End Building Ban Injunction," *Miami Herald*, March 14, 1948.

7 *World Book Encyclopedia*, 1991 edition, Vol. 8, 276.

8 Advertisements, *Miami Herald*, March 12, 1948.

9 "New Year With Sun as Usual," *New York Herald Tribune*, Jan. 5, 1947.

10 "Hotels on Beach Hit Hard by Big Storm," *Miami Daily News*, Sept. 18, 1947.

11 Interview with Hank Meyer by author, March 19, 1992.

12 "Special Committee to Investigate Organized Crime in Interstate Commerce," Sen. Estes Kefauver (D-Tenn.), chairman; 82nd Cong, 1st sess., Report No. 307, 1952, 31.

13 "Katzentine Led Fight on Mobs," John Pennekamp column, *Miami Herald*, March 29, 1960.

14 "Miami Beach Bookie Syndicate Is Proud of Its 'Civic' Record," *Miami Herald*, March 21, 1948.

15 Third Interim Report of the Special Committee to Investigate Organized Crime in Interstate Commerce, 36.

16 Estes Kefauver, *Crime in America* (London: Victor Gollancz, 1952), 86.

17 *Ibid.*, 87.

18 Third Interim Report of the Special Committee to Investigate Organized Crime in Interstate Commerce, 29–30.

19 *Ibid.*, 30–32.

20 *Ibid.*, 34.

21 "Modest Fine Drawn by Ex–S and G Pair," *Miami Daily News*, July 15, 1955.

22 *Ibid.*

CHAPTER EIGHTEEN

1 Morris Lapidus, *Architecture of Joy* (Miami: E. A. Seemann Publishing Company, 1979), 17.

2 *Ibid.*, 125.

3 "Newest Hotel Opens Friday," *Miami Herald*, Dec. 12. 1949.

4 Lapidus *Architecture of Joy*, 131.

5 "Beach Zoning Case Continued," *Miami Herald*, Nov. 28, 1947.

6 "Firestone Estate Zoning on Docket," *Miami Herald*, Feb. 22, 1949.

7 "Feiner Advocates Firestone Estate for City Park," *Miami Beach Sun*, March 19, 1950.

8 "Syndicate Buys Firestone Estate," *Miami Daily News*, July 21, 1952.

9 "Sun 'N' Sea Stockholders Suing Over Firestone Estate Contract," *Miami Herald*, Jan. 1, 1953.

10 On Dec. 11, 1953, the Florida Supreme Court ruled that Miami Beach had the right to restrict an 8,000-foot strip of oceanfront land to residential construction. This was a reversal of a lower court decision that would have allowed the land to be used for hotels and apartments. The courts kept making decisions and then reversing themselves. In

April 1954, the Florida Supreme Court upheld a lower court decision permitting Sam Kay and Samuel T. Haas to rezone their property north of the Firestone Estate for hotel building.

11 "Beach OKs Oceanfront Rezoning," *Miami Herald*, June 3, 1954.
12 "Luxury Hotel Planned," *Miami Herald*, Dec. 30, 1953.
13 "Work Begun On Beach's Biggest Hotel," *Miami Daily News*, Jan. 17, 1954.
14 "It Will Be Florida's Largest, Most Luxurious Hostelry by Fall," *Miami Herald*, Feb. 21, 1954.
15 Lapidus, *An Architecture of Joy*, 135.
16 *Ibid.*, 137.
17 *Ibid.*
18 *Ibid.*
19 *Ibid.*, 137–141.
20 Interview with Harold Gardner by author, April 7, 1994.
21 Lapidus, *An Architecture of Joy*, 142.
22 *Ibid.*
23 "Firestone Mansion To Give Way," *Miami Herald*, Oct. 24, 1954.
24 "Everything at Fontainebleau Hotel is Super-Colossal," *Miami Herald*, Dec. 19, 1954.
25 "Doors Swing Open At Fontainebleau," *Miami Daily News*, Dec. 19, 1954.
26 "Guests Jam Fontainebleau for Benefit Opening," *Miami Herald*, Dec. 21, 1954.
27 *Ibid.*
28 Lapidus, *An Architecture of Joy*, 161.
29 "Meet Our Most Controversial Architect," *Miami Daily News*, Oct. 7, 1956.
30 Lapidus, *An Architecture of Joy*, 164.
31 "Architect Blasts Modern Design as Cold, Heartless," *Miami Herald*, April 24, 1955.
32 "Don't You Call My Hotel Names," *Miami Herald*, May 9, 1963.
33 *Ibid.*
34 "Paper Swings Wrecking Ball at Hotels, Lapidus Says: I'm Not Ashamed of Them," *Miami News*, Oct. 23, 1979.

CHAPTER NINETEEN

1 "Jumbo Fish Tales," *London Times Literary Supplement*, Nov. 6, 1959, as quoted by William R. Linneman and Harriet Fether in "Miami Beach Hotel Names," American Speech, Oct. 1964, Vol. XXXCIX, No. 3.
2 William R. Linneman and Harriet Fether: "Miami Beach Hotel Names," *American Speech*, Oct. 1964, Vol. XXXCIX, No. 3.
3 *Ibid.*
4 Interview with Hank Meyer by author, March 19, 1992.
5 "Tomorrow's The Big Day Here as Thousands Await `Live' TV," *Miami Daily News*, June 29, 1952.
6 Godfrey had hip implant surgery in 1954
7 "Why Did Godfrey Do It?" *Miami Daily News*, May 31, 1953.
8 "Godfrey `Converts' Beach Hotel Into Giant Television Studio," *Miami Daily News*, April 12, 1953.
9 "Wind Blows Godfrey Indoors," *Miami Daily News*, April 13, 1953.
10 *Ibid.*
11 Interview with Hank Meyer by author, March 19, 1992.
12 "Millions See Godfrey (And Miami Beach)," *Miami Daily News*, April 14, 1953.
13 "Lions Want Causeway Named for Godfrey," *Miami Daily News*, April 19, 1953.

14 "Causeway Named for Godfrey OKd," *Miami Daily News*, April 26, 1953.
15 The causeway, in 1964, was named in honor of John F. Kennedy.
16 "Godfrey Plugs Stir Interest," *Miami Daily News*, April 23, 1953.
17 "Why Did Godfrey Do It?," *Miami Daily News*, May 31, 1953.
18 "Jewish Group Honors Godfrey at Dinner," *Miami Herald*, Jan. 29, 1954.
19 *Ibid.*
20 "Godfrey Back Here for Show," Miami News, Feb. 24, 1964.
21 "Fiery Godfrey Lashes Out on Viet War," *Miami Herald*, Jan. 17, 1967.
22 Interview with Hank Meyer by author, March 19, 1992.
23 "Godfrey Keynotes Brotherhood Theme," *Miami News*, Feb. 25, 1972.
24 *Ibid.*
25 "TV, Radio Personality Arthur Godfrey Dies," *Miami Herald*, March 17, 1983.

CHAPTER TWENTY

1 By 1962, air departures from Havana were at a peak. They were halted in June 1963 when commercial air traffic was cut off, and ultimately resumed as a U.S. government-sponsored airlift on Dec. 1, 1965.
2 Interviews with Mario and Pedro Menocal by author, August 10, 1993.
3 "6,500 Cubans A Week Arrive in Miami to Spend Vacations," *Miami Daily News*, June 27, 1947.
4 *Ibid.*
5 "Beach to Double Its Convention Business", *Miami Herald*, Jan. 1, 1960.
6 "Biggest Summer Seen For Miami," *Miami Herald*, April 18, 1960.
7 *Ibid.*
8 Interview with Ramon A. Mestré by author, Nov. 23, 1993.
9 *Ibid.*
10 Interview with Bernardo Benes by author, April 13, 1994.
11 *Ibid.*
12 *Ibid.*
13 *Ibid.*
14 "Last Curtain's Fallen on `Papa's' Beauties", *Miami Herald*, Jan. 29, 1959.
15 "Walters is Dean of Show Producers And Glorifier of Feminine Pulchritude", *Miami Herald*, March 23, 1965.
16 Interview with publicist Harold Gardner by author, April 7, 1994.
17 "Meyer Lansky Dies, Eluding Law a Final Time", *Miami Herald*, Jan. 16, 1983.
18 Hank Messick: Syndicate in the Sun, 1968, 139.
19 "Mob Money: Silent Host in Beach Hotels," *Miami Herald*, Jan. 29, 1967.
20 *Ibid.*
21 "Fontainebleau, Herald Agree on Dismissal," *Miami Herald*, April 21, 1968.
22 "FBI on Lansky: Grudging Respect for Favorite Hood," *Miami Herald*, Jan. 16, 1983.
23 "Lansburgh, Cohen Sentenced To One Year for Conspiracy", *Miami Herald*, April 28, 1974.
24 "Hotelman, Promoter Morris Lansburgh, 60," *Miami Herald*, Feb. 11, 1977.
25 "The Million Dollar Rascal," *Restaurant South Magazine*, February 1959.
26 Leo Rosten, *The Joys of Yiddish*, (New York: Pocket Books, 1968), 230.
27 Interview with publicist Beverlye Keusch Weinberger, April 4, 1994.

28 Wolfie Cohen later opened the Rascal House restaurant in Sunny Isles and served as a Miami Beach city councilman. He died in 1986.
29 "Carl Fisher's Estate Leased," *Miami Herald*, July 24, 1949.
30 "The Shadows Fade Away to Let In Today," *Miami Daily News*, Oct. 11, 1961.
31 "Big Day July 11: Mall Job Begins", *Miami Herald*, July 3, 1960.
32 "Pair of Decisions Will Shape Lincoln Road Future," *Miami Herald*, July 10, 1994.
33 Max Orovitz came to Miami during the Boom with $12 in his pocket and a law degree from Emory University. He began work with the Commercial Bank and Trust Company. In 1930, he became director of the new City Bank of Miami Beach. Involved with several other Miami businesses, he also became involved in the young state of Israel as part of the Miami Group, which invested in hotels, housing developments, banks and oil wells there. In Miami, he plunged into civic and philanthropic activities, particularly with Mount Sinai Hospital and the Greater Miami Jewish Federation.
34 Paul George, *Mount Sinai Medical Center of Greater Miami, 1949-1984*, (Privately published, Undated) 23.
35 *Ibid.*, 77.

CHAPTER TWENTY ONE

1 Interview with Hank Meyer by author, March 19, 1992.
2 "4 Beatles Fly Into Miami and Set Off Teenage Riot," *Miami Herald*, Feb. 14, 1964.
3 *Ibid.*
4 "Meet The Beatles," *Miami Herald*, Feb. 5, 1984.
5 "Fraud in the Afternoon: Beatles and Boxer Feud," *Miami Herald*, Feb. 19, 1964.
6 "On Extra Tickets—Wasn't Ed's Fault," *Miami Herald*, Feb. 19, 1964.
7 *Ibid.*
8 "Oldsters Outdo Kids at Beatle–TV Show," *Miami Herald*, Feb. 17, 1964.
9 "20 Years Ago, Mop–Tops Wanted to Hold Our Hands," *Miami News*, Feb. 3, 1984.
10 Ferdie Pacheco, *Muhammad Ali, A View from the Corner* (New York: Birch Lane Press, 1992), 39.
11 *Ibid.*, 74.
12 *Ibid.*, 79.
13 "It's Definite; Gleason Moving Show to Beach," *Miami Herald*, Feb. 18, 1964.
14 Interview with Hank Meyer by author, March 19, 1992.
15 *Ibid.*
16 W. J. Weatherby, *Jackie Gleason, An Intimate Portrait of the Great One*, (New York: Pharos Books, 1992), 142.
17 "It's Definite; Gleason Moving Show to Beach," *Miami Herald*, Feb. 18, 1964.
18 W. J. Weatherby, *Jackie Gleason. An Intimate Portrait of the Great One*, 141-142.
19 Gleason obtained his divorce from Genevieve in Florida, but by the time that took place, Honey had long since lost her patience—and married Las Vegas singer Dick Roman.
20 W. J. Weatherby, *Jackie Gleason, An Intimate Portrait of the Great One*, 142.
21 *Ibid.*
22 *Ibid.*, 147.
23 *Ibid.*
24 *Ibid.*, 216
25 *Ibid.*

CHAPTER TWENTY TWO

1 *Presidential Elections Since 1789*, (Washington, D.C.: Congressional Quarterly, Inc., 1983), 63.
2 "Heavy Security Creates Air of Vigilance in City," *New York Times*, Aug. 6, 1968.
3 The Julia Tuttle Causeway (I-195) across Biscayne Bay and the bridge from the north over Haulover Cut (AIA) are fixed bridges
4 "Maybe Chicago and Miami Beach Were Just Bad Dreams," *Miami News*, July 14, 1976.
5 "Racial Violence Erupts in Miami; Abernathy and Kirk Ask Calm," *New York Times*, Aug. 8, 1968.
6 "3 Negroes Killed in New Miami Riot," *New York Times*, Aug. 9, 1968.
7 World Book Encyclopedia: 1969 Year Book, p307.
8 "War Foes Build `Dike' As Protests Flow On," *Miami Herald*, July 13, 1972.
9 "Troops, Non-Delegates Prepare to Fold Tents," *Miami Herald*, July 14, 1972.
10 "500 Driven Back at Hotel; Vets Quell Nazis at Park," *Miami Herald*, Aug. 21, 1972.
11 "Cubans, Anglos Scuffle," *Miami Herald*, Aug. 22, 1972.
12 "Beach March Turns Rowdy—and 212 Arrests Follow," *Miami Herald*, Aug. 23, 1972.
13 *Ibid*.
14 "More Than 800 Are Arrested After Spreading Street Chaos," *Miami Herald*, Aug. 24, 1972.
15 *Ibid*.
16 *Ibid*.
17 "Controlling Crowd is a Routine Stint for ex-Beach Chief," *Miami Herald*, July 17, 1988.

CHAPTER TWENTY THREE

1 "Never-Ending Squabbles Hurt Miami Beach," *Miami Herald*, Nov. 1, 1983.
2 "Despite Vote, South Beach Redevelopment Still Needed," *Miami News*, Nov. 12, 1979.
3 "Beach Politics: Stunts, Tricks, Venom—Again," *Miami Herald*, June 30, 1985.
4 "Frink Files $100,000 Slander Suit Against Golub For His Klan Charge," *Miami Herald*, June 4, 1949.
5 "Probers Call Faust's Hand On Accusation of Frink," *Miami News*, May 31, 1949.
6 *Miami Beach Sun*, June 6, 1949.
7 "Frink Files $100,000 Suit Against Golub For His Klan Charge," *Miami Herald*, June 4, 1949.
8 "KKK Charge Results in Libel Case," *Miami Herald*, June 7, 1949.
9 Interview with Gerald Schwartz by author, April 21, 1994.
10 "Beach Politics: Stunts, Tricks, Venom—Again," *Miami Herald*, June 30, 1985.
11 "Richard Cries 'Foul' in Election," *Miami News*, June 2, 1953.
12 "Two New Men Named to Beach Council," *Miami News*, June 3, 1953.
13 Interview with Beverlye Keusch Weinberger by author, April 21, 1994.
14 "Election Climaxes Bitter Campaign," *Miami News*, June 4, 1957.
15 "Wolfie Is In, Lincoln Road Loses Traffic," *Miami News*, June 3, 1959.
16 Patricia Peabody Roosevelt, *I Love a Roosevelt* (Garden City, N.Y.: Doubleday & Co., 1967) 368–9.
17 *Ibid.*, 329-30.
18 "It's Mayor Roosevelt on Miami Beach Now," *Miami News*, June 2, 1965.
19 Patricia Peabody Roosevelt: *I Love a Roosevelt*, 326.
20 Interview with Beverlye Keusch Weinberger by author, April 11, 1994.
21 "It's Elliott, Dermer in Runoff," *Miami News*, May 17, 1967.
22 In late May and early June 1939, the St. Louis sailed from Germany to Cuba, its Jewish passengers assured of entry through a previous deal. When the ship arrived in Havana, they were refused entry. The St. Louis sailed in Florida waters for several days in hopes that the U.S. would accept the refugees. When President Franklin Roosevelt did not act, the ship returned to Europe, much to the chagrin of American-Jewish groups.
23 "Beach Latin Quarter Urged by Roosevelt," *Miami News*, Dec. 31, 1969.
24 Roosevelt moved from Miami Beach to a home near South Miami. As if on an odyssey, he later moved to Portugal, then England, Seattle, California and Arizona. He died on Oct. 27, 1990, in Scottsdale.
25 "The Gadfly," *Tropic Magazine*, *Miami Herald*, March 13, 1994.
26 Plissner stayed at it until he died at the age of 90 on Aug. 19, 1991.
27 "Beach Revives Move to Secede From Dade, Form Own County," *Miami News*, Aug. 19, 1978.
28 Dermer died at the age of 54 of a heart attack on April 5, 1984.
29 Powell arrived in Miami Beach in 1922. With his father and brother Al, they went into the real estate business as L. L. Powell and Sons, first at Meridian Avenue and Fifth Street, later at 921 Lincoln Road. In 1942, he was contacted after councilman Baron deHirsch Meyer resigned to go into the Army and asked to serve the remainder of the term. He did and was elected outright following that—elected constantly until retiring in 1971.
30 "Powell: A Battler in Beach's Early Days," *Miami News*, Jan. 28, 1980.
31 *Ibid*.
32 "D. Lee Powell to Leave Beach Council," *Miami Herald*, Sept. 23, 1971.
33 "Dermer Vows to Name Those in 'Alliance'," *Miami News*, Sept. 2, 1971.
34 " 'Unholy Alliance' Runs Beach But Can Be Destroyed—Dermer," *Miami Herald*, Sept. 27, 1971.
35 *Ibid*.
36 "Targets Reject Charges," *Miami Herald*, Sept. 27, 1971.
37 Hank Meyer took the city's public relations private when he resigned on March 22, 1967, after 18 years on the city job, then captured a private contract to handle its public relations. He gave it up shortly thereafter, opening the field to others.
38 "Schwartz Falls Out With Fromberg, Vows to Unseat Him," *Miami News*, Sept. 25, 1984.
39 "Beach Sees Bitter Brawl For Mayor," *Miami Herald*, Nov. 1, 1985.
40 "South Beach Power Makes A Comeback in New Coalition," *Miami News*, Nov. 7, 1985.
41 "Daoud Pleads Guilty to 4 Charges," *Miami Herald*, July 1, 1993.
42 Paul was to stand trial himself for diverting $3.2 million of CenTrust customers' funds to his private use—and Daoud was to be a witness for the prosecution, testifying as to how Paul bribed him.
43 "Daoud Gets Five Years for `Big Mistake'," *Miami Herald*, Sept. 9, 1993.
44 "Gelber New Beach Mayor by Landslide," *Miami Herald*, Nov. 20, 1991.

CHAPTER TWENTY FOUR

1 "Jewish Imagep [sic] Hank vs. Jerry," *Miami Beach Daily Sun*, March 31, 1965.
2 "Drive to Lure Young Families Pays Off At Beach," *Miami News*, Dec. 4, 1967.
3 "Socio-Economic Diagnostic Study of the South Shore Area of Miami Beach, Florida," Welfare Planning Council of Dade County, Florida, November 1968.
4 "Beach to Decide on Renewal Authority," *Miami Herald*, Feb. 12, 1976.
5 "The Most Powerful Man in Miami Beach," *Tropic Magazine*, *Miami Herald*, July 9, 1978.
6 "Novack Gets One Last Chance to Save Hotel," *Miami Herald*, Aug. 4, 1977.
7 "Fontainebleau's New Owner May Close Hotel for Repair Soon," *Miami News*, Dec. 3, 1977.
8 " 'Mr. Fontainebleau' Reflects on Decline, Fall of Empire," *Miami Herald*, Nov. 18, 1983.
9 *Ibid*.
10 When he headed the Greater Miami Sports Authority, Muss and his commission were considering a site on Miami's riverfront for a sports arena when the *Miami Herald* revealed on May 23, 1981 that Muss had a contract to purchase part of the site and build a shopping center rather than an arena there. Later, when Muss led his commission to recommend a site in Miami that was the little-used Florida East Coast Railway yards for a new football/baseball stadium, the *Herald* said it was a straight line across the Julia Tuttle Causeway from the Fontainebleau-Hilton Hotel to that site and, thus, Muss would profit from it. Muss chose to remove the target. He quit the Sports Authority, went back to his hotel and let others pursue the fruitless quest of an in-city sports stadium.
11 "Beach to Decide on Renewal Authority," *Miami Herald*, Feb. 12, 1976.
12 "Panel Picks New Head," *Miami Herald*, March 1, 1978.
13 "South Beach Sees Tomorrow as a Waterway Wonderland," *Miami Herald*, July 19, 1976.
14 City of Miami Beach Summary of Landlords' Rights and Obligations Under the Rent Stabilization Law, July 9, 1975.
15 "Last-Ditch Effort to Save Rent Controls Voted Down," *Miami Beach Sun Reporter*, June 10, 1977.
16 "Why Bulldoze Our New Building, They Ask," *Miami Herald*, Nov. 5, 1976.
17 "South Beach Sees Tomorrow as a Waterway Wonderland," *Miami News*, July 19, 1976.
18 "Low-Cost Units Gain Beach OK," *Miami Herald*, Aug. 13, 1977.
19 *Ibid*.
20 "South Beach's Facelift 'On the Two-Yard Line'," *Miami News*, July 18, 1978.
21 "Major Firms 'Signing Up' For S. Beach," *Miami Herald*, Aug. 12, 1976.
22 "Beach Redevelopment Gets a Helping `Handshake,' " *Miami Herald*, Dec. 31, 1979.

23 "Standoff on South Beach," *Miami Herald*, May 28, 1981.

24 "A Shaper of Miami Beach Walks Away From the Spotlight," *Miami News*, April 22, 1982.

25 "South Beach Renewal Plan Abandoned," *Miami Herald*, Dec. 14, 1982.

26 *Ibid.*

27 "Stephen Muss: Miami Beach Moses?" *Miami News*, March 6, 1979.

28 *Ibid.*

29 "A Shaper of Miami Beach Walks Away From The Spotlight," *Miami News*, April 22, 1982.

30 "Beach Ends Fuss on Muss Center," *Miami Herald*, Sept. 7, 1989.

31 *Ibid.*

32 " 'Condo Conversion' Trend Away From Rentals Adds to Suicide Rate, Legislators Told," *Miami News*, Aug. 27, 1979.

33 Interview with Stuart Blumberg by author, April 22, 1994.

34 *Ibid.*

35 "Resort City is Suffering Worst Slump," *Miami Herald*, Sept. 18, 1983.

35 "No Fun In The Sun: Beach Hotels Suffering," *Miami Herald*, July 10, 1983.

36 *Ibid.*

37 *Ibid.*

38 *Ibid.*

39 "Beach Tenements Ranks First On List of Crime Hot Spots," *Miami Herald*, March 9, 1983.

40 "Ciment's Plan Ignores Facts About Refugees," *Miami Herald*, Sept. 24, 1983.

41 *Ibid.*

CHAPTER TWENTY FIVE

1 "She's The First Lady of Art Deco. . . But Last in Developers' Hearts," *Miami News*, Feb. 19, 1981.

2 Barbara Capitman, *Deco Delights*, (New York: E. P. Dutton 1988), 16.

3 "Design Forum Planned," *Miami Herald*, Sept. 12, 1976.

4 *Ibid.*

5 Capitman, Kinerk and Wilhelm, *Rediscovering Art Deco U.S.A*, (New York: Viking Studio Books, 1994), 1.

6 *A Guide to the Architecture of Miami* (Miami: South Chapter, American Institute of Architects, 1963.)

7 Capitman, Kinerk and Wilhelm, *Rediscovering Art Deco*, 17.

8 *Ibid.*

9 Interview with Jo Werne by author, Sept. 1, 1993.

10 "Art Deco Fans, Owner Dispute Building's Charm," *Miami Herald*, Aug. 25, 1978.

11 *Ibid.*

12 "Art Deco Plan Wins Support," *Miami Herald*, Dec. 14, 1978.

13 "Art Deco Foes Come Out of Woodwork To Protest Size of Preservation Area," *Miami Herald*, Feb. 1, 1979.

14 *Ibid.*

15 "Victory for Art Deco Proves That the Past Has a Future," *Miami Herald*, May 15, 1979.

16 *Ibid.*

17 "Beach Art Deco—New Guide Tells All," *Miami News*, Oct. 18, 1979.

18 "League to Order Master Plan for Saving Historic District," *Miami Herald*, Jan. 6, 1980.

19 "Art Deco Demolitions Draw Protests," *Miami Herald*, Jan. 13, 1980.

20 "Builders Buck Ordinance, Ask 'Where's the Money?' " *Miami News*, Feb. 6, 1980.

21 *Ibid.*

22 "Good Times Run Out For Boulevard Hotel," *Miami Herald*, March 26, 1980.

23 *Ibid.*

24 "Art League Copes With Funding Cut," *Miami Herald*, Oct. 2, 1980.

25 "Revamped Hotel Debuts With Deco Fantasy Ball," *Miami Herald*, Dec. 15, 1980.

26 "To Hotel Wrecker, Beauty is in the Eye of the Deco Defender," *Miami Herald*, Jan. 8, 1981.

27 *Ibid.*

28 "Free Enterprise is as American as Old Art Deco," *Miami Herald*, Jan. 22, 1981.

29 "Deco District on the Beach Could Be Draw," *Miami Herald*, Jan. 29, 1981.

30 "Both Sides Agree: We Love New Yorker Hotel Deal," *Miami Herald*, Feb. 19, 1981.

31 *Ibid.*

32 "Art Deco New Yorker Tumbles," *Miami Herald*, April 24, 1981.

33 "Biscaya Served Many Masters," *Miami Herald*, March 16, 1987.

34 "Preservationists Mourn Hotel's Demise," *Miami Herald*, Oct. 16, 1988.

35 *Ibid.*

36 Interview with Nancy Liebman by author, July 17, 1994.

37 "Ocean Drive Becoming Mecca of Cafe Society," *Miami Herald*, July 10, 1986.

38 "The Changing Face of Ocean Drive," *Miami Herald*, Jan. 2, 1994.

39 "Art Deco's Grand Dame Fought to End," *Miami Herald*, April 1, 1990.

40 Nancy Liebman, successor to Barbara Capitman as executive director of the Miami Design Preservation League, credits six members with refocusing the league. They were Richard Hoverman, Joe Fleming, Stanley Levine, Ernie Martin, Mickey Wolfson and Liebman.

41 Interview with Nancy Liebman by author, July 17, 1994.

42 *Ibid.*

43 "Cocowalk's Developer Buys Bancroft Hotel Site in Beach," *Miami Herald*, Feb. 3, 1994.

44 "Luxury, Suburbia Big Markets," *Miami Herald*, May 7, 1993.

45 "Hot Properties," *New Times*, April 7–13, 1994.

46 "Tycoon Thomas," *New Times*, Dec. 16–22, 1992.

BIBLIOGRAPHY

BOOKS

Akin, Edward N. *Flagler: Rockefeller Partner and Florida Baron*. Kent, Ohio: Kent State University Press, 1988.

Ballinger, Kenneth. *Miami Millions:*. Miami, Fla.: Franklin Press, 1936.

Bass, Jo Ann, and Sax, Richard. *Eat at Joe's*. New York: Clarkson Potter/Publishers, 1993.

Belth, Nathan C. *A Promise to Keep*. New York: Times Books, 1979.

Benét, William Rose. *Benét's Reader's Encyclopedia*. Third edition. New York: Harper and Row, 1987.

Blackman, E. V. *Miami and Dade County, Florida*. Washington, D.C.: Victor Rainbolt, 1921.

Blake, Nelson M. *Land into Water—Water into Land*. Tallahassee, Fla.: University Presses of Florida, 1980.

Bonawit, Oby. *Miami Florida Early Families and Records*. Miami, Fla.: privately printed, 1980.

Bramson, Seth. *Speedway to Sunshine*. Erin, Ontario: Boston Mills Press, 1984.

Brinton, D. G., M.D. *Library of Aboriginal American Literature*. Philadelphia, 1884.

Brown, Jefferson. *Key West, The Old and the New*. St. Augustine, Fla.: The Record Company, 1912.

Bryan, C. D. B. *National Geographic Society: 100 Years of Adventure and Discovery*. New York: Harry N. Abrams, 1987.

Capitman, Barbara, Kinerk, Michael D., and Wilhelm, Dennis W. *Rediscovering Art Deco U.S.A*. New York: Viking Studio Books, 1994.

Capitman, Barbara. *Deco Delights*. New York: E.P. Dutton, 1988.

Cash, W. T. *The Story of Florida, Vol. III*. New York: American Historical Society, 1938.

Chapin, George M. *Florida 1513–1913, Past and Future*. Chicago: S. J. Clarke Publishing Company, 1914.

Chardon, Roland. *Biscayne Bay: Past/Present/ Future: A Geographical History of the Biscayne Bay Area*. Coral Gables, Fla.: University of Miami, 1976.

Cox, James M. *Journey Through My Years*. New York: Simon and Schuster, 1946.

Cutler, Harry Gardner. *History of Florida, Past and Present, Historical and Biographical*. Chicago and New York: Lewis Publishers, 1923.

De Brahm, William Gerard. *The Atlantic Pilot*. A facsimile reproduction of the 1772 edition. Gainesville, Fla.: University Presses of Florida, 1974.

Devaney, John and Barbara. *The Indianapolis 500*. Chicago: Rand McNally, 1976.

Fisher, Jane. *Fabulous Hoosier: A Story of American Achievement*. New York: Robert M. McBride, 1947.

Florida Editors Association. *The Book of Florida.*. Florida Editors Association, 1925.

Fontaneda, d'Escalante. *Memoir of Don d'Escalante Fontaneda Respecting Florida., ca.1575*. Translated from the Spanish with notes by Buckingham Smith. Washington, D.C., 1854. Edited by David O. True. Reprinted. Coral Gables: Glade House, 1945.

Georgano, G. N., editor. *Encyclopedia of Motor Sport*. New York: Viking Press, 1971.

George, Paul. *Mount Sinai Medical Center of Greater Miami, 1949–1984*. Miami Beach, Fla.: Mount Sinai Medical Center, 1985.

Giller, Norman. *An Adventure in Architecture*. Miami, Fla.: Norman Giller, 1976.

Guide to the Architecture of Miami. Miami, Fla.: Florida South Chapter of American Institute of Architects, 1963.

Harlee, William Curry. *Kinfolks: A Genealogical & Biographical Record*, Vol. II. New Orleans, La.: Searcy and Pfaff, 1934–37.

Hauser, Thomas. *Muhammad Ali: His Life and Times*. New York: Touchstone Books, 1991.

Hokanson, Drake. *The Lincoln Highway*. Iowa City, Iowa. University of Iowa Press, 1988.

Kefauver, Estes. *Crime in America*. London: Victor Gollancz, Ltd., 1952.

King, Rev. Elisha A. *Planting a Church in a National Playground: Miami Beach, Florida*. Miami, Fla.: Personal Help Library, Miami, 1942.

Kleinberg, Howard. *Miami: The Way We Were*. Miami, Fla.: Miami Herald Publishing Co., 1985.

Kobler, John. *Capone: The Life and World of Al Capone*. New York: Da Capo Press, 1992.

Kofoed, Jack. *Moon Over Miami*. New York: Random House, 1955.

Lamme, Vernon. *Florida Lore Not Found in the History Books*. Boynton Beach, Fla.: Star Publishing Co., 1973.

Lapidus, Morris. *Architecture of Joy*. Miami, Fla.: E. A. Seemann, 1979.

Liebman, Malvina W. and Liebman, Seymour B. *Jewish Frontiersmen*. Miami Beach, Fla.: Jewish Historical Society of Southern Florida, Inc., 1980.

Lights! Camera! Florida! Ninety Years of Moviemaking and Television Production in Sunshine State. Tampa: Florida Endowment for the Humanities, 1987.

Lincoln Highway Association. *The Lincoln Highway*. New York: Dodd, Mead & Company, 1935.

Linehan, Mary Collar. *Early Lantana, Her Neighbors and More*. St. Petersburg, Fla.: Byron Kennedy, 1979.

Lummus, J. N. *The Miracle of Miami Beach*. Miami, Fla.: Miami Post Publishing Co., 1940.

McIver, Stuart B. *The Greatest Sale on Earth*. Miami, Fla.: E.A. Seemann Publishing, 1980.

Messick, Hank. *Syndicate in the Sun*. New York: MacMillan, 1968.

Morrissey, Pat, editor. *Miami's Neighborhoods*. Miami, Fla.: The Miami News, 1982.

Muir, Helen. *Miami, U.S.A.* Coconut Grove, Fla.: Hurricane House, 1953.

Munroe, Ralph Middleton, and Gilpin, Vincent. *The Commodore's Story*. Reprinted from 1930 edition by the Historical Association of Southern Florida. Northberth, Pa.: Livingston Co., 1966.

Nash, Charles Edgar. *The Magic of Miami Beach*. Philadelphia: David McKay, 1938.

National Cyclopaedia of American Biography. New York: James T. White & Co., 1931.

Pacheco, Ferdie. *Muhammad Ali: A View from the Corner*. New York: Birch Lane Press, 1992.

Parks, Arva Moore. *The Forgotten Frontier*. Second printing. Miami, Fla.: Banyan Books, 1980.

Parks, Arva Moore. *Miami: The Magic City*. Miami, Fla.: Centennial Press, 1991.

Peters, Thelma. *Biscayne Country*. Miami, Fla.: Banyan Books, 1981.

Phillips, P. Lee. *Notes on the Life and Works of Bernard Romans*. A facsimile reproduction of the 1924 edition. Gainesville, Fla.: University Presses of Florida, 1975.

Pierce, Charles W. *Pioneer Life in Southeast Florida*. Edited by Donald Walter Curl. Coral Gables, Fla.: University of Miami Press, 1970.

Presidential Elections Since 1979. Washington D.C.: Congressional Quarterly, Inc., 1983.

Reardon, Leo. *The Florida Hurricane & Disaster*. Miami, Fla.: Miami Publishing Co., 1926. Reprinted. Miami, Fla.: Arva Parks & Co. with Tulsa, Oklahoma: Lion & Thorne, 1986.

Redford, Polly. *Billion-Dollar Sandbar*. New York: Dutton, 1970.

Ridolph, Edward. *Biscayne Bay Trolleys*. Forty Fort, Pa.: H. E. Cox, 1981.

Rodriguez, Ivan, Ammidown, Margot, and Dieterich, Emily Perry. *From Wilderness to Metropolis*. Second Edition. Metropolitan Dade County Office of Community Development, Historic Preservation Division, 1992.

Roosevelt, Patricia Peabody. *I Love a Roosevelt*. New York: Doubleday & Company, 1967.

Root, Keith. *Miami Beach Art Deco Guide*. Miami Beach, Fla.: Miami Design Preservation League, 1987.

Roseberry, Cecil R. *Glenn Curtiss: Pioneer of Flight*. Garden City, N.Y.: Doubleday, 1972.

Rosten, Leo. *The Joys of Yiddish*. New York: Pocket Books, 1968.

Schoenberg, Robert J. *Mr. Capone: The Real and Complete Story of Al Capone*. New York: William Morrow, 1992.

Sewell, John. *Miami Memoirs*. 1933 edition republished by Arva Moore Parks. Miami, Fla.: Arva Parks & Co., 1987.

Sloan, Raymond P. *On a Shoestring and a Prayer*. Garden City, N.Y.: Doubleday & Company, 1964.

Small, John K. *From Eden to Sahara, Florida's Tragedy*. Lancaster, Pa.: Science Press Printing Company, 1929.

Stearns, Frank. *Along Greater Miami's Sun-Sea-Ara*. Miami, Fla.: F. F. Stearns, 1932.

Weatherby, W.J. *Jackie Gleason: An Intimate Portrait of The Great One*. New York: Pharos Books, 1992.

Weigall, T.H. *Boom in Paradise*. New York: Alfred H. King, 1932.

World Book Encyclopedia. Chicago, 1991.

World Book Year Book 1969. Chicago: World Book Encyclopedia, 1969.

Writer's Program. *Indiana: A Guide to the Hoosier State*. New York: Oxford University Press, 1941.

PERIODICALS AND PAMPHLETS

American Speech, Vol. XXXCIX, No. 3, October 1964.

Bath Club charter, by-laws, house rules. 1937.

Biscayne Bay: Past/Present/Future. Papers prepared for Biscayne Bay Symposium, April 2–3, 1976. University of Miami Sea Grant, Special Report 5, April 1976.

Chardon, Roland. *Geoscience and Man, Vol. XVIII, Cartographic Analysis of Coastal Change: Natural and Urban.* Baton Rouge, La.: Louisiana State University, 1977.

City directories, Greater Miami and Miami Beach, 1922, 1925, 1926, 1931, 1933, 1938, 1939, 1940, 1941, 1942, 1949, 1954, 1971.

Congressional Quarterly.

Dixie Highway Magazine, October 1916.

Funk, Ben, and Monahan, James. "Happy Where the Heart Is." *Reader's Digest,* June 1954.

London Times Literary Supplement.

McCloskey, Mark A., and Rickman, Thomas H., Jr. *Professional Study of the Serviceman's Pier, Branches and Branch Services.* Miami Beach, Fla.: privately published, 1946.

Miami Beach Improvement Co., *The Bridge.* Miami, Fla.: Miami Beach Improvement Co., 1915.

Miami Beach Pictorial, Jan. 27, 1929.

Miami Beach Public Library and Art Centre, *The John S. Collins Memorial.* Miami Beach, Fla.: Miami Beach Public Library and Art Centre, 1938.

"Miami Worries About Another Boom." *Life.* Feb. 12, 1945.

New Jersey Coast in Three Centuries. Genealogical and historic-biographical appendix, Vol. III, 1902.

Pancoast, J. Arthur. "A Successful Failure." *Tropic.* September 1914.

Panorama, 1950-54.

Peters, Thelma. "Log of the Biscayne House of Refuge." *Tequesta* (Journal of the Historical Association of Southern Florida) XXXVIII, 1978.

Phillip Morris Magazine, November-December 1990.

Sessa, Frank B. "Anti-Florida Propaganda and Counter-Measures During the 1920s." *Tequesta* (Journal of the Historical Association of Southern Florida). XXI, 1961.

Society Pictorial, 1933–1942.

Spanish River Papers, Boca Raton, Vol. IX, No. 3, May 1981.

"Steve Hannagan's Girls," *Life.* Nov. 30, 1946.

Sunday Pictorial, 1929-1931.

Tequesta.

The Million-Dollar Rascal. Restaurant South Magazine, February 1959.

The Typhoon, Year Book of Miami Beach High School, 1940, 1941. 1942, 1943. Possession of James Snedigar.

Time.

"We Call It Patriotism" and "Getting Results." *The Beach Breeze,* Miami Beach High School student newspaper. Feb. 25, 1942.

World Almanac, 1993.

NEWSPAPERS

Florida Sun and Riviera Times, 1950
Miami Beach Register.

Miami Beach Sun, 1950, 1965.
Miami Beach Sun-Reporter, 1977, 1979.
Miami Daily News & Metropolis, 1923–1926.
Miami Daily News, 1926–1957.
Miami Evening Record, 1902,1905.
Miami Herald, 1903–1994.
Miami Metropolis, 1896–1923.
Miami Morning News, 1903.
Miami News, 1957–1988.
New Times, 1992-93.
New York Herald Tribune, 1947.
New York Journal-American, 1944.
New York Times, 1922, 1968.
Red Bank, New Jersey, Register, 1895.
Tropical Sun, 1892.

MANUSCRIPTS AND LETTERS

Fisher, Carl Graham: Collection of letters, other documents. Historical Museum of Southern Florida, Miami, Fla.

History of Biscayne Bay House of Refuge, MS, Records of the United States Coast Guard, National Archives.

Letter. Avery Smith to Miami Herald, Aug. 28, 1912.

Letter. D. W. Griffith to E. G. Sewell and E. E. Brackett, July 11, 1921.

Letter. John Wescott to Col. Coryell, Jan. 14, 1882. Transcribed by Dr. Joe Knetsch, Division of State Lands, July 28, 1992; Florida Collection, Florida State Library, Tallahassee, Fla.

McGregor, A. James. *A ceramic chronology for the Biscayne Bay Region of southeast Florida..* Thesis. Florida Atlantic University, 1974.

Pierce, Charles W. Manuscript of *Pioneer Life in Southeast Florida.* Palm Beach Historical Society.

PUBLIC DOCUMENTS:

United States

Florida Hurricanes, U.S. Department of Commerce, 1967.

Miscellaneous letters to Surveyor General, 1883. Department of Natural Resources, Tallahassee, Fla.

Monmouth County, New Jersey, Census, 1880.

Sanborn Insurance Company map of Miami Beach, 1918. Library of Congress, Map Division.

Sanborn Insurance Company map of Miami Beach, 1921. Library of Congress, Map Division.

Sanborn Insurance Company map of Miami Beach, 1943. History Archives, Miami Beach City Clerk's office.

Third Interim Report of Special Committee to Investigate Organized Crime in Interstate Commerce. New York: Arco Publishing Co., 82nd Congress, 1952.

United States Census, 1920.

U.S. Department of Commerce. *Memorable Hurricanes of the United States Since 1873*, 1973.

State of Florida

Florida Department of Natural Resources.

Florida Hurricane Survey Report 1965.

Minutes, Board of Trustees, Internal Improvement Fund of the State of Florida.

Parks, Arva Moore. *Where the River Found the Bay: Historic Study of the Granada Site.* Miami, Fla.: Florida Division of Archives, History and Records Management, 1979.

Records Department, Division of State Lands of Florida, Florida Department of Natural Resources.

Dade County

County Commission minutes, March 3, 1942.

Deed Record Books, A–Z.

Miscellaneous Book A.

Mortgage books 33 and 39.

Plat book, various.

Socio-Economic Diagnostic Study of the South Shore Area of Miami Beach, Florida. Miami, Fla.: Welfare Planning Council of Dade County, Fla., 1968.

City of Miami Beach

City Council minutes, July 29, 1918.

City Ordinance 457, Nov. 4, 1936.

History archives, Miami Beach City Clerk's office.

RESOURCE PERSONS

Aristole Ares
Dr. Joe Knetsch
Gerald Schwartz
Harold Gardner
Richard Kumble
Olive Delahunt
Jo Ann Bass
Beverly Keusch Weinberger
Harold Rosen
Kay Pancoast
Harold Kassewitz
Leonard Abess
Sally Hopkins Woodruff
Norman Giller
Ramon Mestré
Bernardo Benes
Russell Galbut
Hyman Galbut
James Snedigar
Hank Meyer
Victor Johnson
Ed Levitt
Elizabeth Jane Gessner Nash
William Theobald
Helen Muir
Stuart Blumberg
Jo Werne
Nancy Liebman
Via Polly Redford audio tapes:
    C. W. (Pete) Chase
    Russell T. Pancoast
    Alfred Barton
    Jane Fisher
    Rose Weiss
Mario and Pedro Menocal
Via Ann Bishop
    Jesse Weiss (1980)
Via Georgia Moretz
    Russell T. Pancoast
(Junior League Interview)
    C.W. Chase
(Conversation with Margaret Nedau (Miami Beach News Bureau), April 20, 1961, Miami Beach City Archives, Miami Beach City Clerk's office.)
Via Marcia Kanner, for Temple Israel
    Mitchell Wolfson

INDEX

ACKNOWLEDGMENTS

The playwright Wilson Mizner once observed that to steal from one is plagiarism, but to steal from many is research. I have done a lot of research for this book.

At the top of my list is Arva Moore Parks, whom I acknowledge as Miami's leading historian. She not only provided me with research material and tracked down all the photographs, she also published this book. We fought a lot— she won, I cursed—but her work on my behalf is immeasurable.

Larry Wiggins, a Homestead newspaper executive, genealogist and researcher *par excellence*, was most generous in sharing much of his Miami Beach files with me. Dr. Joe Knetsch, historian with the Florida Department of Natural Resources in Tallahassee, enthusiastically opened the doors to Miami Beach's unwritten past. Stuart Blumberg, president of the Miami Beach Resort Hotel Association, prodded me to do this book—for which I never will forgive him. Special thanks goes to the Pillars of the Miami Beach Chamber of Commerce without whose sponsorship, this book would not have been possible.

Those who assisted in my research are legion. They include Jim Snedigar, son of former mayor Red Snedigar; longtime City of Miami Beach employee Aristotle Ares; Miami Beach's great publicist Hank Meyer; old friend and Beachite Dick Kumble; Mrs. Charles Nash, the widow of the author of Miami Beach's first history book; nonagenarian Olive Delahunt, who has lived uninterrupted in Miami Beach since 1922; former County Commissioner Jim Redford, widower of Polly Redford; Miami-Dade Community College president, husband of Arva Moore Parks and patient friend Bob McCabe; Miami Beach Mayor Sy Gelber; City Manager Roger Carlton; Jesse Weiss' daughter Jo Ann Bass, the extraordinary lady of Joe's Stone Crab; history buff and son of an early Miami Beach merchant, Alvin Samet; Rebecca Smith and Dawn Hugh of the Historical Museum of Southern Florida; Sam Boldrick, archivist of the Florida Room at the Miami-Dade Public Library.

Also, Otto Richter/University of Miami Library archivist William Brown; Miami Beach Art Deco activist and City Commissioner Nancy Liebman; former Miami Beach press agents Beverlye Keusch Weinberger and Harold Gardner; publicists Gerald Schwartz and Stu Newman; Dade County Archeologist Bob Carr; genealogist Ann Armstrong; Mike Kinerk of the Miami Design Preservation League; Miami Beach City Clerk Richard Brown and his assistants, Natalie Harvey and Patricia Ridgely; historian Donald Walter Curl of Florida Atlantic University; historian Louis DeVorsey of the University of Georgia; Bill Theobold of the Florida Department of Agriculture; Jane Catanzaro of the Monmouth (N.J.) Public Library; Don Curry, deputy clerk of the Dade County Public Records Library; TV news icon Ann Bishop—and Carl Fisher, himself, for leaving behind a wealth of correspondence.

Without them, I would have had to resort to plagiarism.

PHOTO CREDITS

Bringing Miami Beach's history to life with photographs was only possible because many people and institutions were generous with their collections. These include: The City of Miami Beach (MB), Richard Brown and Dorothy Merante; The Historical Association of Southern Florida (HASF), Rebecca Smith and Dawn Hugh; The State of Florida Photographic Archives (SPA), Jody Norman; *The Miami Herald,* (MH) Dave Lawrence, Bill Whiting and Gay Nemeti; Burt Zuckerman, Kenneth Laurence, Bob Lafferty; Beach pioneers, their children and grandchildren: Marty Pancoast Grafton and Lester Pancoast (Pancoast Family), the late Nell Smith (Smith), Connie MacLeod Bischoff (Chase Family), Alvin Samet, Susan Powell, Andrea Lynch Cole, Jo Ann Bass, Jim Snedigar, and Olive Delahunt. Special thanks goes to John Gillan for his beautiful color photographs of Miami Beach today, to Mary Alice Graves Baer who shared the heretofore unknown early photographs of her aunt, photographer Alice Wood, Mary Munroe for her constant dedication to the work of Ralph M. Munroe and Bob Sabin of Polaroid Corporation.

J. N. Lummus strikes the first blow for the demolition of the Lummus Building in 1941. The City of Miami Beach was incorporated here on March 15, 1915. It later became a gambling casino and a Jewish home for the aged. (SPA)